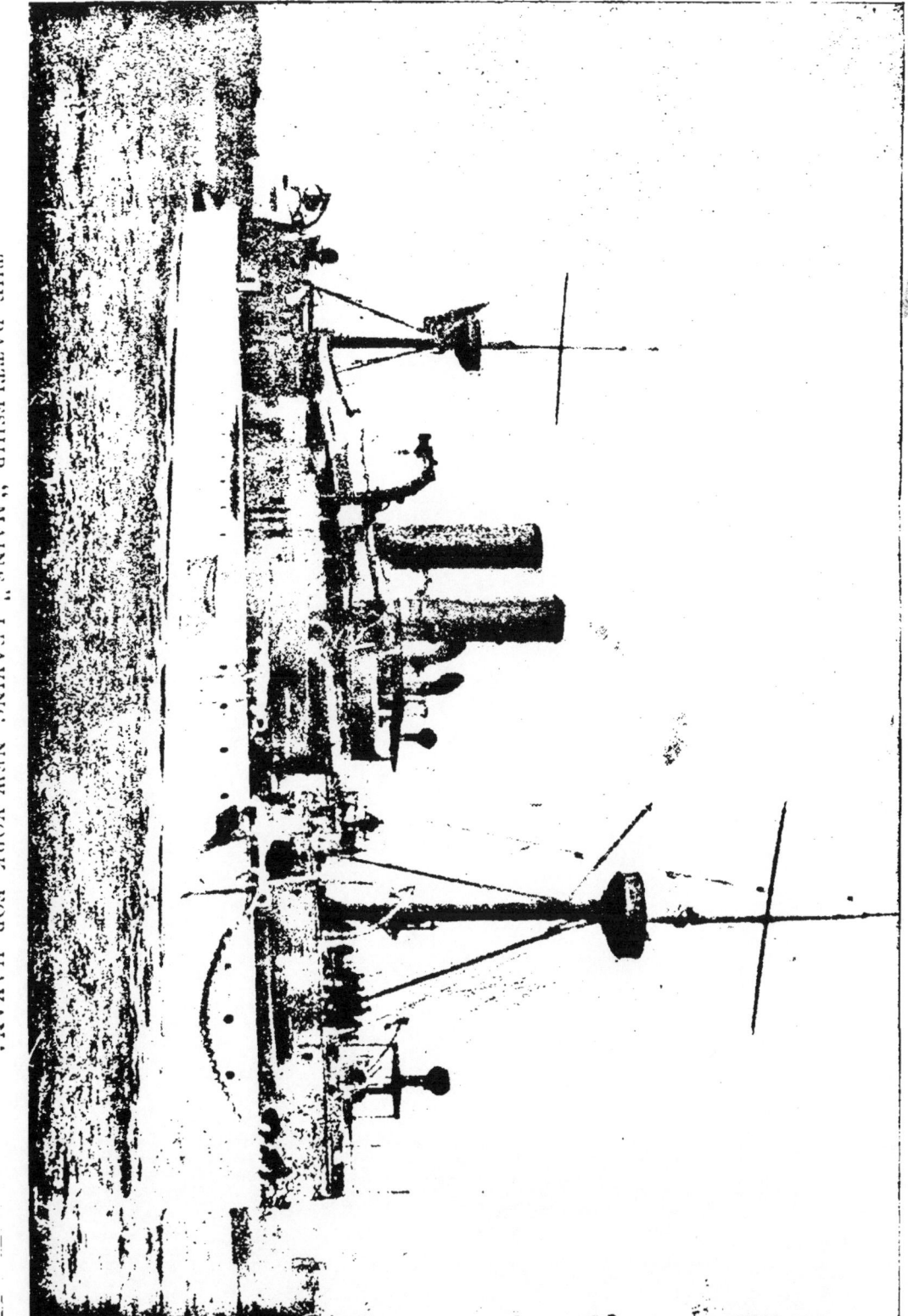

H.M.S. BATTLESHIP "MAINE," LEAVING NEW YORK FOR HAVANA.

Blue Jackets of '98

Blue Jackets of '98

A History of the Spanish-American War

By Willis John Abbot

Author of " Blue Jackets of '76," " Blue Jackets of 1812,"
"Blue Jackets of '61," The Battlefields Series
" The Life of Carter Henry Harrison "

New York
Dodd, Mead and Company
1899

Copyright, 1899,
BY DODD, MEAD AND COMPANY.

All rights reserved.

University Press:
JOHN WILSON AND SON, CAMBRIDGE, U.S.A.

Contents

CHAPTER I

THE FAR-REACHING CAUSES OF THE WAR WITH SPAIN — HOW THE SPANISH EMPIRE IN AMERICA WAS FOUNDED AND FORFEITED — THE UNITED STATES AS SPAIN'S GUARDIAN — THE DIPLOMACY OF THE CUBAN QUESTION — THE VIEWS OF JEFFERSON AND MONROE — THE OSTEND MANIFESTO — THE THREAT OF THE HOLY ALLIANCE — THE UNITED STATES SAVING CUBA FOR THEIR OWN 1

CHAPTER II

WHY SPAIN AND THE UNITED STATES CLASHED — THE ISLAND OF PERPETUAL REVOLUTIONS — THE "SOLES DE BOLIVAR" AND THE "BLACK EAGLE" — LOPEZ AND HIS FILIBUSTERS — HOW A KENTUCKIAN DIED — THE TEN YEARS' WAR — THE COMPROMISE OF ZANJON AND ITS REPUDIATION — THE EXECUTION OF THE "VIRGINIUS" PRISONERS — JOSE MARTI AND HIS CONSPIRACIES — THE NEW REVOLUTION OF 1895 — CAMPOS AGAIN AND HIS FAILURE — WEYLER, "THE BUTCHER," AND HIS FAILURE — CHARACTER OF THE CUBAN LEADERS — WHAT RECONCENTRATION MEANT — THE APPOINTMENT OF BLANCO — AMERICAN AID TO THE STARVING — THE COMPLICATIONS THAT LED TO THE VISIT OF THE "MAINE" 13

CHAPTER III

THE DISASTER TO THE "MAINE" — CAPTAIN SIGSBEE'S DESPATCH — THE STATE OF PUBLIC OPINION — WHY THE "MAINE" WAS SENT TO HAVANA — HER RECEP-

TION THERE — PRECAUTIONS AGAINST ATTACK — THE EXPLOSION — FRIGHTFUL LOSS OF LIFE — PERSONAL NARRATIVES OF SURVIVORS AND EYE-WITNESSES — THE OFFICIAL INVESTIGATIONS — ATTITUDE OF THE SPANIARDS — THE FINDING OF THE COURT OF INQUIRY — "REMEMBER THE 'MAINE'" 41

CHAPTER IV

AT THE NATIONAL CAPITAL — THE COURSE OF THE CUBAN QUESTION IN CONGRESS — ITS TREATMENT BY PRESIDENT CLEVELAND — IT CONFRONTS PRESIDENT MCKINLEY — THE MISSION OF GENERAL STEWART L. WOODFORD — FAIR PROMISES OF THE SPANISH MINISTRY — THE FAILURE OF AUTONOMY — THE DE LOME LETTER AND ITS RESULT — PREPARATIONS FOR WAR — CONGRESS VOTES A $50,000,000 EXTRAORDINARY CREDIT FOR PURPOSES OF NATIONAL DEFENCE — THE REPORT OF THE "MAINE" COURT OF INQUIRY . . . 67

CHAPTER V

THE NAVIES OF SPAIN AND THE UNITED STATES — THE GLOOMY ESTIMATES OF THE EXPERTS — SHIP HUNTING IN EUROPE — WHY A NAVY CANNOT BE EXTEMPORISED — YACHTS AND AUXILIARY VESSELS — THE BLOCKADE OF CUBA — LIEUTENANT ROWAN'S EXPEDITION — THE FIRST CAPTURE — HOT WORK AT MATANZAS — THE ATTACK ON CARDENAS — DEATH OF BAGLEY — THE FIGHT AT CIENFUEGOS 89

CHAPTER VI

SPAIN'S POSSESSIONS IN ASIA — UNEXPECTED SCENE OF AMERICAN NAVAL ACTIVITY — THE PHILIPPINE ISLANDS AND THEIR PEOPLE — RENDEZVOUS OF THE ASIATIC SQUADRON AT HONG KONG — COMMODORE GEORGE DEWEY — THE DEPARTURE FOR THE PHILIPPINES — THE SPANISH FLEET AT MANILA — THE BATTLE AND COMPLETE VICTORY OF THE AMERICANS — NO MEN LOST — DEWEY MADE AN ADMIRAL —

Contents

AGUINALDO AND THE INSURGENTS — TROUBLE WITH GERMANY — A VIGOROUS MESSAGE — THE FRIENDLINESS OF ENGLAND 117

CHAPTER VII

SPAIN'S CAPE VERDE FLEET — THE COASTS OF THE UNITED STATES MENACED — HOW THE NAVAL FORCE OF THE UNITED STATES IN THE ATLANTIC WAS EMPLOYED — THE SEARCH FOR CERVERA — BOMBARDMENT OF SAN JUAN DE PORTO RICO — ENTRAPPED IN SANTIAGO DE CUBA — THE SAMPSON-SCHLEY CONTROVERSY — THE VOYAGE OF THE "OREGON" — THE BLOCKADE OF CERVERA 141

CHAPTER VIII

SANTIAGO DE CUBA — THE PLAN TO BOTTLE UP CERVERA — THE VOLUNTEERS — PREPARATIONS FOR THE SACRIFICE — THE STATIONS OF THE MEN — UNDER FIRE — THE STEERING GEAR DISABLED — THE TORPEDOES SHOT AWAY — SINKING OF THE "MERRIMAC" — SURRENDER OF HOBSON AND HIS MEN — ADMIRAL CERVERA'S COURTESY — IN MORRO CASTLE — THE BOMBARDMENT 162

CHAPTER IX

THE ARMY IN THE WAR — PREJUDICE AGAINST A STANDING ARMY — REGULARS AND MILITIAMEN — CHARACTER OF THE UNITED STATES SOLDIER — THE CALLS FOR VOLUNTEERS — THE ROUGH RIDERS — THE "SONS OF SOMEBODY" — MOBILISATION OF THE TROOPS — THE FIFTH CORPS AT TAMPA — THE "GUSSIE" EXPEDITION — PREPARING FOR THE INVASION OF CUBA — THE DELAYS AND THE START — ARRIVAL AT SANTIAGO — CONFERENCE OF SHAFTER, SAMPSON, AND GARCIA — THE LANDING 177

CHAPTER X

THE LANDING AT DAIQUIRI — FLIGHT OF THE ENEMY — GOOD FORTUNE ATTENDING THE INVADERS — DIFFICULTY OF LANDING STORES — THE ADVANCE INTO THE INTERIOR — CONFERENCE AT SIBONEY — MARCH OF THE ROUGH RIDERS — FIGHT AT GUASIMAS — BRAVERY AND HEAVY LOSS OF THE AMERICANS — THE REGULARS IN ACTION — THE LOSSES AND THE VALUE OF THE VICTORY 199

CHAPTER XI

SAN JUAN, EL CANEY, AND AGUADORES — WAITING FOR SUPPLIES — THE POSITION AT EL CANEY — GENERAL LAWTON'S DISPOSITIONS — EFFECT OF MAUSER BULLETS — STORIES OF THE BATTLEFIELD — THE CAPTURE OF EL CANEY — THE ATTACK ON SAN JUAN — PLAN OF THE BATTLE — THE SLAUGHTER IN THE SUNKEN ROAD — THE CHARGE ON THE HILL — EXPOSED POSITION OF THE AMERICANS — THE QUESTION OF RETREAT — THE SCENES AT BLOODY BEND — THE DEMAND FOR THE SURRENDER OF SANTIAGO — NEWS OF CERVERA'S DEFEAT 218

CHAPTER XII

RIGIDITY OF THE BLOCKADE — THE BOMBARDMENTS — THE MARINES AT GUANTANAMO — CERVERA'S DASH FOR LIBERTY — THE FLEET ALERT — ABSENCE OF THE FLAGSHIP AND THE ADMIRAL — THE CONTROVERSY OVER THE HONOURS — DESTRUCTION OF THE "INFANTA MARIA TERESA" — CAPTURE OF ADMIRAL CERVERA — GALLANT FIGHT OF THE "GLOUCESTER" — THE ANNIHILATION OF THE TORPEDO DESTROYERS — THE "ALMIRANTE OQUENDO" BEACHED — THE END OF THE "VIZCAYA" — MAGNIFICENT WORK OF THE "OREGON" AND "TEXAS" — THE "CRISTOBAL COLON'S" FIGHT FOR LIFE — THE END OF THE SPANISH SQUADRON — EFFECTS OF AMERICAN GUNNERY — THE DISPOSAL OF THE PRISONERS 248

Contents

CHAPTER XIII

CLOSING IN — THE SUFFERINGS OF BELEAGUERED SANTIAGO — THE LAGGING NEGOTIATIONS FOR SURRENDER — THE OUTPOURING OF REFUGEES — THE BOMBARDMENT — SURRENDER OF THE SPANIARDS — THE STARS AND STRIPES ABOVE SANTIAGO — THE WRECKING OF THE ARMY BY SICKNESS — THE FLIGHT TO THE NORTH — THE INFAMY OF THE TRANSPORTS — MONTAUK POINT AND CAMP WIKOFF — FEVER CAMPS IN THE UNITED STATES 292

CHAPTER XIV

THE PORTO RICO CAMPAIGN — TROOPS EMPLOYED — THE BOMBARDMENT OF NIPE — LANDING AT GUANICA — PLAN OF THE CAMPAIGN — CAPTURE OF PONCE — FRIENDLINESS OF THE INHABITANTS — CAPTURE OF GUAYAMO, COAMO, AND MAYAGUEZ — THE ENEMY'S STAND AT ABONCITO — THE NEWS OF PEACE — COMPLETE SUCCESS OF THE CAMPAIGN — THE PEACE NEGOTIATIONS — THE PROTOCOL — EVACUATION COMMISSIONERS 309

CHAPTER XV

THE PHILIPPINES AGAIN — DEWEY'S POSITION IN MANILA HARBOUR — HIS WORK IN DIPLOMACY AND WAR — THE PART PLAYED BY AGUINALDO — THE COMING OF THE AMERICAN TROOPS — THE QUARREL WITH THE GERMANS — THE CAPTURE AND OCCUPATION OF MANILA — GROWING DISCONTENT OF THE FILIPINOS AND THEIR FINAL REVOLT — THE PROBLEMS PRESENTED TO THE UNITED STATES BY THE SITUATION IN THE PHILIPPINES 325

CHAPTER XVI

THE PEACE COMMISSION AT PARIS — THE COMPLETION OF THE TREATY — THE STRUGGLE IN THE AMERICAN SENATE — SOME LESSONS OF THE WAR — THE WORK OF THE TORPEDO BOATS — THE NEED FOR A PERMANENT STAFF ORGANISATION — THE PART PLAYED BY THE MILITIA — THE FUTURE OF THE ARMY 355

Blue Jackets of 98

CHAPTER I

THE FAR-REACHING CAUSES OF THE WAR WITH SPAIN — HOW THE SPANISH EMPIRE IN AMERICA WAS FOUNDED AND FORFEITED — THE UNITED STATES AS SPAIN'S GUARDIAN — THE DIPLOMACY OF THE CUBAN QUESTION — THE VIEWS OF JEFFERSON AND MONROE — THE OSTEND MANIFESTO — THE THREAT OF THE HOLY ALLIANCE — THE UNITED STATES SAVING CUBA FOR THEIR OWN.

THE Spanish war of 1898 was the result of inexorable causes which had their manifestations as early as the opening of the nineteenth century. The phrase "manifest destiny" has been sorely abused and degraded to a partisan cry, but half a century ago the destiny of the Spanish possessions in this hemisphere was manifest. The causes which impelled a peace-loving nation to declare war upon Spain in April, 1898, existed even in the time of Pizarro and of Cortez. Spanish cruelty and rapacity have ever been at odds with the dominant spirit of our western hemisphere, and the decree for Spain's expulsion from the West Indies was writ large in the history of the nineteenth century long before the destruction of the "Maine" and the starvation of the reconcentrados hastened its execution. A free and enlightened republic and a mediæval despotism are inevitably quarrelsome neighbours. To the Cuban victims of Spanish tyranny the United States offered always an example of the blessings of a democracy and of the fruits of successful revolution, while to the people of the great republic the condition of Cuba was a constant irritant, resulting in repeated unlawful but well-meant private expeditions planned to overthrow Spain's authority in that island.

One hundred years ago the Spanish authority was supreme over all South America except Brazil and Guiana. In North America, the Floridas and all that vast expanse of territory west of the Mississippi and extending to the golden shores of California were recognised by all nations as Spanish. In twenty-five years this noble domain had dwindled to the islands of Cuba and Porto Rico, with a few near-by islets. To-day even that pitiful remnant of the empire which Columbus won for Spain is lost. With everything in its favour, with its customs, its language, and its sons still dominating more than half of the western hemisphere, Spain can no longer exercise authority over one foot of American soil. The sons of Spaniards threw off the Spanish yoke, for the free air of America stimulated their ambition and taught them that the political and social ideas of the Dark Ages have no place among the nation builders of to-day. The pathetic phase of the obliteration of Spain as a world power is justly obscured by the fact that Spanish power has always stood for oppression, cruelty, rapacity, and ignorance. When Spain has been great the progress of the world in science, art, and industry has stood still until the fighting men could administer a check to Spanish aggressions. In our own hemisphere, Cortez and Pizarro destroyed civilisations more advanced than any which Spain has founded in their stead. The ravaged fields and burned cabins of "pacified" Cuba are but the latest evidences of that national spirit of savagery which three hundred years ago left a like impress on Peru in ruined palaces and obliterated cities.

The story of the foundation and the overthrow of Spanish power in America, the narrative of the series of successful revolutions which resulted in the establishment of the galaxy of republics in Central and South America is not to be told here. It demands volumes of its own — volumes of which page after page will necessarily be given over to stories of such revolting cruelty as stain the annals of no other people. The bigotry of the Inquisition accompanied the greed of the spoliator. The fagot and the stake awaited such of the aborigines as refused to yield up their simple beliefs, while the sword or the torture was the portion of the chiefs who stubbornly clung to their treasures demanded by the men of Velasquez, Cortez, or De Soto. The Indian chief bound to a stake by Velasquez, and awaiting the fiery death decreed by a remorseless conquerer, expressed bitterly the hatred with which the Spaniards had inspired his people:

"Do not you wish to go to Heaven?" asked the priest who stood at his elbow.

"Are there Spaniards there?" asked the victim.

"Certainly."

"Then let me go somewhere else," cried the unhappy savage, who could conceive of no hell more cruel than that which Spanish cruelty had ordained for his people on earth.

I have said that the United States and Spain were by the very antagonism of their institutions quarrelsome neighbours, but had it not been for the United States, Spain would have been deprived of her West Indian possessions long before the event did actually occur. It has long been the conviction — usually unexpressed — of our leading statesmen that Cuba was naturally a part of our territory and would inevitably become a part of the United States. Thomas Jefferson more than seventy-five years ago discerned this fact and declared of that island that "her addition to our confederacy is exactly what is wanted to round out our power as a nation to the point of its utmost interest." And John Quincy Adams, when Secretary of State, wrote in a letter to the United States minister at Madrid that, "It is scarcely possible to resist the conviction that the annexation of Cuba to our federal republic will be indispensable to the continuance and integrity of the Union itself."

But though the question of the control of Cuba and the relations of the United States to the nation owning the island have furnished themes for the state papers of almost every President and Secretary of State since the times of Jefferson, the actual question of annexation either by force or by purchase has seldom had frank treatment. Reading between the lines, we may well discern that it was in the mind of every public man, but international comity, for one reason, prevented its utterance. Moreover, the question of slavery came in later days to complicate the problem and to divide public opinion. If there was to be annexation, how would Cuba enter the Union? The North vowed as a free state only; the South insisted that the existing institution of slavery — it was destroyed in Cuba only as lately as 1886 — should be accepted with the island. This radical difference between the sections of the United States long prevented annexation, though more than one President urged such a policy upon Congress. In 1848, when Europe had its hands full, trying to repress a wave of republicanism which seemed likely to sweep all thrones away before it, President Polk instructed the minister at Madrid to offer one hundred million dollars for the sovereignty of the island. It is characteristic of the Spanish temperament that the offer was not only refused, but treated as an affront, though even then the Cubans were in revolt, as indeed they have been, with but brief intermissions, ever since. And again Presidents Pierce and Buchanan urged upon Congress the wisdom of annexation by purchase, but were unable to enlist the favourable attention of the national legislature, which feared the slavery issue involved. "It is required," wrote President Buchanan in his message of 1859, "by manifest destiny that the United States should possess Cuba, not by violence, but by purchase at a fair price." This President spoke from a knowledge of his subject based on careful and prolonged study, for in 1854 James Buchanan, then minister to England, joined with the ministers to Spain and France in the celebrated "Ostend Manifesto." This document, prepared by the three diplomats after a conference at Ostend, declared that if Spain should stubbornly refuse to sell Cuba, national prudence and national self-preservation would make it imperative for the United States to conquer and annex the island, lest it be made by successful negro revolt a second San Domingo. Notwithstanding this vigorous representation, the Congress to which the Ostend manifesto was sent was as unwilling to authorise Cuban annexation as was that of six years later, when Minister Buchanan had become President. It is apparent that however favourably the Presidents have looked upon the project of annexation, — and many have either recommended or discussed it, — Congress has always regarded it with suspicion or even with hostility.

The annexation of Cuba to the United States has, therefore, never become a matter of international discussion. However earnestly it may have been desired by individual statesmen, it never attained such force as a national movement as to compel the attention of foreign governments. But the relations of the United States to Cuba, and to Spain in her capacity of owner of Cuba, have been the matter of grave diplomatic consideration abroad, and have more than once threatened serious complications. The position assumed by the United States until the year 1898 was much that of the fabled dog in the manger. As a nation, we have persistently declared that we did not want Cuba, but that, under no circumstances, would we ever permit any nation other than Spain to acquire it. More than this, and more indefensible unless on the ignoble ground of national selfishness, we have at all times, until after our own civil war, frowned upon the efforts of the Cubans to win independence. The antagonism of the governing powers of the United States to the aspiration of the Cubans for independence sprung, of course, from the consciousness that a republic in which slavery was prohibited, despite the presence of great numbers of blacks, would be an annoying neighbour to the slave states of the Union. This opposition to Cuban independence disappeared with slavery in the United States, and it is perhaps fair to say that if the South was so long potent in delaying Cuban freedom, its representatives far outdid the spokesmen of our Northern communities in urging action in behalf of the patriots in 1898. To-day, by the act of the United States, Cuba is offered an opportunity to essay self-government. Whether the trial shall end in that annexation to the United States which Jefferson hoped for and Buchanan foresaw, immediate history will tell. It will not take another century to determine the final constitution of Cuba.

American opposition to the independence of Cuba — opposition which it must be remembered was that of prudent statesmen rather than of the masses of the people — ended with our own civil war and the destruction of slavery. But antagonism to the acquirement of sovereignty by any other power was more deeply rooted and, having its first expression in a famous state paper by President Monroe, has continued until the present day. This feature of the relations of the United States to its island neighbour has been of such supreme importance in the national code of the United States that it merits special attention from all who would understand the motives and principles which have animated and still direct the United States in its dealings with neighbouring powers. It is the story of the origin and development of a clause in our national creed scarcely less revered than the preamble to the Declaration of Independence itself,— the story of the MONROE DOCTRINE.

In 1815 Europe, having crushed Napoleon, undertook the task of undoing the work of the French Revolution, and extirpating what the despotic monarchs were pleased to consider the pestilential germs of democracy from all European lands. Russia, Austria, and Prussia formed a coalition to this end, giving it a title which would be blasphemous if it were not ridiculous, — "The Holy Alliance." In 1818 France, being again under the rule of the Bourbons, joined the coalition, and England secretly approved its purposes, though without giving open adherence to it. The embers of the fire of republicanism which had blazed so fiercely during the opening years of the nineteenth century were still smouldering. In Naples and Piedmont the people were in revolt, and in 1821 Austria performed her part of the "holy" agreement by suppressing with the sword these embryonic efforts for popular government. In 1823 France joined in taking away from the Spanish people the small measure of liberty which a constitutional monarchy secured for them, and restored absolutism in the Iberian peninsula. Nor was the Holy Alliance content to confine its endeavours to its own side of the Atlantic. Its intervention in Spain suggested to its members that in the Spanish-American colonies there were menacing signs of the republican spirit which should engage the thoughtful and forceful attention of a league devoted to the protection of all the divine rights of kings, — and all rights of kings must be divine, else they cannot be rights at all, as the people have no share in granting them. Throughout the Spanish states of South America, revolution was at that time in the high tide of successful accomplishment. Bolivar, the Washington of South America, was at the most glorious period of that wonderful career of agitation and generalship by which so much of South American territory was wrested from European control. Cuba was honeycombed with republican conspiracies, though no open revolt was then in progress. The secret association of the "Soles de Bolivar" had enlisted the sympathies and co-operation of the best and most patriotic of the white natives of the island. A correspondence with Bolivar was in progress, his sympathy and aid assured, and a day set for striking the first blow. The blow was not struck, however, for treachery betrayed the leaders, and the conspiracy went to pieces; but the investigation that followed alarmed the champions of absolutism by the evidence it gave of the extent and force of the democratic heresy in Cuba.

It occurred, therefore, to the zealous servitors of monarchy in Europe that Cuba offered a point of vantage whence to conduct the war upon democracy in America. An allied army there would effectually discourage any further spread of the pernicious doctrines of Washington, Jefferson, and Bolivar in that island, and thence expeditions might be despatched to regain the ground lost in South America. A hint of this plan reached our department of state as early as July, 1818, when Richard Rush, the American minister at the Court of St. James, was told by Lord Castlereagh of a proposition made by Spain for the mediation of England, in association with the Holy Alliance, with the rebellious Spanish colonies. "Mediation," being a milder word than coercion, is much in favour with diplomats; but the real essence of the proposition was that the Spanish colonies should be reconquered for Spain, and the purpose of Lord Castlereagh's communication was to find out what the United States thought of the project. The answer of Rush, which was that the United States would have no part in the affair unless its purpose was to secure the independence of the colonies, suggests that the habit of frankness, which in the latter end of the nineteenth century has been described as diplomacy in shirt-sleeves, is not wholly a new development of American diplomatic methods.

That the United States would neither permit other nations to strengthen the hands of Spain in the western hemisphere, nor allow the Spanish colonies to be transferred to stronger sovereignty, may have been a doctrine new to European diplomatic circles, but it had been definitely determined upon at home. In the Jefferson manuscripts, preserved at the national capital, is a memorandum of action taken at a cabinet meeting in 1808. The cabinet then, wrote Jefferson, "unanimously agreed in the sentiments which should be unauthoritatively expressed by our agents to influential persons in Cuba and Mexico; to wit: 'If you remain under the dominion of the kingdom and the family of Spain, we are contented; but we should be extremely unwilling to see you pass under the dominion or ascendancy of France or England. In the latter case, should you choose to declare independence, we cannot now commit ourselves by saying we would make common cause with you, but must reserve ourselves to act according to the then existing circumstances; but in our proceedings we shall be influenced by friendship to you, by a firm feeling that our interests are intimately connected, and by the strongest repugnance to see you under subordination to either France or England, either politically or commercially!"

This, it will be noted, was the determination of Jefferson's cabinet, not openly declared in any state paper. It clearly holds the germ which after various stages of evolution finally developed into the Monroe Doctrine.

In 1822 Lord Castlereagh, who had been rebuffed by Rush in the matter of "mediation" with the Spanish colonies, committed suicide. His successor, Canning, a more adroit diplomat, approached Minister Rush anew, but with vastly more skill. The story of the diplomatic advances by which the British minister sought to ingratiate himself with the American diplomat is an amusing one. No social art, no warmth of flattery, no professions of admiration for republican principles and for the men who were giving them effect in America was left untried. But at the end came the same proposition, "Would the United States join England in a European Congress to determine what should be done with Spain's rebellious American people?" Rush declined, declaring that the United States had already recognised the independence of the South American states, and had, furthermore, no intention of entangling itself in European politics.

"You could not have met Canning's proposals better," wrote President Monroe to the envoy, on learning of this colloquy, "if you had had the whole American cabinet at your right hand." But having posted this despatch to the American minister at London, Monroe wrote to Jefferson and Madison to ask them what they thought of Great Britain's proposition and of Rush's reply.

Madison replied cautiously. Jefferson sent a letter, parts of which have been incorporated in what may be called our code of national political wisdom. "Our first and fundamental maxim should be," he wrote, "never to entangle ourselves in the broils of Europe. Our second, never to suffer Europe to meddle in cis-Atlantic affairs. America, North and South, has a set of interests distinct from those of Europe and peculiarly her own. She should therefore have a system of her own, separate and distinct from those of Europe. While the last is labouring to become the domicile of despotism, our endeavour should surely be to make our hemisphere that of freedom." Nevertheless Jefferson, a man of inconsistencies as varied as his talents, was willing to make an exception to his sweeping declaration against foreign entanglements in behalf of Great Britain which he was popularly supposed to regard with especially distrust and aversion. "Cuba alone," he wrote in another letter to Monroe, "seems at present to hold up a speck of war to us. Its possession by Great Britain would indeed be a great calamity to us. Could we induce her to join us in guaranteeing its independence against all the world, except Spain, it would be nearly as valuable as if it were our own. But should she take it, I would not immediately go to war for it; because the first war on other accounts will give it to us, or the island will give itself to us when able to do so."

Shortly after this President Monroe sent to Congress his

TORPEDO BOAT "TALBOT."

famous message in which, referring to the supposed designs of the Holy Alliance upon the integrity of the new or embryonic states of South America, he declared that, "We should consider any attempt (of the allied powers) to extend their system to any portion of our hemisphere as dangerous to our peace and safety."

Thereafter the position of the United States toward Cuba and the Spanish domination therein was clear and easily to be understood. We were ready to defend Spain's authority against all interlopers — did indeed defend it against Mexico and Colombia, which in 1825 formed a project for the invasion of Cuba. In 1830 Van Buren, Secretary of State under President Jackson, gave formal notice that Mexico would not be allowed to acquire Cuba. In 1825 Henry Clay, in a circular to the American ministers in Europe, said:

"You will now add that we could not consent to the occupation of these islands (Cuba and Porto Rico) by any other European power than Spain, under any contingency whatever."

Five years later, as though to show that the aversion of the United States to any change in the governmental conditions of Cuba was not directed against European aspirants for conquest alone, Martin Van Buren, Secretary of State under Andrew Jackson, warned off Mexico with a curt notification that the United States would not permit her to acquire Cuba. And so, year after year, and administration after administration, the word went forth to all the peoples and courts of the world that the United States would defend the title of Spain to Cuba against all comers. But it made no pledge to protect Spain against her own subjects, nor did it promise to abstain from taking the island for itself. Edward Everett, Secretary of State in 1852, in restating the American position, announced frankly that the United States would not bind itself not to take the island if, because of the evils of Spanish rule, this should become necessary or prudent. "But," he wrote, "the President would consider its acquisition by force, except in a just war with Spain (should an event so gravely to be deprecated ever take place), as a disgrace to the civilisation of the age."

With this final word from Edward Everett, we may well let the story of diplomatic discussion in which our Spanish neighbour has involved the United States rest. Our national course in this matter has been singularly straightforward and consistent since the days of Jefferson. The latter half of the century brought no change in the policy which had been formulated in its youth. Our civil war and the problems growing out of it quieted Cuban agitation for thirty years; but when it became acute once more, and the war which Everett more than hinted at became inevitable, the despatch of the Secretary of State in 1852 might have been put in the preamble of the resolutions by which war was declared, without in any degree misrepresenting the popular sentiment which compelled that challenge to Spain.

CHAPTER II

Why Spain and the United States Clashed — The Island of Perpetual Revolutions — The "Soles de Bolivar" and the "Black Eagle" — Lopez and his Filibusters — How a Kentuckian died — The Ten Years War — The Compromise of Zanjon and its Repudiation — The Execution of the "Virginius," Prisoners — Jose Marti and his Conspiracies — The New Revolution of 1895 — Campos Again and his Failure — Weyler, "the Butcher," and his Failure — Character of the Cuban Leaders — What Reconcentration meant — The Appointment of Blanco — American Aid to the Starving — The Complications that led to the Visit of the "Maine."

THERE are many kinds of bad neighbours. The aggressive and quarrelsome fellow who intrudes upon the rights of those who live about him may be the worst, but he is not the only undesirable one. There are the family that maintains a constant nuisance, the family that quarrel perpetually among themselves to the disturbance of peace and the scandal of the neighbourhood, and the family whose children are untrained and undisciplined, a terror to neighbouring young people and a menace to everything breakable in the vicinity. The policy of the United States was successful in preventing a neighbour of the aggressive sort from settling down in Cuba; but by protecting Spain there we submitted ourselves to every other species of annoyance that a neighbour could inflict. From the beginning of the century, Cuba was in revolt. Spanish misrule and extortion made rebellion the normal condition of the island, and compelled the sympathy of Americans, even if considerations of state did make the active intervention of the government impossible. A colony which is regarded only as a mine to be worked, a cow to be milked, a field from which all produce is to be taken and nothing returned for fertilising, a slave whose portion is all hard work and lashes,— such a colony is naturally rebellious and justified in rebellion.

It was upon such principles that Spain administered her colonies, and particularly Cuba.

Never was there more biting irony than the conferring upon Cuba of the title "The Ever Faithful Isle." The phrase had its origin in 1808, when Napoleon drove the Bourbon dynasty from Madrid. In Havana then the Spanish officials met and declared their loyalty to the exiled sovereign, and defied the conqueror,— things perhaps not very audacious when done at 4,000 miles distance from the seat of war. But even at that moment a conspiracy for the overthrow of Spanish authority was in progress, and they who affirmed their loyalty to the exiled Bourbons were not Cubans but Spanish officials,— carpet-baggers, as we should call them in the United States, whose protestations meant only that they would be unflinchingly loyal to the power which had conferred upon them their positions.

This distinction between the Spanish office-holders, mostly in Havana, and the Cubans should be kept constantly in mind. One of the great reasons for the persistence of the Cuban dissatisfaction with the Spanish government has been that the officials, even to the administrative clerks, have usually been Spaniards sent out to the colony and animated only by a desire to get rich and go home again.

In 1823 the first serious attempt to overthrow the authority of Spain was made. Prior to that year the Cuban uprisings, such as they were, had originated with negroes, and had sprung from the agitation for the abolition of slavery. But it was the very flower of the young Cuban whites who joined in the plot of the "Soles de Bolivar" in 1823, having for its purpose the independence of the island

and her enrolment among the free republics which the genius of Bolivar had created on the great continent to the south. The conspiracy, as I have already noted, was short lived. Betrayed by traitors, the conspirators were apprehended, and many of them executed. The spirit that animated these young patriots, however, was not destined to perish. In three years, a new rebellion was planned, the ring-leaders being men who had figured in the abortive conspiracy in the name of Bolivar. This, too, was short lived, but it appears to have spread sufficiently to affright the Madrid government, which took steps to strengthen the hands of the colonial governor against future conspiracies, by giving him unqualified power to put the island, or any part of it, under martial law whenever he saw fit. At any time he could order the arrest and trial by court-martial of any citizen or body of citizens whom he might suspect, and the courts were powerless to protect them. He could exert the right of search and seizure in time of absolute peace, as though the country were a town in a state of siege. Of course the effect of this grant of power, which was freely exercised, was to increase the dissatisfaction of the people with Spanish rule and to multiply conspiracies. It has ever been that the effort of despotism to stifle discontent by becoming more despotic has failed. In Cuba, citizens who had held aloof from all previous revolutionary movements now joined in the plots against the Spanish power. The third of the organised conspiracies which quickly followed, was that of the order of the "Aguila Negra," or Black Eagle, and it met the same fate as its predecessors.

It is perhaps not too early in this chronicle to say that from the first the Cubans showed themselves better at conspiring than in giving their conspiracies effect, better at rebelling against authority than in overthrowing that authority. In proportion to the number of Cubans who sympathised with Gomez, Maceo, and Garcia in the rebellion which by the aid of the United States became finally the revolution, the army was surprisingly small. And in proportion to the size of the army, the number of men who actually appeared in battle was even more disappointing.

We may pass hastily over the successive riots and revolts which kept Cuba in a turmoil for half a century. By 1840 the discontent of the islanders had come to be so general that adventurous persons in the United States, taking seriously the Cuban ambition for freedom, began to consider whether some advantage might not be gained by taking to the island armed bodies of men and inciting the Cubans to successful revolt. In the main these filibusters, as they came to be called, were animated by selfish and mercenary motives. They were true soldiers of fortune, attracted no doubt in part by the romantic notion of helping to build up a new nation, but not at all blind to possible profit for themselves in the government of it. The first of these expeditions was that of Narciso Lopez, in 1848. Lopez had made his essay at rebellion in Cuba with the usual results, and after escaping to the United States, organised there a society of Cuban refugees. Among the members of this society, and among Americans who were actuated by motives as various as men have mental characteristics, Lopez organised a filibustering expedition. The United States authorities got wind of it, and suppressed it, as was clearly the duty of a nation friendly to the government de facto in Cuba. That was the beginning of the war of the United States government on men who were trying to make Cuba free,— a warfare which the practices of civilised nations made compulsory, but which was repugnant to the officials who directed it, the officers who were actively engaged in it, and the people who paid the bills.

Undaunted by his first failure, Lopez made preparations for another effort. He gathered together some six hundred men at an island near Yucatan. Thence by steamer the expedition, well armed and provisioned for a campaign, proceeded to Cardenas, where it landed and threw up entrenchments. Lopez was a visionary,—a man of the John Brown type in some respects. Like the hero of Harper's Ferry, he thought that a people suffering under tyranny would rise and fight for freedom. He did not know his own people. Instead of flocking to his standard, they left him severely alone. They had neither courage for the fight, nor manliness enough to brave the martial law which they knew would be declared on the news of the landing of the expedition. Havana was full of soldiers, and a railroad ran thence to Cardenas. If some patriot had destroyed a section of this road, Lopez might have had time to rouse the country and begin a Fabian warfare like that which Garcia and Gomez afterward made effective. But the patriots were all in the cafés, and two thousand and five hundred Spanish soldiers went down the railroad to attack the invaders. They retreated practically without resistance, and the United States government seized Lopez's steamer and put him on trial, but failed to convict him of any punishable offence. Juries were not much moved by the crime of filibustering then.

We must admire the persistence of Lopez, though his actual accomplishments were inconsequential. In 1851 he was again equipped with a steamer, arms, provisions, and an army of four hundred and fifty men. This time he had a company of more formidable soldiers. Forty-nine were Americans, adventurous men from the West and South who knew how to fight and, as they proved, how to die. Several Hungarians, Germans, and Poles, flotsam from the European revolutions of '48, were in the party, one General Pragay being second in command. Bungled from the first, the expedition perished miserably. The pilot intrusted with the task of finding a landing place nearly took the filibusters into the lion's jaws at Havana, but, escaping this peril, landed them at Bahia Honda. As usual, the force of Cubans which had been expected to join failed to appear, and Lopez committed the fundamental error of dividing his force in the face of the enemy. At the coast were left one hundred and fifty men under command of Colonel Crittenden, a Kentuckian of distinguished family. Lopez, with the main body, pushed on into the interior, hoping to rally the natives to the banner of free Cuba. The Spanish soldiery were quickly on the heels of both parties. Crittenden's party, after a running fight in the woods in which they suffered severely, were captured. In accordance with the inhuman practice of the Spaniards, the survivors, some fifty in all, were sentenced to be shot. Blindfolded and kneeling with their backs to their executioners, they died wretchedly. Crittenden met his end with a flash of defiance on his tongue. "A Kentuckian never turns his back on an enemy and kneels only to his God," he said, when ordered to prepare like the others for death, and he faced his fate like a brave man. Lopez was overtaken by the pursuers at Las Pozas, where he repelled an attack of the enemy, but was so sorely weakened that in his retreat he was compelled to leave his wounded to be murdered by the Spaniards. At Las Frias, soon after, in another battle the filibusters fought bravely and won a second victory. But their little triumphs were without avail. In every fight they lost heavily, and no recruits came to their standards, while the Spaniards, re-enforced daily, kept up the pursuit. Gradually the invaders were reduced to mere scattered bands of miserable fugitives, fleeing through the woods and incapable of further resistance. Lopez and some of his companions were captured and died by the garrote at Havana. The fate of the rest is known only to the impenetrable jungles of Cuba and to the hideous land crabs and loathsome vultures that rend the flesh of the helpless and the dead lying there.

Too many Americans had fallen in the ill-fated Lopez expedition for its fate to be thought of with indifference in the United States, and the gallant words of Crittenden stirred the blood of many who thought such a youth too fine a type to be a victim to Spanish bloodthirstiness. Henceforward the irritation of the United States was great whenever Spain offended in any degree, and offence was constant. Spain began suspecting a filibuster in every American ship in Cuban waters. The constant challenge of our merchantmen angered our sailors, and every incident of this kind was made the most of by the anti-Spanish party, which was coming to be a recognised force in the United States. By firing upon United States ships, opening mail-bags at Havana consigned to this country, detaining merchantmen unlawfully, and seizing them on frivolous allegations of fraud upon the customs, Spain made herself obnoxious to an extent that threatened war. The Ostend Manifesto, already referred to, which frankly discussed the wisdom of taking Cuba from Spain by force, grew out of the irritation these repeated aggressions aroused among our people. But our own war between the States saved Spain for a time.

In 1868 the discontented Cubans rose again in revolt, and this time proclaimed boldly the Cuban Republic. The island was full of soldiers, both the Spanish regulars and the so-called volunteers recruited carefully among the Spanish sympathisers. Nevertheless a lawyer of Bayamo, one Carlos M. de Cespedes, with the knowledge of all the rebellions that had miserably failed, took the field with one hundred and twenty-eight men, half-armed, and bade Spain defiance. But this time the Cubans who had so often disappointed those who strove to free them were readily roused. The years of comparative immunity from armed revolt had been employed by Spain only in making existence more intolerable for the people of the island. Taxes had been increased to a point bordering on confiscation, and the carpet-bagging tax-gatherers swindled the government as they fleeced the tax-payers. The force of "volunteers" was a heavy burden upon the colony. Though a militia body, its members were paid for service. It was recruited largely among the families of those holding office under the home government, and was carefully limited to men of whose loyalty to Spain there could be no question. Besides their military duties, the volunteers quickly began to assume political functions. They became what we call in the United States a machine, dictating nominations for the few electoral offices and monopolising for themselves all the offices of emolument. The native Cuban was practically denied all share in the government of his own province. He was the tax-payer; the Spaniards, the tax-eaters. As the appetites of the latter were voracious, and as the government at Madrid was not without a zest for spoils, the debt of Cuba mounted up until its interest alone was $6.39 per capita, and the amount of revenue which it was sought to extract from the island for 1868 was $40,000,000. This was more than the people could raise, and payment was not made easier by the spectacle of enormous salaries paid to corrupt officials. A Captain-General with a salary of $50,000 a year, when the President of the United States was getting $25,000, and two archbishops at $18,000 each, with other salaries of like extravagance, made the Cuban planter see that he was being impoverished for the enrichment of an office-holding aristocracy. Touched in the pocket, he responded more forcefully to this new appeal for action against the Spanish oppression than he had when the "Soles de Bolivar" had appealed to his desire for freedom, or when the brave and unfortunate Lopez had sought to set up an independent state.

The war that followed was one of endurance rather than of action. The insurgents were confined mainly to the forest clad hills of the interior whence they descended on frequent forays, attacking some Spanish post, capturing and often burning some little town, desolating a province or killing at wholesale men known to be in league with the Spaniards. All the evils of guerrilla warfare were suffered by the unhappy islanders for ten years. The Cubans were weak, ill-armed, and poor. Their chief

"THE MORRIS," TORPEDO BOAT OF THE SMALLEST TYPE.

weapon was the machete,—a heavy sword-like knife. They knew that to give pitched battle to the enemy would be to invite annihilation, so they maintained an irregular warfare in the hope of exhausting Spain's resources of men and money. The Spaniards for their part did not push hostilities with any vigour. To Spanish general officers a war has always meant great profits, and the long duration of the Ten Years War is believed to have been due in part to the willingness of some officers in high command to make money in contracts and by falsified pay-rolls. But as it dragged along the cost to Spain became tremendous, while to the people of the island it meant ruin. Spanish statistics are notoriously incomplete, but not less than 150,000 men were sacrificed in this effort to make Cuba submissive. The Cubans suffered in proportion, and were made the victims of peculiarly cruel orders and murderous outrages at the hands of the Spanish troops. In 1898 what was known as the "reconcentration policy" of General Weyler had much to do with producing the inhuman conditions which led to the intervention of the United States; but Weyler was anticipated in 1869 by General Balmaceda, whose reconcentration proclamation included such cruel ordinances as this: "Every *man* from the age of *fifteen years* upwards found away from his habitation who does not prove a proper reason therefor will be shot." In the effort to crush the Cuban by cruel and murderous methods the volunteers of Havana took an active and infamous part. In 1871 they seized a number of school-boys accused of defacing the glass on a tomb containing the body of a Spanish soldier, tried them by a court-martial which had no official character,—a veritable mock court,—and shot eight dead the following morning in execution of the sentence. For these wholesale murders the members of the politico-military organisation were never punished. They were indeed superior to the law and had just forced a regularly appointed Captain-General to return to Madrid.

In this insurrection, as in all others, the sympathy of the people of the United States was earnestly with the Cubans. Pressure was brought to bear on the administration from many sources for the recognition of the insurgents and for active intervention in their behalf. But then, as thirty years later, the insurgents suffered from being unable to show an organised government which could command respect, or a capital that could be reached by an envoy. These facts President Grant pointed out in his message of 1869, but shortly afterward the distressing situation in Cuba compelled him to send in to Congress a special message detailing the unhappy condition of the island and noting that if the insurgents had made no progress in winning liberty, Spain had made none toward suppressing the revolt. There were then the same reasons for intervention that recurred in 1898, and the arguments against it employed by President Grant were almost literally those used later by Presidents Cleveland and McKinley.

Not even the one great crime against the lives of Americans which, in the sinking of the "Maine," in 1898, had so potent a share in bringing on war, was without a prototype in 1873. Filibustering expeditions having for their purpose the supplying of arms, recruits, and munitions of war to the insurgents were common during the earlier revolt as in the days of the later one. In October, 1873, an American side-wheel steamer, the "Virginius," was engaged in one of these expeditions. Off the southern coast of the island, she was sighted by a Spanish gunboat, and despite all efforts to escape was overhauled and captured. One hundred and sixty-five men were taken prisoners, and with the ship were taken in to Santiago de Cuba. Then began a series of unlawful and cruel executions which were in fact assassinations, and which should have resulted in an instant declaration of war by the United States. Within three days of their capture, three Cubans and one American were taken from among their fellows in prison and shot, — not after trial, but summarily, upon order of the Spanish commander, General Burriel. Again three days, and thirty-seven more, including the ship's commander, Captain Frey, were lined up, blindfold and kneeling before a company of marines, and shot dead. Against this execution the consuls of both the United States and England protested in vain. Several of the victims were British subjects, but the Spaniards, with the fatuous indifference which has ever characterised them, gave as little heed to the nationality of the men they slaughtered, as they did to the international law bearing upon their cases. In the face of the combined protest of the consuls, twelve more men were shot on the day following. Then the executions abruptly ceased, for the captain of the British man-of-war "Lorraine" ran into Santiago harbour with shotted guns and men at quarters, threatening to bombard the town if another prisoner was slain.

Then followed diplomacy and delay, until the blood of the American people, roused rightly to the fighting point by these murders, had time to cool. In the end Spain agreed to surrender the "Virginius"— and did it by delivering her in a filthy and sinking condition; to punish the officials engaged in the massacre,— and did it by promoting Captain Burriel; and to pay a small indemnity for the victims of the massacre, — as though lives could be paid for. There was hot indignation at the termination of the affair then, and it is not pleasing reading now, even after the bloody annihilation of Spain's proudest squadron within sight of the spot where the men of the "Virginius" were slain has in some degree atoned for the crime. In 1873, however, the nation had no navy, and before a Spanish tribunal no cause not backed with show of force seemed to meet with justice. It cannot be maintained, however, that any considerations of fighting strength could have made the course of the United States in dealing with the government responsible for the "Virginius" outrage wise or prudent. The duty neglected then had to be performed thirty years later. It was necessary that at some time Spain should be taught to observe the customs of civilised peoples and to treat her neighbours with respect. It is a curious coincidence, by the way, that the public wish for the recognition of the insurgents, which naturally was very strong immediately after the "Virginius" affair, was balked by the Secretary of State, Hamilton Fish, whose grandson, bearing the same name, was the first man shot dead on Cuban soil in the Spanish war of 1898.

When even the affair of the "Virginius" failed to result in intervention by the United States, the rebellion lagged. Then as in later years the Cubans recognised that their one hope of winning freedom lay in the possibility that their great neighbour would make their cause its own. Disappointed in this hope, they fell to bickering among themselves, and at the same time the disordered conditions in Spain which had contributed much to the advantage of the insurgents were cleared up by the firm re-establishment of the Bourbon dynasty on the throne, With peace at Madrid, the suppression of the Cubans was believed to be easy, and a distinguished soldier, General Martinez Campos, was sent to the island with 25,000 veteran troops and the unqualified authority of the Captain-General. Campos was astonished at the magnitude of the task committed to him. The Cubans were as elusive as foxes in the thickets, and as fierce and unexpected in their attacks as panthers. With ambushes, night assaults, sudden raids, the harrying of the country and the destruction of provisions, they demoralised the regulars, who were all unused to guerrilla warfare. After a year of this sort of hostilities, finding the island no nearer pacification than at the outset, Campos determined to try the methods of compromise. The first Cubans with whom he communicated and who undertook to present his overtures to their comrades were promptly killed by their fellows, who construed even a willingness to carry proposals from the enemy as a sort of treachery. In the end, however, an agreement was reached known as the treaty of Zanjon, which ended the Ten Years War. It promised on behalf of Spain radical reforms, a large measure of self-government, and immunity to all who took part in the rebellion. It is unnecessary to enumerate in detail all the provisions of this treaty, for almost without exception they were violated by Spain either in letter or in spirit. One clause provided that any persons who had participated in the recent insurrection who desired to leave the island might do so at the expense of Spain. This was taken advantage of by several of the leaders, including some of whom the world was destined to hear more, — Maximo Gomez and Antonio and Jose Maceo. Those who remained soon discovered that the blood shed in the Ten Years War had been wasted, for Spanish perfidy nullified all the concessions which had been exacted from the Madrid ministry. It was the recollection of the deception practised at this time which made the Cuban patriots and their friends in 1898 absolutely deaf to the engaging promises of autonomy and reform with which the Spaniards sought to quiet the last revolution.

A tricked and humiliated people will never rest quietly under the domination of their deceivers. Plans for a new Cuban revolution were under way before the wounds incurred in the Ten Years War were fairly healed. Spain was quick to furnish the excuse. She sent out hordes of Spanish office-holders bent only on spoliation. She organised anew the Spaniards in Cuba, making them a class apart from the Cubans and giving them all the profitable places. Spanish manufacturers were given a virtual monopoly of the trade of the island, and the bread of Cuban children was made dear that Spanish millers might be rich. Taxes went up again to the point of extortion, and indeed all the conditions which had led to the earlier revolt were renewed and made more burdensome.

The patriots who had left the island under the provisions of the treaty of the Zanjon were the active organisers of the new outbreak. They formed revolutionary clubs in the United States, the West Indies, and South America. Funds were raised, an active correspondence maintained, arms purchased. Jose Marti, a graduate of the University of Madrid, was the active organiser in this work. He chartered ships, penetrated Cuba in disguise, — he would have been hanged if caught — went over to San Domingo to see the veteran Gomez and to Costa Rica to meet the Maceos. By February, 1895, his plots were sufficiently matured for the first blow to be struck. On the 24th of that month it was reported at Havana that another rebellion had begun. A small band of rebels had appeared at Ybarra, in Matanzas, and the other sections of the island reported the defiance of authority by parties of armed men. "Only a negro uprising," said the Spanish authorities. It was preposterous to suppose that the authority of Spain, supported as it was by 20,000 regular troops and 60,000 enrolled volunteers, could be seriously menaced by a few bands of ragamuffins. But before that insignificant revolt had enlisted the aid of the United States, Spain, in the effort to suppress it, had put about 200,000 men in the field, and had lost by death, wounds, and sickness not less than 105,000 of them, while the expense in money of the war had reduced the nation to the verge of bankruptcy.

The story of this war, which within three years compelled the intervention of the United States, is much like that of its predecessor. The insurgents grew rapidly in numbers and in confidence. The exiles of the Ten Years War returned enthusiastically to join in the new effort for free Cuba. First to come was Antonio Maceo, an educated mulatto and a born soldier, the only leader in the old days who had refused to concur in the treaty of Zanjon, but kept in the field for two months after all others had submitted. Soon after came Marti, and Maximo Gomez from San Domingo, the former to fall in the very first skirmish, the latter to fight to the end and to march proudly into Havana, the hero of the assembled Cubans, when that capital was entered by the soldiers of the United States and their allies. Third in importance among these devoted leaders, was Calixto Garcia, another veteran of the Ten Years War, a man of seventy years, whose soldierly bearing compelled the respect of all the trained soldiers who in later days met him. These leaders of high character and of long experience gave to the new movement for free Cuba a more impressive appearance in the eyes of the world. They remembered the weakness of their earlier effort, springing from the lack of a government and a capital, so they called a constitutional convention, adopted a form of government, and elected a ministry of which Salvador Cisneros was president. In form the government was all that could be asked, in fact it was mainly on paper, and the capital was as elusive as a will-o'-the-wisp. No seaport town could be held by the Cubans for lack of a navy, nor could they establish themselves permanently in any interior city which was easy of access to an enemy which outnumbered them.

Skirmishes and raids made up the military history of this war as of the earlier one. The Spanish government, quickly taking alarm, recalled Captain-General Calleja, and sent in his place Martinez Campos, the negotiator of the repudiated compromise of 1878. This appointment did not tend to allay the irritation of the Cubans; but Campos brought with him 25,000 Spanish regulars, a force which it was thought would suppress all disorder. Before the year had ended thrice as many more had come from Spain, and the rebellion was stronger than ever. Gomez, who was supreme in command of the insurgents, early adopted a general plan of campaign by which the innumerable bands of insurgents were to be guided. It was a plan of avoidance of pitched battles and of constant irritation to the Spaniards. All small posts were to be attacked to the end that arms might be captured, and every Spaniard who delivered up his arms was to be set free. Railroad and telegraph lines were to be cut wherever found. All crops of sugar-cane and all cane mills were to be destroyed unless the owners contributed to the Cuban campaign fund. As in the latter event the Spaniards destroyed crops and mills, the making of sugar soon came to an end in Cuba. Finally the farmers were to be prevented from sending food to the city unless they paid a tax to the insurgent treasury. Above all things, no band of insurgents was to risk a battle in which the odds were against them. A policy which would starve and weary the Spaniards, and so harass the country that it would become unendurable was the Cuban plan of campaign,— the only one which with their limitations the insurgents could have made effective. Accordingly, we look unavailingly for battles. Even when considerable forces met, the fighting was not stubborn. Early in the war, Campos and Maceo came into conflict near Bayamo with from 1500 to 2500 men each. An inconclusive battle was fought. "The enemy suffered severely," was the report of each side, for the statistical methods of both Spaniard and Cuban were alike in their endeavour to minimise their own losses and multiply those of the foe. The most notable thing about the accounts of the battles of the insurrection, from whichever side emanating, is their complete inaccuracy. Major Grover Flint, a young American who joined Gomez, tells a story which fairly indicates the Spanish method of finding "victories" to chronicle. "There had been a court-martial in Lacret's camp the morning of the skirmish," writes Major Flint. "A mulatto lieutenant named Sanchez — a brave man, too, they told me — had been found guilty of assault on a negro girl of the neighbourhood and condemned to death. He was hung under the porch of a deserted cottage, with a placard on his breast giving his name, the offence, and the finding of the court. I saw the body and the Spaniards saw it too. A week later, in a bundle of Havana newspapers that came to us, we read that the cabecilla (or chieftain) Sanchez had fallen in battle and had been left dead on the field by Lacret's retreating bands." The incident is of value, too, as showing how drastic was the discipline in the insurgent camps. They were rebels but not ruffians. Though outlawed by Spain, they were obedient to the laws which civilised people impose. It is unhappily too well established that Spain judged her soldiers more leniently for the offence for which the rebel Sanchez was hanged.

By the end of 1895 the revolution had spread to all parts of the island, and the Spaniards were secure in possession only of the large cities. The imported soldiers from Spain sickened and died in the deadly summer climate, and the repeated drafts were beginning to make the Spanish people impatient. It was determined at Madrid that the policy of Campos lacked force and vigour, and General Valeriano Weyler y Nicalau, Marquis of Teneriffe, was commissioned in his place. Weyler was a man of infamous record. A professional soldier, he had made war murderous under the plea of making it decisive. He was notorious equally for the cold brutality of his nature and for his rapacity. He was no less a robber than a murderer. In the previous war in Cuba he had gained an execrable name by the commission of unnameable barbarities. In the Philippines he had not only appalled the people by his utter indifference to the plainest dictates of humanity, but had robbed the government by wholesale. His appointment to Cuba meant that the war would be conducted with the utmost barbarity, but did not promise speedy peace. Weyler found his profit in a state of war, and could not be expected to make haste to end it.

In fact it was soon seen that the boasted energy of the new Governor-General was without results. The insurgents continued as before harrying the country, checking all production, and thus cutting off Spanish revenues. Maceo burned Batabano and terrorised the province of Pinar del Rio after the Governor-General had pronounced it pacified. Gomez, at Camaguey, defeated General Castillanos, though the Spaniards outnumbered him four to one. Then Weyler adopted the celebrated device of the "trocha," a line of defence composed of trenches, barbed wire, and blockhouses extending across the island from Mariel to Majana. Two months were spent in building this trocha, and 15,000 men employed. The theory of it was that it would cut the insurgent forces in two, that they could never cross it to unite, and that thus severed they would be easily defeated. As a matter of fact the troops both of Gomez and Maceo crossed it repeatedly. But in one of his expeditions, a most audacious one extending into Havana Province itself, Maceo fell into an ambush and was killed. A surgeon on his staff, Dr. Zertuccha, is charged with having betrayed him, but of this there is doubt. A gallant soldier, a strict disciplinarian, a man of a high sense of honour and one who struggled unceasingly to prevent the revolution degenerating into a mere outbreak of lawlessness, Maceo was a sore loss to the Cuban cause. He had been second in command to Gomez, and upon him the leader of the revolution had relied implicity. His place was to some degree taken by General Calixto Garcia, who reached Cuba soon after.

While the warfare of General Weyler on the insurgents gave not the slightest promise of a suppression of the insurrection, it was his methods which hastened the end in the way it came. Upon the manner of warfare which came to be described as Weylerism, the people of the United States looked with indignation and growing wrath. In the field his men were murderers more than soldiers. Neither women nor children were spared on their raids, and the desolate thickets of Cuba witnessed many a scene of revolting cruelty that vied in horror with the incidents of our early Indian wars. But chief of all the offences accredited to Weyler, and most potent in rousing the United States to action, was the policy of reconcentration which formed the subject of his first order on reaching Havana.

The theory of this policy was simple. Weyler saw that certain provinces were held by the insurgents, who lived on the country. They refused battle except when in such numbers that their victory was certain. Lurking in the forests, they would dash out, strike, and disappear. Months of ordinary campaigning made no impression upon them, and there seemed to be no reason why they could not prolong this species of warfare indefinitely. It must be admitted that the problem which confronted General Weyler was one not easily solved. His method of treating it was to make the country in which the insurgents were operating a desert, to destroy its crops and its homes, to remove its peaceable inhabitants to the neighbouring towns, to prohibit any further farming or cattle-raising until the rebels were starved out and ready to surrender. The results of this policy were shocking to the civilised world, but in itself it was not a new device in warfare. To ravage a country upon which the enemy is living is a primary proposition in strategy. Our own General Sheridan once reported that he had so desolated the Shenandoah Valley, "that a crow flying over it would have to take his rations with him."

But the effect of this policy in Cuba was only to cause the deaths from starvation and disease of tens of thousands of unoffending people. The weak and aged, the women and children were the sufferers, while the insurgent ranks were swelled doubly by the men who had seen their fields laid waste and their roofs burned. The decree would have been cruel had it merely ordered the destruction of homes; but it went further and compelled the "pacificoes" thus brutally dispossessed to gather in the nearest towns, where there was no way for them to earn a living nor any methods, save those of mendicancy, for getting either shelter or food. One clause of the order, which was a mere invitation to murder, prescribed that all pacificoes who did not within eight days come into the towns would be treated like enemies, — that is, be outlawed and killed wherever found.

The blood of Maceo, the life-long planning of Marti, the gallant service of Garcia and Gomez with all their followers did less for free Cuba than this one decree.

From the moment the effects of reconcentration began to be apparent, the fortunes of the insurgents in the field were of no importance. They kept the field, for in a country so rich in vegetation as Cuba a persistent force of men willing to endure hardships cannot be starved out, and the Cuban patriots lived patiently on fruits and roots and fought on. But the people gathered in the cities died miserably, and soon the newspaper correspondents from the United States, instead of sending vague accounts of battles between the Spaniards and the Cubans, with a paucity of details and a loud claim on the part of the former that each had been a glorious victory, began visiting towns where the reconcentrados were gathered and telling of their condition to the people at home with only too much detail. Babies starving to death in their mothers' arms, the bodies of starved women and little children lying in the filthy street where they had fallen in their last agony, helpless people by the thousand crowded together in filthy corrals without shelter, without food, and destitute of the ordinary decencies of life — conditions such as these, " in the very dooryard of the United States," as the phrase went, were intolerable. Our people were incredulous for a long time. Such barbarity was incredible in these days of civilisation, but the evidence multiplied day by day. To the testimony of the correspondents was added that of unprofessional observers who went to Cuba to satisfy themselves that the newspapers lied, and came back white with horror and with rage. The growing perfection and wide use of photography added materially to the volume of proof of Spain's barbarities. The camera does not take things that do not exist, and the pictures of emaciated children showed one phase of the Weyler policy, while other photographs of pacificos tied hand and foot and bleeding from fatal wounds of the machete inflicted while they were thus helpless denoted another. Even in the enormous mass of exaggerated and often wholly imaginative stuff sent out from Cuba in the guise of news, there was enough which bore unmistakably the stamp of truth and which related stories of outrage, barbarity, and murder to inflame public opinion in the United States to the point of war. General Weyler saw the danger and tried to avert it characteristically, not by reforming his course, but by imprisoning and expelling from Cuba the correspondents who had exposed it. This was of no avail. Put on their mettle, the journalists redoubled their activity, and by this time their reports had ample authentication from official sources. The endeavours of the charitable to care for the destitute gave convincing indication of the extent of destitution. The Spaniards themselves were forced to join in the work of mercy. Early in the war the Spanish army, probably under compulsion, raised a fund for this purpose, Campos giving $2,000 and each soldier contributing one day's pay. After Weyler's departure, General Blanco, his successor, secured a fund of $100,000 for the starving, and the city of Havana by taxation raised nearly as much for the same end. In every considerable city of Cuba committees were formed for the relief of the reconcentrados, but the situation soon became too much for the utmost endeavours of private charity to cope with. When 400,000 people are beggared and starving, when all industry and commerce in the nation are wrecked by war, the few who have a livelihood left to them are neither numerous enough nor rich enough to relieve the unfortunate. There was but one way to restore even a semblance of prosperity to the island, and that was to permit the reconcentrados to return to their farms. That Weyler would not do, and when his successor, General Blanco, repealed the reconcentration order it was too late.

By that time the survivors had not means to procure seed for a new crop nor to support themselves while making it. Nor had many of them enough strength left to take up the tasks of life again even if permitted. Of about 400,000 reconcentrados more than half had died when the United States intervened. How many perished thereafter cannot be told, perhaps never will be. Anticipating somewhat the course of the narrative, it may be said that the effort of the United States to rescue the reconcentrados from their impending fate was absolutely unsuccessful. We found it as impossible to wage war without inflicting suffering on innocent people as had Weyler himself. The first act of our war was to declare a blockade of Cuba which lasted four months, thus literally increasing the difficulty of getting food for the unfortunates. Just prior to the beginning of the war some relief was effected by charitable contributions from the United States, from Spain secured through the urgency of the United States, and from the people of the United States acting through the Red Cross society. But the declaration of war stopped this at once.

In a succeeding chapter the progress of the Cuban question through Congress is traced. Here it is necessary to note only certain of the incidents which created and kept alive that public sentiment which impelled Congress to act. Chief of all these was the visit of Senator Redfield Proctor, of Vermont, to Cuba and his report, delivered in a speech in the senate, of the scenes he had witnessed there. Other men had seen like horrors and had told of them. Journalists had been recounting tales like his for months; a number of gentlemen representing both houses of Congress had made a trip to the "pacified" provinces as the guests of the owner of the "New York Journal" and had told of what they saw; the consuls in various Cuban cities had described as graphically as the deportment of the state department would permit the agonies of the people. But Senator Proctor's speech carried more weight

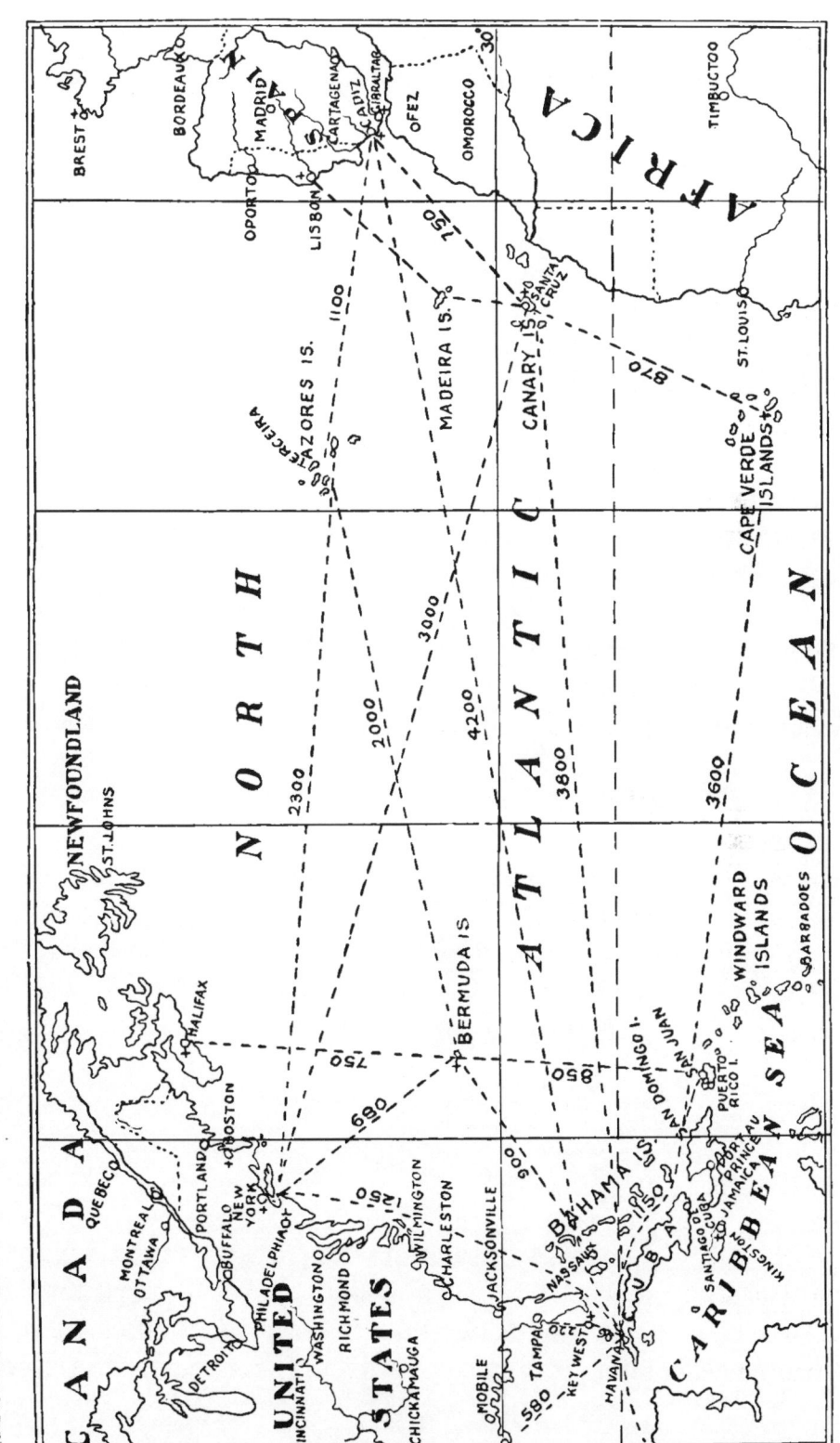

THE NORTH ATLANTIC OCEAN.

than all. He had been Secretary of War, he was a man of substance in the nation, and had not been held a violent Cuban sympathiser. So when in the Senate he expressed himself in words like those herewith quoted, not only his colleagues but the whole people felt the time had come for action. Quoting Weyler's reconcentration order, the Senator said:

"Many doubtless did not learn of this order. Others failed to grasp its terrible meaning. It was left largely to the guerrillas to drive in all who did not obey, and I was informed that in many cases a torch was applied to their homes with no notice, and the inmates fled with such clothing as they might have on, their stock and other belongings being appropriated by the guerrillas. When they reached the town they were allowed to build huts of palm leaves in the suburbs and vacant places within the trochas, and left to live if they could. Their huts are about ten by fifteen feet in size, and for want of space are usually crowded together very closely. They have no floor but the ground, no furniture, and after a year's wear, but little clothing except such stray substitutes as they can extemporise, and with large families or with more than one in this little space, the commonest sanitary provisions are impossible. Conditions are unmentionable in this respect. Torn from their homes, with foul earth, foul air, foul water, and foul food, or none, what wonder that one half have died, and that one quarter of the living are so diseased that they cannot be saved. A form of dropsy is a common disorder resulting from these conditions. Little children are still walking about with arms and chests terribly emaciated, eyes swollen, and abdomen bloated to three times the natural size. The physicians say these cases are hopeless.

"Deaths in the streets have not been uncommon. I was told by one of our consuls that they have been found dead about the markets in the morning, where they had crawled, hoping to get some stray bits of food from the early hucksters, and that there had been cases where they had dropped dead inside the market, surrounded by food. These people were independent and self-supporting before Weyler's order. They are not beggars even now. There are plenty of professional beggars in every town among the regular residents, but these country people, the reconcentrados, have not learned the art. Rarely is a hand held out to you for alms when going among their huts, but the sight of them makes an appeal stronger than words."

This condition was the fruit of Weyler's régime, but it continued long after the Spanish government, alarmed at the outcry against the "butcher," recalled him and sent the more humane General Blanco in his stead. It must be remembered, too, that this state of indescribable misery and suffering existed at a time when the Spanish government insisted that there was no war in Cuba, nothing but a slight rebellion which would speedily be suppressed, and declared that for our government to recognise a state of war and concede to the Cubans the rights of belligerents would be an unfriendly act.

By December of 1897 the actual warfare between the Spaniards and the insurgents had ceased to be a matter of interest in the United States. In comparison with the colossal crime of starving a whole people into subjection, the raids and skirmishes which were dignified by the name of battles were regarded as of no importance. The Weyler régime too had been fruitful of actual outrages upon the persons and property of citizens of the United States. The most celebrated of these cases was that of the so-called "Competitor" prisoners, a number of men whom the Spaniards had captured on a filibustering vessel of that name, and whom Weyler proposed to shoot after their condemnation by a court-martial organised to convict. The stout protest of Fitzhugh Lee, the United States consul-general at Havana, saved the prisoners from this fate, but they were kept imprisoned for months without opportunity to see counsel for their defence, despite General Lee's vigorous protests. More unlawful still was the Spanish treatment of Dr. Ruiz, a naturalised American who for some suspected offence was thrown into prison and there brutally murdered by his guards. This case was so heinous that the United States government made of it a grave issue, with the result that thereafter Americans suspected of political offences were turned over to General Lee, who sent them forthwith to the United States. It is just to note here that so large a proportion of these Americans bore Cuban names and spoke English with difficulty it was apparent many had taken advantage of our liberal naturalisation laws to secure American protection in their enterprises against Spain.

In August, 1897, Weyler was recalled. The assassination of the Spanish premier Canovas had led to a change of ministry, and the new government determined to try methods of concession with the Cubans. But the time for concessions had passed. The evil that Weyler had done could no more be undone than the dead he had starved could be brought to life. General Blanco promptly cancelled the reconcentration order, but, as has been explained already, the starving and dying multitude was in no condition to profit by this belated clemency. As Consul-General Lee said, "In the first place these people have no place to go to; their houses have been burned down; there is nothing but the bare land left, and it would take them two months before they could raise the first crop. In the next place they are afraid to go out from the lines of the towns, because the roving bands of Spanish guerrillas, as they are called, would kill them. So they stick right in the edges of the town, just like they did, with nothing to eat except what they can get from charity." Nor was the aid belatedly provided by Spain and the government of Cuba properly employed in alleviating the sufferings of the reconcentrados. There is only too much evidence that some of this money, and some of the provisions sent by charitable people of the United States, was diverted to the uses of the Spanish soldiery.

General Blanco also endeavoured in good faith to check the growing antagonism between the United States and the Spanish in Cuba. The efforts for the amelioration of the reconcentrados were part of this effort. The release of the "Competitor" prisoners was a second step in the programme, but it came too late. Curiously enough, the effort to feed the starving had much to do with making the relations of the two nations more critical, for the Spaniards in Havana — uncompromising and haughty at all times — looked upon the acceptance of contributions from the United States and the permission to the Red Cross Society to engage in relief work as a sort of implied admission of American right of intervention. They manifested their disapproval by riots in the streets of Havana and by threats of mobbing the American consulate. Out of this grew the visit of the "Maine" and the calamity that made war inevitable.

Chief, however, of the features of the new policy upon which Blanco relied to avert the impending conflict was the offer to Cuba of a system of autonomy. This was in some degree a concession to American demands, as will be seen, but the concession, however pleasing to the administration at Washington, was received with suspicion and positive hostility in Cuba. There was complaint that a mere semblance of home rule was offered and that the whole purpose of the revolution would be lost if the overtures were accepted. But more effective even than this argument was the appeal of the insurgent leaders to history. Garcia and Gomez both had fought in the Ten Years War. Both had accepted then in good faith the promise of reforms with which Spain had purchased peace. Both had seen the promise violated, the reforms withdrawn or deprived of all beneficial effect by the methods of administering them. With this bitter knowledge fresh in their memory these Cuban leaders did not waste time in discussing the apparent merits of the plan of autonomy which Spain proffered, but rejected it at once. "Nothing but absolute independence" was their cry, and they declared that for a member of the insurgent army to discuss autonomy would be equivalent to treason. They declined to receive envoys from Blanco, and announced that anyone sent to offer a compromise based on the new concessions would be treated as spies. It was difficult for the Spanish authorities to believe that this threat was seriously meant, but the insurgents soon proved they were in deadly earnest. Colonel Joaquin Ruiz was selected to make the first effort to win over an insurgent band to peace and autonomy. Under a flag of truce he proceeded to the camp of the Cuban leader, Aranguren, choosing him because of a personal friendship dating back to before the war. In spite of the old-time friendship, in spite of the flag of truce, the messenger was seized and shot in accordance with the general order which had been given publicity, and which Ruiz had ignored. "A savage murder," cried the anti-Cuban party in the United States. "A justifiable act of war," responded the Cuban sympathisers. Whichever it was, it at least showed that Spain's belated offer of autonomy had no chance of acceptance.

Events such as these, occurring day by day, kept the attention of the people of the United States riveted on Cuba. Every day the popular demand for recognition of the insurgents or for actual armed intervention grew more forceful. It was seen that Spain could never suppress the revolt, and it was evident that while the effort continued, the United States navy would be employed in chasing filibusters, our interests in the island, which were heavy, would go more and more to ruin, our citizens would be exposed to insult and actual injury at the hands of Spanish soldiers, and above all, the inhuman and intolerable spectacle of a whole nation being wantonly starved to death at our very doors without protest on our part would be presented to the world. The voice of the people arose almost as that of one man in the demand that this condition should be remedied, cost what it might. Only from a very few, and those mostly men who were controlled by the ignoble influences of the stock-market, did there rise a sound of dissent. A group of men of enormous wealth, and of corresponding political influence, fought strenuously against any action which might " unsettle values " — their conception of the one unbearable thing. Long they held the Washington government back from the plain discharge of its duty to man and to God. But in the end, they fell back, and the American people marched on in an unbroken column to fulfil its mission — to purge the new world of the last vestige of Spanish power and Spanish brutality.

CHAPTER III

THE DISASTER TO THE "MAINE" — CAPTAIN SIGBEE'S DESPATCH — THE STATE OF PUBLIC OPINION — WHY THE "MAINE" WAS SENT TO HAVANA — HER RECEPTION THERE — PRECAUTIONS AGAINST ATTACK — THE EXPLOSION — FRIGHTFUL LOSS OF LIFE — PERSONAL NARRATIVES OF SURVIVORS AND EYE-WITNESSES — THE OFFICIAL INVESTIGATIONS — ATTITUDE OF THE SPANIARDS — THE FINDING OF THE COURT OF INQUIRY — "REMEMBER THE 'MAINE.'"

THE American newspapers of the morning of February 16, 1898, blazed with news that stirred the hearts of the people as had no intelligence since the first shot was fired at Fort Sumter; news of a calamity so great as to plunge a nation in mourning — a disaster so unprecedented, so mysterious, surrounded with so many suspicious circumstances as inevitably to suggest to the most judicial mind the instant thought of treachery blacker and more infamous than any of which Cortes or Pizarro was guilty. The official information, hurriedly given out by the Washington authorities in order that its more restrained tone might counteract the wrathful surmises of the press, was given in this despatch to the Navy Department from Captain Sigsbee, commanding the United States battle-ship "Maine":

"'Maine' blown up in Havana harbour at nine-forty to-night and destroyed. Many wounded and doubtless more killed or drowned. Wounded and others on board Spanish man-of-war and Ward Line steamers. Send lighthouse tenders from Key West for crew and the few pieces of equipment above water. None has clothing other than that upon him. Public opinion should be suspended until further report. All officers believed to be saved. Jenkins *and Merritt not yet accounted for. Many Spanish officers, including representative of General Blanco, now with me to express sympathy.* SIGSBEE."

Captain Sigsbee's appeal for a suspension of judgment, greatly as it redounded to his credit as a cool and prudent man in an hour of awful strain, was but partly acceded to. There was suspension of action but not of opinion. In Congress, while all men were discussing in private conversation the frightful deed, official utterances were confined to resolutions of sympathy and regret. The executive authorities, beyond making the necessary arrangements for saving whatever of value remained on the wreck, caring for the survivors, burying the dead, and providing for a searching inquiry into the cause of the disaster, showed no sign of recognising in the event a new and potent factor in the Spanish-American problem. But the masses of men were swift to judge, and to-day there are but few to question the righteousness of their judgment. They recalled the nature of the Spaniard, cruel and treacherous from all historic times. They told each other that never in the history of the United States navy had a ship been destroyed by the accidental discharge of her own magazine, and they grimly suggested that the coincidence of a superheated magazine operating for the first time in a Spanish harbour was a little too much for credulity. And as day after day the newspapers, searching indefatigably for clews, unearthed this or that suspicious circumstance, the public conviction hardened in the form that it took instantly upon getting the news — a stubborn, ingrained belief that the battle-ship had been destroyed and her crew assassinated by the deliberate and prearranged plan of a Spaniard. A popular navy officer, Captain Evans, widely known as "Fighting Bob," was credited in the newspapers with a remark which well expresses the public sentiment. He was said to have been talking to the Secretary of the Navy.

"If I had been in command of the fleet at Key West instead of Admiral Sicard," said he, "I would have taken my entire squadron into Havana harbour the next morning, and then I would have said to them, 'Now we'll investigate this matter and let you know what we think about it at once.'"

"If you had done that you would have been severely reprimanded," responded Secretary Long.

"Perhaps so," was the response, "but the people would have made me President at the next election."

Possibly the story is apocryphal. At any rate the officer referred to has always refused to authenticate it. But it serves its turn in showing what was the popular feeling at the time of the destruction of the "Maine," for it was told and retold with hearty approval all over the land.

Let us go back now a little and consider the reasons for the presence of the "Maine" in Havana harbour and the foundation for the general belief, which probably will never be changed, that she was blown up by the enemy.

In an earlier chapter some reference has been made to the increasing friction between the Spanish authorities and the Americans whose business interests kept them in Cuba. It has been the custom of civilised nations since the earliest days of international relations to send warships to protect their citizens resident in foreign lands whenever a disordered state of society or the collapse of government makes protection by the local authorities impossible or improbable. The United States, by reason of their comparative freedom from foreign complications, have seldom had this duty to perform, though occasionally revolutions in South American states have compelled the sudden despatch of a protecting man-of-war. At no time has such a precaution as this been regarded as indicative of hostility toward the established government of the state to which the vessel has been sent. It is probable that no month passes without the employment of a British or French man-of-war to protect the interests of the citizens of that nation in some foreign land, yet the event is not held to suggest unfriendliness of any kind. In the case of Cuba, however, peculiar conditions made the stationing of a war-ship at Havana take on a special and unusual significance. That which did most to produce this unfortunate result was the prolonged delay in taking this action. Either President Cleveland or President McKinley, in the early days of his administration, might have sent a ship to Havana and kept one there continuously without awakening the resentment of the Spaniards, had the act been done promptly and quietly. As it was, newspaper clamour was aroused by the delay, the American papers most hostile to Spain being most noisy in their demands for the presence of a ship at Havana. What should have been merely a perfunctory and conventional precaution was made to take on the proportions and character of an act of hostility and defiance. The diplomats were involved. Spain protested. The President hesitated. The newspapers shrieked. And so, when popular pressure and the real vital necessities of the case compelled the President to act, the sending of the ship was hailed by American jingoes and most Spaniards as an actually unfriendly act. The very precautions taken to divest it of this air only strengthened the popular conviction. The Spanish government was consulted and gave its formal acquiescence to an act which perhaps never before in the history of nations had been made the subject of diplomatic negotiations. The correspondence between the State Department and the Spanish minister was made public to show how thoroughly friendly was the episode, and arrangements were made to have a crack Spanish cruiser, the "Vizcaya," visit New York as an offset to the American ship at Havana.

The ship finally selected to undertake the mission was the second class battle-ship "Maine." Built in 1895, this ship was one of the most modern and efficient vessels in the navy at the time of her assignment to this service. She was 324 feet long, of 6650 tons displacement, with a trial speed of 17.45 knots and armoured with twelve inches of steel on the hull, and eight inches on the turrets. In each turret were two ten-inch rifles and in addition she had six six-inch rifles, seven six-pounders and eight one-pounders. She carried a crew of 26 officers, commissioned and warranted, and 330 men. For some weeks before her actual despatch to Havana the " Maine " had been stationed at Key West, her commander, Captain Sigsbee, being in constant cable communication with Consul-General Lee and under orders to proceed immediately to Havana if summoned by that official. It was well known at Key West and at Washington that the situation at the Cuban capital was grave and that at any moment some outbreak of mob violence might put the lives of the many Americans in jeopardy. Day after day Captain Sigsbee and General Lee exchanged cable messages on the most trivial topics, the purpose being to keep the cable constantly tested for interruptions. The understanding between the two officers was that on the receipt of the message " two dollars " Captain Sigsbee should have his ship ready to sail within two hours, or on the receipt of another pre-concerted despatch. In his own story of the events leading up to the loss of his ship Captain Sigsbee says that this preliminary message did in fact come one night and that, after ordering all hands to report aboard at the sound of a gun, he went ashore with a number of his officers to attend a dance, that all suspicion of the possible movement of the night be averted. The second message did not come, however, and the destiny of the " Maine " worked itself out in a different way. Not until late in January when the battle-ship was at sea with the squadron of Admiral Sicard, did the order to go to Havana come, and then it came from Washington. On the 25th of that month the ship steamed into the harbour of the Cuban capital. Even more than the ordinary ceremony of courtesy was observed. The officers were clad in semi-dress uniforms and the crew in blue. A local pilot took the vessel to the buoy selected by the harbour master, and as soon as she was moored a Spanish lieutenant arrived to make the customary visit of ceremony. From him Captain Sigsbee satisfied himself that a salute fired to the Spanish flag would be returned, and accordingly salutes both to the flag and to Admiral Manterola were fired and speedily acknowledged. The next day Captain Sigsbee, accompanied by General Lee, paid his visit of ceremony to the Governor-General. It is worthy of record now that the American officer has said: "All visits were made without friction and with courtesy on both sides, and apparently with all the freedom of conversation and action usually observed." Even in the demeanour of the people on shore Captain Sigsbee noticed nothing out of the way. "I thought the people stolid and sullen, so far as I could judge from an occasional glance. I noted carefully the bearing of the various groups of Spanish soldiers I passed. They saluted me, as a rule, but with such an appearance of apathy that the salute really went for nothing. They made no demonstration against me, however, not even by look."

It was hardly to be expected, however, that there should not be some resentment in the Spanish mind against the naval representatives of a nation which was notoriously in sympathy with the efforts of the insurgents to win their freedom, and that some expression of this resentment should not occasionally break forth. Captain Sigsbee's own story of the events of his stay inspires rather wonder that the Spanish temperament, always impetuous and passionate, did not result in more open insults to the Americans during the short time that was to elapse before the destruction of the ship. He relates that no Spanish officers visited the ship except on calls of ceremony; that the bumboat men in the harbour did not seem to wish the custom of the "Maine's" sailors; that at a bull-fight he "detected glances at himself (me) that were far from friendly," and that from passing ferries in the harbour derisive shouts and whistles were sometimes raised at sight of the "Maine." These are but trifles, less important by far than the discourtesy with which a mayor of New York treated Captain Eulate, of the "Vizcaya," when that officer made his visit of ceremony. Nor was the circular thrust into the hands of Captain Sigsbee one day, a translation of which follows, much more significant.

SPANIARDS!

LONG LIVE SPAIN WITH HONOUR!

What are you doing that you allow yourselves to be insulted in this way? Do you not see what they have done to us in withdrawing our brave and beloved Weyler, who at this very time would have finished with this unworthy, rebellious rabble who are trampling on our flag and on our honour?

Autonomy is imposed on us to cast us aside and give places of honour and authority to those who initiated this rebellion, these low-bred autonomists, ungrateful sons of our beloved country!

And, finally, these Yankee pigs who meddle in our affairs, humiliating us to the last degree, and, for a still greater taunt, order to us a man-of-war of their rotten squadron, after insulting us in their newspapers with articles sent from our own home!

Spaniards! the moment of action has arrived. Do not go to sleep. Let us teach these vile traitors that we have not yet lost our pride, and that we know how to protest with the energy befitting a nation worthy and strong, as our Spain is, and always will be!

Death to the Americans! Death to autonomy!

Long live Spain! Long live Weyler!

Notwithstanding the comparative courtesy with which they were treated and the efforts made to preserve at least an appearance of amity with the Spanish authorities and people, the Americans understood that they were in what was practically a hostile port. On the "Maine" most of the precautions against attack which would have been taken in time of war were observed. To patrol the harbour, or to use search-lights would be to give offence, but the less obvious precautions were taken. An extra watch was kept on deck at night. Sentries were posted at every point of vantage on the ship and the most minute reports were made to the commander. Ammunition was kept ready for the rapid-fire guns and an extra supply of shells for the six-inch guns, while double steam was kept up in order that the turrets might be at all times movable. Though visitors to the ship were encouraged without reference to their nationality, a careful eye was kept on each, and particular attention was given to such as brought parcels aboard, lest dynamite or an infernal machine might be left in some vital part of the ship. The court of inquiry which examined into the cause of the explosion found, as we shall see later, that every imaginable precaution had been taken to guard against treachery.

It was the night of February 15th. The harbour of Havana, always beautiful despite the miasmatic ooze with which it is bottomed, was never more enchanting to the senses. The soft tropic air just stirring with the westerly trade wind barely ruffled the surface of the water in which were reflected the brilliant stars of the southern heavens. An arc of shining lights against a dark background told where the city with its thronged cafés and its starving reconcentrados lay. The harbour was dotted with ships. The "Maine" at her moorings had swung around broadside to the city — "in the position in which she would have been sprung to open her batteries on the shore fortifications," is the significant way Sigsbee afterwards described it. A little distance astern was an American liner, the "City of Washington," while to the starboard were the two Spanish men-of-war "Alfonzo XII" and "Legazpi." On the decks of all the ships men were sitting and the quays of the city were thronged with people seeking the open air. Captain Sigsbee was sitting in his cabin writing, as he tells us, to his wife, apologising for having carried a letter of hers in his pocket for a year — how curiously do some of the little things of life jostle the great events that determine the course of history and make or unmake nations! As he was putting the letter into its envelope there came a terrifying explosion and about the ship all was darkness. To him "it was a bursting, rending, crashing sound or roar of immense volume, largely metallic in character. It was followed by a succession of heavy, ominous, metallic sounds probably caused by the overturning of the central superstructure and by falling débris. There was a trembling and a lurching motion of the vessel and a list to port, and a movement of subsidence. The electric lights, of which there were eight in the cabin where I was sitting, went out. Then there was intense blackness and smoke."

Rushing through the darkness to reach the deck the captain encountered a man. In the impenetrable gloom he could not see whom he had met, but it proved to be his orderly, William Anthony, who reported the ship blown up and sinking. In the contemporaneous accounts of the disaster Anthony was described as having given a formal salute, come to attention, and said, " Sir, I have to report the ship blown up and sinking." Amplified with much picturesque detail, this story went the rounds of the newspaper press, made Anthony a hero of melodrama, and might have passed into history had not Captain Sigsbee himself demolished it with the remark that if a salute had been made it could not have been seen in the intense blackness of that compartment. But the captain goes on to say that no salute nor any melodrama was needed to add to the heroism of this private of marines who kept his head and did his duty with calmness and efficiency. It was at nine-forty P. M. the explosion occurred. Writing long after the fact, and with the full testimony taken by the board of inquiry available, we know now much that to Captain Sigsbee when he reached the flame-lighted deck was unknown and problematical. Despite the smoke which hung over all the ship like a pall he could see that the forward part of the "Maine" was shattered to pieces, that flames were leaping up amidships and that the wreck was sinking. He found about him most of his officers, though cries of agony from the water and from the fast sinking berth-deck gave melancholy certainty that among the crew great loss of life must have occurred. He has recorded that his first order was to post sentries about the wreck to guard against attack, for he instantly believed what in due course of time was proved, that the "Maine" had been blown up from outside, and he ascribed it to an enemy. It was but a few moments before discipline and the habit of command and obedience asserted themselves among the survivors. The magazines were flooded lest any remaining explosives should be discharged. Boats were lowered to search for survivors in the water, in which task they were aided by boats from the Spanish man-of-war and the American liner. Slowly to the captain on the still tenable quarter-deck came reports showing the terrible extent of the disaster. Officers reported the machinery wrecked, the bow under water, the fire gaining on the after magazines and the great body of the crew lost — nobody knew how many until that dreadful night was far spent. The ship settled slowly until the deck on which Sigsbee and the executive officer, Lieutenant Wainwright, stood was level with the water. Then, as the fire still threatened the magazines all stepped into a boat, the captain being last to leave, and were rowed away to the "City of Washington" whence Captain Sigsbee sent the despatch to the Secretary of the Navy which heads this chapter. There too he received the report of the first muster which showed that only eighty-four or eighty-five survivors could be found, and

FORWARD THIRTEEN-INCH GUN ON BATTLESHIP INDIANA.

thither General Lee hurried when news of the disaster reached him. Not until the hospitals had time to tell their stories of painful recoveries and pitiful deaths was the full measure of the disaster taken. In all on that fatal night 254 men were killed outright, while thirteen others died long after in hospital. In this one disaster — or as it may fairly be said, by this one crime — more than seventeen times as many men were killed as fell in the United States navy during the whole course of the war.

The official inquiry into the causes of the explosion, which was begun shortly after the disaster, not only sifted thoroughly all obtainable facts bearing on the destruction of the "Maine" and resulted in a verdict which accorded with the first instinct of the people, but it brought out from survivors and eye-witnesses of the disaster picturesque and graphic accounts of the occurrences of that dreadful night. Some of the testimony in this hearing may be quoted in part, showing as it does how instantaneous and complete was the calamity, and how the discipline among both officers and men asserted itself even before the extent of the ruin could be imagined. Perhaps most interesting of all the testimony given was that of Lieutenant John Hood, of the "Maine," who was on deck at the time of the explosion. In part it follows:

"I was sitting on the port side of the deck, with my feet on the rail, and I both heard and felt — felt more than I heard — a big explosion, that sounded and felt like an underwater explosion. I was under the impression that it came from forward, starboard, at the time. I instantly turned my head, and the instant I turned my head there was a second explosion. I saw the whole starboard side of the deck, and everything above it as far aft as the after-end of the superstructure, spring up in the air, with all kinds of objects in it — a regular crater-like performance, with flames and everything else coming up. I immediately sprang myself behind the edge of the superstructure, as there were a number of objects flying in my direction, for shelter. I ran very quickly aft, as fast as I could, along the after-end of the superstructure, and climbed up on a kind of step. I went under the barge, and by the time I went up on the superstructure this explosion had passed. The objects had stopped flying around. Then I saw on the starboard side there was an immense mass of foaming water and wreckage and groaning men out there. It was scattered around in a circle, I should say about a hundred yards in diameter, off on the starboard side. I immediately proceeded to lower the gig, with the help of another man. After I got that in the water several officers jumped in it, and one or two men. In the meantime somebody else was lowering the other boat on the port side. I heard some groans forward, and ran forward on the quarter-deck down the poop-ladder, and I immediately brought up on an immense pile of wreckage. I saw one man there, who had been thrown from somewhere, pinned down by a ventilator."

THE COURT. "May I interrupt Mr. Hood a moment? He said several officers jumped into the gig. He does not say for what purpose or what they did. That might leave a bad impression unless he states what the object was."

ANSWER. "They jumped into the gig, commanded to pick up these wounded men whom we heard out in the water. The orders had been given by the captain and the executive officer to lower the boats as soon as they came on deck. I spoke of lowering the gig because I was on the deck before they got up there, and began to lower it anyway, to pick up these men. As I was saying a minute ago, I found this one man lying there on the quarter-deck in this wreckage, pinned down by a ventilator. With Mr. Blandin's help we got him up just in time before the water rose over him. The captain and the executive officer ordered the magazines to be closed [flooded]. We all saw at once that it would be no use flooding the magazines. We saw that the magazines were flooding themselves. Then the captain said he wanted the fire put out that was starting up in the wreckage. I made my way forward through the wreck and debris, up to the middle superstructure, to see if anything could be done toward putting out this fire. When I got there I found nothing could be done, because the whole thing was gone.

"When I climbed up on this wreck on the superstructure I saw similar piles of wreckage on the port side which I had not seen before, and I saw some men struggling in that, in the water; but there were half a dozen boats there, I suppose, picking them up and hauling them out; and after pulling down some burning swings and things that were starting to burn aft, to stop any fire from catching aft, I came aft again out of the wreckage. There was no living thing up there at that time. Shortly after that we all left the ship. There were two distinct explosions, — big ones, — and they were followed by a number of smaller explosions, which I took at once to be what they were, I suppose — explosions of separate charges of the blown-up magazine. The instant this first explosion occurred I knew the ship was gone completely, and the second explosion only assisted her to go a little quicker. She began to go down instantly. The interval between the two was so short that I only had time to turn my head and see the second. She sank on the forward end — went down like a shot. In the short time that I took to run the length of that short superstructure aft, the deck canted down, showing that her bow had gone at once.

"At the same time the ship heeled over considerably to port, I should say about ten degrees the highest amount, and then the stern began to sink very rapidly, too; so rapidly that by the time I got that gig lowered, with the assistance of another man or two, the upper quarter-deck was under water, and the stern was sinking so quickly that when I began to pick this man up, whom I spoke of on the quarter-deck, the deck was still out of water. Before I got this ventilator off him — it didn't take very long, as Mr. Blandin assisted to move that to get him up — the water was over my knees, and just catching this fellow's head, the stern was sinking that quickly.

Two officers only went down with the "Maine," for the explosion occurring directly under and in the forward part of the ship left the officers' quarters and their stations on the quarter-deck almost intact. Lieutenant Friend W. Jenkins, unhurt by the first explosion, was rushing forward to his post of duty when the second eruption of steel and giant explosives occurred, and in it he met his death. Assistant Engineer D. R. Merritt was sitting in the junior officers' quarters in the steerage with Naval Cadet D. F. Boyd when the infernal roar broke upon them. The steerage, being forward of the ward-room, or officers' mess, was nearer the seat of the explosion and suffered more accordingly. Cadet Boyd, in his testimony, tells the story of Merritt's death:

"Assistant Engineer D. R. Merritt and I were sitting in the steerage when I heard a dull report, followed by the crashing of splinters and falling of the electric light fixtures overhead. The lights were extinguished at the first report. I was struck by a small splinter and dazed for a moment. I grasped Mr. Merritt by the arm, exclaiming: 'Out of this! Up on deck!' Together we groped our way out of the steerage, and along the bulkhead in the after torpedo room, where we met a cloud of steam and tremendous rush of water. The force of the water separated us, and as I was lifted off my feet I caught a steam-heater pipe, and reached for the steerage ladder. It was gone. I worked my way along the steampipe until I reached the port side of the ship. Water was rushing through the air-ports, and as I reached the side, I heard some one cry: 'God help me! God help me!' I think it must have been Merritt. At that moment I found the two torpedoes that were triced up under the deck-beams, and, twining my legs around them, I worked my way inboard. The water was then at a level of about one foot from the deck-beams. At that moment some burning cellulose flared up, and I was able to reach the hatch-coaming and work my way up on deck. I rushed on the poop, and there found Captain Sigsbee, Lieutenant-Commander Wainwright, Lieutenants Holman and Hood, and Naval Cadet Cluverius. The remaining boats were away, picking up these men in the water. Lieutenant-Commander Wainwright and I then went on the quarter-deck awning and on the middle superstructure to help out any wounded."

About the death of Lieutenant Jenkins there has been some mystery, cleared up only in part by the testimony at the inquiry. At the moment of the explosion he was sitting with three other officers in the ward-room, far from the actual seat of the explosion. His companions were saved, but of him, or of his body, nothing has been seen since. It has been made apparent, however, that in following the path of duty he met death. The coloured waiter of the officers' mess, who was in the pantry adjoining the mess-room when the shock occurred, tells of the last seen of Lieutenant Jenkins in homely but graphic phrases:

"I met Mr. Jenkins in the mess-room, and by that time the water was up to my waist, and the water was running aft. It was all dark in there, and he hollered to me, and he says: 'Which way?' I don't know what he meant by that. I says: 'I don't know which way.' He hollered again: 'Which way?' I says, 'I don't know, sir, which way.' And he hollered the last time; he says: 'Which way?' I says: 'I don't know, sir.' Then I was groping my way, and the water was up to my breast. Mr. Jenkins started forward, and then the whole compartment lit right up. That whole compartment where the torpedoes were lit right up, and I seen Mr. Jenkins then throw up both hands and fall, right by the steerage pantry. Then I groped my way aft, and got to the captain's ladder — the ladder coming out of the ward-room — just as you come out of the ward-room to go up in the cabin. When I got there the ladder was carried away, and somehow or other the manrope kept fast upon the deck, but the ladder got adrift from it down below in the water. By that time the water was right up even with my chin. Then I commenced to get scared, and in fooling around it happened that a rope touched my arm, and I commenced to climb overhand and got on deck."

Immediately above the magazine which was exploded nearly three hundred men swung sleeping in their hammocks. More than two hundred and fifty of these were slain instantly or drowned by the rapid sinking of the ship. Some were blown to atoms as they slept, never recognising the abrupt transition from life to death. Some were so stunned that after regaining consciousness in the hospital at Key West they had no recollection of the disaster, and thought themselves still on board the good ship then deep in the foul ooze of Havana harbour. Those immediately above the roaring crater were obliterated. Captain Sigsbee relates that on the roof of the berth-deck there was the impression of two human bodies ground to powder against it by the force of the blast. The report of the court of inquiry is full of the narratives of those who escaped with their full faculties undimmed, but to most of the men the shock came so suddenly and out of such a peaceful environment, that the memory of a roar and the sense of finding themselves struggling in the water were all that remained. A fireman, William Gartrell, told a story of escape that seems almost miraculous. He was, at the moment of the disaster, in the steam steering-room, two decks below the officer's mess-room. That is as if, taking the gun-deck of the ship as the first floor of a building, he was three stories under ground. To get as far up as the officers' mess-room, or the steerage, whence as we have seen officers and men escaped only with the greatest difficulty owing to the inrushing water, "he had to run forward about twenty feet, spring across to a ladder, climb up two flights of ladders, and pass through another doorway"—thus Captain Sigsbee describes his path to life and goes on to say of it that it "was a narrow and difficult route under the best of conditions." But Fireman Gartrell followed it to safety and thus tells the story of his flight.

"I could see through the door, sir. It was a kind of a blue flame, and it came all at once. The two of us jumped up, and I went on the port side up the engine-room ladder, and Frank Gardiner he went up the starboard side — at least, he did n't go up, because he hollered to me. He struck the door right there where the partition separates the two doors, and he must have struck his head. He hollered to me; he says: 'O

Jesus, Billy, I am gone.' I didn't stop then, because the water was up to my knees. I made a break as quick as I could up the ladder, and when I got up the ladder into the steerage-room the ladder was gone. Everything was dark. I couldn't see nothing; everything was pitch-dark, and I gave up, or I started to give up. There was a coloured fellow with me; I didn't know his name until afterward. His name was Harris. We got hold of each other. I says, 'Let's give up; there is no hope.' I started in to say a prayer the best I knew how, and I heard a voice. It must have been an officer; it couldn't have been a man's voice, because he says, 'There is hope, men.' I knew from that that he was an officer. After that I seen a little light. It looked like an awful distance from me, but I made for that light, and when I got there it seemed like I could see the heavens. I got jammed in the ladder. My head was right up against the deck. I seen the ladder, and I caught hold of Harris, and the two of us hugged each other. . . . The ladder was hung crossways on top. There wasn't no ladder that we could walk up. The ladder was up above us. . . . I don't know whether I got out first, or this coloured fellow, but when I did get out I tried to say a prayer. I looked where I was, and I saw the heavens and everything, and I tried to say a prayer or something, and I fainted away. I felt some one picking me up, and they throwed me overboard."

From the principal sleeping place of the crew on the berth-deck forward only two men escaped, for it was directly above the magazine that was exploded by the external shock — whatever that may have been. That any should have come alive from that spot is no whit short of miraculous, for the deck above and below them was rent as by a volcanic shock, great masses of steel were lifted high in air and turned jagged edges on every side to tear the flesh of men thrown against them. One of the men who came still living through that fiery furnace explained his escape with the remark: "I think I must be an armour-piercing projectile." The other, Charles Bergman, boatswain's mate, gave to the court of inquiry a somewhat incoherent but still interesting account of his experience. He was sleeping in his hammock, he said, when he heard a terrible crash.

"Something fell, and then after that I got thrown somewhere in a hot place. Wherever that was I don't know. I got burned on my legs and arms, and got my mouth full of ashes and one thing and another. Then the next thing I was in the water — away under the water somewhere, with a lot of wreckage on top of me that was sinking me down. After I got clear of that I started to come up to the surface of the water again, and I got afoul of some other wreckage. I got my head jammed in, and I could n't get loose, so I let myself go down. Then it carried me down farther. I suppose when it touched the bottom somewhere it sort of opened out a bit, and I got my head out and started for the surface of the water again. I hit a lot of other stuff with my head, and then I got my head above the water. I got picked up by a Spanish boat, one of these shore boats, I think."

The testimony of officers and passengers on merchant ships lying in the harbour also throws some light on the appearance of the ship at the moment of the explosion. The captain of a British bark, lying from a quarter to a half a mile away, said that he was writing in his cabin at the moment, and the shock was so great that he thought his ship had come into collision. The transoms of his cabin doors were knocked out of place, and the concussion affected his head painfully. That was with the first shock. Rushing on deck, he arrived just in time to see the second explosion. "The débris ascended," he said, "one hundred and fifty or one hundred and sixty feet up in the air. It seemed to go comparatively straight until it reached its highest point of ascent; then it divided and passed off in a kind of rolls or clouds. Then I saw a series of lights flying from it again. Some of them were lights, — incandescent lights. . . . The colour of the smoke I should say was a very dark slate-colour. There were fifteen to twenty of those lights that looked like incandescent lights. The smoke did not seem to be black, as you would imagine from an explosion like that. It seemed to be more a slate-colour. Quantities of paper and small fragments fell over our ship, and for some time after."

The American steamship "City of Washington" was lying at anchor about a quarter of a mile from the "Maine," and at the moment of the explosion several of her passengers were sitting on deck enjoying the tropical night. One of these, Mr. Sigmund Rothschild, delivered very important testimony at the inquiry. In the brief excerpt here printed, his insistence upon the resemblance of the sound of the first explosion to that of a shot is very noticeable:

"I had brought my chair just about in this condition [indicating], and had not sat down, when I heard a shot, the noise of a shot. I looked around, and I saw the bow of the 'Maine' rise a little, go a little out of the water. It couldn't have been more than a few seconds after that noise, that shot, that there came in the centre of the ship a terrible mass of fire and explosion, and everything went over our heads, a black mass. We could not tell what it was. It was all black. Then we heard a noise of falling material on the place where we had been, right near the smoking-room. One of the life-boats, which was hanging, had a piece go through it, and made a big hole in it. After we saw that mass go up, the whole boat ['Maine'] lifted out, I should judge, about two feet. As she lifted out, the bow went right down. . . . We stood spellbound, and cried to the captain [of the 'City of Washington']. The captain gave orders to lower the boats, and two of the boats, which were partly lowered, were found broken through with big holes. Some iron pieces had fallen through them. Naturally, that made a delay, and they had to run for the other boats, or else we would have been a few minutes sooner in the water. Then the stern stood out like this, in this direction [indicating], and there was a cry from the people: 'Help!' and 'Lord God, help us!' and 'Help! Help!' The noise of the cry from the mass of human voices in the boat ['Maine'] did not last but a minute or two. When the ship was going down, there was the cry of a mass of people, but that was a murmur. That was not so loud as the single voices which were in the water. That did not last but a minute, and by that time we saw somebody on the deck in the stern of the ship, and it took about a few minutes when the boats commenced to bring in the officers."

When day dawned after that night so full of horror and of death, the Americans on shore and on the ships could see only a shapeless mass of twisted and blackened steel where twenty-four hours earlier had been one of the proudest of the United States battle-ships. A cloud of smoke hung over the wreck, for the cellulose with which the sides were packed, and the wood in such portions of the cabin as were still above water, were slowly burning. All that was recognisable as a part of a ship was the after military mast, which, with its fighting-top and the national flag floating at half-mast, protruded above the scene of disaster. Boats crowded the harbour. Sightseers were out in swarms, patrol boats from the Spanish ships guarded the wreck, and the surviving American sailors were out in craft of all kinds on the solemn duty of recovering the dead as they slowly came to the surface. During the day, the United States despatch boat "Fern," and the lighthouse tender "Mangrove," came into the harbour from Key West, bringing supplies and surgical aid. It is worth noting, in passing, that while Captain Sigsbee urged a suspension of judgment on the part of the people as to the cause of the explosion, he was swift to form his own conclusions. He asked that lighthouse tenders, rather than a man-of-war, be sent him, because he believed that the "Maine" had been deliberately blown up, and he did not wish the nation to risk losing another ship in the same way on the eve of a war that had now become inevitable.

Events now proceeded rapidly toward the final submission of the issues between the two peoples to the arbitrament of the sword. Investigations into the causes of the explosion of the "Maine" were set on foot by Spain and the United States both. The Spaniards were promptest with their inquiry, beginning it within an hour after the disaster; but as it proceeded it was apparent that it was undertaken less to find the real cause of the explosion than to clear the Spaniards of any complicity in it. In default of proof of incompetence or negligence on the part of the officers of the wrecked ship, the responsibility for the disaster rested with the Spaniards, for among all civilised people a ship in a foreign port is supposed to be entitled to police protection by the local authorities. The "Maine" lay at a buoy selected for her by the Havana harbour master. The port was, technically at least, a friendly one. If the discipline and system aboard were such as to make it impossible that she had been destroyed by the accidental explosion of one of her own magazines, the responsibility for the disaster — which under such circumstances would be a crime — would necessarily rest with the Spaniards. This responsibility would be all the heavier for the fact that the city and port were in fact under military rule. For months no explosives of anything like the power necessary to set off the magazines of an armoured battleship had been in the possession of, or obtainable by, any private person in the city. Some years earlier, in the port of New York, an adventurous swimmer, to advertise a species of aquatic suit he had invented, swam out at night and affixed a dummy torpedo to the hull of a British man-of-war lying at anchor. Such an exploit might have been possible at Havana at other times, though the suspicion with which the officers and men of the "Maine" regarded their surroundings and their hosts made it impossible at this moment. But the theory that the act was one of private malice only is shaken by the fact that martial law strictly prohibited to any private citizen the possession of explosives.

The feeling of resentment against the Spanish which naturally grew out of this calamity was not a little increased by the attitude and utterance of the people of

Havana, including many of the high officers in the Spanish army. It is proper to say here that the Spanish navy officers, living up to the traditions of courtesy which seem to characterise that branch of the armed service of every nation, did not offend in this regard, but, on the contrary, were punctilious in their avoidance of anything which might seem like gloating over the misfortune of the Americans, or criticism of the methods of discipline on the "Maine." But the very night of the wreck, while our men were still fighting for life in the engulfing waters, the cafés of Havana were crowded with Spanish army officers drinking deep draughts of champagne to the downfall of the Yankees. When the cruiser "Vizcaya" reached Havana shortly afterwards, her captain called on Captain Sigsbee and showed something more than official and perfunctory sorrow for the calamity which had befallen the American sailor, but the cry from the docks as the Spanish cruiser entered the harbour was, "Down with the Americans!" and the sunken "Maine" was contrasted with the trim Spanish ship, as if the difference between the two nations was thereby typified.

Calmly however, while the work of recovering and burying the dead was in progress the United States proceeded with the task of inquiring into the causes of the disaster. A court of inquiry composed of Captain (afterwards Admiral) William T. Sampson, Captain French E. Chadwick, Lieutenant Commander William P. Potter, and Lieutenant Commander Adolph Marix, judge-advocate, was appointed and convened at Havana in the cabin of the "Mangrove" on the 21st of February. Divers were then at work on the "Maine," and had been for some time gathering evidence for the court and striving to recover the bodies of the dead. In this work in and about the wreck the Americans were systematically hampered by the Spanish authorities, who at one time went so far as to attempt to prescribe to Captain Sigsbee the times and manner in which he should visit the wreck of his own ship. This, and the persistence with which the Spaniards, by innuendo or direct charge, advanced the theory that the ship had been blown up through the fault of her own officers, added to the tension between the representatives of the two countries.

Into the details of the evidence submitted to the court of inquiry it will not be necessary to go. That portion of it other than the accounts of eye-witnesses to the tragedy, some of which we have quoted, was of a scientific and technical character intended to determine whether the ship had been blown up from without or by an internal explosion. It is obvious that had the latter been the case, the keel and bottom would have been bent out and downward. Upon the divers who examined the wreck determination of this all-important problem rested, and in recognition of its importance several navy officers, though untaught in the art of diving, volunteered to don the submarine armour and go down into the mud and darkness to study the question for themselves. Permission was, however, refused them, and reliance was placed upon the reports of the professional divers, some of whom were enlisted men in the navy. The manner in which evidence was deduced from their reports was interesting. Serving on the "Fern" at the time was a young navy officer, Ensign W. V. N. Powelson. His training had been that of a scientific naval constructor, and his life had been given to the study of the structure of ships. With a set of detailed drawings of the "Maine" before him, he would have the divers measure pieces of the frame which were affected by the explosion. Comparison of these measurements with the drawings would show exactly the place in the ship at which the plate belonged, though when found it might have been blown many yards from its proper position. After painstaking work in the collation and comparison of evidence occupying one month, the court presented its report, which was in effect that the bottom of the ship had been forced up some 35 feet in a way that could only have been possible by the employment externally of some powerful explosive. It declared that there were two explosions with an appreciable space of time between them and distinctly different in character.

"The first explosion was more in the nature of a report like that of a gun, while the second was more open, prolonged, and of greater volume. This second explosion was, in the opinion of the court, caused by the partial explosion of one or more of the forward magazines of the 'Maine.'" The court went on to declare that the condition of the bottom of the ship as disclosed by the divers "could have been produced only by the explosion of a mine at about frame 18 and somewhat on the port side of the ship." It further declared that "the loss of the 'Maine' was not in any respect due to fault or neglect on the part of any of the officers or members of the crew of said vessel," but that "the 'Maine' was destroyed by the explosion of a submarine mine which caused the partial explosion of two or more of her forward magazines."

The report of the Spanish board of inquiry ascribed an internal cause to the explosion, and inferentially accused the American officers of faulty discipline and incorrect methods. But this document, though published widely in the United States, did not shake the public conviction that the act was that of a Spaniard, though there was no inclination to charge the Spanish authorities with complicity in the execrable crime.

Great as was the wrath and hot the hatred bred of the destruction of the "Maine," it was in no sense the cause of the war which speedily followed. It is not easy to say whether it hastened or delayed the inevitable conflict. The slow deliberation of the court of inquiry, and the fact that all felt that a declaration of war before the findings of that court were complete would be something in the nature of "snap judgment," deferred for a month acts which probably would have been more hastily taken otherwise. Public sentiment had become pretty generally fixed in the opinion that the inhuman conditions prevailing in Cuba could only be remedied by the intervention of the United States, and political conditions in Spain were such that such intervention would have led infallibly to war. There were, it is true, people and publicists in the United States who were so strongly of the opinion that the "Maine" and the "Maine" alone brought on hostilities that they even went the length of accusing the Cuban patriots of committing the crime in order to inflame Americans against Spain. This unjust and incredible suspicion, however, was held only among those known as "the peace at any price men," and it was scarcely the most discreditable opinion enunciated by them during the general public discussion that preceded the war.

It is probable that history in coming ages will concede what the public men who urged on the war claimed, that it was a struggle entered upon for the most unselfish purposes; that it was a war for humanity, a war undertaken to free a neighbouring people from a rule which was offensive to every civilised instinct; a war from which could come no profit, and which would necessarily be costly, both in blood and treasure. The unexpected and possibly undesirable fruits of the victory which the diplomats and politicians held for the nation at the end of hostilities may obscure but do not disprove the entire unselfishness with which the nation entered upon the struggle. It was not a war of revenge, any more than it was intended to be a war of conquest. Though the newspapers harped continually upon the fate of the "Maine," and the impression was created that the battle signal in the American navy was, "Remember the 'Maine,'" the thought of revenge was far distant from the minds of American commanders. No United States vessel went into action flying that signal. It was hoisted but once, without authority, by an enlisted man of the coast signal service, and he was promptly reprimanded for it. As Captain Sigsbee well said, "I should like to make the point . . . that this great and free country, with its education, good intention, and universal moral influence, may go to war to punish but not to revenge. Improperly applied, the motto, 'Remember the "Maine,"' savours too much of revenge, too much of evil for evil."

CHAPTER IV

AT THE NATIONAL CAPITAL — THE COURSE OF THE CUBAN QUESTION IN CONGRESS — ITS TREATMENT BY PRESIDENT CLEVELAND — IT CONFRONTS PRESIDENT MCKINLEY — THE MISSION OF GENERAL STEWART L. WOODFORD — FAIR PROMISES OF THE SPANISH MINISTRY — THE FAILURE OF AUTONOMY — THE DE LOME LETTER AND ITS RESULT — PREPARATIONS FOR WAR — CONGRESS VOTES A $50,000,000 EXTRAORDINARY CREDIT FOR PURPOSES OF NATIONAL DEFENCE — THE REPORT OF THE "MAINE" COURT OF INQUIRY.

WHILE the court of inquiry was holding its sessions at Havana and Key West, the tide of events at Washington was setting slowly but irresistibly toward war. In both Houses of Congress, even before the destruction of the battle-ship, the war party was strong. The feeling that upon the nation rested a solemn duty to interfere in behalf of suffering humanity at its very doors was too forceful for party ties, and Republicans vied with Democrats in urging upon the administration a vigorous and immediate policy of intervention. The student of contemporaneous history as set forth in the newspapers of the day will discern a seeming party division; but it was more apparent than real. The Executive, being charged with the heavy responsibility of determining upon war or peace, naturally and properly proceeded with the utmost deliberation, as though desirous of exhausting the last peaceful remedy before accepting the final arbitrament of the sword. As the President was a Republican, the great majority of the Senators and Representatives of that party were in loyalty bound to uphold his policy and await his pleasure. It appeared then, that the Democrats were urging on the war and the Republicans holding back;

but when the President gave the signal, both parties were as one in their response. It was a war in which political differences were forgotten and sectional antagonisms obliterated.

The date of the beginning of the active agitation which finally resulted in war may be set at December, 1896, when President Cleveland in his last message to Congress reviewed at some length the situation in Cuba growing out of the insurrection, recapitulated the various propositions that had been made for securing to the Cubans relief from their intolerable ills, and referred, though without approval, to the demand for armed intervention. He went on to inform Congress that the Executive had suggested to Spain a plan for home rule in Cuba, and had offered to guarantee its execution if accepted. This guarantee was regarded as essential, since the perfidy of Spain in failing to fulfil the reforms by the promise of which it had quelled the last prior revolution made it unlikely that the insurgents would again trust to Spanish good faith. Though the message was addressed to Congress, one phrase in it was evidently intended as a hint to Spain. "It cannot be reasonably assumed," said the President, "that the hitherto expectant attitude of the United States will be indefinitely maintained. . . . By the course of events we may be driven into such an unusual and unprecedented condition as will fix a limit to our patient waiting for Spain to win the contest either alone, and in her own way, or by our friendly co-operation." And, continuing, he said that a situation might be presented "in which our obligations to the sovereignty of Spain will be superseded by higher obligations which we can hardly hesitate to recognise and discharge."

Spain was not deaf to the hint of the President, but the threat aroused her antagonism and increased her stubbornness rather than stimulating her government to seek an honourable and practicable way out of the hopeless situation in which the nation was placed. The Prime Min-

CAPTAIN MAHAN   CAPTAIN CROWNINSHIELD   SECRETARY LONG   ADMIRAL SICARD

THE NAVAL BOARD OF STRATEGY; 1898.

ister, Canovas, responded at once with an interview which sounded the note of defiance. "No concession of any kind," said he, "will be made until the insurrection in Cuba is put under control. Spain is strong enough to carry on the campaign in Cuba and the Philippine Islands until peace is restored, no matter how long the struggle may last."

And so the Cleveland administration went out of office leaving the Cuban trouble as a legacy to its successor. Meanwhile the agitation of the question grew in volume throughout the nation. A great section of the American press, comprising the newspapers of the largest circulation, if not of the greatest influence, made the cause of the Cubans its own. Havana was filled with American correspondents who telegraphed to their papers graphic descriptions of the cruelty of the Spanish soldiery and the wanton destruction of property to the permanent impoverishment of the island. Some of these correspondents joined the insurgent forces and made the American people familiar with the character of such patriot leaders as Gomez, Garcia, and Maceo. Others fell foul of Spanish authority in Havana, and were cast into Morro castle, whence they were released only after long diplomatic negotiations. No campaign for the Presidency was ever fought by American newspapers with more persistence than the fight for recognition of the Cuban republic.

In official circles at Washington the incoming of a new administration gave brief pause to discussion of Cuba. Among the practical politicians, the distribution of post-offices and consulships then took first place. But the administration undertook immediately the work of securing the release of all Americans in Cuban jails, and pressed it with such zeal that by the end of April all were free. The Senate, on the 20th of May, passed a joint resolution recognising the belligerency of the Cuban insurgents, a measure which had it been given effect would have done away with the friction resulting from filibustering expeditions. It was, however, left to die in the Foreign Affairs Committee of the House. A day or two later, however, the Cuban question appeared again in Congress, being brought up by a special message from the White House. The President said that from special reports obtained from the American consuls in different parts of the island, it was learned that many American citizens were suffering as the result of the reconcentration policy of the Spanish military authorities. He asked that an appropriation of $50,000 be made for their relief, which was accordingly done. The discovery that, in order to check the rising ambition for liberty in Cuba, Spain was starving not only her own people, but our citizens as well, did not tend to allay the growing abhorrence of Spanish methods in the United States.

At this juncture, General Stewart L. Woodford was appointed United States minister to Spain, and given instructions to pursue a most diplomatic and amicable course, keeping ever in view the end of restoring peace and settled conditions in Cuba, but exhausting every resource of diplomacy in the endeavour to accomplish it by peaceful methods. For a time it seemed that fate smiled on the purpose of the mission. Before General Woodford reached his post, an assassin struck down the Prime Minister, Senor Canovas, a man of the Bismarckian type, a man of blood and iron. To him succeeded Sagasta, and the liberal party, which was believed to be more ready to pursue a conciliatory policy toward the Cubans, came into office. The change in the attitude of the Spanish government was immediate. General Woodford presented the demands of the United States to the new ministry, receiving instead of the cold rebuff with which Canovas had met all representations from this government, an assurance that Spain would consider and act upon them. The essential part of Minister Woodford's instructions were to demand the recall of General Weyler and the abandonment of the policy of reconcentration. He was also directed to inform the

Spanish government that the war should have been ended long before, and to ask that a date be set prior to December, 1897, when it would be stopped. The representations of the United States envoy were met with diplomacy more characteristic of Spain than the direct, if brusque and haughty, methods of Canovas. The policy of procrastination and evasion was at once brought into play. Weyler was indeed recalled, returning to his country, there to become a popular hero and a menace to the ministry that recalled him, but, despite the most plausible promises, the system of reconcentration was not abandoned, and the work of starving Cuba into subjection continued. To the demand that a date be set for the close of the war, Spain replied that such action would be impossible; and, as a return concession for the recall of Weyler, time was asked to put into operation in the island a new system of autonomy. It is enough to say of this project that it failed wholly of fruition. The Cubans had gone too far on the path to complete freedom to be coaxed back into allegiance to Spain by any device of home rule, however alluring, and the system of autonomous government for the island proffered by the Sagasta ministry was on its face hollow and unsatisfactory. In the early days of the war, much was made by the peace party in the United States of the apparent concessions wrung from Spain by Minister Woodford, and the assertion was generally made that a continuance of diplomatic negotiations would have secured for Cuba all that was won by the barbaric and expensive method of war; but the facts cannot be said to bear out the argument. The Woodford mission was in all essentials a failure. The one thing accomplished was the recall of General Weyler, and his successor, General Blanco, varied little from his methods, though he succeeded in inspiring less antagonism in pursuing them. The hand of iron still held the Cubans in a grip no less remorseless because the glove of velvet had been donned.

In Congress and by the people at large the slow progress

of General Woodford's diplomacy was regarded with general impatience. Day after day the news from Cuba was of women and children slowly starving to death under the merciless operation of the reconcentration system. A plague, like that which appears in India at the time of famines, broke out among the unhappy islanders, and the scenes described by travellers and correspondents shocked the sense of humanity of our whole people. Our navy was kept busy at heavy expense in defeating the efforts of Americans to land arms and munitions of war for the use of the insurgents, and the courts sentenced to imprisonment two ship captains found guilty of commanding such expeditions. This use of the new navy bitterly offended the nation, which saw the ships built to carry to all lands the emblem of liberty and popular government made the effective aids to the maintenance of as corrupt and barbaric a despotism as the world has ever seen, while the sentence to the penitentiary of men convicted of aiding a neighbouring people in a struggle for liberty, however much in accord with the strict letter of the law it may have been, caused a cry of protest, indignation, and reproach to arise from every part of the republic. And so when Congress met in December ready to receive the President's message, the whole country looked with chief interest for that part of it which should treat of the Cuban question and the attitude of the new administration toward the patriots who were trying to do for Cuba what Washington and his men did for the colonies of North America.

There was universal disappointment when it appeared that the whole sum and substance of the advice of the Chief Executive was, "Wait." The message was one of information rather than of suggestion. The intolerable situation in Cuba was described in detail, and with caustic comments upon the Weyler administration. But there was no suggestion of immediate action by the United States, but rather a plea for delay. The autonomy plan which few, either in the United States or Cuba, had taken

PRESIDENT McKINLEY.

seriously, seemed to have impressed Mr. McKinley favourably, and he apparently expected a great change for the better under General Blanco. Only in so far as it set forth unmistakably the President's conviction that the United States possessed the right to intervene in Cuba when the proper time should arrive, did the message satisfy the American people. But as it did not declare that time arrived, it was disappointing on this side of the water, while in Spain the very enunciation of the right of intervention at any time added to the hostility felt for the United States. The President himself was speedily undeceived as to the condition of the people of Cuba, for on Christmas Eve, he issued an appeal to the country for contributions in aid of the starving Cubans, — unhappy reconcentrados who were starving as fast under the "humane" Blanco as under the cruel Weyler.

The first month of the new year saw little official action in any branch of the United States government bearing upon the fast growing quarrel with Spain. Between the people of both countries the antagonism was fast becoming more bitter under the influences of the causes which I have detailed in an earlier chapter, but the President was still fighting for delay and the House of Representatives, under the masterful domination of the speaker, Mr. Thomas B. Reed, systematically held without action all resolutions sent thither by the more radical Senate. Toward the end of January, the executive took the significant step of sending to Key West and the Dry Tortugas, within six hours steaming of Havana, the ships of the North Atlantic squadron, — so plain a menace that many high authorities have declared it equivalent to a declaration of war.

February had hardly come in when an event occurred that ruffled the calm that seemed to be settling over official circles at Washington, and gave the diplomats of the world something to talk about. The very day when President McKinley was penning his appeal to the American people for aid for the suffering Cubans, the Spanish minister at Washington, Señor Dupuy De Lome, was writing a letter to a Spanish journalist in which he described the President of the United States as a "low politician who wishes to leave a door open for himself, and to stand well with the jingoes of his party." The President was further accused of catering to "the rabble." This letter was stolen by an emissary of the Cuban Junta in New York, and given to the American press.

Now the people of these United States are not always observant of the proprieties in speaking of their Presidents, and it is entirely probable that in more than one newspaper which printed with condemnatory headlines the De Lome letter, there may have been editorial comments on the President quite as disrespectful as those which the Spanish envoy permitted himself. Just about that time a great section of the American press was berating Mr. McKinley very vigorously for what seemed to be his lethargy in taking up the Cuban question. He was accused of being dominated by the financial interest of the country, and of being more alive to the sound of the Wall Street stock ticker than to the bitter cry of starving Cuba. But while Americans said these things of their President, and read them in their own journals with entire complacency, they experienced quite another sensation when they discovered a minister from Spain putting forth so very unfavourable an estimate of the qualities of the nation's chief magistrate. The outcry against De Lome was immediate and noisy, and that hapless individual, quick to recognise the extent of his offence, forestalled the penalty which he knew would be inflicted, by cabling his resignation to Madrid before Minister Woodford could deliver the President's request for his recall. This was regarded by the Spaniards as a diplomatic triumph on his part, and as Spain refused to apologise for his letter on the ground that it was purely a private communication, the affair ended without any formal reparation having been made for the affront. De Lome was neither recalled, ordered out of the country by our government, nor was apology made for his letter. On February 15th, the day of the explosion of the "Maine," the appointment of Señor Luis Polo y Bernabe as minister to succeed De Lome was announced by the Spanish ministry.

Naturally this incident did not tend to allay the growing aversion with which the American people regarded the Spaniards, and the agitation for swift action in Cuba's behalf was greatly aided by some frank and illuminative passages in this same letter which showed that the promises of autonomy so glibly made to Minister Woodford were meant only to deceive and to gain time. It was remembered too that the employment of the best ships of the United States navy to check filibustering, that so irritated our people, had been conducted practically under the directions of this envoy who was thus convicted of insulting and deceiving our government. But the De Lome incident was swept out of the mind of the people while it was still fresh in their memory by news of the awful and murderous destruction of the "Maine."

Strangely enough the assassination of this noble ship produced a calm rather than a storm in the National Legislature. A distinguished United States Senator, Mr. Henry Cabot Lodge, who was himself foremost in the fight for Free Cuba, has well written:

"Scarcely a word was said in either House or Senate, and for forty days the American people and the American Congress waited in silence for the verdict of the board of naval officers who had been appointed to report on the destruction of the 'Maine.' To those who understood the American people, this grim silence, this stern self-control, were more threatening than any words of public sorrow or anger could possibly have been."

This reticence of Congress, this unwillingness to appear to prejudge in any way the report of the court of inquiry justifies the assertion that the disaster to the "Maine" delayed rather than hastened war. One single instance gives striking illustration of the care which was taken to avoid anything which might seem like acting under the influence of the natural wrath and indignation which the destruction of the war-ship aroused. The very day before news of the disaster arrived, Congress had called for information as to the state of affairs in Cuba, having particular reference to the condition of the reconcentrados and other peaceful victims of a cruel, cruel war. The President had this information at hand, it having been prepared by the American consuls in Cuba in response to instructions from the state department. It told a sad story of suffering, spoliation, and starvation, but the President withheld it from Congress until the first hot fire of wrath over the destruction of the "Maine" had been given time to cool.

In the midst of this silence on the immediate matter of the disaster, however, Congress took definite action in preparation for the war which all but the most short-sighted could see now was sure to come. On the 9th of March both Houses, without a dissenting vote, appropriated as an emergency fund to be placed at the disposal of the President, $50,000,000.

Thus provided with needed funds, the executive departments began the work of preparing for war. It was evident from the first that the brunt of the conflict would fall upon the United States navy. For Spain to invade the United States with any considerable army was obviously impossible, and equally so was any invasion of the Iberian peninsula by the American forces. Whatever land fighting there was to be, would occur in Cuba and Porto Rico, and it was not to be expected that any very great army would be necessary for the establishment of American supremacy in those islands. Indeed the commanding general of the army estimated that 90,000 men would suffice. But the vast coast line of the United States, dotted with rich and populous cities, offered a rich and tempting field for Spanish naval operations, and it was of prime importance that the navy should be sufficiently reinforced to be equal to any emergency that might arise. Accordingly, experienced officers were sent abroad to purchase such war-ships as might be found in the market and to secure additional supplies of munitions of war. It was necessary that this work should be done with the utmost expedition, for immediately upon the formal declaration of war it would become the duty of all neutral nations to prevent by all methods in their power the sale of war material to either of the belligerents.

There is a notable lesson for the future in the very slender success which our representatives abroad had in their efforts to purchase ships. They had practically unlimited means and more than a month in which to conduct negotiations, yet they secured only one ship which was a really considerable addition to our navy. This was the cruiser " Amazonas," built in England for Brazil, a protected cruiser, with a displacement of 3,600 tons and a speed of twenty knots. In her armament this was a notable vessel, for she mounted Armstrong guns which possess a greater muzzle velocity and a greater striking energy than ours of the same class, — the six-inch Armstrong being, in fact, equal in efficiency to our eight-inch rifles. The ship was also provided with smokeless powder, something that the American navy was without and the lack of which seriously affected the efficiency of our forces by land and sea. The " Amazonas " on being put into commission under the Stars and Stripes was renamed the " New Orleans." With her was bought a sister ship, the " Abrouail," but this vessel, which was renamed the " Albany," was caught unfinished by the declaration of war, and pinned up in a British ship-yard during the continuance of the conflict. A very good torpedo boat destroyer — a class of vessel in which the United States navy is exceedingly deficient — was trapped in the same way. We secured, however, a little sixty-foot torpedo boat, and an 1,800 ton gun-boat built in England for Portugal, which we renamed the "Topeka." From Brazil was also purchased the "Nictheroy," an American merchant ship, bought by the Brazilians years ago and remodelled for naval purposes. She was hardly a valuable addition to the American navy.

This virtual failure to materially strengthen the navy by purchase abroad, though money was plenty, time ample, and all the rest of the world at peace with no immediate need for men-of-war, should not be forgotten by the people of the United States. Had our quarrel been with a well-equipped nation, and one disinclined to delay the beginning of hostilities until we had ransacked the ship-yards of Europe, even this slender measure of re-enforcement would have been lacking.

At home the purchase of vessels proceeded with more satisfactory results. In the great passenger ships of the American line the navy department had ready to its hand four swift liners easily convertible into cruisers. This line enjoys from the United States government a large and most remunerative contract for the carriage of the trans-Atlantic mails, in consideration of which its ships are to be held subject to the government's right of charter in time of war. Two of the vessels, the "St. Paul" and "St. Louis" were built in American ship-yards and specially designed for conversion into cruisers. All four vessels were chartered, at an average cost of more than $2,000 a day apiece, and hurriedly remodelled. The British-built ships were renamed "Yale" and "Harvard," and were speedily presented with colours and machine-guns by the delighted students of those colleges. The best of the coast-wise steamships of other lines were also bought by the government and converted into cruisers, transports, or hospital ships, while a great number of slim and speedy yachts were bought for torpedo boats. In all, more than 50 vessels were thus purchased, ranging from the great 16,000 ton Atlantic liners down to trim and

HURRY-WORK AT NIGHT ON MONITOR "PURITAN" AT LEAGUE ISLAND NAVY YARD, PHILADELPHIA.

pigmy yachts hardly big enough to carry a one-pounder rapid-fire gun.

While the navy department was thus busy, the war department was not idle. The sites for camps had to be examined with reference to their hygienic condition, their propinquity to strategic points, and their railroad facilities. Contracts with railroads for the carriage of troops and munitions of war were to be prepared, and preliminary arrangements with the great purveyors of food products to be made for army rations. While Congress seemed to be hesitating, and the people were getting impatient with the prolonged delays of diplomacy in the face of certain war, the days seemed to those charged with the duty of preparation to fly all too fast. That the nation was not prepared was matter of current notoriety. In the United States the government is too constantly under the search-light of the press for the nation ever to be deceived, as were the French in 1870 with the famous report that the army was ready "to the last button on the last gaiter." We knew we were short of ammunition, of artillery and rifles, and of men, but in spirit the people were ready. For the military capacity of Spain there was a general contempt, which the subsequent events showed to be not unjustified.

Towards the end of March the war party in Congress began to show renewed activity. On the 17th of that month the speech of Senator Proctor, recounting what he had seen in Cuba, was made in the Senate, and in both Houses of Congress at about the same time the members of a commission sent to the devastated island by the proprietor of the "New York Journal," described the scenes of starvation and horror there. Senator Proctor's speech was particularly effective, as he had been at an earlier period Secretary of War, and had not prior to the time of his address been prominently identified with the pro-Cuban party. His impassioned appeal for action made the pressure of Congress on the President more forceful than ever. On the 28th, the report of the "Maine" Court of Inquiry came in, accompanied by a message from the President still pleading for delay. A day earlier he had submitted to Spain a proposition by the terms of which the United States would undertake to conduct negotiations with the insurgents for peace, and a reconciliation with the mother country, Spain meanwhile declaring an armistice to continue until October 1st. It was also requested that the reconcentrados be permitted to return to their farms, while the United States would look after their immediate wants. The proposition met with cold rejection from Spain, — most happily; for it is apparent now that, had the President succeeded in that or any of his well meant but unwise efforts to avert war, the sufferings of the Cubans would have been indefinitely prolonged and the war only deferred, not avoided. But the "Maine" report put an end to Congressional patience. A majority of the Senate had been for months openly at odds with the President on account of his dilatory policy, but without the concurrence of the House could not resort to compulsion. The parliamentary usage in the House is such that the speaker can absolutely dictate what business shall be done, and almost what matters shall be spoken of. Speaker Reed was avowedly opposed to any action on the Cuban question. Even to the day of the declaration of war, he was at least a passive opponent of the pro-Cuban party, while in the earlier days of the discussion his power was sufficient to block all that the Senate wished done. Party discipline for a long time kept even those Republicans who believed in the justice of the Cuban cause docile under the speaker's masterful domination, but after the report on the "Maine" there were threats of a revolt which he could not ignore. The country had forced Congress into line, and the representatives saw clearly that they must compel the speaker to cease obstruction, or Republican candidates before the people at the next election would encounter public disapproval and defeat. Speaker Reed saw that the moment for his capitulation had come, and the President recognised that without the power of the speaker to defend him he would be at the mercy of a Congress which had long been hungry for more drastic measures. Accordingly he prepared a message in which he virtually turned the determination of the whole policy of the government toward Spain over to Congress. But though news of the imminence of this message was conveyed to the capital, the document itself was held until the American consuls could be withdrawn from Cuba, lest its publication should provoke the Spaniards there to riot and perhaps to murder. It was the 11th of April when the message finally reached Congress. Pending its transmission, the ambassadors of Great Britain, France, Germany, and Italy, the Russian *charge d'affairs*, and the Austrian minister waited upon the President and presented him a joint note appealing "to the feelings of humanity and moderation of the President and the American people in their existing differences with Spain," and expressing a hope that further negotiations will lead to an agreement, which, while securing the maintenance of peace, will afford all necessary guarantees for the re-establishment of order in Cuba." There was some criticism among public men of the action of the President in receiving the diplomats, as it seemed to give an inferential acquiescence to the theory that our national quarrel was fit subject for the interference of European governments. But the President's reply, prepared carefully in advance, was so worded as to avoid this construction, making it clear that the United States regarded the communication as one in the interests of humanity only, and expressing confidence that " equal appreciation would (will) be shown for its own earnest and unselfish endeavours to fulfil a duty to humanity by ending a situation, the indefinite prolongation of which has become insufferable."

At noon on the 11th of April, the long expected message on the condition of affairs in Cuba was sent to Congress. The galleries in both chambers were crowded and every Representative and Senator who was able to be out was in his seat. From Maine to Alaska, the nation was on the alert for what was expected to be a historic document, the first formal step toward the entrance of the United States upon its first war with a nation of continental Europe, — a war that would be epoch-making in all history for the lofty purposes for which it had been undertaken.

The message was long, with an infinity of detail and without effort at oratorical style. After rehearsing the history of Spanish rule in Cuba, and describing the conditions which the United States had at last determined to correct, the President went on to enumerate the reasons which justified the intervention of the United States. These were fourfold:

First. Humanity, or the duty of checking the wanton sacrifice of human life in Cuba.

Second. The obligation of the United States to protect the lives and interests of its citizens resident in Cuba, or the property on that island owned by citizens and residents of the United States.

Third. The necessity of putting an end to the damage to American commerce caused by the existing state of disorder and war.

Fourth. The wisdom of terminating a situation which was a constant menace to our national peace, and which involved the nation in heavy expense in its effort to preserve the laws of neutrality.

In the presence of these considerations, therefore, the President declared that the time for intervention had at last come. He declined to recommend the recognition of the Cubans as belligerents, and made an elaborate argument against the recognition of the Cuban Republic, but asked of Congress authority to take such steps as seemed to him wisest to the end of restoring a stable government in Cuba, and insuring peace and protection to its people and to our own citizens there resident. And he asked that he be empowered to employ the army and navy of the United States in giving effect to his plan.

The well-disciplined administration majority in the House passed within twenty-four hours, and almost without debate, the resolution which the President had asked; but in the Senate there was more delay. There the President's unwillingness to accord recognition to the Cuban Republic caused much dissatisfaction and an acrimonious debate, at the end of which a resolution was adopted which, besides conferring upon the executive the authority requested, declared the Island of Cuba free, recognised the Republic, and demanded the withdrawal of Spain's troops and the relinquishment of Spanish authority. The House then passed this resolution, with the proviso for the recognition of the Republic stricken out. That necessitated sending the resolution to a conference committee, whence it emerged in the following form, and was adopted on the 19th of April by both Houses:

"Joint resolution for the recognition of the independence of the people of Cuba, demanding that the government of Spain relinquish its authority and government in the island of Cuba, and withdraw its land and naval forces from Cuba and Cuban waters, and directing the President of the United States to use the land and naval forces of the United States to carry these resolutions into effect.

"WHEREAS, The abhorrent conditions which have existed for more than three years in the island of Cuba, so near our own borders, have shocked the moral sense of the people of the United States, have been a disgrace to Christian civilisation, culminating, as they have, in the destruction of a United States battle-ship, with 266 of its officers and crew, while on a friendly visit in the harbour of Havana, and cannot longer be endured, as has been set forth by the President of the United States in his message to Congress of April 11, 1898, upon which the action of Congress was invited; therefore be it resolved,

"First — That the people of the island of Cuba are, and of right ought to be, free and independent.

"Second — That it is the duty of the United States to demand, and the government of the United States does hereby demand, that the government of Spain at once relinquish its authority and government in the island of Cuba and withdraw its land and naval forces from Cuba and Cuban waters.

"Third — That the President of the United States be, and he hereby is, directed and empowered to use the entire land and naval forces of the United States, and to call into the actual service of the United States the militia of the several States to such an extent as may be necessary to carry these resolutions into effect.

"Fourth — That the United States hereby disclaims any disposition or intention to exercise sovereignty, jurisdiction, or control over said island, except for the pacification thereof, and asserts its determination when that is accomplished to leave the government and control of the island to its people."

The Cuban question was thus rapidly passing into the Spanish war. At home and abroad recognition of this fact was almost universal. Friends of peace and devotees of the stock market continued despairingly their efforts to avert the conflict, but it was apparent to the most sanguine that all hope of a peaceful adjustment was ended. Political conditions in both Spain and the United States forced the unwilling executives into war. The activity of the Democrats in this country in urging on the war, and the evident determination of the people that humane conditions should be restored in Cuba, even though by force of arms, caused some of the strongest influences about the President to be exerted in favour of immediate hostilities. In Spain the ministry saw that to yield to the demands of the United States would be to invite overthrow, even if it did not give supporters of Don Carlos, a pretender to the throne, a chance to embark upon a successful revolution. The signature by the President of the resolutions the day following their passage put an end to all doubt, and instantly upon this action an ultimatum was sent to Minister Woodford at Madrid for presentation to the Spanish government. In this document the substance of the congressional resolutions was restated, and the demand made that Spain at once relinquish its authority in Cuba and withdraw its land and naval forces thence. Three days were given for an answer to this demand, and a copy of the document was given to the Spanish minister at Washington.

To the ultimatum of the United States, no answer was ever returned other than the very insufficient ones offered by the guns of Montojo and Cervera at Manila and Santiago. One of those diplomatic "triumphs" so dear to the hearts of the Spaniards was accomplished by the ministry at Madrid. Swift upon the passage of the resolutions by Congress, the watchful Spanish minister at Washington cabled the news to his government. Before Minister Woodford had an opportunity to present the ultimatum cabled him from Washington, he received from Pio Gullon, the Spanish Minister of Foreign Affairs, his passports, with a note informing him that diplomatic relations between the two nations must be considered at an end, because Congress had passed a resolution which "denies the legitimate sovereignty of Spain and threatens immediate armed intervention in Cuba,—which is equivalent to a declaration of war." This was on the 21st of April. The day before at Washington Minister Polo had been notified by a messenger from the State Department of the character of the resolutions passed by Congress, and of the nature of the instructions sent to Minister Woodford. He at once responded by a demand for his passports, saying that "the resolution is of such a character that my permanence in Washington becomes impossible." That very night he took a train for Canada, while Minister Woodford, no less prompt in abandoning a hostile country, took train from Madrid to the French frontier.

The Spaniards, like all Latin peoples, are more fond of

the picturesque and romantic than we, and attach vastly more importance to the trivialities of etiquette than do any Anglo-Saxon people. To them the fact that Minister Woodford had never been able to present the ultimatum of the United States was a matter of prime importance. Taken in connection with the Spanish minister's voluntary departure from the United States, while the American minister was ordered out of Madrid, it took almost the proportions of a great victory, and when to these two incidents was added the further diplomatic triumph won by Dupuy De Lome in resigning before the President of the United States could ask for his recall, the sum was as inspiring as a successful war. The contrast between the Spanish and the American character is strikingly shown by the difference in the treatment of the departing ministers. Senor Polo left Washington unattended, except by a crowd of newspaper reporters. General Woodford was escorted to the railway station at Madrid by the mayor of the city, who treated him with the gravest courtesy until the train started, then turned and led the assembled crowd in a cheer for Spain. But Minister Polo reached the Canadian frontier without insult or assault, while the train of the American envoy was stoned at Valladolid.

So ended the political and diplomatic preliminaries to the war. It is true that the formal declaration of war by the United States Congress was not made until the 25th of April, but the 19th may be taken as the date of the actual beginning of hostilities. It was so regarded by Spain, for it was the act of that day that impelled the Spanish ministry to send Minister Woodford his passports and to withdraw Minister Polo from Washington. Indeed the United States navy committed the first overt act of war without awaiting the formal declaration by Congress, for four days prior to the declaration of war the blockade of Cuba was begun, and the first capture on the high seas effected.

Before closing the account of the political events leading up to the war, some account of the manner in which the statesmen of Spain met the fateful issue is necessary. Looking back upon the ease with which the United States won the victory in the conflict, and remembering that even before the issue was joined cool observers in either country must have been able to discern the great disparity of force between the two, one thinks that there must have been great trepidation among responsible leaders in Spain as to the outcome of the conflict. It is just to say, however, that if any doubt existed among the ministry or the leaders of the Opposition of the perfect ability of Spain to meet and honourably resist her giant adversary it was manfully suppressed. The Spaniards bore themselves as a brave, if not a prudent people. Madrid met the news of the outbreak of hostilities with enthusiasm. The Queen Regent, accompanied by the boy King, Alfonzo XIII, being then but fourteen years old, went to the Senate chamber, cheered as they passed along the streets of Old Madrid by an enthusiastic throng. The boy wore full military uniform, the regalia of the Cadets with the insignia of the Golden Fleece. As they entered the great hall, the assembled multitude broke into frantic cheering. Probably no man there was ignorant, if he but stopped to think, of the immense superiority of the antagonist that Spain was about to meet, but there was no sign of trepidation. Nations are always self-confident, — happily so, else the best fights that ever have been fought for human liberty would have been left untried. Nor is any nation often doubtful of the entire justice of the cause it defends, nor harassed by any doubt that the divine favour is especially bestowed upon it. So the Queen Regent, standing at the threshold of a war destined to deprive her country of its most cherished colonial possessions, announced to the Cortes the " indomitable purpose which inspires my government to defend our rights," and professed confidence that the support of Heaven would be given to so just a cause. Three days later war was an accomplished fact, and with a final appeal to the Great Powers of Europe for sympathy and aid in this struggle against aggressive democracy, Spain entered upon a conflict from which she was destined to retreat crippled financially, bleeding from a score of deadly wounds, and stripped of her most precious colonial possessions in two hemispheres, — possessions won for her by the two great explorers who, though neither of them was a Spaniard, under the patronage of Spain's greatest monarchs, Ferdinand and Isabella, and the Emperor Charles V, made the name of Spain glorious, — the lands won by Christopher Columbus in the Atlantic and Ferdinand Magellan in the Pacific.

CHAPTER V

THE NAVIES OF SPAIN AND THE UNITED STATES — THE GLOOMY ESTIMATES OF THE EXPERTS — SHIP HUNTING IN EUROPE — WHY A NAVY CANNOT BE EXTEMPORISED — YACHTS AND AUXILIARY VESSELS — THE BLOCKADE OF CUBA — LIEUTENANT ROWAN'S EXPEDITION — THE FIRST CAPTURE — HOT WORK AT MATANZAS — THE ATTACK ON CARDENAS — DEATH OF BAGLEY — THE FIGHT AT CIENFUEGOS.

AMONG the people of the United States the navy has always been held in high favour. Perhaps this sentiment had its origin in the War of 1812, when the frigates commanded by Hull, Bainbridge, and Porter won stirring victories on the sea, and in some degree obliterated the memory of the shameful disasters to the American arms on shore. Or perhaps the ancient aversion of the fathers of the republic to a standing army has concentrated upon the navy all the popular affection that in other nations is divided between the two branches of the armed service. At any rate the American people have always shown to the navy a favour denied to the army, and if they have not been as liberal in their appropriations to its support as navy officers might wish, they were not, in the decade preceding the Spanish-American war, at any rate niggardly. For this reason, when the war with Spain was fairly upon us, the naval preparations of the United States may be said to have been adequate.

Some slight outline and comparison of the respective strength on the water of the combatants will be useful here, though to go into detail would be of little service to the civilian reader. So many factors go to make up the sum of a warship's efficiency that a comparison perfectly lucid to a naval expert is only confusing to the landsman. The number of guns, the weight of the broadside, the proportion of rapid-firing rifles, the torpedo equipment, the weight of armour or other protection, the speed of the ship, the character of the powder, and a host of other considerations combine in a technical estimate of a warship's power. Such an estimate may well be omitted here.

The sea power of Spain at the breaking out of the war may be broadly indicated by the following facts: In battle-ships Spain was decidedly ill-equipped, but two vessels of her navy coming in this class. One was of antiquated type, the other, the "Pelayo," was a modern steel battle-ship of 9900 tons, with a strong armament. In first-class cruisers Spain was strong. Of these she had seven, ranging in size from the "Emperador Carlos V" of 9235 tons to the "Cristobal Colon" of 6840 tons. The 11-inch Hontoria rifles, which formed the main batteries of these ships, are regarded by navy officers as exceptionally efficient ordnance. Of second-class cruisers Spain had eight, and of smaller cruisers and gunboats some thirty or more, a few of them being wooden and antiquated. In torpedo boats and torpedo destroyers Spain was vastly superior to the United States, and at the opening of the war this fact created something like a panic among Americans. The efficiency of the torpedo boat, having never been subjected to the actual test of war, was universally overrated, and most dolorous predictions of the disaster which awaited our ships in the encounter with the waspish pygmies were common in the American newspapers. Of torpedo-boat destroyers Spain had six, ranging from 220 to 255 feet, and from 380 to 400 tons displacement. These were really formidable vessels, uniting the qualities of a torpedo boat with those of a gunboat, and useful therefore on the blockade and on service requiring a greater coal capacity than any torpedo boat possesses. The United States was wholly without any of this class of vessels. Of torpedo boats proper, Spain had ten of the first class, six of the second class, and seven of a mongrel type, but thoroughly serviceable. It may be pertinent to note at this juncture that throughout the war not one United States ship was destroyed, touched, or even seriously menaced by a torpedo.

Let us consider now, in equally general terms, the navy of the United States at the outbreak of the war. The report of the Secretary of the Navy for 1897 showed that the United States had in effective condition four battle-ships of the first class, two of the second class (one of these was the ill-fated "Maine"), two armoured cruisers, sixteen cruisers, fifteen gunboats, six double-turreted monitors, one ram, one dynamite gunboat, one despatch boat, and five torpedo boats. There were at the time of the secretary's report under construction five battle-ships of the first class, sixteen torpedo boats, and one submarine boat. None of these was completed in time to be of service during the war. In connection with the effective strength of the navy should be considered the so-called auxiliary fleet, or merchant ships under subsidy and liable to naval service. In all, twenty of these were borne on the navy rolls. The great number of swift yachts owned by citizens of the United States and readily convertible into torpedo or patrol boats was also an element in the naval supremacy of the United States.

Apparently, therefore, the navy of the United States was vastly more powerful than that of Spain. But to skilled students of naval affairs the disparity of the two adversaries did not appear so great. Captain Alfred T. Mahan, admittedly the greatest living expert on "Sea Power," refers to the comparative strength of the combatants in an article written after the war had demonstrated the superiority in fact of the United States navy, thus:

"The force of the Spanish navy — on paper, as the expression goes — was so nearly equal to our own that it was well within the limits of possibility that an unlucky incident, the loss for example of a battle-ship, might make the Spaniard decisively superior in nominal, or even in actual, available force. An excellent authority told the writer that he considered the loss of the 'Maine' had changed the balance; that is, that, whereas with the 'Maine' our fleet had been slightly superior, so, after her destruction, the advantage, still nominal, was rather the other way."

Captain Mahan charitably refrains from making public the name of the "excellent authority" whose estimate of the nominal strength of the United States navy proved so sadly at fault when its actual power came to be exerted. He was not alone, however, in his error. The English reviews printed many articles signed by men of supposed authoritative position among naval experts, depicting the struggle that was to come between the navies of the United States and Spain as a very close one, and in many cases giving all the elements of superiority to Spain. Our ships were described as unseaworthy, and our sailors, because of the admixture of nationalities which the whole people of the United States represent, were expected to lack that sense of national pride and patriotism which would enable them to stand fire. If the masses in the United States were a little braggart and flamboyant in their certainty of American superiority, the expert proved that the academic estimate is not the one necessarily correct.

Moreover, the outcome of a naval war is not wholly dependent upon the comparative numbers of vessels in the hostile navies, for brilliant strategy may enable the weaker power to still outnumber the enemy in some decisive battle, or to reduce to impotence the fleet of its adversary by menacing manœuvres without offering battle at all. In the accounts of the great naval battles of the war, I will contrast more fully the comparative strength of the two

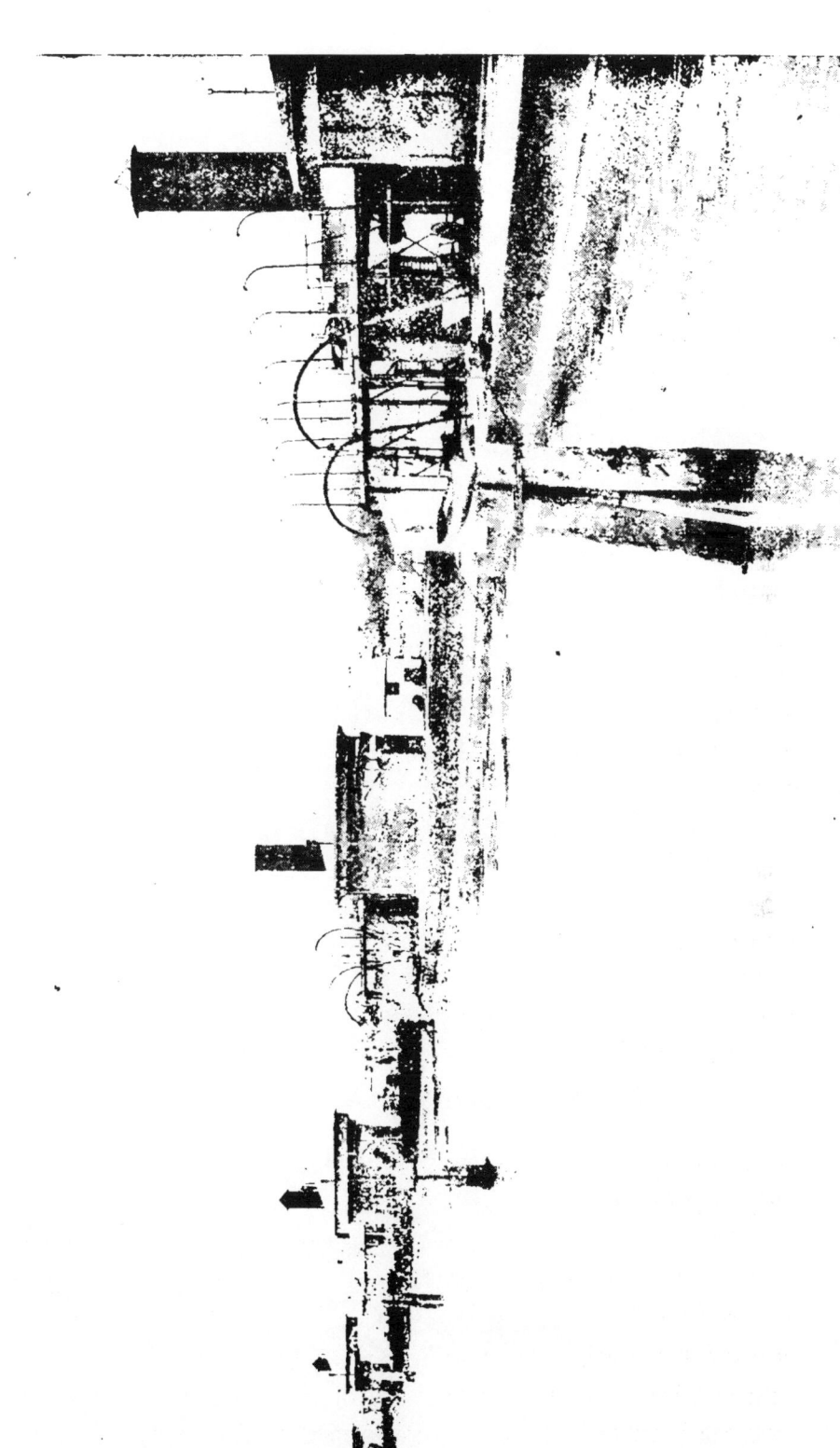

MONITORS AT LEAGUE ISLAND NAVY YARD, PHILADELPHIA.

adversaries. It is proper to note here two elements of strength for Spain, and of weakness for the United States.

The proximity of Cuba to the United States made it certain that the theatre of war would be on our coast. This being the case, it was highly advantageous for Spain that her colonial possessions in the West Indies supplied her with coaling stations and bases of supplies. If the United States had been compelled to press an offensive war on the coast of Spain, our commanders would have been handicapped from the very first by the lack of such facilities. The efficiency of a modern man-of-war is absolutely limited by its coal capacity. A battle-ship sent from our coast to Spain would exhaust two-thirds of its coal supply in crossing the Atlantic. Until that was made good, its condition would be most perilous, and as the tendency of modern custom is to declare coal contraband of war, the bunkers of a United States ship in wartime could not be replenished in any foreign port, except under such limitations as would prohibit further offensive operations. The difficult and perilous device of coaling at sea from colliers sent from home ports would have to be relied upon, and would offer to an alert enemy most promising opportunities for an effective attack. Again, our long coast-line, plentifully dotted with flourishing cities, was difficult to guard, and tempting to the audacious and daring naval commander, while Spain's coast is almost destitute of large cities. Our exposed coast cities, though never in fact attacked, or even menaced, still compelled the employment of a certain number of vessels as scouts and for harbour defence, reducing the force available for active operations against the enemy. Such a coast-line as ours adds immensely to the effectiveness for an enemy of what the naval authorities call a "fleet in being." That is, a fleet, organised and in commission, and which may at any moment strike at any one of a number of points. Such a fleet the Spaniards maintained at Cadiz through the greater part of the war, and because of it our government was at all times apprehensive of an attack on some one of our northern coast cities. Doubtless had the Spanish character been more adventurous, our coastwise towns would not have got off scot free as they did. Efficient as were our scouts, and alert as our intelligence department was, it is certain a seaman of the Paul Jones type, with a swift cruiser and a roving commission, would have found somewhere between Portland, Maine, and the Gulf of Mexico a spot to strike and flee from before a superior enemy could be called to give him battle. But Spain had no Paul Jones.

On the afternoon of the 21st of April, the harbour of Key West off the southwestern point of the Florida peninsula was full of ships of war. There lay the North Atlantic squadron, under command of Rear Admiral William T. Sampson, who was appointed to this all-important command upon completing his duty as President of the "Maine" court of inquiry. In his fleet were the "New York," which flew the admiral's flag, the battle-ships "Iowa" and "Indiana," the double-turreted monitors "Puritan," "Terror," "Miantonomah," and "Amphitrite," the cruisers "Marblehead," "Montgomery," "Detroit," and "Cincinnati," the gunboats "Helena," "Castine," "Newport," "Nashville," and "Machias," the torpedo boats "Foote" and "Porter," and a number of colliers, despatch boats, supply boats, and other plebeians of a naval column. The little town, deadly dull usually and given over to Cuban cigar-makers and the native "conchs" who lead an amphibious life, had enjoyed three months of such life as it had not seen since the days of the civil war. Its streets were crowded with officers, seamen, and alert newspaper correspondents. These enforced visitors found less pleasure in the situation than did the natives, for Key West is, at the best, a dreary stopping-place for men accustomed to the activities of the great world, and for weeks, from the officers and followers of the fleet, fervent prayers had daily arisen for action. No community in the whole land watched more impatiently the slow progress of Congress, and the suspense was increased by the difficulty with which full and prompt information of what was doing at the capitol was received. The Northern papers were two days old by the time they reached the sandbar on which some two thousand navy officers and men, with an army of civilians, were marooned, and the meagre details which the managing editors at home telegraphed for the guidance of the correspondents with the fleet only whetted the appetite for more. Nevertheless, it was from one of these correspondents that the admiral commanding first learned of the action of Congress, and that his fleet was to be ordered at once to begin the blockade of Cuba. Swiftly following the despatch to the correspondent came a long communication from the Secretary of the Navy, Hon. John D. Long, to Admiral Sampson, containing an order to sail, and with it the full text of the President's proclamation of blockade. Then there was stir in Key West. All officers and men were recalled to the ships, and the wharves were crowded with supplies bought by the ward-room stewards in anticipation of a long tour of sea service. The newspaper boats, of which there were a dozen or more, were darting nervously about the harbour, visiting one ship after another in search of elusive news. When night fell, the masts of the vessels glowed with winking parti-coloured eyes, that silently, but with infinite meaning, transmitted messages from one commander to the other. The great battle-ships lying farthest out toward the mouth of the harbour swept sea and land with the long, bright beams of their search-lights, vigilant ever lest some hostile torpedo boat should slip in to the destruction of some American vessel. At daylight, the smoke began rising, first in faint wreaths, and then in rolling clouds, from the stacks of the vessels, and the sun was not yet risen when a line of bright-coloured flags flying from the signal mast of the flagship told the watchers on shore that some order was being delivered. The signal was answered instantly by the piping of the boatswain whistles on all the ships, and the clanking of heavy chains as the anchors were dragged up from their sandy beds. Soon the whole fleet was under way, in two parallel columns, and moving out to sea in perfect silence. Not a gunshot signalised this first movement of an American fleet against a European foe, no bugle-call noted the opening act of an epoch-making war. Not even a cheer told the men on ship and shore that a new page in history was being turned by a people long renowned for the victories of peace rather than those of deadly conflict. The scene was wholly peaceful. The yachts employed by the newspapers as despatch boats gave even a festal air to the squadron, while a number of fishing smacks and merchantmen plied, as in ordinary days, about the harbour.

For some of the merchantmen, however, the ordinary days were past and the era of war-time disaster at hand. The fleet had hardly left Key West below the horizon when a wreath of smoke on the sky-line showed a steamer approaching. She was watched, as everything afloat is watched from a man-of-war, but little heed was given to her, nor would have been, perhaps, except for the mistaken courtesy of her captain.

"I saw that fine fleet of American warships," he said afterwards, gloomily recounting his tale to the newspaper correspondents, "and said I to the mate: 'Pedro, get the colours, and we will salute those beautiful ships.'" So, in the innocence of his heart, and wholly ignorant of the fact that his country was at war with the United States, Captain Lazaraga, of the steamer "Buena Ventura," bound from Pascagoula, Mississippi, to Bilboa, Spain, with a cargo of lumber, ran up his best Spanish flag and dipped it thrice in seamanly courtesy to the fleet he so much admired. The answer was hardly what he expected, nor can it be termed chivalric. None of the warships dipped its colours, but to the foretop of the leading one ran up a number of little balls of bunting, breaking out into some kind of a signal which

Captain Lazaraga could not understand. Immediately he saw one of the American vessels, which he afterwards learned to be the "Nashville," turn aside from the column and steam towards him. Soon she fired a blank cartridge towards the "Buena Ventura."

"A curious way of saluting, those Yankees have," said the captain, and kept his ship on a course. Then came another shot, this time sending a shell screaming before the bows of his ship. At this juncture he concluded to stop and see what the affair meant, and his vessel was presently boarded by an ensign and a prize crew, from whom he learned of the war, and that his ship, in pursuance of a barbaric custom still in vogue on the high seas though abandoned on land, was a prize to the American navy. The ship was sent into Key West, where she was received with great enthusiasm, and the newspapers of the nation, just then being in hysterical mood, made as great ado over taking this hapless merchantman as if some deed of unparalleled valour had been done.

From time immemorial it has been the usage of nations to hold private property at sea in the ship of an enemy fit subject for capture, and navy officers have been enriched by the prize-money thus obtained. Yet civilised nations respect private property of an enemy on shore, and an army traversing an enemy's country will even punctiliously pay for supplies taken from the inhabitants for its support. Why this distinction should be drawn cannot be satisfactorily explained. As the better natures of men have been developed, — and there is no doubt that man grows better as the world becomes more civilised, — effort has been made to do away with this practice of capture at sea. Though the poverty of Spain's merchant marine resulted in making the prizes of the American navy very few and of very little value, there was evident among the American people a feeling of aversion to the whole system of marine spoliation. Had an American army invaded Spain, our soldiers would not have looted the houses and shops and divided the booty. Why, then, asked our people, should a Spanish property afloat be less sacred than that ashore? Could the salt water wash out the stain of the theft? This sentiment was so very general among the people that it is probable the movement to exempt private property, not contraband of war, from capture at sea will receive a great impetus as a result of the Spanish war.

The duty upon which Admiral Sampson's squadron was now despatched by the President to undertake was the most arduous and the least stimulating that ever falls to the lot of a navy officer. To maintain a blockade is to be a sentry with a beat at sea, and with no relief. Steaming slowly up and down, near enough to a shore to be in danger should a sudden hurricane burst upon the sea, but unable ever to land; close enough to the enemy to be in constant danger from torpedoes or other methods of stealthy attack, but without hope of a fair battle, ship to ship and man to man, the blockaders suffer stupid monotony without relief from constant apprehension of disaster, and have all the routine and work of warfare without hope of glory. In this service, so thankless yet all-important, the United States navy has made a record that challenges the admiration of the world. During the long years of the war between the States the navy kept the ports of the Confederacy locked like a bank's vaults. Bound in that circle of steel and iron, the South was fairly starved into subjection. Europe said it could not be done. The best naval authorities of the Old World scoffed at the idea of making an effective blockade of a coast more than two thousand miles long and full of practicable harbours. Nevertheless it was done, and though Europe, angered by interrupted trade, watched vigilantly for even a day's break in the blockade, such as would permit it to be declared ineffective, the break never came. In the war with Spain the problem before the navy was almost as great, though as no nation showed any great desire to have the Cuban ports reopened the diplomatic difficulties were less

SPANISH MERCHANT STEAMER "CATALINA," CAPTURED BY CRUISER "DETROIT," APRIL 24, 1898.

grave. The island has a coast-line of two thousand miles, but the harbours are comparatively few, and the dense undergrowth that made an impassable wall along the water front made the use by blockade runners, of any except the improved and recognised inlets, impossible. But the task of the navy was not to be confined to the maintenance of a blockade. A landing place for the American army that was to invade Cuba had to be prepared, and the Spanish fleet was to be found and destroyed. For many weeks, however, owing to the slow preparation of the army and the dilatory policy of the administration, the blockade alone engaged the attention of Admiral Sampson. All blockades are monotonous — this one was deadly dull. The prizes were few and of little value. The most notable one of these was the steamship " Panama," of Barcelona, a large steamer mounting two 14-pound guns and one machine gun. This vessel fell a prey to the " Mangrove," a little lighthouse tender, hastily fitted up for blockading duty, and far inferior to the " Panama " in armament, in the size of the crew, and in tonnage. So small was the " Mangrove's " crew that a prize-crew had to be borrowed from the " Indiana," which lay in the offing, to take the prize into port, while the boarding officer had to borrow a revolver to overawe the captives. Beyond doubt, had the " Panama " shown fight she might have beaten off the audacious pygmy that made her heave to; but the fleet of huge ships of war in the distance gave to the mandate of the " Mangrove's " captain an authority that under other circumstances the Spaniard might have been more willing to disregard. Another prize of considerable value, taken by the torpedo boat " Terror," was the " Bolivar," with about $70,000 in silver aboard.

While the blockading fleet was steaming up and down before Havana in plain sight of the lights of the town by night, and the steeples and chimneys by day, the people of the city were being urged by General Blanco to hold themselves loyal to Spain, and to resist the invaders to the death. Havana was full of Cuban sympathisers, but as the official class, with whom all authority rested, were strongly pro-Spanish, the patriots dared not express themselves. Not until after the war was over, and the gallant Cuban General Gomez entered Havana with the American troops, did the feeling of Cuban patriotism break out in wild enthusiasm. Until American authority was there established, an expression of sympathy for the insurgents was likely to land the citizen in Morro, if indeed it did not end in his lying dead by the sea-wall as the firing squad marched away. So when war was declared, General Blanco met with what was, ostensibly at least, a hearty response to his appeals to the loyalty of the citizens. The town was decked with the Spanish colours, and a great body of citizens marched in procession to the Army headquarters, where their spokesmen pledged to General Blanco their lives and fortunes in defence of the Spanish crown. The general responded in a speech of characteristic Spanish quality. He described in terrifying phrase the barbarity of the foe, and called upon them to save all that they held dear — their lives, their property, and the honour of their women — by repelling the invaders, who were even then at the very walls of Morro. As for himself, he swore that death only could put an end to the stubborn resistance he intended to offer. Unhappily for General Blanco the war was ended, and Spain expelled from Cuba without his ever seeing the American lines, or having any opportunity to perform any of the deeds of valour he promised the citizens of Havana.

While the American fleet was standing guard at the doorway to the Cuban capital and the military authorities in that city were fighting the war with volleys of eloquence, an officer of the United States army was prowling through Cuba, gathering topographical information for the expected army of invasion, and making arrangements with the Cuban insurgents for co-operation. The officer was Lieutenant Andrew S. Rowan, who had entered Cuba the day of the declaration of war. Avoiding all the frequented lines of travel, he had crossed in an open boat from Jamaica, guided by a boatman who was half fisherman, half smuggler, and all outlaw. Eluding the Spanish patrols, who would have promptly hanged him as a spy had they caught him, Rowan made his way to a camp of insurgents, by whom he was taken through the forests to General Garcia at Bayamo. He was the first official visitor from the United States to the camps of the patriots, and his arrival awakened the wildest enthusiasm. Through the Junta — or Cuban revolutionary committee — in New York, leaders like Garcia and Gomez had been kept informed of the generous interest which the people of the United States took in the Cuban struggle for liberty, and of the efforts making in Congress to aid them in their aspirations. This young officer, a soldier every inch, brought to the veterans of the revolution the first assurance that the long fight was won — for all knew that the aid of the great republic meant victory, certain and inevitable. They did not know, nor did Rowan, that when the visitor entered their camp, war was already existing, and the Americans had begun making captures; but the visitor was able to assure them that when he left Washington the breach between the two countries was certain, and the formal beginning of hostilities only a matter of days. And if the coming of Rowan was an encouragement to the revolutionists, the circumstances in which he found them offered justification for his mission and all that lay behind it. They occupied the ancient city of Bayamo, a place of 30,000 inhabitants. On every side were the smouldering ruins of forts, whence the Spaniards had but recently been driven. Through the gates of the city poured in a returning throng of its inhabitants, who had been driven from home by the barbarities of Spanish occupation, but for whom the victorious patriots had opened a way again to their homes and firesides. The scene gave the lie to all the Spanish assertions of the collapse of the revolution, and offered to the messenger from the United States a picture of patriotism triumphant, of a great victory in a good fight for liberty. All day Rowan spent with Garcia, of whose high qualities as man and soldier he, like all who met that life-long champion of Cuban liberty, speaks in terms of admiration. Plans were interchanged, maps for the guidance of an invading army prepared, and the military situation carefully canvassed. Doubtless the stories Rowan brought of the doings of the world beyond the blockaded coasts were of surpassing interest to the general so long condemned to life in the Cuban thickets, but Garcia was a soldier, and in deadly earnest. He wasted no time, and gave his guest but a brief resting-space. "At five o'clock," says Rowan, " he said he had his despatches ready, and asked if I could start North at once, as he wished to get his replies to the United States government as soon as possible. He detailed General Callazo, Colonel Hernandez, and Dr. Dietas an expert on the diseases of that section, to accompany me." The four started after nightfall, and threading the woods with the greatest care, travelled through jungles and across rivers and swamps for two days, when they reached a large town in ruins, but surrounded by fortifications which were held by about 500 Cubans. This was Vittoria de las Tunas. Pressing on again through the dense forest, and at one time scaling a lofty peak whence they enjoyed a view of the ocean, which for them meant safety, they came at last to the coast. There they found a flourishing salt works, conducted for the Cuban army and manned by men under arrest for some breach of army discipline. A little boat, not big enough for the whole party, but the best obtainable, was here put at Lieutenant Rowan's service, and with sails made of hammocks, and a mere makeshift for a mast, they put to sea — Dr. Dietas having been sent back for lack of room. In the distance, soon after setting sail, Rowan discerned the fleet of

Admiral Sampson, then on its way to Porto Rico, for it was then the 5th of May. But without halting the fleet, the party continued its course for the coast of the United States, and, having by good fortune overhauled a sponging schooner, its crew of negroes were with some difficulty, and after many threats, persuaded to take them to Nassau. To reach home from that point was easy. In the course of this perilous expedition, Lieutenant Rowan had crossed Cuba from south to north. He had discovered that a province which the Spaniards claimed to control was, in fact, in the hands of the revolutionists; he had seen for himself that the Cuban army was organised, disciplined, ready to fight, and confident; he had found the territory laid waste and depopulated, giving only too striking evidence of the fact that the war was making of Cuba a desert. All this he had done at the hourly risk of his life, at the peril indeed of a death commonly held to be ignominious, for in military law he was a spy, and would have been hanged within a few hours of his capture. Yet, for all his bravery, he holds no unique position among his fellows. The annals of the United States army are full of such deeds of courage as his exploit.

And now to return to the blockade. When the navy had fairly set itself to the task assigned it, the conviction became general that very insufficient tools had been furnished for a very hard job. Monitors with a speed of ten knots are not the most efficient engines with which to close a number of ports against merchantmen that make fifteen knots under easy steam; and torpedo boats that carry coal enough for perhaps three days' steaming are apt to be a source of embarrassment on a blockade where a coal capacity sufficient for a month's stay outside the blockaded port is a great desideratum. Nevertheless, the blockade was made effective, though no doubt that was largely due to the comparatively small temptation which Cuban commerce offered to those who otherwise might go in for the exciting and profitable sport of blockade running. Not only was every considerable merchantman that came within suspicious distance of Havana or adjacent ports captured or warned off, but wretched little fishing smacks and boats with garden stuff for the beleaguered town were sternly sent about their business, while a Yankee tug once fiercely tried to bring to the British man-of-war "Talbot" with a blank cartridge. Officers and correspondents with the fleet report that so accustomed had the islanders and the Spaniards themselves become to the murderous system of warfare which had been practised under Weyler that the prisoners taken by the navy could hardly comprehend their good fortune in not being at once shot, and the amazement of a Spanish officer who was captured as he was going off on a leave of absence to be married, when he was released on parole, was picturesque and almost laughable in its effusiveness. But the occasional captures were not of sufficient importance to relieve the tedium of the blockade, and once or twice the sight of a warship on the horizon was hailed with enthusiasm by officers and men as seeming to promise a fight. But it always turned out to be the ship of a friendly nation — once an Italian, whose nationality was not made out until she began to salute the admiral's flag, and again the British ship "Talbot." The latter vessel, an armoured cruiser of 5600 tons, was twice zealously pursued as a possible enemy, once by the gunboat "Nashville," 1371 tons, and once by the "Scorpion," a converted yacht.

Once in awhile two or three of the ships would run a little bit inshore and throw a few shells at some earthwork over which the Spanish flag was flying. As a rule little damage was done on either side, for the Spanish were not good marksmen, and while the shooting of the Blue Jackets was true, it was shown early in the war, and not disproved during its continuance, that earthworks cannot be reduced nor silenced for long by fire from ships.

BATTLESHIP "IOWA" IN DRY-DOCK.

But at home in the cities the news of these inconclusive affrays was eagerly read and commented upon as if a battle had indeed been fought. The newspapers of New York gave almost as much space to the first event of this sort, the bombardment of Matanzas, as in 1861 they did to the battle of Bull Run. Yet it was an affair only worthy of a place in history, because it was the first attack with really modern naval weapons upon a fort. The attacking vessels were the " New York," " Puritan," and the " Cincinnati." The batteries were uncompleted earthworks, and it was to prevent their completion, and perhaps to afford his men a little relief from the boredom of the blockade, that Admiral Sampson concluded to throw a few tons of iron and explosives at them. The " New York" opened fire at about 4000 yards, and the officers watching from the bridge saw the yellow dust fly. But from the ports of the ship, from every turret, sponson, and shield in which there was a gun in action the yellow powder smoke flew too, and it was very quickly evident to those who sighted the guns and who watched the effect of the shots, that the great weakness of the United States Navy in the war was going to be the lack of smokeless powder. The whole ship was wreathed in hot, stifling smoke. It choked and scorched the lungs of the gunners, and it hid the enemy from their sight. Though the batteries were worked with furious speed, much of the shooting was necessarily at random, for through the smoke was no vision possible, and there was no waiting for it to clear away before the next shot was fired. The officers in charge of the turret guns would run from the turret to a point on deck where the vapour was less dense, and there getting their bearings would rush back to train their guns. The firing continued for twenty minutes, and at the end the batteries, though silenced, were still effective. One shot from the big 12-inch gun of the " Puritan" was seen to strike immediately under one of the Spanish cannon, which rose in the air out of the cloud that attended the exploding shell, but the rest of the projectiles, so far as could be seen, stirred up the dust and frightened the defenders, but did no damage that a gang of men with spades and wheelbarrows could not repair in an afternoon.

When the news of this bombardment reached the United States it was hailed as a great victory. When the American ships stopped firing and drew off, the Spaniards on their part claimed a great victory, and celebrated it with oratory and fireworks. " Our loss, one mule," was the Spanish bulletin cabled to Madrid. It was in fact little more than half an hour's target practice. Not one of the ships engaged was hit.

There were several incidents of this sort, all largely celebrated in the American newspapers, but none of which had other than a passing and merely journalistic interest. On the 29th of April the batteries at Cienfuegos, on the southern coast of the island, were engaged by the "Marblehead," and the day after, the forts at Cabanas near Havana were attacked and materially injured by the cruiser " New York." It was good target practice for the Yankee gunners, and perhaps it played its part in the great *dénouement* that came at Santiago on July 3d, but for the immediate moment it was a prodigious use of powder and shot for a pygmy result.

As the days wore on and the purpose of the United States developed, the tedium of the blockade was relieved by opportunities for service of a more dashing character — service for employment in which the officers of the squadron vied eagerly with each other, and in which a few found both glory and death.

On the northern coast of Cuba, some seventy-five miles from Havana, lies the little town of Cardenas. It possesses a picturesque and difficult harbour, and was well fortified by the Spaniards in the days preceding the declaration of war. Within the harbour, protected partly by the batteries but more by the fact that the channels were too shallow to permit the entrance of the larger United States cruisers, were a number of Spanish gunboats of light draught, which every now and then would run out, inspect the blockading fleet, and then dash back into their safe retreat. There was little harm in this, as none of the enemy's ships was big enough to menace even the smallest ship the Americans had on that part of the blockade, but there was an air of defiance, of bravado, about the Spanish procedure which irritated the men on the blockading squadron, and it was determined to teach them a lesson. The process of education proved expensive.

The next time the Spaniards came out the torpedo boat "Foote" made a dash at them. The guns she mounted were of course no match for those on the enemy, but the American sailors had already become contemptuous of Spanish markmanship, and it was thought that the 'Foote" could get within torpedo range, let slip her projectile, and get away unscathed. The attack was hardly begun, however, before it was found that these Spaniards had learned to shoot, and the "Foote" withdrew, for the game was not worth risking a torpedo boat for. On the 11th of May, the gunboat "Wilmington" joined the vessels on this part of the blockade. As her draught was light enough to permit her to enter the bay it was determined to explore the entrance, and if possible inflict some damage on the enemy. All buoys had been removed from the harbour, and it was believed that the channel had been mined, but with the help of a Cuban pilot, the "Wilmington," torpedo boat "Winslow," and the auxiliary tug "Hudson," picked their way in toward the city, which was soon in plain sight, its red roofs, white walls, and green trees presenting a beautiful prospect. At the wharves could be seen two large, square-rigged vessels, and a trim white steamer, which the men on the three war vessels already looked upon as prizes. Nothing could be seen of the gunboats, which had evidently found some hiding-place close to the shore. To lure them from their retreat the little "Winslow," armed only with one-pounders, steamed gallantly in towards the wharves. The bay was perfectly clear, and the water calm. In the city there seemed to be no sign of excitement, and the stillness of a summer's day hung over land and sea, over nature and the homes of men alike. Suddenly the peace was broken. From behind the corner of a wharf, where no battery appeared nor any menace of danger, came a flash and sharp report, and a shell whizzed past the "Winslow." Hastily her helm was put hard down, but before she could turn shots came from three or four other places, with increasing precision. No smoke betrayed the position of the batteries, and the noise made by the shells, no less than the obvious precision of the arms employed, showed that the enemy was equipped with the most modern ordnance. The Americans answered swiftly and vigorously, even the little "Winslow" banging away with her one-pounders. But about the ships of war hung dense clouds of yellow smoke, obscuring their aim, and making it impossible for them to discern each other's signals, while the Spanish use of smokeless powder concealed the location of their batteries and made the task of the navy gunners doubly hard. It was soon demonstrated that the attack proceeded from the Spanish gunboats, which were shielded behind solid wharves, and therefore made almost impregnable. From their retreat they directed their fire almost exclusively against the "Winslow." She was nearest in shore, more vulnerable than the "Wilmington" and more valuable than the "Hudson." The Spaniards determined to make the best of their opportunity. One of their first shots struck and partly disabled her, but she fought on in the midst of a rain of shot and shell, until at last, with her steering gear cut and nearly unmanageable, her commander, Lieutenant J. B. Bernadou, determined to take her out of action. The "Hudson" coming near at this moment, he informed her commander of his purpose.

"Do you need any help?" shouted the commander of the tug, seeing the battered state of the torpedo boat.

"No, only plenty of room to work in," responded the commander of the "Winslow." "We are crippled, and she does not mind her helm well."

The "Hudson" then drew off and returned to her engagement with the enemy, but in a few moments saw that the "Winslow" was drifting helplessly toward the shore, while a signal man was vigorously wigwagging some message to the flagship. Again the "Hudson" ran down upon the torpedo boat, and this time a heavy line was thrown across to her. At the first cast it fell short. A brisk breeze had by now sprung up, and the drift of the disabled vessel toward the shore grew more rapid, while as she drifted the accuracy of the enemy's aim improved until she was in a position fairly murderous. Again the rope was thrown. A shot knocked a great splinter of steel from the deck, which buried itself in Bernadou's groin, inflicting a painful and dangerous wound; but wrapping a towel about it to stanch the blood, the plucky officer ran aft to get the hand-steering gear to work, as by this time the steam gear had been hopelessly wrecked. Before the necessary changes could be made the hand gear too was shot away, and the last vestige of hope for saving the craft under her own gear was destroyed. Meanwhile the "Hudson" drew near again. On her rail was perched an officer swinging the line he was about to throw. Amidships on the "Winslow" were a group of men in charge of Ensign Bagley, a boyish young officer just out of the naval academy.

"Hurry up," cried Bagley, laughingly; "it's getting too hot for comfort here."

The words had scarcely left his mouth when with a deafening crack a shell exploded just above his head. Instantly the group of men that a moment before had stood there, alert, cool, expectant, inspirited by the calm and cheerful demeanour of the boy who commanded them, vanished. Five were instantly killed. One, sorely mutilated, was blown almost overboard, and died as his comrades were drawing him back. Ensign Bagley was struck in the head by a bit of the shell and instantly killed — the first officer to fall in the war.

Meanwhile the Spaniards were not slackening their fire in any degree. Though the full measure of the destruction done by their shells on the torpedo boat could not be discerned from their position, they could see through their glasses that the "Winslow" was disabled, that the "Hudson" was handicapped by having to care for her, and that their range was accurate. Accordingly they redoubled their efforts. It was said after the battle that certain buoys in the harbour which our men took to mark the course of the channel were in fact planted by the Spaniards to indicate the range, and that this accounts for a precision of aim, which was equalled by their artillery or naval gunners in no other battle of the war.

The hawser being at last made fast, the "Hudson" started out of the harbour, towing the sorely shattered torpedo boat with her freight of dead and wounded. From the town flames and smoke were beginning to rise, and weeks after deserters from the Spanish army coming off to the ships reported that had the attack been kept up a few minutes longer, town, gunboats, and shipping must have surrendered. A story told by Lieutenant Ernest Mead, the navigating officer of the "Hudson," shows something of the spirit of the men that manned the "Winslow" that May morning:

"While securing the 'Winslow' the second time, an incident occurred which forces itself through the crush of sad memories and causes a smile. One of the 'Winslow's' crew was conspicuous for his quickness, knowledge, and adaptability. He knew where everything was, and how to do everything, and he was usually there to do it. But, from the time the first line was made fast until we were miles out of range of the shore, his sole idea was to get another shot at the Spaniards. The minute he could drop the work before him he would jump to a gun, throw in a shell, elevate the gun as far as it would go, and let drive, caring nothing of where the shot landed so long as it went in the direction of the shore."

It seemed as though the death of Ensign Worth Bagley brought home to the people of the United States for the first time the conviction that it was a real war upon which the nation had entered, and that war meant death, and sorrowing homes, and desolated hearts. To his widowed mother in her North Carolina home came the expressions of regret and sympathy from a whole nation. The neighbours and boyhood friends of the dead lad paid to his body the honour of a hero's funeral, and a noble monument marks his resting-place. And even before the final ratification of the treaty of peace put a definite end to the war, the Congress of the United States, without dissenting voice, adopted a resolution creating five additional cadetships at the national naval academy in order that one might be given to the younger brother of the brave officer slain at Cardenas. Republics are not wholly ungrateful, nor surely could any nation not wholly lost to a sense of admiration for patriotism fail to reward with honour the sacrifice of a mother who meets the loss of her first son in warring for his country by consecrating her second to the very service in which the elder met his untimely though heroic death.

While the guns were roaring at Cardenas, American seamen and Spanish soldiery were engaged in hot conflict on the other side of the island of Cuba. On that southern coast one port only, that of Cienfuegos, was blockaded. In its configuration this harbour was not unlike the one where Bagley went to his death. The town, completely hidden from the sea by high hills, lay back some distance from the ocean, and was reached by a channel full of tortuous turnings. Its importance from a military standpoint arose from the fact that two cables had their ground connection there — one extending to Santiago de Cuba and another to Batanabo. It was determined to cut these cables, and the task fell upon the men of the blockading squadron, then composed of the " Marblehead," the " Nashville," and the revenue cutter " Windom." The work of cutting cables in order to isolate General Blanco from the world had been actively pressed on the northern side of the islands, and it was believed that by severing the lines at Cienfuegos he would be shut off from all outside communication. This proved to be an erroneous expectation, for never during the war was the Spanish general in Havana without full and speedy communication with his home government. In view of the complete information which our government had of the location of these cables and the facilities which we possessed for cutting them, it seems inexplicable that Blanco should have retained this privilege unless for some reason it was the policy of our government to leave him in communication with Madrid. At the final surrender the terms were made by stipulation with the Madrid ministry, and it seems probable that had the commanding general at Santiago been left to act upon his own responsibility, his defence might have been more stubborn and protracted. As we shall see, the order which sent Cervera to his destruction came from the Spanish capital, and was insisted upon despite the admiral's protest. In fact, therefore, it was a fortunate thing that all communication between the generals in Cuba and the governing authorities in Spain was not interrupted; but whether its continuance was due to prevision on the part of our government or a mere failure to find and cut the cables cannot as yet be determined.

To the men on the ships steaming up and down before Cienfuegos none of these considerations was of any importance whatever. They were ordered to find and cut the cables leading into that city, and they set about doing it. The point of attack was clearly indicated by the little house on the beach to which the cables led. To make the attack effective it had to be made from small boats, as on that coast the water shoals very gradually, and the large vessels could not approach the shore. Accordingly, early in the morning of May 11th, just as the ships at Cardenas were getting ready to enter the harbour, the three vessels outside Cienfuegos steamed as near to the shore as their draft would permit and let slip their launches and boats. Two steam launches, two smaller ones, and half a dozen boats were quickly crowded with men, who swarmed down the sides of the men-of-war, eager for action. On the launches were machine guns, the row-boats being unarmed. The plan was for the men in the small boats to go as near inshore as might be necessary to pick up the cables. They were to do no fighting, but give their attention wholly to the work in hand. If there should be an attack from the shore, the launches with their machine guns were to protect the workers and drive away their assailants. It was quite evident at the very outset that the Spaniards were entirely alive to the importance of their cables and intended to fight stubbornly for their defence. As the vessels came nearer the shore rifle pits could be made out, and bodies of infantry and cavalry could be seen forming about the cable-house.

In command of the expedition was Lieutenant C. M. Winslow, a son of the man who sunk the "Alabama," with Lieutenant E. A. Anderson as second. The men were all volunteers, but not all of the volunteers, for when the word of the expedition was passed along the decks of the ships every man offered to go, and the process of selecting the fortunate ones almost bred a riot.

As the boats drew off from the ships the latter opened a heavy fire with shell upon the line of bushes along the shore in which the enemy were thought to be concealed. There was silence for a time on shore, save for the bursting of our own shells, for the Spaniards fled from the heavy fire without response; but when the line of boats came within two hundred feet or so of the sand, the ships were obliged to cease firing. Then the enemy crept back to his line of low earthworks concealed in the bushes, and presently opened fire with rifles and machine guns. The position of the Americans was a most desperate one. Each boat, crowded with men, lying on a tranquil sea only a few hundred feet from a sheltered and unseen enemy, was an easy target. The row-boats were within ninety feet of the shore, within point-blank range of over a thousand Spaniards armed with modern weapons. About the little craft the water was lashed into fury by a storm of bullets, the jets springing up on every side as they do when some summer hail-storm pelts the surface of a quiet lake. Winslow stood quietly in his boat, a conspicuous target, urging on his men. Their task was one that required deliberation and care. The cable had first to be found, as it lay on the bottom, with grappling irons, then hauled across a boat, and a section, usually about the width of the boat, chopped out of it with axes and chisels. The men engaged in this task had to suffer the fire of the enemy without responding. For them was all the peril of battle, without any of the stimulus and excitement which the act of fighting brings. They were as helpless as a pigeon before the gun of a noted trap-shooter. Out a hundred feet or so beyond them the launches were fighting manfully, with their one-pounders and rapid fire guns, to drive the Spaniards away; but the latter had the advantage of cover and of numbers and stuck to their work. The ships in the distance joined in the affray, taking such positions and choosing such targets as enabled them to fire without endangering their own men. A lighthouse on the shore was filled with Spaniards, who were firing from its windows. "Cut it down," said Captain McCalla to the gunners of the "Marblehead," and soon down it came in ruins. The cable-house collapsed when a shell from the "Nashville" exploded in it. A block-house near by tumbled to pieces under the hot fire. How many of the Spaniards fell is not known now, perhaps it never

BOMBARDMENT OF MATANZAS, CUBA, BY THE "NEW YORK," "CINCINNATI," AND "PURITAN,"
APRIL 27, 1898.

will be, for Spain will not take pains to publish the records of a war in which she won no glory. But hot as was the fire from the sea, that from the land never slackened. The bullets still sung in the air above the busy workers at the cables, and splashed in the water in seemingly undiminished numbers; but the sailors noticed that the enemy seemed to be getting the range. The thud of the striking bullet and the groan of the stricken man began to be heard too often. Lieutenant Winslow was hit in the hand, but tied up his wound and went on with his work. Men were seen to topple over in the boats. Eight were seriously wounded, one of them dying on the way to the ship. One brave fellow sitting at his oar attracted the attention of a neighbour by his singular silence. Beneath him was discovered a great pool of blood, and he was found to have borne a grave wound silently lest complaint might interrupt the progress of the work. Two hours and a half this fierce fire was endured, and then, two cables being cut, the signal was given from the flagship to withdraw. One man killed, two wounded seriously, one of whom died, and six slightly wounded was the official report. A curious hurt was sustained by Captain Maynard of the "Nashville," who was struck on the chest by a bullet which had already passed through the shoulder of an ensign.

Trivial affairs, of course, as viewed in the great theatre of war, were these two battles of the 11th of May, 1898, but to the men engaged in them, to those who imperilled their lives and perhaps lost them, to those who as a result of their service to their country and to humanity through her met cruel wounds, these battles were as great as any Waterloo. If too the loss was light, so was it throughout the war to the Americans. One shell at Cardenas slew, on the little torpedo boat "Winslow," one third of the men killed afloat in the whole war. More fell there than died with Dewey at Manila and Schley at Santiago combined.

In the two fights of the 11th of May, there fell more men than were lost elsewhere by the navy during the whole war; more navy men than fell either afloat or ashore, saving only the six marines who died at Guantanamo. As Bagley was the first, so he remained the last commissioned navy officer to die in battle during the war for the freedom of Cuba; and so, if the importance of battles be, like most other things, relative, we must concede something more than mere passing importance to the good fights well fought by the United States navy at Cardenas and Cienfuegos on the same day.

CHAPTER VI

SPAIN'S POSSESSIONS IN ASIA — UNEXPECTED SCENE OF AMERICAN NAVAL ACTIVITY — THE PHILIPPINE ISLANDS AND THEIR PEOPLE — RENDEZVOUS OF THE ASIATIC SQUADRON AT HONG KONG — COMMODORE GEORGE DEWEY — THE DEPARTURE FOR THE PHILIPPINES — THE SPANISH FLEET AT MANILA — THE BATTLE AND COMPLETE VICTORY OF THE AMERICANS — NO MEN LOST — DEWEY MADE AN ADMIRAL — AGUINALDO AND THE INSURGENTS — TROUBLE WITH GERMANY — A VIGOROUS MESSAGE — THE FRIENDLINESS OF ENGLAND.

DURING the lagging days of debate and diplomacy that preceded the declaration of war, there was of course eager discussion among the people of the probable strategy of the impending conflict and of the point at which the first blow would be struck. All agreed that Havana would be the first objective. That taken, some thought that in the event of continued resistance by the enemy our fleets might even be ordered to the coast of Spain. Hardly anywhere was there the slightest idea that the first crushing blow of the war would be delivered in Asiatic waters, where the flag of the United States was seldom seen, and where Spain had a populous and rich colony, then almost an unknown land to English-speaking peoples. When the news came that Admiral Dewey had run into the harbour of Manila, May 1st, and destroyed a Spanish fleet, the nation was first dumb with astonishment, and then hilarious with joy. Little was known about Manila or the Philippine Islands and less about Dewey, but a decisive victory won within ten days of the declaration of war, and in an unexpected quarter, stirred the nation as it was perhaps not stirred again during the course of the war.

The Philippine Islands were won for Spain by the famous explorer Magellan under the patronage of the great Emperor Charles V in 1521, in the course of a voyage which ended in the circumnavigation of the earth. The colony had suffered more than three hundred years of Spanish domination, and showed all the signs of arrested development, and even decay, that characterise Spanish provinces wherever they may be placed. The usual rebellion had been in progress there for years, fought on the part of the insurgents as they fought in Cuba, with raids, skirmishes, and the avoidance of battles, and on the part of the Spaniards with wholesale executions, torture, and barbarity. In the Philippine Archipelago are 1400 islands, most of them wholly uncivilised and never brought under the control of any government. In all some eight million people, mostly savages, some having a rudimentary civilisation, were ruled by the Spaniards, who applied to them the methods which had driven Cubans to beggary first, and then to desperation. The "carpet-bag official" was there in all his inefficiency and rapacity. The collection of taxes was farmed out, with the result that the maximum amount was exacted from the people and the minimum paid in to the government. There was absolutely no pretence at applying the revenues to public improvements. Such things were unknown. Bridges once burned were not rebuilt, roads were mere trails, most of the towns were mere aggregations of huts with unpaved streets and only a big church to suggest the presence of any European authority. Out of the presence and the power of the church sprang many of the evils of which the Filipinos justly complained. The priests were in effect part — and a very powerful part — of the government. The Archbishop of Manila exerted more authority than the Governor-General. This would have been less hurtful had the tone of the church been as high, and its influence exerted as positively for good as is usual in civilised countries. But, far away from the central authorities, the church functionaries in the Philippines too generally forgot the duties imposed upon them by their priestly functions. They were often immoral, rapacious, cruel, and dishonest. The misdeeds of the friars, who were scattered all through the islands, formed one of the chief counts in the revolutionists' indictment of Spain.

At the moment of the declaration of war with the United States no revolution was in active progress in the Philippines. In December, 1897, Spain had applied to the insurgents there the methods which had proved successful under Campos in Cuba in 1869, and had effected a compromise by promising reforms and paying a large sum of money to the insurgent leaders, chief among whom was a young man, General Emilio Aguinaldo, in consideration of their leaving the islands. As usual, the promises of the Spaniards were not kept. The reforms were insolently repudiated, and such of the revolutionary leaders as had trusted in Spanish honour and remained in the islands were cruelly put to death. Aguinaldo and his colleagues, who had gone to Hong Kong, noted these infamies from afar, and, having at their command the very considerable sum which Spain had paid them, began preparations for a new revolt.

In Hong Kong at this same moment was a man destined to do more toward freeing the Filipinos from the domination of Spain than could any junta of revolutionists. This was Commodore George Dewey, U. S. N., who had with him a fleet, not of prodigious strength it is true, but which exceeded in power anything the United States had ever before had in those far away waters. Not by accident was Dewey there, nor was it by accident that he was so " well heeled," as the fighting phrase goes. In war, the unexpected ought not to be permitted to happen, and nothing occurred in those far-away Pacific waters which was unexpected to the authorities at Washington, however surprising it may have been to the people of the United States. The selection of Commodore Dewey to command the Asiatic squadron, which was made in January, was in no sense an accident. If the people overlooked the fact that Spain had a fleet and colonies in Asiatic waters, the Navy Department did not, and a man of proved gallantry and skill in battle was chosen to direct the United States forces there. Dewey had graduated in two good schools — at Annapolis in 1854, and under Farragut on the Mississippi River in 1862. A veteran and a fighter, he was selected for the Asiatic squadron as soon as the probability of war was unmistakable, and it is said that he was bitterly disappointed at the choice, expecting that all the sea fighting would be done on the Atlantic. The Navy Department, however, thought otherwise, and begun hurrying ships to the Asiatic station weeks before the rupture between the nations became imminent. By the eighteenth of April Commodore Dewey had his full squadron assembled in the British port of Hong Kong. These six fighting-ships comprised the fleet:

"Olympia": protected cruiser; armament, four 8-in., ten 5-in., twenty-four rapid fire; complement, 466. "Baltimore": protected cruiser; armament, four 8-in., six 6-in., ten rapid fire; complement, 395. "Boston": partly protected cruiser; armament, two 8-in., six 6-in., ten rapid fire; complement, 272. "Raleigh": protected cruiser; armament, one 6-in., ten 5-in., fourteen rapid fire; complement, 200. "Concord": gunboat; armament, six 6-in., nine rapid fire; complement, 150. "Petrel": gunboat; armament, four 6-in., seven rapid fire; complement, 100. "McCulloch": revenue cutter; armament, four 4-in.; complement, 130.

Several colliers, purchased with their cargoes at Hong Kong before the declaration of war shut off this method of securing supplies, completed the fleet. Warned day by day by cable from Washington of the progress of the

ADMIRAL GEORGE DEWEY.

quarrel, Dewey put his ships in war paint, sent ashore all movables, instructed his officers in his plans, and was ready to strike when the word should come. The first official warning came from the authorities of Hong Kong. War had been declared, and Great Britain had issued its proclamation of neutrality. Even without orders from Washington, that fixed the only course that Commodore Dewey could take. Under the law of nations he was compelled to leave Hong Kong within twenty-four hours. Whither should he go? The nearest United States port was San Francisco, seven thousand miles away. To enter another foreign port meant another brief resting space of twenty-four hours, and then a polite request to leave. And coal? That prime essential of a modern ship was construed as contraband of war, and accordingly no neutral power would permit him to take in any of its harbours more than a sufficient supply to carry his ships back to the United States by the most direct route. Evidently one course only was open to the American fleet — the orders from Washington could be of only one tenor. A Spanish harbour somewhere in Asiatic waters must be captured and made a naval base. First, however, it was necessary to heed the British note of warning and leave Hong Kong. Accordingly, anchors were hove up and the fleet, with flags flying and bands playing, steamed out to sea. The British residents of the city made no secret of their sympathy with the Americans thus going out to early battle, but crowded the quays and shipping, cheering and saluting as the warships passed.

This first voyage of the fleet was but short. Mirs Bay, a Chinese harbour only a few miles to the northward had been selected as the anchorage where orders from home would be awaited, and the "McCulloch" was left behind to fetch them when they should arrive. The delay was but short, for the next day the revenue cutter steamed up to the new rendezvous bearing this message, dated Washington, April 24th:

"*Dewey, Asiatic Squadron:*

War has commenced between the United States and Spain. Proceed at once to Philippine Islands. Commence operations at once, particularly against the Spanish fleet. You must capture vessels or destroy. Use utmost endeavours. LONG."

For this, Admiral Dewey had been waiting and planning ever since his arrival on the station in January, and there was now no delay. A short conference with the captains on board the flagships filled out the evening, and shortly after midnight the fleet sailed on its errand of battle. Prows were turned south towards the Philippine Islands, lying 620 miles away. Speedy ships were in the squadron, but so too were slow ones, and the latter — the "Petrel" with a speed of barely seven knots holding the unenviable distinction — fixed the speed of all. Three days passed before the line of the coast — the Island of Luzon — was made out. Then Subig Bay, where it was reported the enemy might be found, was carefully reconnoitred, but without success. The fishermen plying their calling about the harbour's mouth had seen no Spanish fleet, and in none of the nooks or corners of the bay was there so much as a gunboat. So on to Manila thirty miles away. It was clear that the Spaniard had taken refuge there, preferring to fight with the aid of shore batteries.

What was this enemy for whom Dewey sought? In naval strength unequal to him, it was true, but not so much so as to make the issue of the battle a foregone certainty. The Spanish ships were comparatively antiquated, but they were not, as a London weekly insisted, wooden. Their guns were as good as those carried by the American ships. They outnumbered the Americans materially — to Dewey's six fighting-ships Admiral Montojo had ten, and two torpedo boats besides. The "Olympia" outclassed anything the Spaniards had, but in skilled hands the numbers of the enemy might be expected to more than make up for this. In batteries the

Americans had the advantage, but not overwhelmingly. To their 57 big guns, the Spaniards had 52; and to their 74 rapid-fire and machine guns, the enemy had 70. These figures eliminate the "McCulloch," which did not go into action, and the Spanish torpedo boats, which were sunk before their guns would bear. But the American big guns were heavier, for the Spaniards had nothing but 6.2-inch cannon to Dewey's 10-inch.

When the battle was fought the first hour showed the immense superiority of the Americans in everything that goes to win victory; but as Commodore Dewey led his fleet along the coast of Luzon toward the harbour where he knew the enemy lay in waiting, he had nothing to expect but a desperate battle with a fleet not greatly his inferior. It must be remembered that the Spanish ships were anchored in a harbour protected by shore batteries. To get at them the Americans had to pass down a channel guarded on either side by powerful forts armed with modern rifles. The harbour to be traversed before reaching the enemy was sixteen miles long, and it was only to be expected that it was plentifully besprinkled with mines. With these facts before him, and with the reasonable expectation that the Spanish fleet would receive his attack at a point where the fire of the forts would be effective, Commodore Dewey could only anticipate a hard fight, with a result subject to the fortunes of war. The measure of a commander's gallantry is fixed by the probable perils he braves, not by the result of the combat.

One seems to read in Dewey's first decision the effects of his training under the great Admiral Farragut. His fleet arrived off the mouth of Manila Bay at night. There was no stop to reconnoitre, no suggestion of " bottling up " the enemy after the Santiago fashion, no waiting until daylight might make it easier to run the gantlet of mines and batteries, no delay of any kind, but a quiet and immediate attack on the enemy. Only a brief wait for the moon to set, and then on, in single file, the "Olympia" leading, the "McCulloch" bringing up the rear, with all lights out except one lantern at the stern of each ship for the next to steer by. Seemingly the Spaniards had no idea that an enemy was at their door. The great light that marked the entrance to the harbour gleamed as though to welcome the grim procession of ghostly gray ships stealing unaware upon their prey. The forts were as silent as though all defenders were dead. To the men on the ships it seemed that their progress was attended with the tumult of a thousand railroad trains. They walked with muffled tread and spoke in whispers lest Spaniards miles away might hear them, and marvelled that the rush of the vessels through the water and the white foam breaking away from the cleaving prows did not attract the attention of the enemy. Yet there came no sound of cannon, nor did any mine rend the plates of any stout ship. The last ship of the column, the "McCulloch," gave the first alarm. From its smoke-stack, when coal was flung on the furnaces below, there flared up a red flame lighting up the waters and the rigging of the ships ahead. All turned expectantly toward the batteries in anticipation of a shot, but no sound came. Again the unlucky beacon flared, and again, and after the third illumination the darkness to starboard was pierced by the flash of a gun on a rock called El Fraile. The shell went wild and the "Concord" responded with the fierce bellow of a 6-inch gun. There was no longer any attempt at secrecy, and cannon roared from the "Boston," the "McCulloch," and the "Concord," the big ships at the head of the line passing on in silent dignity. The shot from El Fraile had done much more good than harm. It gave to the commodore, who with a Filipino insurgent by his side stood on the bridge of the "Olympia" piloting in the fleet, a clear idea of how the shore lay. That battery once passed, all the defences of the harbour's mouth were left behind, and there was nothing more to apprehend until the city, with its

DEWEY'S VICTORY—THE NAVAL FIGHT IN MANILA BAY, MAY 1, 1898.

forts at Cavite, was reached, — nothing, that is, except mines, against which no skill could avail and which might therefore be ignored. "Perhaps they'll make it all the hotter for us when they do begin," said Dewey, commenting on the quiescence of the Spaniards. So the ships steamed sullenly on up the bay, the tension measurably lessened by the little spurt of fire, but with every man alert for the next development of the morning — for by this time the sudden dawn of the tropics was breaking.

Nothing but the undeniable facts of the case could make credible the amazing inefficiency which characterised the Spaniards, not only at Manila but at other points attacked by American fleets. Thus early in Dewey's advance on Manila the defenders had sacrificed one advantage without effort to make use of it. The mouth of the bay which the Americans entered without resistance was well fortified. A strait about five miles wide is broken by the islands Corregidor, Caballo, and El Fraile — all fortified, and armed with Krupp guns. On the mainland Limbones and San José points on either hand bear more forts and more steel rifled cannon. Nevertheless, all were passed within easy range and with only an ineffective fire from one battery. If there were contact mines in the channel, they failed to explode. If there were electric mines, the officers intrusted with their discharge failed to wake up. In the hands of a power of ordinary military attainments the defence of the entrance of Manila Bay would have cost the invader a ship or two.

The swift coming of day discovered to the eager gazers from the American ships not only the old town of Manila with its clustering low roofs and towering cathedral, but a sight which they had come all this way to see — the Spanish fleet — ten great ships with military tops showing across a low neck of land — lying at anchor under the batteries at Cavite, a suburb of the city where the navy yard, arsenal, and other military and naval establishments were placed. There was silence on the ships as the stirring spectacle was presented, and the men, many of whom had slept on the run in from the harbour's mouth, crowded to the points of vantage to gaze on it. With a glass, the roofs and quays of the city could be seen to be crowded with spectators; so it was evident that the short engagement with the battery at El Fraile had alarmed the city. As the men gazed, others passed up and down the decks of the men-of-war, distributing cups of hot coffee and biscuit by orders of the commodore, who had no intention of having his sailors go into action hungry. The plan of the battle had been worked out already, and only a few signals from the flagship were necessary to place the fleet in the formation agreed on. As the signals fluttered from the gaff, black balls mounted to every peak on all the vessels, and breaking out displayed the great battle-flags. At that the enemy growled out a word of warning with the 9-inch guns of Fort Lunetta, and the attacking column moved suddenly on to closer quarters. "Hold your fire," was the word passed on from the flagship, and save for two shots from the "Concord" no answer was made to the forts. Onward toward the Spanish fleet, which was maintaining a like silence, the fleet sped. A sudden muffled roar and a great volume of mud and water springing into the air right before the flagship told that the dreaded mines were near, and in an instant another exploded. Neither did any hurt, and with the explosion of the two the Spanish resources of that sort seemed to be exhausted. By this time the fleet was approaching the enemy nearly. On the bridge of the "Olympia" stood Commodore Dewey, Captain Gridley and Flag-Captain Lambert at his side. Though the Spanish ships now joined the forts in pouring a fire on the advancing foe, there was still no response. Just as the sun rose, red and glaring with midsummer heat, the commodore turned to the officer at his side and said, quietly, " You may fire now, Gridley, when ready." Gridley was ready, and almost on the instant an 8-inch shell hurtled out through the yellow smoke toward the enemy, now about 4500 yards away. Presently a signal from the flagship conveyed to all the vessels a like permission, and the whole fleet was soon engaged.

On the flagship, before opening action, Dewey had assembled his men and given them this final word: "Keep perfectly cool, and pay attention to nothing but orders." This was the watchword throughout the American fleet that morning, and, as the result, the fire was deliberate and deadly. The column — "Olympia," "Baltimore," "Raleigh," "Petrel," "Concord," and "Boston," in the order named — steamed along parallel to the Spanish ships, working every gun that could be brought to bear, and receiving the fire of ships and forts in return. The fire of the enemy was, as Dewey put it in his report, "vigorous, but generally ineffective." It was a succession of brilliant misses, of shots that came so near hitting that it was a constant marvel that the American ships were escaping destruction. One shell struck the bridge gratings of the "Olympia;" one narrowly missed the commodore himself. The fire became so hot that Captain Gridley, who stood exposed by the commodore's side, was directed to go into the conning tower in order that both might not be killed or disabled at once. On the "Boston," a shell burst in a stateroom setting it afire. Through both sides of the "Baltimore's" unarmoured hull a shell sped, happily hitting no one in its course. A 6-inch gun was disabled, and a box of ammunition was exploded on the same ship. Down past the Spanish line the squadron moved, the port side of every ship a mass of flame and smoke, then circling around in a grand sweep — that made the Spaniards think for a moment they were pulling out of action — the column returned again on its course, and the men of the starboard batteries had a chance to try their skill while their fellows rested. Each turn brought them nearer the enemy; each broadside found the American gunnery improving. Five times the circuit was made, and then a signal fluttered from the yard of the

"Olympia," and the fleet turned away to the other side of the harbour, where the "McCulloch" and the colliers had been lying. The Spaniards raised a resounding cheer at the sight of what they supposed to be a retreat, and a telegram was instantly sent off, that the enemy had been compelled to haul off for repairs. On the American ships, where the purpose of the order was not understood, there was much grumbling. "Breakfast," growled one of the gunners, who had been told that was the purpose of the intermission; "who the —— wants any breakfast? Why can't we finish off the Dons, now we 've got them going?" Breakfast, however, was not the object of the delay. A misinterpreted signal had caused the commodore to believe that ammunition for the 5-inch guns was running short, and as the smoke made it difficult, if not impossible to ask each ship-captain by signal how much he had, it was determined to haul off and redistribute the ammunition if it was required. In the end, however, no necessity was found for this, and as there was time then for breakfast, the meal was served.

In the portion of the engagement prior to the intermission, the "first round," it might be called, the Spaniards had suffered heavily. The American fire had been both rapid and accurate. With the glasses, the shots could be seen striking the thin iron hulls of the Spanish ships, and by the time the third circuit had been made three were in flames. Stung into fury by the losses inflicted on his squadron, Admiral Montojo, just as the Americans were turning to begin their third circuit, slipped the cables of his flagship, and under full steam darted out as if with the intention of ramming the "Olympia," or at any rate coming to close quarters. The dash was magnificent, but it was futile. As the "Reina Cristina" swung away from her fellows, the fire of the whole American fleet was concentrated upon her. As she clung stubbornly to her course, the storm of projectiles swept down upon her, pierced her hull like paper, swept her decks, and, bursting, spread death and fire of every side. Her bridge was shot away, her engines wounded. Superhuman gallantry could bear the punishment no longer, and, responding with difficulty to her helm, she turned to seek her former position. Just as her stern was presented to the American fire, an 8-inch gun on the "Olympia" was trained upon her, and its projectile sped forth on a murderous errand. It struck the Spaniard full in the stern, tore its way forward, killing men, shattering guns, exploding ammunition, piercing partitions and tearing up decks, until it exploded in her after-boiler. The wound was mortal. With flames leaping from her hatches, and the shrill screams of agonised men rising above the thunder of the battle, the "Reina Cristina" staggered back. One hundred and fifty of her men lay dead, and nearly a hundred wounded, — most of them sacrificed in Montojo's gallant effort to rush the American flagship. Another heavy loss fell upon the Spaniards while this act in the drama of battle was progressing. Thinking, no doubt, that the attention of the "Olympia," would be wholly centred upon the "Cristina," the two Spanish torpedo boats slipped out, and made a run for the American fleet. One headed for the supply-ships, but was caught by the "Petrel," which first drove her ashore, and then pounded her with rapid-fire guns until she blew up. The other, advancing on the "Olympia," was struck amidships by a shell, broke in two, and disappeared like a broken bottle. So at Manila, as later at Santiago, it was demonstrated that torpedo boats are not the dangerous engines of war that had been thought, — at least not when they are in Spanish hands.

Three hours' intermission was taken by the American sailors after that first round. A leisurely breakfast, a critical examination of all guns and machinery that had been under strain, and the work of preparing an ample supply of fresh ammunition occupied the time. Then out fluttered the signals again, the crews went to their quarters, the great screws began to revolve, and once more the fighting ships bore down upon the unhappy enemy. This was to be the wind-up. Before those ships returned again to their anchorage it was the intention of the quiet little man on the "Olympia's" bridge to comply literally with the orders he had received from the Secretary of the Navy and destroy or capture the Spanish fleet. He took up the task just where he had left it, and in the same manner. Again the fleet revolved in a great circle of smoke and fire, though at closer range than before. The Spaniards, whose hopes had been roused by the stoppage of the action, were demoralised by its renewal. Their fire was wild, their resistance half-hearted. The "Reina Cristina"—no longer the flagship, for Montojo had transferred his flag to the "Isla de Cuba"—was blown up by the shells of the "Baltimore." After her, speedily followed the "Don Juan de Austria," her *coup de grâce* being administered by the "Raleigh." The little "Petrel" ran into the shoal water and set fire to the "El Correo," the "Marques del Duero," the "Don Juan de Austria," "Isla de Luzon," "Isla de Cuba," and "General Lezo," all of which had been disabled by the fire of the fleet, and most of which had been run ashore after surrendering. Admiral Montojo with great gallantry fought his second flagship until her guns were silenced and the flames were making her decks untenable. Then he abandoned her to her fate and escaped to the city, whence, it is said, a great concourse of people had come out that morning to see the "pigs of Yankees" annihilated. Finally, the "Don Antonio de Ulloa," the last ship left fighting, sunk with her flag still nailed to her mast, and a well-placed shot entered the magazine at Cavite, ending the resistance of the shore batteries. Then the signal was flung out from the flagship "The enemy has surrendered," the hot, weary, and smoke-begrimed men swarmed cheering out of turrets and up from the bowels of the ships, the flagship's band broke out with the "Star Spangled Banner," and the victory of Manila, the first victory in the war with Spain, was won. And at how light a cost! The story told by Mr. E. W. Harden, who was on the "Olympia" and witnessed that he tells of, recounts perhaps the most remarkable occurrence in naval warfare up to that time; it was repeated at Santiago: —

"As each captain came over the 'Olympia's' side, he replied to the eager query 'How many killed?' in a manner that indicated a very much mixed state of mind. Mingled with satisfaction at having lost no man, was an evident desire to have it understood that the lack of loss was no proof of an absence of danger.

"'Only eight wounded,' replied Captain Dyer of the 'Baltimore' — 'none seriously. But six shells struck us, and two burst inboard without hurting any one.'

"'Not a dashed one!' was the rollicking way the next captain reported.

"'None killed and none wounded,' was the apologetic reply of the next one; 'but I don't yet know how it happened. I suppose you fellows were all cut up!'

"'My ship was n't hit at all,' was the next report, made with a sort of defiant air, as if the speaker would like to hear it insinuated that he had had any part in keeping his men in a safe place.

"When the 'Boston's' captain came alongside it was feared that he for certain would have a serious list of casualties, for it was known that his ship had been on fire. And when he announced neither killed nor wounded, the news quickly spread through the flagship, and the men cheered vociferously."

The description of the course followed by one shot which struck the "Baltimore" makes this complete immunity of our men seem miraculous. This was a 60-pound armour-piercing projectile, fired from a land battery. It struck the ship about two feet above the upper deck between two guns which were being served; pierced two plates of steel one quarter of an inch thick each; then ploughed through the wooden deck, striking and breaking a heavy beam by which it was turned upwards; passed through a steel hatch-combing; disabled a 6-inch gun; hurtled around the semicircular shield which surrounded the gun, missing the men at it; reversed its course and travelled back to a point almost opposite that at which it had entered the ship, and thus passed out. It had passed between men standing crowded at their quarters and had touched none, but it exploded some loose ammunition by which eight were wounded.

For the Spaniards there was no such immunity as attended the Americans. No miracles interposed between them and the American shells, perhaps because the latter were more skilfully directed. The exact losses in Admiral Montojo's squadron are not known. His ten ships and two torpedo boats were totally destroyed, and the report of General Augustin, the Governor-General, put the number of killed and wounded at about 618, though there is reason to believe it was nearer a thousand. The ships lost and their armament are summed up in the following table:

	Description.	Armament.	
Reina Cristina	Steel cruiser.	Six 6.2-in., two 2.7, 13 R. F.	352
Castilla	Wooden cruiser.	Four 5.9, two 4.7, two 3.4, two 2.9, 12 R. F.	349
Don Antonio de Ulloa .	Iron cruiser.	Four 4.7, 5 R. F.	159
Don Juan de Austria .	Iron cruiser.	Four 4.7, two 2.7, 21 R. F.	179
Isla de Luzon	Steel protected cruiser.	Six 4.7, 8 R. F.	156
Isla de Cuba	Steel protected cruiser.	Six 4.7, 8 R. F.	156
Velasco	Iron cruiser.	Three 6-in., two 2.7, 2 R. F.	147
Marques del Duero . .	Gunboat.	One 6.2, two 4.7, 1 R. F.	96
General Lezo	Gunboat.	One 3.5, 1 R. F.	115
Argos	Gunboat.	. . . . . .	87
			1796

The official report of the battle by the Spanish admiral gives a graphic picture of the accuracy and effect of the American fire. After describing the fleets and the circumstances under which the battle opened, he says:

"The Americans fired most rapidly. There came upon us numberless projectiles, as the three cruisers at the head of the line devoted themselves almost entirely to fight the 'Cristina,' my flagship. A short time after the action commenced one shell exploded in the forecastle and put out of action all those who served the four rapid-fire cannon, making splinters of the forward mast, which wounded the helmsman on the bridge. In the meantime another shell exploded in the orlop, setting fire to the crew's bags, which they were fortunately able to control. The enemy shortened the distance between us, and rectifying his aim, covered us with a rain of rapid-fire projectiles.

"At half-past seven one shell destroyed completely the steering-gear, another exploded on the poop, and put out of action nine men. Another destroyed the mizzen-mast head, bringing down the flag and my ensign. A fresh shell exploded in the officers' cabin, covering the hospital with blood, destroying the wounded who were being treated there. Another exploded in the ammunition-room astern, filling the quarters with smoke and preventing the working of the hand steering-gear. As it was impossible to control the fire, I had to flood the magazine when the cartridges were beginning to explode.

"Amidships, several shells of smaller calibre went through the smoke-stack, and one of the large ones penetrated the fire-room, putting out of action one master-gunner and twelve men serving the guns. Another rendered useless the starboard bow gun. While the fire astern increased, fire was started forward by another shell which went through the hull and exploded on the deck.

"The broadside guns, being undamaged, continued firing until there were only one gunner and one seaman remaining unhurt for firing them.

"The inefficiency of the vessels which composed my little squadron, the lack of all classes of the personnel, especially master-gunners, and seamen-gunners, the inaptitude of some of the provisional machinists, the scarcity of rapid-fire cannon, the strong crews of the enemy, and the unprotected character of the greater part of our vessels, all contributed to make more decided the sacrifice which we made for our country.

"Our casualties, including those of the arsenal, amounted to three hundred and eighteen men killed and wounded."

Ordinarily after so signal a victory as this, a commander might reasonably expect relief from responsibility and a respite from perplexing problems. Commodore Dewey's situation was not so comfortable. He held Manila at the mercy of his guns, but to bombard it would be to kill scores of innocent people, many citizens of friendly nations. If he compelled the city to surrender by a threat of bombardment, he had no troops with which to hold it. If he drove out the Spanish troops, he had no means of preserving order and protecting property. All this doubtless occurred to him as he watched the final scenes in the annihilation of the enemy's fleet, and soon thereafter it was formally presented for his consideration by the British consul, who came off in a boat to ask that the city should not be bombarded. After consideration the commodore contented himself with sending word to the Captain-General that the town would not be harmed unless the fleet was fired upon. This convention was scrupulously adhered to, and the fleet lay long in the harbour, with the Spanish flag floating in plain view and in easy range over the city. Cavite, however, with its arsenal and forts, was surrendered on the 2d of May, under threat of bombardment. The same day the cable connecting Manila with Hong Kong was cut, though Admiral Dewey offered to spare it and permit the Spaniards to use it in communicating with Spain if they would allow him to use it in communicating with Washington. This offer Augustin refused, happily for Dewey, perhaps, for he was thereby freed in great measure from the control of a Board of Strategy at Washington and of an Administration which was rather a clog than a spur to the operations of the army and navy on the Atlantic coast. As a result of the destruction of the cable, the people of the United States received their first news of the victory from Madrid, incomplete and garbled of course, as coming through Spanish sources.

Dewey was not in haste to send word of his achievement, but waited until everything that could be done at that moment was completed. Monday morning the little "Petrel" ran in near Cavite, and Captain Lambert went ashore to receive the formal surrender of the fort, which had hauled down its flag the day before. There was some Spanish quibbling, and an effort made to disprove that the flag had ever been struck, but Lambert was equal to the occasion. Before leaving his ship he had directed that unless he returned in an hour the works should be bombarded. Forty-five minutes had been consumed in argument when the captain pulled out his watch. "Unless you surrender unconditionally so soon that I can get back to my ship in fifteen minutes," he said, "the 'Petrel' will open fire on your works." Then there was a speedy surrender, and priests and nuns came humbly to beg the American commander to restrain his men from murdering all the wounded in the hospitals — something which they had been assured was the invariable practice of the barbarous "Yanquis." The next day the "Raleigh" and "Baltimore" went down to the mouth of the bay and, after a brief attack, captured the forts on Corregidor and Sangley Point. The guns in these works were destroyed by wrapping them with guncotton and exploding it with electricity. It is interesting to learn that when the officer in command at Corregidor went to the "Raleigh" to surrender himself he was greatly alarmed to find the ship drifting in the main channel, or Boca Grande, and demanded that he be put ashore. Asked for an explanation, he said that the channel was full of contact mines, and that, while the Americans might brave death if they so desired, it was not fair to expose a prisoner to almost certain destruction. It was through that channel that the American fleet had entered the harbour.

With all the harbour defences in his command, Dewey now sent off to Hong Kong the "McCulloch" bearing his first despatches to Washington, four days after his victory. Thus it was one week after the first rumours from Madrid before the American people received definite information in these reports

"MANILA, May 1.— Squadron arrived at Manila at daybreak this morning. Immediately engaged the enemy and destroyed the following Spanish vessels: 'Reina Cristina,' 'Castilla,' 'Don Antonio de Ulloa,' 'Isla de Luzon,' 'Isla de Cuba,' 'General Lezo,' 'Marques de Duero,' 'Cano,' 'Velasquo,' 'Isla de Mindanao,' a transport and water battery at Cavite. The squadron is uninjured and only a few men are slightly wounded. Only means of telegraphing is to American consul at Hong Kong. I shall communicate with him.

"DEWEY."

"MANILA, May 4.— I have taken possession of the naval station at Cavite, Philippine Islands, and destroyed the fortifications. Have destroyed fortifications at bay entrance, Corregidor Island, paroling the garrison. I control the bay completely and can take the city at any time. The squadron is in excellent health and spirits. The Spanish loss not fully known, but is very heavy. One hundred and fifty killed, including captain, on 'Reina Cristina' alone. I am assisting in protecting Spanish sick and wounded. Two hundred and fifty sick and wounded in hospital within our lines. Much excitement in Manila. Will protect foreign residents.

"DEWEY."

To these despatches the immediate response of the Secretary of the Navy was a message of congratulation in the name of the President and the people of the United States and the information that the President had appointed the victorious admiral-commodore a rear admiral. The morning after the "McCulloch" brought that despatch to Manila Bay, watchful eyes on many ships turned to the flagship to see what flag would be run up to the mainmast. It was the blue flag as of yore, but instead of one star there were two, and the guns of the squadron roared out a salute to the new admiral.

Manila, which now lay at the mercy of the American

IRONCLADS IN ACTION.

fleet, is a city of some 250,000 people, chiefly of course natives, although Chinese and Spaniards are there by the thousands, with a few Americans and Englishmen and a large body of half-breeds. It was at this time fortified heavily on its landward side, as the insurgents were active and threatened to capture the town now that the fleet was gone and the harbour defences were falling into the hands of the Americans. The presence of the insurgents was at once an advantage and an embarrassment to the Americans. They were in a sense our allies, as we had a common foe — the Spaniard; and accordingly a certain degree of countenance was given to their most capable leader, Aguinaldo, whom Dewey gave passage down from Hong Kong on the second trip of the "McCulloch." He was received on the flagship with the utmost courtesy and admitted in no small degree to the admiral's counsels. Setting up headquarters in Cavite immediately on his arrival, Aguinaldo began recruiting for the insurgent army and was provided with a certain amount of arms and ammunition from the captured stores by the order of the admiral. But with increasing power the insurgent leader became more self-assertive and his relations with the Americans became strained. It would have been unwise to permit his followers to capture the city, even had they the power, for as yet the admiral had no hint as to the purposes of his own government in dealing with the Philippines. He could not look on and see the insurgents establish a government *de facto* which the Washington government might have to overthrow. The question of the attitude of other powers was also pressing. Shortly after the battle, English, French, and German warships came flocking into the bay. The two latter nations had throughout the war manifested a guarded and restrained unfriendliness for the United States, and there was every reason to apprehend that unless order was maintained in Manila they would land forces to protect the interests of their citizens resident there. Forces so landed are slow to retire — witness the British in Egypt. Therefore it was Admiral Dewey's study to see to it that nothing should happen in the city which would justify European intervention. Bad as the Spaniards were, they had an organised government, and might be expected to maintain order better than the half-disciplined hordes of Aguinaldo. Accordingly, before very many days the Americans were put in the attitude of protecting their enemies the Spanish against their allies the Filipinos. The intricacies of policy do not appeal to the half-savage mind, and this attitude was not unnaturally the cause of some bitterness in the insurgent camps.

The foreign ships, particularly those of Germany, were a source of constant worry to the admiral. It is the custom of nations to permit the warships of a friendly power to enter and move about a blockaded harbour as they will, and equally it is the custom of navy officers who are cognisant of the etiquette of their profession to receive this concession as a privilege rather than a right, and to exercise it in a way that will harass the blockading fleet as little as possible. The Germans in Philippine water seemed to study methods of annoying the Americans. Their ships were constantly entering and leaving Manila Bay, at all hours and on the most frivolous pretexts. Their launches more than once ran about the harbour after nightfall in a way that justified the apprehension of the American lookouts that they might be Spanish torpedo boats. A shot at one of the intruders might have created the gravest international complications. The German navy officers, even after the defeat of Montojo, made of the Spanish officers their chosen companions. They were continually going ashore, fraternising with the enemy in the Manila cafés and giving every possible indication that their sympathies were strongly pro-Spanish. If they did not actually betray the confidence reposed in them by using their opportunities for observation of the American fleet to give information to the Spaniards, they were at least exceedingly indiscreet, for lights that looked like signals, and errands which seemed undertaken in Spain's behalf were frequent. More than once the feeling between the Americans and the Germans seemed to be leading inevitably to an armed conflict, for Admiral Dewey would not sacrifice a single right nor abate in any degree the rightful dignity of the commander of a United States squadron in possession of the bay of Manila. One of these instances was that of the German ship "Princess Wilhelmina," the captain of which prohibited the insurgents from undertaking a certain expedition they had planned. Dewey sent a ship to the spot, and the expedition was carried out under the protection of its guns. Mr. J. L. Stickney, a correspondent who was with the admiral on the flagship, tells a story which he declares he obtained from a "perfectly authentic source." The admiral learned that one of the German vessels had landed provisions in Manila, thereby violating neutrality. He summoned the flag lieutenant of the "Olympia" to his cabin.

"Oh, Brumby," said he, when the officer appeared, "I wish you to take the barge and go over to the German flagship. Give Admiral von Diederich my compliments, and say that I wish to call his attention to the fact that the vessels of his squadron have shown an extraordinary disregard of the usual courtesies of naval intercourse, and that finally one of them has committed a gross breach of neutrality in landing provisions in Manila, a port which I am blockading."

The lieutenant saluted and turned to go. The admiral called him back, his voice, which had thus far been quiet and gently modulated, rising with an intonation of wrath.

"And, Brumby," continued he, "tell Admiral von Diederich that if he wants a fight he can have it right now."

The message had its effect, and thenceforward the annoyance from the Germans was materially lessened, although in some degree it continued until the end of the war, when the German Emperor himself, seeing the danger and the folly of pursuing a course which was creating hostility to

Germany all over the United States, intervened and ordered the German ships away from Manila, intrusting the protection of the German citizens there to the United States authorities,— a sort of belated diplomacy adopted when it was found that the methods of the mailed fist could not be safely employed.

In contrast to the attitude of the German officers was that of the English. Great Britain had in Manila Bay a squadron quite equal to that of Germany,— the latter being rather superior to that of the United States. The British officers lost no opportunity to show their friendship for the Americans, and it is reported that, when on one occasion the German admiral, planning a stroke, asked Captain Chichester, the British commander, what the English would do in case the Germans should protest against an American bombardment of Manila, the messenger received the answer: " Say to Admiral von Diederich that he will have to call on Admiral Dewey to find out what the British ships will do in such an event. Admiral Dewey is the only man authorised to answer this question."

Perhaps there is exaggeration or incorrectness of detail in these stories and in others like them that were current in war-times. It is undeniable, however, that the hostility of the Germans and the friendliness of the English were generally recognised in the fleets, and the international imbroglio finally took the significant form of sailors' fights in Hong Kong, in which Yankee and British Blue Jackets fought shoulder to shoulder against the seamen of the Kaiser.

CHAPTER VII

Spain's Cape Verde Fleet — The Coasts of the United States Menaced — How the Naval Force of the United States in the Atlantic was Employed — The Search for Cervera — Bombardment of San Juan de Porto Rico — Entrapped in Santiago de Cuba — The Sampson-Schley Controversy — The Voyage of the "Oregon" — The Blockade of Cervera.

WHEN war was declared, Spain had at the Cape Verde Islands a very considerable fleet. To these islands, as a sort of outpost, the Spanish Minister of Marine had begun sending men-of-war when the despatch of our North Atlantic squadron to the Dry Tortugas and Key West seemed to suggest a threat. By the middle of April, the Spanish fleet under Admiral Cervera numbered four fine large vessels and three torpedo-boat destroyers. The most powerful ship of the squadron was the "Cristobal Colon," a battle-ship of the second class, mounting two 10-inch guns, ten 6-inch, and six 4.7-inch. That is to say, this was her main battery as set forth in the naval reports, but the Spaniards, with characteristic improvidence, had failed to mount the two 10-inch rifles. As a ship, she was a magnificent structure, "perhaps the finest of her class afloat," writes Captain Chadwick of the "New York," with whose opinion many of the first naval experts of Europe agreed. The three cruisers in Cervera's fleet were sister-ships: the "Almirante Oquendo," the "Infanta Maria Teresa," and the "Vizcaya." They were of 7000 tons displacement each, with a 12-inch armour belt and 3-inch protective deck, and mounted two 11-inch rifles, ten 5.5-inch, and the usual secondary battery of small calibres and machine guns. What appeared to give these ships a notable advantage was their estimated speed of twenty knots an hour. When the day of battle came, however, this speed was found to be as non-existent as the big guns on the "Oquendo." With this fleet Admiral Cervera had further three torpedo-boat destroyers, or large torpedo boats, the "Furor," "Terror," and "Pluton." Of this class of ships the "United States" was wholly destitute. Built in British ship-yards, of the most approved modern patterns, having a speed of thirty knots an hour, and adding to the terrifying torpedo armament a very respectable battery of rapid-fire and machine guns, these were really formidable vessels. They had in combination the sinister qualities of the serpent, which can deliver a fatal stroke and slip noiselessly away, and of the snarling panther, which if cornered can fight viciously for its life. Much was feared from them by the navy officers of the United States; much was hoped of them by Spain. They accomplished nothing.

For some days after the declaration of war, this fleet clung to the protection of the harbour of St. Vincent in the Cape Verde Islands. Portugal, which exercised sovereignty over those islands, was ostensibly a neutral power, and the duty rested with it to order Cervera away within twenty-four hours of the declaration of war. But in fact the sympathies of the Portuguese government were strongly with their Spanish neighbours, and they stretched the code of neutrality to the utmost in giving Cervera sanctuary. The Spaniards were in no hurry to reach Cuban waters. Cervera, an old and able sailor, knew the faults of the ships under his command if the Ministry of Marine did not. In a Spanish magazine the story is told that a year before the war a visitor to Admiral Cervera said to him of this very squadron:

"You appear to be indicated, by professional opinion, for the command of the squadron in case war is declared."

"In that case," replied Cervera, somewhat ruefully, "I

ADMIRAL SAMPSON'S FLEET OFF PUERTO RICO, IN SEARCH OF CERVERA'S VESSELS, MAY 1, 1898.

ADMIRAL CERVERA'S FLEET APPROACHING SANTIAGO, MAY, 1898.

shall accept; knowing, however, that I am going to a Trafalgar."

"And how could that disaster be avoided?" inquired the visitor, with natural anxiety.

"By allowing me to spend beforehand fifty thousand tons of coal in evolutions, and ten thousand projectiles in target practice. Otherwise we shall go to a Trafalgar. Remember what I say."

But the Spanish national character was not favourable to such wise preparation as the admiral wished. With fatuous self-confidence the responsible authorities, as well as the people, thought the navy invincible, and looked with contempt upon the ships and men under the stars and stripes. A former minister of marine, two weeks before the war, expressed through a Madrid newspaper these views as to the probable outcome of the contest upon the sea:

"We shall conquer on the sea, and I am now going to give you my reasons. The first of these is the remarkable discipline that prevails on our warships; and the second, as soon as fire is opened, the crews of the American ships will commence to desert, since we all know that among them are people of all nationalities. Ship against ship, therefore, a failure is not to be feared. I believe that the squadron detained at Cape de Verde, and particularly the destroyers, should have, and could have, continued the voyage to Cuba, since they have nothing to fear from the American fleet."

The marked divergence of opinion between the politicians and people of Spain and the trained officers of the Spanish navy was not without a parallel on this side of the water. While our Navy Department and the officers of our ships showed calm confidence of their ability to cope with Cervera's advancing fleet, the people of some of our sea-coast towns manifested something like a panic. Delegations from nearly all the seaport cities descended upon Washington, headed by their Congressmen, to demand additional protection. Each wanted batteries and a coast-defence vessel. Had the authorities given heed to the apprehensive appeals of Boards of Trade, Chambers of Commerce, Aldermen and Mayors, the United States navy would have been split up into small flotillas and scattered along the coast from Eastport to Jupiter Inlet, while the army would have been converted into a number of small garrisons for harbour defence. Rich citizens of Boston packed up their silver and valuable papers and sent them off to inland safe deposits. Summer cottages along the shore were a drug in the market, and the summer colonists, with remarkable unanimity, developed a liking for mountain air. That in modern warfare unfortified towns are never bombarded did not seem to reassure the timid ones, and the absurdity of fearing that a warship would let fly a $2000 projectile at a peaceful $500 cottage did not appeal to their sense of humour.

Nevertheless, there was some slight foundation for the popular apprehension of danger from the enemy's fleet. When that squadron left St. Vincent on April 29th, being hastened in its departure by a pointed communication from the United States minister to Portugal that neutral customs were being strained to the breaking-point, it disappeared absolutely from view. The Navy Department had apparently made no arrangements for tracing its wake, and the last definite news for many days was that a newspaper boat had followed it for some hours, and left it still headed westward. Of course, the supposition was that it was making the best of its way to West Indian waters, and it was estimated that it should arrive there about the 9th of May.

The distribution of the American fleets in the Atlantic at this moment is a matter of much interest as indicative of the measures of reconnoissance and defence adopted by the naval authorities when the coast was actually menaced by a powerful fleet. At the probable seapoint of battle, with Cape Haitien as a base of information, was

ARMORED CRUISER "NEW YORK" ON HER WAY TO PUERTO RICO.

Admiral Sampson, with the battleship "Iowa," the monitors "Terror" and "Amphitrite," the unarmoured cruisers "Detroit" and "Montgomery," the torpedo boat "Porter," the collier "Niagara," and the armoured cruiser "New York" as flagship. It was a slow-moving squadron, for the monitors, though good in battle, are but sluggish steamers and had to be towed by some of the larger ships.

The part of the squadron left on the blockade was put under command of Commodore Watson, who, with the two monitors, "Puritan" and "Miantonomah," lay off the entrance to Havana with a fleet of gunboats and auxiliaries reaching out to the east and west. Cruising about Martinique and Guadaloupe were the swift converted liners "Harvard" and "St. Louis," while the "Yale" was sent to scout the seas about Porto Rico.

Meanwhile the coast of New England and the Middle States was left with so scant a guard that in some degree the panic of the townsmen was justified. At anchor in Hampton Roads lay what was known as the Flying Squadron, organized early in the war for the protection of the coast, and put under command of Commodore Winfield Scott Schley. In this squadron were the "Brooklyn," "Texas," "Massachusetts," "Minneapolis," and "Columbia," — two battle-ships, two armoured, and one unarmoured cruiser. Circling about, far off the coast, were the auxiliary "St. Paul," and a horde of converted yachts, whose duty it was to scour the sea in search for the enemy, and, discovering him, to make all speed for the nearest telegraph point and summon the Flying Squadron to the rescue. Rumours of an enemy these scouts found in plenty, and day after day the newspapers reported mysterious ships seen off divers vulnerable points on the northeastern coast; but while nobody knew where Cervera was, the Navy Department soon became convinced that he was not in Northern waters, and despatched the Flying Squadron to the Gulf, — an action that raised a bitter outcry on the

North Atlantic coast, where the "Columbia" alone, of the formidable ships, was left.

When the first week in May passed and the enemy failed to appear at any of the points where arrangements had been made to give him a warm welcome, there was a sense of growing anxiety at Washington. A fleet of four great ships and three torpedo boats seemed too big to disappear so completely when the ocean was covered with scouts on the outlook for it. Had Cervera outwitted us, and was he engaged in some secret adventure of sinister purpose? The newspapers were filled with speculations, and the opinion of every naval expert was eagerly sought. Rumours of the most terrifying nature were abroad. Cervera had been sighted off Nova Scotia, and was about to desolate the New England coast. He had gone to the far southwest to intercept and destroy the gallant battleship "Oregon," then making a race from San Francisco to Key West, of which we shall have more to say. One day there came explicit news that the enemy had returned to Cadiz, and Ambassador Hay, at Paris, cabled home that he had positive private information that the big ironclads were lying in the harbour of Cadiz in plain sight for all to see. This was so definite, so official, that authorities and people rested content with the theory that "Cervera had turned tail and sneaked home again," until it was emphatically disproved.

It was the hard-working squadron in the Gulf that finally determined the facts. Admiral Sampson, with the fleet above enumerated, and without more definite knowledge concerning the location of the elusive Spaniards than had the rest of the world, appeared before San Juan, Porto Rico, on the 12th of May. He had expected to find the Spaniards there when he began his voyage, but the information he received at Cape Haitien, where despatches from Washington were received, left little promise of that. Nevertheless, he concluded to go ahead and make an attack on the defences of the port, in the ex-

BOMBARDMENT OF SAN JUAN, PUERTO RICO, MAY 13, 1898.

pectation of uncovering the Spanish fleet if it was indeed within. The topography of the harbour and town is like that of most of the Spanish cities in the West Indies. The town lies at the head of a long, narrow bay, which is defended at its entrance by batteries on the high hills, including, of course, the inevitable Morro. The interior of the harbour cannot be examined with passing the defences at its mouth, so that the question of the presence of the fleet there could only be determined by an attack. The action, though the most considerable one yet fought in West Indian waters, was of slight importance. The admiral, transferring his flag to the battle-ship "Iowa," led the "New York," "Amphitrite," and "Terror" thrice into the harbour, and out by the westward channel, pounding away with their heavy guns as they passed the three batteries. It was early dawn when the attack began, and as the ships crept in toward the glimmering lights of the city, which were beginning to pale in the face of advancing day, every man who had a port to look out of gazed eagerly about the harbour for the enemy's fleet which they hoped to find. It was not there. The scene was one of perfect peace. The light was burning in the lighthouse, as though the people had no fear of guiding a foe to their homes. In the forts on the hills even the sentries seemed to be sleeping, for from them came no sign of life until the ships opened fire with their great guns. Morro Castle stood, dark and gloomy, on the crest of a sixty-foot bluff. Behind it lay the town; opposite, the battery on Cabras Island. From the "Iowa" a 6-inch gun broke the silence, and the projectile crashed against the worn masonry of Morro. Slowly the ships steamed in procession, firing broadsides, and receiving doggedly the return of the forts, which did not seem to wake to the situation until at least four broadsides had been discharged. The "Detroit," within easy range of Morro, fairly pelted that ancient stronghold with projectiles from her rapid-fire guns, driving the defenders to the bomb-proofs, and enveloping the castle in a cloud of flying fragments of masonry. Though wholly unarmoured, she went boldly within rifle range, and when the larger ships, completing their first turn, seemed to be steaming out of the harbour again, the Spanish gunners turned their attention exclusively to her. There was a good chance for disaster to the "Detroit," for she was vulnerable not only to the projectiles of the modern rifles, but to the old smooth-bores, of which the Spaniards were employing several. But she stuck to her position, and when the hail of missiles about her seemed fiercest, her commander, Captain Dayton, as though anxious to do a little shooting himself, pulled a revolver from his belt, and, standing on the bridge under that fierce fire, shot calmly at a sardine-can his servant had thrown overboard. The witnesses of this bit of by-play report that his nerve was good, and that he hit the target five times before it sunk.

The "Montgomery," an unprotected cruiser with a main battery of ten 5-inch guns, had been ordered before the beginning of the action to take Fort Canuelo under its especial charge and silence it if it opened fire. This task the cruiser accomplished with ease, although the battery against which it was pitted was well placed, heavily armed, and should have been able to drive an unarmoured ship away. But the marksmanship of the Spaniards was wretched, and their eagerness to seek cover in face of a lively and well-directed fire, even though little execution was done, was most unsoldierly. All the factors in the engagement except skill and discipline favoured them. Their batteries, besides possessing the advantage that land batteries invariably enjoy over ships, were on such high ground that their gunners were favoured by a plunging fire, while on the ships the guns had to be pointed at such an unusual elevation that the aim of the gunners was materially injured, and the structure of the vessels racked. The practice of our men with the larger guns was especially bad, doubtless for this reason, but the vigour and skill with which the secondary batteries were worked proved enough to quiet the enemy. Two only of our ships were struck, one shell bursting on the deck of the "New York," killing one seaman and wounding three others. Three men on the "Iowa" were wounded. With that the casualties on the attacking fleet ended, though the battle was hotly fought at close range for more than three hours. But on the other hand the enemy escaped as lightly. His forts were not materially injured, and it is not probable — though exact data are not obtainable — that his troops suffered seriously. The engagement simply added one more bit of evidence to the already complete proof that ships cannot reduce earthworks. When the enemy seemed silenced a brief intermission in the American fire would result in the Spaniards returning to the guns they had abandoned, and taking up the fight again. It is true that Admiral Sampson might have passed the forts — indeed he did so repeatedly in the course of his manoeuvring. He might indeed have taken the city, for it lay open to his guns and at the mercy of a landing party. But the capture of small towns was not what that fleet was in the West Indies for. It was hot on the trail of Cervera, and finding that he was not at Port San Juan, the admiral pulled down his battle-flags, left the enemy to repair damages, and set sail again. On the way the torpedo boat "Porter" was sent into Cape Haitien for despatches.

The "Porter" came back at the top of her speed with signals flying to show that she brought important information. When she entered Cape Haitien her people, like all on the American fleet, supposed that the report of Ambassador Hay that Cervera had returned to Spain was correct, but at the United States consulate the landing officer found an accumulation of despatches for the admiral that told most significant tidings. Cervera was in American waters. The American consul at Curaçoa cabled that the Spaniards were there, short of coal and provisions;

a later despatch reported they had left that point for an unknown destination. From Secretary Long were a number of cables. One reported the Spanish fleet as off Martinique, the torpedo-boat destroyer "Terror" being left at Fort de France on that island. This despatch was definite enough to remove all further doubt, and the admiral promptly sent a despatch, ordering the "Yale" and "St. Paul" to cruise in the triangular passage between Jamaica, Haiti, and Cuba; the "Harvard" to guard the Mona passage and the north side of Porto Rico; while the "St. Louis" was sent to cut cables at Santiago and neighbouring points on the south side of Cuba. Admiral Sampson was convinced in his own mind, by a certain instinct, that Cervera would make for Santiago, and he so warned the captain of the "Harvard" in a despatch. To the commodore commanding at Key West, he sent a cable directing that all ships on the south side of Cuba be warned that the enemy might appear there at any moment. This prevision is a striking illustration of the way in which a trained mind, proceeding from fragmentary and insufficient information, will reach a correct conclusion. As for the squadron under his own immediate command, Admiral Sampson made all possible haste to take it back to Key West, proceeding in advance of it himself in the swift "New York." Arriving there, he found the Flying Squadron under Commodore Schley already in port, and the whole fleet tremulous with the knowledge that the enemy was in our waters and the decisive conflict could not long be delayed. There was a fluttering of telegrams to and from Washington, and a vast deal of wigwagging from ship to ship, while at night the electric lights blinked their party-coloured eyes from the foremast of the flagship, and the typewriter in the admiral's cabin below ticked away restlessly. When it was all done Schley was in possession of orders to take his squadron at once by way of the Yucatan channel to the southern coast of Cuba, pick up the "Iowa" and "Marblehead" at Cienfuegos, and find the enemy if possible. The three ships with which Schley started, the "Brooklyn," "Massachusetts," and "Texas," were passing out of Key West harbour when the last of the slow-going fleet which Sampson had had at San Juan entered. "I congratulate you in advance," the admiral signalled to the outgoing ships. "I believe you are going to meet and defeat the Spaniards."

Through the sapphire seas of that tropic region the great warships ploughed heavily, making their relentless way to the port where all expected to find the enemy with whom the fight was to be fought to the death. At the western end of Cuba two fellow-cruisers, the "Cincinnati" and "Vesuvius," were sighted. They were going back to Key West for coal, and had seen nothing of Cervera. The "Marblehead" and "Nashville" also came up, and were equally ignorant of the enemy's whereabouts. Cienfuegos was reached on the 21st. It is one of the blind harbours of which the West Indies are full. Were the Spaniards inside? That question was destined to worry Commodore Schley for some days to come. It was at night that he reached the port, and early the next morning every man on the fleet who had a glass or whose eyes were sharp was studying the entrance to the harbour in search of signs of the enemy's presence. Nothing could be seen. Grim batteries guarded the narrow entrance to the bay, and high hills cut off all vision. But the night before the commodore had heard guns which he thought to be fired in welcome to the Spanish fleet. He saw, furthermore, heavy smoke rising from the inner harbour as though a fleet were at anchor there with fires up. Impressed with the belief that the enemy was within, he determined to blockade the port for a time, sending the fleet "Scorpion" on to Santiago to learn what the big ship scouting in that neighbourhood might have discovered. That day the "Iowa," with "Fighting Bob" Evans on the bridge, came up to join the blockaders, and on the next day the converted yacht "Hawk," the gunboat "Castine," and the collier "Merrimac" arrived. Up to this time Schley was confident that he had the enemy trapped, though it is said that a majority of his officers disagreed with him. Certainly little had been done in the two days to settle the point. No boat, not even a launch, had tried to force the harbour on a voyage of discovery, nor had any officer been put ashore to spy out the land, as we shall find Lieutenant Blue doing at Santiago.

But the "Hawk" brought news which destroyed Schley's confidence in his present position, and made him fear for the safety of the "Scorpion." It reported that the "Minneapolis" had seen the Spanish fleet enter Santiago harbour on the 19th, and had hastened to Hayti to cable the news to Washington, whence it had been telegraphed to Key West, arriving there just after Schley had sailed. Shortly after the arrival of this intelligence the British ship "Adula" came to the mouth of Cienfuegos harbour, for the avowed purpose of taking away British refugees. Her captain told the commodore that Cervera had left Santiago; he had heard it authoritatively at Jamaica. This left the American commander undecided again. The report coming by the "Hawk" might be both correct and incorrect. The "Minneapolis" might have seen the Spaniards enter Santiago harbour, but they might have come out and reached Cienfuegos later. Accordingly a despatch was sent off to the admiral in which the commodore, after relating all these things, said, "I shall therefore remain off this port."

Admiral Sampson at Key West was as firmly convinced that Cervera was at Santiago as Schley was that he had him cooped up in Cienfuegos, and out of this delay at the mouth of the latter harbour grew a controversy among zealous partisans of the two officers which has not been pleasant reading for admirers of the navy.

The next day, the 24th, the "Marblehead," "Eagle," and "Vixen" joined Schley. The commander of the

ADMIRAL WILLIAM THOMAS SAMPSON.

former, Captain McCalla, had been long on the Cuban blockade and had made the most of his opportunities. Ever since the squadron had been off the port, three fires had burned on a certain hill by night, and three horses were seen tethered below by day.

"There is a band of insurgents there," said McCalla, and he went ashore to see them. They told him positively that Cervera was not in the harbour, and with this final and convincing bit of evidence Schley ordered the squadron to get under way and proceed to Santiago. It was a run of four hundred miles, and the fleet was within sight of Morro Castle, that guarded the entrance to the harbour, by five o'clock on the afternoon of the 26th, finding there the "St. Paul," the "Minneapolis," and the "Yale." The former of these vessels reported the capture of a British collier under the very guns of the Spanish batteries. She was freighted with coal for Cervera, and her presence at Santiago should have dispelled the last doubt in the commodore's mind as to where his prey was to be found. Seemingly, however, he did not grasp the situation, for that night without making any effort to reconnoitre the harbour, or seek further for the enemy he displayed the signal :

"Destination Key West as soon as collier is ready, via south side Cuba and Yucatan channel. Speed nine knots."

This order, coming when most of the men on the ships were expecting a signal to prepare for a dash at the enemy early the following morning, caused astonishment and something like consternation in the fleet. The more outspoken captains condemned it bitterly. A correspondent reports that, soon after the signal had been displayed, "Fighting Bob" Evans shouted from the deck of the "Iowa" to Captain Philip of the Texas:

"Say, Jack, what do you think of it?"

"Beats me," was the response; "what do you think of it?"

"Damned if I know," answered Evans, whose reputation for profanity was quite as well won as his reputation for gallantry. "But I know one thing — I'm the most disgusted man afloat."

The order was unquestionably a grave error. Out of it sprang that controversy which raged for a long time in the halls of Congress and in the public prints. The friends of Commodore Schley insisted that the plan of returning to Key West to coal was but the fulfilment of orders given by Admiral Sampson. The partisans of the latter officer charged Schley with having, through stupidity or a lack of dash, narrowly escaped giving Cervera an opportunity to get out to sea and ravage our northern coasts. After the battle of Santiago, in which Schley bore the most active part, the question of the rewards to be given the victorious commanders came up in Congress, and there the contest raged fiercely. Admiral Sampson, in recommending promotions, declined to recommend Schley, pronouncing his conduct "reprehensible." There were stinging innuendos, hints of cowardice, of suppressed despatches, of orders the dates of which were changed after the sequel had proved them to have been unwise, and all the other scandalous charges that zealous politicians trying to build up one man at the expense of another know so well how to array. The essence of the controversy does not appear to be matter worthy the dignity of history, and the manner of it reflected little credit on the friends of the two chief figures whether in Congress or in the navy. As we shall see, the search for Cervera was entirely successful and his destruction complete. The remark of Commodore Schley, when, the last Spanish ship being then blazing on the beach, some one raised the question of to whom the honour of the victory belonged, "There is glory enough in it for all of us," was manly and honourable. It is a pity that all discussion of the affair might not have been conducted in this spirit, for it is in this way that history

FORWARD DECK OF THE DYNAMITE-GUN VESSEL "VESUVIUS."

will view it after the petty dissensions and jealousies of men great enough to win an epoch-making battle have been forgotten.

It is enough to say here that the order to return to Key West was never carried out. Before the collier could be put into condition to make the return voyage, more definite orders arrived from Washington directing the commodore to maintain the blockade at all hazards.

Let us return briefly to Admiral Sampson, whom we left at Key West when Schley's squadron steamed away for the south side of Cuba. The admiral left the rendezvous with the purpose of cruising in the seas that Cervera might fairly be expected to pass through. At Key West he gathered up one or two of the blockading vessels and started for St. Nicholas channel with a fleet that included, besides the flagship "New York," the battle-ship "Indiana," the monitors "Puritan" and "Miantonomah," the cruisers "New Orleans," "Detroit," and "Montgomery," and several torpedo boats and auxiliaries. On the 27th the dynamite cruiser "Vesuvius," the cruiser "Cincinnati," and the monitor "Amphitrite" joined his fleet. St. Nicholas channel extends along the northern coast of Cuba. Sampson was therefore within comparatively easy communication with Washington, torpedo boats plying constantly between the fleet and the nearest cable station, or even running back to Key West on occasion. At the moment of beginning this cruise the admiral was without definite information that the enemy had taken refuge in Santiago, and he chose his cruising-ground, therefore, so as to be able to intercept Cervera should he make for Havana from the east, without going so far as to be unable to return and check the enemy should the Spanish fleet come around the western end of Cuba and seek to make Havana from that direction. Holding thus the key to Havana, he cruised up and down the channel, alert for the appearance of the enemy.

The Spaniards, however, did not put in an appearance; but the admiral's days were plentifully filled with the despatches that poured in upon him from Washington and from Schley. As the conviction grew stronger both at the Navy Department and in the mind of the admiral that the Spaniards were in Santiago, the successive despatches from Schley reporting his continued presence at Cienfuegos, or his purpose of going to Mole St. Nicholas or even Key West to coal, created the most lively apprehension that the enemy would escape. Communication with Schley either from the fleet or from Washington was difficult. By the time an order was despatched a message would come from the commodore indicating such a change in the situation that the order evidently stood in need of correction. On the 28th, apparently doubting that Schley's representations of the necessity for coaling certain of his ships and the impossibility of accomplishing it in the heavy swell of the open sea were well founded, Admiral Sampson sent the "New Orleans" to Santiago with the collier "Stirling," with instructions to Schley to sink the latter vessel in the channel, and by that means to "bottle up" the enemy. Under no considerations was Schley to leave the mouth of the harbour. Thereupon Sampson himself returned to Key West, that he might be in more immediate communication with the Navy Department. There on the 29th he received a despatch from Santiago reporting that smoother weather had enabled the sailors to coal the "Marblehead" and "Texas." This was a relief to the admiral, who straightway wired back congratulations on the achievement, and reiterated his instructions to hold the position at all hazards. Meanwhile the admiral had been seeking from Washington permission to go himself to Santiago, and, succeeding, started with the "Oregon," the "Mayflower," the "Porter" and the flagship. On the way the "St. Paul" was met and from Captain Sigsbee was obtained a copy of a despatch he was carrying to Mole St. Nicolas to be cabled to Long. It was this:

"[Dated] 7 P. M. May 29th.

"Enemy in port. Recognised 'Cristobal Colon' and 'Infanta Maria Teresa' and two torpedo boats moored inside Morro, behind point. Doubtless the others are here. We are short of coal. Using every effort to get coal in. Have about 3,000 tons of coal in collier, but not easy to get on board here. If no engagement next two or three days, Sampson's squadron could relieve this one to coal at Gonaives or vicinity of Port au Prince. 'Brooklyn,' 'Iowa,' 'Massachusetts,' 'Texas,' 'Marblehead,' 'Vixen,' and collier compose squadron here.

"SCHLEY."

The presence of one of the ships with Sampson requires some explanation. In March the battle-ship "Oregon" lay at anchor in the harbour of San Francisco, where she had been built. She is a sea-going battle-ship of 10,228 tons, with an estimated speed of fifteen knots, a main battery of four 13-inch and eight 8-inch rifles, and a full complement of those swift and furious distributors of death known as the secondary battery. To the authorities at Washington the absence of this magnificent ship from the probable theatre of war on the Atlantic coast was a situation not to be risked. It was then thought that the balance of strength between the Spanish and United States fleets was so delicate that the presence or absence of one ship might change it, and it was determined to bring the "Oregon" on the long journey around Cape Horn. We shall see that her presence off Santiago did materially affect the strength of the American fleet, though, as the day went, she might perhaps have been spared.

On the 19th of March the "Oregon" left San Francisco. War was not yet declared, but everybody understood the purpose for which the gallant battle-ship turned her stern to the coast which she had not left since the day of her launching, and sped off to the southward. For her officers and crew, though the diplomats might cry, "Peace! Peace!" there was no peace. Every precaution that would have been observed in time of war was taken. The first port reached was Callao, a run of 4000 miles in 16 days. It was a Spanish-American town, full of people who spoke the language of Spain, and were more in touch with the habits and customs of the nation whose yoke their fathers threw off than they were with the free institutions of the United States. Captain Charles E. Clark, commanding the "Oregon," with the memory of the "Maine" fresh, neglected no precaution he would have taken in an avowedly hostile port. The bunkers had to be filled afresh, but every lump of coal passed under the scrutiny of a cadet engineer, lest some infernal machine should find its way into the furnaces. About the ship all night steam launches filled with armed men kept watchful patrol, and doubled watches on every part of the ship stood guard, ready to shoot at the slightest sign of danger. Swiftly on the completion of the task the anchors were raised, and the ship began again her race against time. One after another the states of western South America were left behind as the restless screws churned mile after mile of the blue waters of the Pacific into a narrow pathway of foam. After leaving Montevideo there was a brief period of excitement and perhaps anxiety, springing from the fact that a Spanish torpedo boat was reported to have lately left that harbour to seek for the American vessel. It was apprehended that the enemy might lie in wait behind one of the capes that extend into the Straits of Magellan, and dash out upon the ship as she was passing through those narrow waters; but no sign of the enemy appeared, and the great battle-ship turned northward with half its journey done and no enemy sighted. But on April 17th at Punta Arenas the tars of the battle-ship turned out on the decks and turrets to cheer as they saw the stars and stripes flying over a trig little gunboat. It was the "Marietta," and she brought to Captain Clark the story of the rapid drift of political events toward war. The narrative only increased the anxiety of all to reach the battle-ground before all should be over. It was not a matter of fearing

"RACING HOME"—THE BATTLESHIP "OREGON" ON HER WAY FROM SAN FRANCISCO TO KEY WEST.

an attack of the enemy, but rather dread lest the enemy should have been defeated without the "Oregon" sharing in the work. So after coaling again, with all hands working day and night, the ship dashed out to sea. Rio Janeiro was entered and left behind. There the news of the declaration of war and Dewey's deeds was received. Bahia, reached on the 8th of May, had despatches from Washington for the ship. The Navy Department sent word of the disappearance of Cervera's fleet and the general apprehension lest it might have sailed south to cut off the "Oregon." Now indeed the "Oregon" was entering the zone of danger. At muster that day Captain Clark addressed the crew, telling them of the power of the enemy that they might at any moment encounter, and saying: "In time of war it is our duty to avoid so superior a force, but if we do meet them we shall impair their fighting efficiency." Then the ship was stripped, her dull war-paint put on, and so out again into the pathless ocean ready to do battle not only with wind and wave, but with any steel-clad fighting-machine that might carry the Spanish flag. In company with the "Oregon" now sailed the "Buffalo," which, as the "Nictheroy," had been purchased from Brazil. But through the perilous waters of the West Indies the two ships steamed without sighting the enemy, and on the 24th Captain Clark communicated with Washington from Jupiter Inlet. "If you have repairs to be made," telegraphed the Secretary of the Navy, "go to Norfolk; otherwise report to Admiral Sampson at Key West." The "Oregon" went to Key West. After a voyage of 14,700 miles at the top of her speed she had arrived in perfect condition, without a rivet sprung or a tube leaking.

Now that ships have become floating machine-shops, great iron tanks full of delicately adjusted and complicated machinery, such an exploit as this is as notable as a victory. What men-of-war have gained in destructive efficiency and in invulnerability to an enemy's shot, they have lost in what may be colloquially called staying capacity at sea. The days when a ship could put out for a three years' cruise, often being out of port for many months, are ended forever. A battle-ship's ability to keep the sea is limited above all things by her coal capacity, so that visits to port at least once in three weeks are essential. But more than this, it is very unusual for a modern warship to be able to make a cruise at all protracted, even under easy steam, without disarranging her machinery to a degree that makes a visit to some navy-yard a necessity. The United States navy has recognised this fact, and has sought to counteract it by building a floating machine-shop, the "Vulcan," which carries all possible appliances for making repairs at sea, so that a blockade or a cruise need not be interrupted.

The voyage of the "Oregon" was, therefore, an exceptional exploit, an achievement that reflected upon its builders and on the engineering staff which had charge of her machinery the credit that in a hot battle falls to the share of the line officers. She was built at the Union Iron Works of San Francisco, a ship-yard which has turned out several vessels of the new navy. Her chief engineer was Robert W. Milligan. No doubt the exploit of carrying the "Oregon" a distance equivalent to half the distance around the earth at the equator had much to do with the passage by Congress, in March of 1898, of a long contested measure by which the engineering force of the navy was given just equivalent rank with the line, and equal opportunities for promotion. It is no derogation to the man behind the gun, whose praises have been widely sung, to say that the man who guards the valves and bearings deep in the bowels of the ship, not knowing how the battle is going above, and without hope of escape in case of disaster, is an equally important and equally admirable figure in modern naval warfare.

All suspense being now over, the little squadron went gaily on, and the next morning found Schley's fleet clustered about the mouth of Santiago harbour. The admiral at once took command of the entire fleet, and the Flying Squadron, as an independent command, went out of existence. Commodore Schley reported that on the 28th he had taken his whole squadron far enough into the harbour to discover the entire fleet of Cervera lying at anchor, with the great " Colon," like a huge mastiff, lying farthest to fore and guarding the entrance. Two days later the Americans opened fire on the harbour defences, but at such long range that no material effect was produced. With this, active efforts against the enemy ended until Admiral Sampson arrived. It was June first that the admiral appeared, and the American fleet settled down to watch the mouth of that narrow harbour as a cat watches a hole whence a mouse is expected to pop out at any moment. Ranged about, ready to pounce upon their prey, were these ships of the United States navy: Battleships: "Massachusetts," "Texas," "Oregon," "Iowa." Armoured cruisers: "New York," "Brooklyn." Cruisers: "New Orleans," "Marblehead." Auxiliaries: "Gloucester," "Vixen," "Mayflower," "Harvard." Gunboat: "Castine." Torpedo boat: "Porter."

CHAPTER VIII

Santiago de Cuba — The Plan to bottle up Cervera — The Volunteers — Preparations for the Sacrifice — The Stations of the Men — Under Fire — The Steering Gear Disabled — The Torpedoes Shot away — Sinking of the "Merrimac" — Surrender of Hobson and his Men — Admiral Cervera's Courtesy — In Morro Castle — The Bombardment.

THE town of Santiago de Cuba is the second in size of the Cuban towns, having a few more than 70,000 people. It is an historic spot, outdating any settlement on the continent, for it was founded in 1514, while that great mainland of North America whence now came swarming these ships and sailors for Santiago's overthrow was still a wilderness, inhabited only by the warring red men. Before the war it was a thriving place, the centre of the mining industry of Cuba and the place of investment of considerable American capital. Its harbour is of the characteristic Cuban type. A narrow channel gives entrance to a bay six miles long and about two broad. At the harbour's mouth steep hills come down to the water's edge on either side. One is crested with Morro Castle, a picturesque, venerable, and wholly obsolete fortress of masonry. On the other side were some earthworks at the entrance, and the Estrella and Catalina batteries farther in. How efficiently these batteries were armed and manned could not be told from the fleet, but Commodore Schley's reconnoissance had discovered the presence of modern rifles, while the narrowness of the channel and the elevation of the batteries made any effort to run in apparently very hazardous.

In a general way the topography of Santiago Bay was familiar to Admiral Sampson before he left Key West.

At that time his presumption was that the American objective, that is, point of main attack, in Cuba would be Havana, and he desired to have all the American battleships and armoured cruisers off that city to aid in the assault upon it. Accordingly, his one study was to discover some method of freeing the fleet from the duty of blockading Cervera, for he did not believe that the Spaniards would come out and offer battle while a superior force lay off the bay. For the Americans to dash in after the fashion of Dewey does not seem to have been considered. The force within was vastly greater than that Dewey had to encounter, the harbour was more difficult and better defended. It occurred to the admiral that a ship might be sunk in the channel in such a way as to bar all egress, and that with the enemy thus bottled up most of the vessels of the blockading squadron could be spared to join in any movement against Havana. This project was broached to a young officer, Lieutenant Hobson, before leaving Key West.

Lieutenant Hobson was known at this time in the navy as a hard student and a man of scientific tastes and attainments. He had graduated at the head of his class in the naval academy, and after two years' service as midshipman on the cruiser "Chicago," was sent to Europe to study methods of planning and constructing warships. When the war broke out he was an assistant naval constructor, with the rank of lieutenant, and was ordered to the "New York" to study and report on the characteristics of the various ships of the North Atlantic squadron and the class of service for which each was best fitted. Because of his technical attainments Hobson was desired by the admiral to prepare a plan for sinking the collier "Merrimac" in the channel. The plan once adopted, the young officer eagerly asked the assignment to carry it out. At first the admiral hesitated. The captain of the "Merrimac" had a presumptive right to command his vessel in any service to which he was assigned, and

Captain Miller strenuously insisted on this right, but in the end the admiral concluded that Hobson, as the originator and author of the plan, would necessarily go to see to its accomplishment, and that Captain Miller would be in effect a supernumerary. As the enterprise was extra-hazardous, permission for the captain to go was refused.

The plan was simple enough; the execution of it simply implied that nine men could be found willing to take a ship into point-blank range of the Spanish batteries and over the Spanish mines, anchor her deliberately across the channel, explode torpedoes under her hull, and escape by means of a small boat through the Spanish zone of fire and past the enemy's picket-boats. It was easy to find the nine men, for there were more than 3000 in the squadron, and upon call, all volunteered. Officers and men pressed about Hobson when the news of the adventure became general, and begged to be chosen. In the end these seven were chosen: Randolph Clausen, Osborn Warren Deignan, Daniel Montague, Francis Kelly, George Charette, George F. Phillips, and Mullen.

The ship was hurriedly prepared for the sacrifice, by being stripped of everything valuable. Torpedoes were fastened to the starboard side and connected with electric wires to the deck. The plan was to enter the channel at full speed, and at a concerted signal the men in the engine room, Phillips and Kelly, were to shut off the engines, open the water connections, and lay up on deck. At a prearranged point in the channel the ship was to be laid athwart the channel and the heavy anchor at the bow let go. Elaborate arrangements were made to bring the strain on this gradually. At the moment it was to be let fall, the ship would be moving at an estimated speed of six knots an hour, and the momentum of so heavy a mass of iron moving through the water would cause the anchor to drag, even if the chain did not part. Accordingly a series of hemp stops, or short ropes, were attached to the chain at different points and then to cleats on the ship, so that

RESPONSE TO THE CALL FOR VOLUNTEERS TO ACCOMPANY HOBSON ON THE "MERRIMAC."

before the full strain fell on the chain it would come upon them one by one. They would resist briefly, then snap, and after the last stop had given way an eight-inch cable would take up the burden, holding it until it in turn parted. By this time it was thought the ship's speed would be so much reduced by these successive checks that the chain cable might be expected to hold. While the vessel was slowly swinging across the channel, the men were to touch off the torpedoes, each man being given an end of an electric wire for that purpose. When she was seen to be sinking, all were to leap overboard and clamber into a boat towing at the stern. They were then to make for the shadow of the shore under Morro Castle, where a launch under command of Ensign Powell was to be prepared to pick them up. It was a desperate undertaking, but one such as at all times in the history of the American navy our Blue Jackets have been eager to engage in. The rivalry of officers and men for a share in this exploit was so lively that the admiral and Hobson were subjected to much embarrassment by the pressure for place. Admiral Sampson, with whom the plan originated, was more hopeful of its execution without loss of life than were most of the officers on the fleet. To a correspondent who asked if it was not sending men to certain death, he responded: "Well, I don't know. You see it will be pretty hard to hit eight men on a big ship like that." As for the men, they did not seem to consider whether there was a chance of escape or not. All they wanted was a chance to join in the attempt. The night before the harbour was entered, the volunteers were summoned to the admiral's cabin for final muster. In a few words the admiral expressed his sense of their bravery and devotion in undertaking so perilous an adventure, but he had hardly stopped speaking when the spokesman of the men answered: "And we want to thank you, sir, for giving us the privilege of going when so many good men volunteered."

On the morning of the 2d of June the ship was ready

for the sacrifice and was under way, just about to make the turn into the harbour, when a torpedo boat came flying from the flagship with instructions to return to the fleet. The disappointment was a bitter one, for until the admiral could be seen Hobson could not tell whether the whole plan might not have been abandoned. To add to the suspense, the "New York" went flying off at daybreak in pursuit of a suspicious vessel seen in the offing, and did not return for some hours. On her return, eager inquiries were made of the admiral. The undertaking was to be postponed only, not abandoned.

About midnight, as the moon was setting, the "Merrimac" was again under way. On the bridge were Hobson and Deignan, in the engine-room were Phillips and Kelly. Murphy was on the forecastle, with instructions to let go the anchor and instantly to fire torpedo number one. A new man this Murphy, taking the place of Mullen, who had broken down with overwork and nervous strain. His was the post of the greatest danger on the ship — if there were one spot more dangerous than another where all stood in continual peril of their lives. Slipping the anchor, he would be in peril from the snapping stops, and the rushing cable. Touching off torpedo number one, which would be immediately under his post, he would be in danger of being blown overboard or even of receiving a wound. All these things were explained to him, but he showed no trepidation. "It shall be done, sir," was his only response. All on deck were to lie on their faces near the rail. A halliard tied to the wrist of each and running to the bridge where Hobson stood was to be the means of making signals. Three decided pulls meant that the torpedoes were to be discharged. For the men below, the signal on the engine-room telegraph to stop served also as a signal to throw open the water-valves and come on deck. Uniforms were simple — underwear, cartridge belts, and revolvers.

The last launch left the ship for the fleet, carrying in it Ensign Powell, who was to stand on and off the harbour's mouth looking for survivors after the deed was done. The moon was high and bright, and in its clear light the contour of the shore and the forts that were to be braved were clearly outlined. It was evident enough that the Spaniards would have no excuse for being surprised, as the great black ship, 400 feet long, was a conspicuous object on the silvery water. The range line that marked the entrance for the channel was reached. The ship swung round and pointed fair and straight down the watery lane it was to follow to its death. Charette ran down below to tell the two in the engine-room that the die was cast and to repeat their instructions by way of precaution. Straight down the appointed course sped the heavy collier. One thousand yards from Morro, and no shot yet. Hobson began to wonder at this ominous silence, which was more trying to the nerves than the clamour of great guns and small that he had expected. Five hundred yards. Ah, there goes the first shot; but it came from the surface of the water, not from the forts, and was quickly followed by another and another. Nothing could be seen except the flash of the gun, but its position showed that it must be a rapid-fire gun on a small picket-boat. The artillerist seemed to be a poor marksman. No sound of striking shot was heard, though he was near enough to hull the ship at every discharge. His projectiles all seemed to pass astern. Suddenly Hobson solved the mystery. The Spaniard, with admirable judgment, knowing that the small calibre of his cannon would make no impression on the ship, was shooting at the exposed rudder and steering-gear. Success in hitting that target meant failure for Hobson. Now, however, began the roar and crash of great guns from the land batteries.

"Steady, men, never mind the batteries." The men were steady. None moved, and the helmsman stood to his wheel as though rooted there. From both sides of the narrow strait came now the din of guns, the leaping jets of flame, and the singing shells. Machine guns and Mauser rifles swept the decks. The hull of the ship quivered under repeated blows. For that part, Hobson now cared little. He was near the point at which the "Merrimac" was to be scuttled, and every hole below or near the water-mark made his task easier. Something struck the bridge and carried part of it away; but the engine telegraph was still there, and through it the signal went to the two brave men down below — "Stop."

Immediately the screw stopped turning and a shiver through the ship told that the sea-connections were opened and the vessel was beginning to fill.

"Lay down to the torpedoes," was the word now passed along, and the men crawled along the deck, each to his appointed station. Then came the discovery of a loss that made all this careful planning, all this heroism fruitless. "Starboard" was the word to the wheelman. Deignan swung his wheel obediently, but the ship hung. "Starboard! I say, starboard!" "The helm's a-starboard, sir." The slow response of the "Merrimac" to the helm was suspicious. Now came the moment to swing into the final position. "Hard a-port," cried Hobson. The answer came calmly, "Hard a-port, sir." The ship made no response. "Hard a-port, I say!" A little excitement now in the lieutenant's tone, as surely was excusable. The well-trained man-of-war's man answered in conventional phrase, "The helm is hard a-port, sir, and lashed." He knew what was the trouble, but he volunteered no remark. Hobson was quick to grasp the situation. The steering gear had been shot away, — afterwards the Spanish lieutenant who commanded the guard boat at the entrance to the harbour claimed credit for this, — and at the critical moment the "Merrimac" was unmanageable.

The one chance now was that the ship's headway and the tide might be used to swing the vessel into position in connection with the anchors. It was desirable, above all things, to get the bow grounded first; that done, there was still hope of swinging athwart the channel. All men were now at their posts, Hobson alone on the bridge, Deignan having left the useless wheel for his torpedo. Murphy on the forecastle felt a warning pull on his line, then three steady pulls, and seizing his axe he cut the cable, and the bow anchor fell with a crash. Turning swiftly, he picked up two electric wires. Their ends were brought into contract, the spark flashed down to the torpedo, and with a crash the bow torpedo exploded. All was going well.

Now for the rest of the torpedoes. Three pulls on the ropes for two and three. No answer. The signal was repeated without success. Crossing the bridge, the lieutenant shouted at the top of his voice, " Fire all torpedoes," but the infernal din of the cannonnade and the bursting shells drowned his cry. In a moment, Charette came running through the storm. " Torpedoes 2 and 3 will not fire, sir; a shot struck the firing battery and the cells are scattered all over the deck." Then off went Number 5, followed in a few moments by the report that 4, 6, and 7 were destroyed by the enemy's fire. The situation was thus desperate. Slow sinking and no steering gear made the project of controlling the vessel's position almost hopeless. Perhaps careful management of the stern anchor might help to gain the day. Hobson left the bridge, and went to the deck, determined to superintend in person this last manœuvre. As he reached the rendezvous amidships where the men were to gather after the duty assigned to each should have been done, he found all there. Then the stern anchor had already been let fall and nothing remained but to trust to chance. The lieutenant was somewhat chagrined; but presumed Montague, the sailor in charge of the anchor, had followed instruction. Long after he learned that a shell from the batteries had burst just above Montague's head and, sparing him, had cut the lashings and let the anchor fall.

Huddled together under the bulwarks, with the shells whizzing and bursting above them, the men now waited for the ship to settle to her last berth. Dense smoke hung over all the deck, and the clamour of the shells made conversation in any ordinary tone of voice impossible. Suddenly out of the mirk appeared a strange figure creeping on all fours toward the rendezvous. "An enemy," was Hobson's first thought, and drawing a revolver he covered the advancing man. From the belt of Charette too flashed a pistol. Luckily neither man fired, for as the crawling form came closer it was made out to be that of Kelly, who had been stunned and thrown violently against the mainmast by a shell that broke immediately above him. Curiously enough, the shock destroyed his memory, and recollecting only that he belonged in the engine-room, he started down the hatch, being recalled to his senses by the sight of water pouring in below in a heavy stream.

All this time the ship was settling but slowly, and as it lay beneath the Estrella batteries at point-blank range, it seemed that nothing but a miracle was saving the little crew from death. The Spaniards had, of course, no knowledge of the helplessness of the craft they were firing upon, and they wasted enough ammunition on the riddled "Merrimac" to sink a battleship. At last a torpedo went off with a stunning shock, and the ship began to settle more rapidly, though even then to Hobson's impatience it seemed supernaturally buoyant. It is curious, as one reads the story of this adventure, to contrast the slowness with which the "Merrimac" sank, despite the efforts of friends on board and foes ashore, with the suddenness with which some great Atlantic liner, like the "Bourgogne" in 1898 for example, goes to the bottom despite every effort made to keep her afloat.

There remained nothing to be done except to consider the possibilities of escape. Some of the men suggested leaping overboard at once and attempting to get away by swimming, but the commander pointed out that the moon was near setting, and that with it down escape would be easier in the darkness; so all lay still on the gradually falling deck, the vessel trembling under the repeated strokes of missiles that found their mark. It is inexplicable that none were hit, for from Mauser rifles to six-inch cannon, every variety of shore and naval gun was levelled on the ship, and torpedoes were fired from the "Pluton" and the "Reina Mercedes." At last came a significant lurch. "She will turn over on us," cried one of the men.

"No," answered Hobson; "she will right herself in sinking, and this will be the last spot to go under." So it proved. Bending down her bow like some great animal lowering its head in token of defeat, the "Merrimac" sank, lifting her stern high in air. But let Lieutenant Hobson himself tell the story of that supreme moment:

"A great rush of water came up the gangway, seething and gurgling out of the deck. The mass was whirling from right to left 'against the sun;' it seized us and threw us against the bulwarks, then over the rail. Two were swept forward as if by a momentary recession, and one was carried down into a coal-bunker, — luckless Kelly. In a moment, however, with increased force, the water shot him up out of the same hole and swept him among us. The bulwarks disappeared. A sweeping vortex whirled above. We charged about with casks, cans, and spars, the incomplete stripping having left quantities on the deck. The life-preservers stood us in good stead, preventing chests from being crushed, as well as buoying us on the surface; for spars came end on like battering-rams, and the sharp corners of tin cans struck us heavily.

"The experience of being swept over the side was rather odd. The water lifted and threw me against the bulwarks, the rail striking my waist; the upper part of the body was bent out, the lower part and the legs being driven heavily against what seemed to be the plating underneath, which, singularly enough, appeared to open. A foot-ball instinct came promptly, and I drew up my knees; but it seemed too late, and apparently they were being driven through the steel plate, a phenomenon that struck me as being most singular; yet there it was, and I wondered what the sensation would be like in having the legs carried out on one side of the rail, and the body on the other, concluding that some embarrassment must be expected in swimming without legs. The situation was apparently relieved by the rail going down. Afterward Charette asked: 'Did those oil-cans that were left just forward of us trouble you also as we were swept out?' Perhaps cans, and not steel plates, separated before my knee-caps.

"When we looked for the life-boat we found that it had been carried away. The catamaran was the largest piece of floating débris; we assembled about it. The line suspending it from the cargo boom held and anchored us to the ship, though barely long enough to reach the surface, causing the raft to turn over and set us scrambling as the line came taut.

"The firing had ceased. It was evident the enemy had not seen us in the general mass of moving objects; but soon the tide began to set these away, and we were being left alone with the catamaran. The men were directed to cling close in, bodies below and only heads out, close under the edges, and were directed not to speak above a whisper, for the destroyer was near at hand, and pulling boats passed near. We mustered; all were present, and direction was given to remain as we were till further orders, for I was sure that in due time after daylight a responsible officer would come out to reconnoitre. It was evident that we could not swim against the tide to reach the entrance. Moreover, the shores were lined with troops, and the small boats were looking for victims that might escape from the vessel. The only chance lay in remaining undiscovered until the coming of the reconnoitring boat, to which, perhaps, we might surrender without being fired on.

"The moon was now low. The shadow of Socapa fell over us, and soon it was dark. The sunken vessel was bubbling up its last lingering breath. The boats looking for refugees pulled closer, peering with lanterns, and again the discipline of the men was put to severe test, for time and again it seemed that the boats would come up, and the impulse to swim away was strong. A suggestion was made to cut the line and let the catamaran drift away. This was also emphatically forbidden, for we should thus miss the reconnoitring boat and certainly fall into less responsible hands. Here, as before, the men strictly obeyed orders, though the impulse for safety was strong to the contrary, and *sauve qui peut* would have been justifiable, if it is ever justifiable.

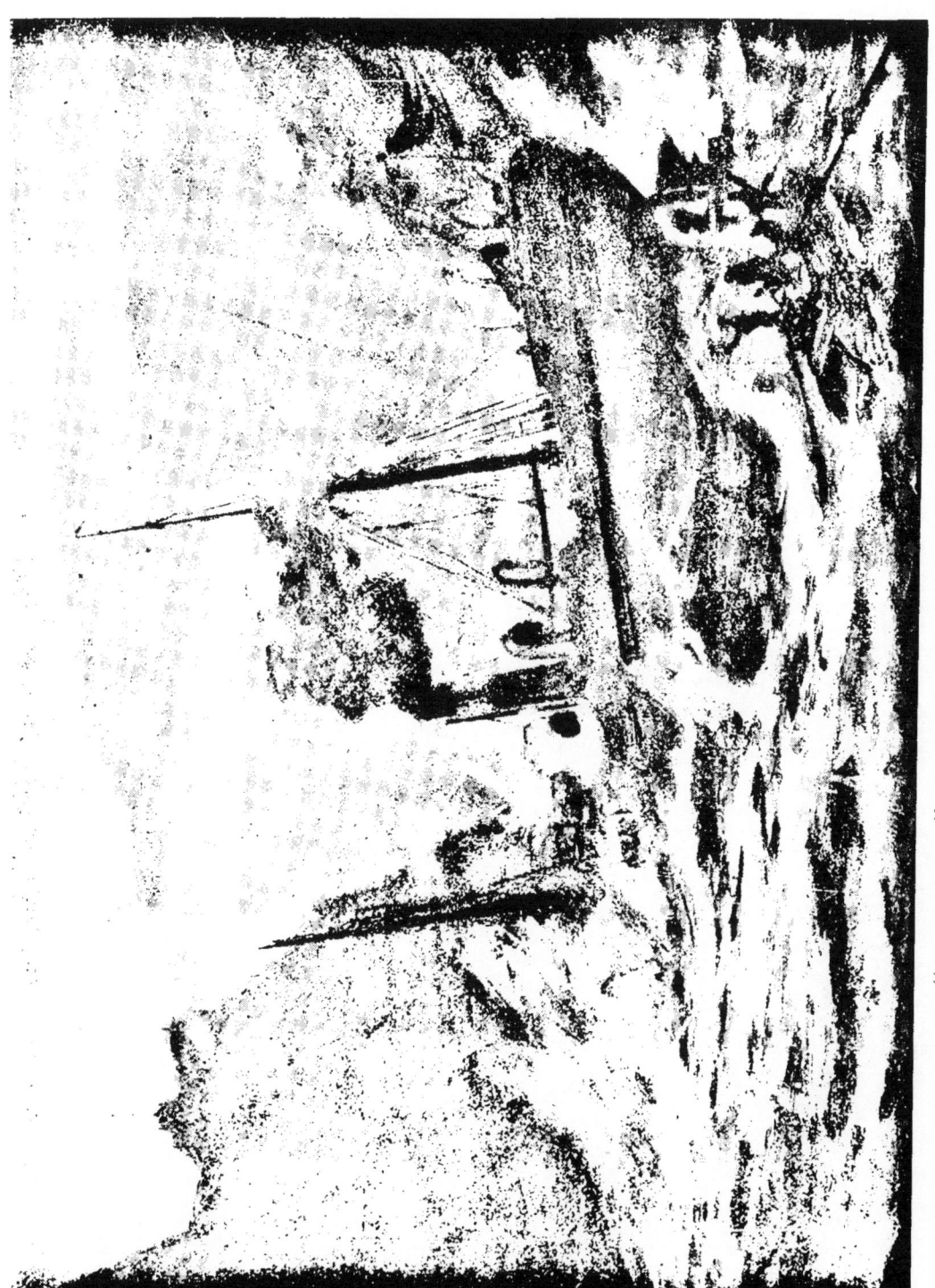
HOBSON SINKING THE "MERRIMAC" IN THE ENTRANCE TO SANTIAGO HARBOR, JUNE 3, 1898.

"The air was chilly and the water positively cold. In less than five minutes our teeth were chattering; so loud, indeed, did they chatter that it seemed the destroyer or the boats would hear. It was in marked contrast with the parched lips of a few minutes before. In spite of their efforts, two of the men soon began to cough, and it seemed that we should surely be discovered. I worked my legs and body under the raft for exercise, but, in spite of all, the shivers would come and the teeth would chatter."

At daybreak the bugles sung from the Spanish forts, and soon the chilled and famished men clinging to the raft heard the sound of a steam launch coming toward the wreck. They were invisible from the launch, for by orders they kept their heads below the rail, and were on the further side of the catamaran. When the launch came near, Hobson hailed in a strong voice.

"Is there an officer on that launch?" he cried. After a moment of surprised silence the answer came in the affirmative.

"An American officer wishes to surrender himself and his men," continued Hobson. At this a file of marines appeared on the bow of the launch with rifles as though about to fire, and all that had been said and written of Spanish cruelty flashed through Hobson's mind. But he was in the hands of a gallant and chivalric enemy. A quiet order was spoken in the launch, the riflemen disappeared, and soon the drenched Americans were being helped aboard, while in the midst of the Spanish conversation that went on among the captors, the prisoners could distinguish now and again the word "valiente," and it needed no knowledge of foreign tongues to enable them to guess what that meant.

The officer on board the launch proved to be Admiral Cervera himself. Without entering into conversation with the prisoners he directed that they should be put aboard the "Reina Regente," where he left them. Here all were treated with that lack of personal animosity with which navy officers of all lands usually regard a foe. For Hobson the executive officer laid out a full uniform, stimulants were offered to officer and men, and a good breakfast served. While Hobson ate, all the officers joined in the general conversation, all the details of his exploit being admiringly discussed. It is interesting to know that at this informal gathering, before a single battle had been fought, the Spanish officers expressed the conviction that Cuba was already lost and that Spain was fighting for honour only.

Presently Hobson sent to Admiral Cervera the request that he might be allowed to send to Admiral Sampson a formal report, a copy of which he enclosed for the Spanish admiral's perusal. This request was naturally declined, but Cervera with generous courtesy sent off a flag of truce to the fleet with news of the safety of the captives. This was happy tidings to the men on the American ships, for Ensign Powell, after having gallantly braved the Spanish fire in his little launch through the whole night and until day-breaking made him an easy target for the gunners on shore, had returned to the flagship with the mournful tidings that not a man had appeared. Perhaps in later days, when Admiral Cervera was himself a prisoner to the American navy, remembrance of this kindly deed had much to do with the general sympathy and good feeling manifested for him by the whole American people. Lieutenant Hobson himself bears testimony to the uniform consideration shown him by the Spaniards. "There can be no question," he writes, "that the Spanish character is deeply sensible to a genuine sentiment. The history of warfare probably contains no instance of chivalry on the part of captors greater than that of those who fired on the 'Merrimac,' and I knew that harshness of treatment could have had its origin only in official consideration." And yet, as we contrast the treatment of these prisoners of war who had behind them the power of a great nation in arms with that meted out to wretched Cubans, non-combatants as well as soldiers, and with the cowardly execution of the crew of the "Virginius," we cannot ascribe the courtesy shown Hobson to Spanish character altogether. Rather it seems that Admiral Cervera was a man of chivalric instincts who had inspired his officers with like sentiments. In part, too, it must be ascribed to that greater mildness of personal temper always notable in the naval service, to which I have already referred. It would seem that the cosmopolitan training of the men who follow the sea teaches them all men are about of a kind whatever their nationality, and that a brave and honourable man is to be honoured and well treated whatever his flag or his condition. It is very noticeable that as soon as the American prisoners were transferred to the charge of the army their discomforts began.

Immured in a cell of Morro Castle, whither they were taken from the "Reina Mercedes," the prisoners awaited a doubtful future. In the main they were treated well enough, though the Spanish sentries jeered the sailors with gestures suggestive of violent death. The Blue Jackets were not in any degree disturbed, however. "We would do it all over again to-morrow, sir," said Charette to Hobson when he met the latter in his cell one morning. From his window the lieutenant could look down into the channel where the "Merrimac" lay, and the sight was one of bitter disappointment, for instead of blocking the channel she had swung lengthwise in it and the gallant exploit was fruitless. From the Spanish officers who paid visits of ceremony he learned many curious incidents of the night. Many Spaniards had been wounded and a few killed, of course by their own guns firing across the strait, for the "Merrimac" carried not a single cannon. As a complement to this illuminating episode in Spanish warfare, may be mentioned the fact that an American patrol boat picked up one of the torpedoes that had been fired at the "Merrimac," and discovered that the warhead, or explosive charge, had not been placed in it, and it was as harmless as a wooden projectile. The Spaniards on their part were very curious about American methods, and were particularly puzzled by the number of foreign-born citizens in our navy. That by the alchemy of the Republic Swedes, Irishmen, Frenchmen, and Germans could be made into American citizens and fight valiantly and well for their adopted country, was to the Spaniards inexplicable.

In Morro Castle Hobson had to undergo the bombardment which after some days was taken up by the fleet. The shells roared and crashed about the decrepit old fort, and brought down great masses of masonry amid blinding clouds of dust. Though the location of his cell was known to the fleet, and every effort was made to avoid striking it, many of the shells struck too near for comfort, and a great gash in the wall within two feet of the window tells to-day the story of his peril. Neither the lieutenant nor any of his companions suffered, however, and they remained snugly caged until the coming of the army in June led to their exchange. Of that more in due course. For the present we may leave the gallant eight closing in Spanish cells an exploit of which Commodore Schley said:

"History does not record an act of finer heroism than that of the gallant men who are prisoners over there," pointing to Morro. "I watched the 'Merrimac' as she made her way to the entrance of the harbour, and my heart sank as I saw the perfect hell of fire that fell on the devoted men. I did not think it was possible one of them could have gone through it alive. They went into the jaws of death. It was Balaclava over again without the means of defence which the Light Brigade had. Hobson led a forlorn hope without the power to cut his way out. But fortune once more favoured the brave, and I hope he will have the recognition and promotion he deserves. His name will live as long as the heroes of the world are remembered."

CHAPTER IX

The Army in the War — Prejudice against a Standing Army — Regulars and Militiamen — Character of the United States Soldier — The Calls for Volunteers — The Rough Riders — The "Sons of Somebody" — Mobilisation of the Troops — The Fifth Corps at Tampa — The "Gussie" Expedition — Preparing for the Invasion of Cuba — The Delays and the Start — Arrival at Santiago — Conference of Shafter, Sampson, and Garcia — The Landing.

FROM the very earliest days of the Republic it has been the pride of its people that no great standing army has been necessary for the maintenance of its authority at home or its influence abroad. A determination to shun anything like militarism was impressed upon the people by Washington and Jefferson, and given renewed emphasis by observation of the lamentable results which the creation and maintenance of enormous armies have entailed upon the peoples of Europe. It is not to be denied that this instinctive dread of an army would be a source of peril to the nation, if the temper of our people, the nature of our interests, and our geographical situation did not all combine to make foreign wars very rare in our history and very improbable for our future. Once only in our national existence have we been embroiled with a foeman at all our equal in resources, — in 1812 with Great Britain. The war with Mexico was a foregone conclusion, and that with Spain hardly less so, although the latter power was vastly our superior in the strength of its army. It had indeed in Cuba alone, when war broke out, a greater military force than our entire regular army, and it had lost in Cuba during the time of the then existing revolution an army four times the size of ours. For years all the military needs of this nation had been amply met by a regular army of about 28,000 men. The gradual disappearance and progressive civilisation of the Indians made the need for soldiery less apparent year by year, and an increasing tendency to employ the United States forces to preserve order in cases of strikes and other labour troubles alarmed thinking people, and stimulated political demagogues. It is probable that the sentiment, essentially a healthy one, against a great standing army was never more forceful in the United States than on the eve of the war with Spain.

But the army we had, if small, was admirable. Its officers were as fine a body of educated soldiers as the world contained. Graduates, in the main, of the military academy at West Point, they had enjoyed a technical education such as no military nation of Europe can outdo for its young soldiers. A considerable number of the older officers had served through the desperate campaigns of the war between the States, and brought the experience of veterans to the guidance of their juniors, while still more had profited by service in Indian wars, which peculiarly fitted them for the bushwhacking tactics that might be expected in Cuba. The rank and file of the army fell in no degree short of the officers in fitness. The small size of the army and the relatively high pay have made it possible for the United States to pick and choose its soldiers to a degree unknown in England, where military service, as here, is voluntary. Man for man, no armed force of Europe could outdo ours in technical skill or discipline, and throughout the war the foreign attachés who followed our campaigns joined in encomiums upon the hard-marching, hard-fighting, uncomplaining American regular.

About this little nucleus of professional soldiers was to be built and moulded into military form and efficiency the volunteer army. For this the foundation was the organised militia of the States, numbering some 410,000. Militia regiments, by the terms of their organisation, are subject only to service when called upon by the governor of the State, commissioning them. To become a part of the army of the United States, they must volunteer in response to the summons of the President. Out of this situation there proceeded some confusion and not a little scandal in the opening days of the Spanish war. There was great disparity in efficiency between the militia organisations of different States and of different localities in the same States. In some of the poorer communities of the South and West the local militia was only partly uniformed and not all armed, while in some of the large and rich cities of the North, where dread of riot had made wealthy citizens liberal to the local regiments, the equipment was not only effective but ornamental. Fate brings its compensations, however. It was not from the action of any half-clad company of a backwoods cross-roads that the sign of unwillingness to serve the country at the front in war-time came, but from the richest regiment in the richest city of the Union.

On the 23d of April, following swift upon the signing of the warlike resolutions of Congress, the President issued his proclamation calling for 125,000 volunteers. These were to be taken from the States and Territories in proportion to the population of each; and although nothing in the proclamation or the law limited volunteers to the existing national guard or militia organisations, yet in practice this first body of soldiers was made up of men already enlisted in the militia. One month later a second call for 75,000 men was issued, and at this time room was found for specially organised regiments, distinct from the National Guard. By special authority of Congress the army was further increased by the enlistment of ten regiments of "immunes," or men, usually negroes, not liable to contract yellow fever; three special regiments of cavalry, to be recruited among the cowboys and pioneers of the far West; and a special engineering command of 3550 men. The maximum strength of the regular army was also raised by congressional authority. The creation of this great body of volunteers gave opportunity for many striking displays of patriotism. As in fitting out the navy with auxiliary craft several private individuals made free gifts of their large and costly steam yachts to the nation, so the army for the liberation of Cuba was made the beneficiary of many generous donors. Mr. John Jacob Astor was the most conspicuous of these, for he armed and organised a magnificent field battery and gave its services to the nation. No touch of self-seeking was in this gift, for he did not even ask the command of the battery, but later accepted a staff appointment. Men of wealth and prominence enlisted in subordinate offices or even in the ranks. Mr. William J. Bryan, a recently defeated Democratic candidate for the Presidency, raised a company in his native town of Lincoln, Nebraska, and was elected the colonel of the Third Nebraska Regiment. The President, in appointing general officers for the army, took pains to select a few representatives of the Confederate veterans in the South. FitzHugh Lee was one of these, though his service as consul-general at Havana in the troublous days just preceding the war gave sufficient reason for his appointment to a major-generalship. General Joseph A. Wheeler, a veteran cavalryman of the Confederacy and a Democratic member of Congress, was also appointed major-general and put in command of a division of cavalry. The courage, physical endurance, and continued pertinacity of General Wheeler in the face of his apparent frailty — he weighed but ninety pounds — and his advanced years, for he had almost attained the Psalmist's limit of threescore years and ten, made him a popular hero. It was inevitable, perhaps, that with the vast number of military places to be filled and the pressure brought for appointment by politicians

GENERAL JOSEPH WHEELER.

and other men of influence, there should have been grave errors of judgment committed. In providing for the necessary personnel for the commissary and quartermaster's departments, most unfortunate appointments were made. Day after day the newspapers recorded the appointment to offices, with the rank of major or higher, of young men without experience or capacity, who were the relatives of senators, cabinet officers, or other men in official station. The scandal of "The Sons of Somebody," as the newspaper phrase ran, grew with each day's reports. It became so notorious that an ex-President of the United States whose son had received one of these appointments was constrained to say publicly that he had not asked the appointment, and, indeed, had urged his son not to take it. It is but just to say that the son became one of the most efficient officers of his army corps.

A picturesque and, as the event proved, most serviceable addition to the army was one of the special cavalry regiments organised at San Antonio, Texas, and soon known the land over as Roosevelt's Rough Riders. When the war began, Theodore Roosevelt, a New Yorker of means, an old-time ranchman, a keen hunter, a politician of no mean skill, and a nervous, restless, adventurous, and, above all, combative man of middle age, was Assistant Secretary of the Navy. He had sought this place expecting war with Spain, and had exerted himself to the utmost in preparing the navy for the conflict. As the time of active hostilities grew near, he looked eagerly about for some way in which to take the field; for to one of his temperament the routine of a bureau, however useful to the nation, would be intolerable when there was opportunity to engage in real war. The act of Congress authorising the enlistment of three regiments of cavalry opened the opportunity, and the colonelcy of a regiment forming at San Antonio, Texas, was presently given to an intimate friend of Mr. Roosevelt's, Dr. Wood, a regimental surgeon in the regular army. A most extraordinary military command this soon became. Having a nucleus of cowboys and plainsmen, it was at once dubbed by the newspapers the "Rough Riders," and began to gather recruits from the most diverse classes of society. Mr. Roosevelt was himself a picturesque character of many dissimilar interests, and former companions of his in very different walks of life flocked to his standard. He was a college-bred man, and into the ranks of the Rough Riders came men who were still undergraduates, men famous on the athletic field or the football gridiron. He had lately been a police commissioner of New York, and members of the famous Broadway squad of giants volunteered to follow him to Cuba. The New York clubs gave some of their most gilded members, and young men went to San Antonio with their valets to become privates in the rough riding cavalry. From the West came men who had hunted the big game of the Rockies with Roosevelt, or rode with him over his ranch in the Bad Lands. From the very first much was made of this regiment forming in the far Southwest by the newspapers, and it had the advantage — for it is an advantage even to a fighting-machine — of wide advertising. A famous shooting sheriff of Arizona, and an actor well known in the theatres of the Northern cities; several veteran Indian fighters and several Indians as well; three former officers of the regular army; four ex-clergymen of the Baptist and Methodist denominations; a few professional gamblers; an internal revenue agent from Tennessee, where gentlemen of his calling are at any time likely to be shot on sight, and a number of rich young men experienced in the pursuit of pleasure in many lands made up this extraordinary regiment.

In the end the First United States Volunteer Cavalry proved to be something more than picturesque. Dismounted, with all their talent for rough riding unemployed, they fought the first fight in the invasion of Cuba, suffered bravely, and acquitted themselves well. Better

Copyright, 1898, by G. G. Rockwood, N. Y.

HON. THEODORE ROOSEVELT.

armed than the majority of the volunteer regiments, and composed of men most of whom were inured to hardship and trained in the use of weapons, this command had most of the good qualities of a regiment of regulars. When it is remembered that many of the volunteers, even those who had been long in service in the national guard, had never fired a gun up to the time they were brought to the camps of concentration, it is easy to appreciate the immense value of a regiment of trained hunters and pistol-shooters such as this. It is worth noting, by the way, that though nominally a cavalry regiment, this command was never furnished with sabres, as it was thought the time employed in teaching the use of an unfamiliar arm would be wasted. It is not improbable that in future warfare this example will be widely followed. Colonel Mosby, the celebrated "rough rider" of the Confederacy, has left his opinion that the sabre is a handicap to the cavalryman when two or more pistols can be carried.

The troops thus gathered from the great cities and from the farms, from workshops, counters, class-rooms, and fields, were gathered together as speedily as might be in great camps, for instruction, drill, and all the processes of making a soldier out of a raw recruit. These camps were scattered about the country, the largest being at Chickamauga, Tennessee, where some thirty-five years earlier the fathers of many of these men now going to fight shoulder to shoulder for the nation had met in deadly battle. But the most important of the great camps was at Tampa, a small settlement on the gulf coast of Florida, convenient to a harbour near the coast of Cuba. Here, by the end of May, were concentrated about 16,000 men, constituting the Fifth Corps, under command of Major-General Shafter. In the main this corps was composed of regulars, for it was intended for the first invasion of Cuba, and the most efficient troops were naturally selected for it. The great body of volunteers was scattered over the country at

Chickamauga, Mobile, Fernandina, Jacksonville, Camp Black, on the wind-swept plains of Long Island, and other points of rendezvous, where officers of the regular army were diligently endeavouring to make the militiaman into a disciplined automaton. In all, before midsummer the army rose to a strength of 274,717 men, of whom 58,688 were regulars. Up to the time of the cessation of hostilities in Cuba less than one-fifth of this army had seen active hostilities, and many regiments were mustered out without having left their camps of instruction. The actual fighting of the war, in the West Indies at least, was done mainly by the little regular army.

The camp of the Fifth Corps at Tampa was unique in many respects among the military posts of history. The chief figure of the little town was a great winter-resort hotel, of those Brobdignagian proportions and that barbaric splendour which characterise the resorts of Florida. Ordinarily it is closed at the season of the year corresponding to that which saw Tampa transformed suddenly into an armed camp, but in 1898 it was open in all its gorgeousness through the glaring summer days. Here congregated the vast array of begilded officers, the swarming correspondents, the observant foreign attachés, artists looking for material, sightseers and the vast army of womankind who flocked to the spot as soon as it appeared that the movement upon Cuba was not to be immediate. War was declared, and the guns of the navy were thundering against the coast of Cuba; but at Tampa the cool drink on spacious porches, the dance in brightly lighted ballrooms to the strains of music from New York, and the quiet flirtation in shady walks were the most martial occupations of the officers. It was the "sound of revelry by night," like that which Byron describes as ushering in the battle of Waterloo. But in the midst of all the gaiety those whose duties were to prepare for the movement of the troops were busy, anxious, and alert.

Indeed, General Shafter and his headquarters staff at

Tampa had confronting them a problem which had never before been presented for solution in the army of the United States. For the first time in the history of the nation a foreign country was to be invaded in force. For the first time all the details of an expedition by sea had to be worked out with due regard to the possibility of interference by the enemy's navy, and the difficulties of subsisting in a hostile and already desolated land. During the war with Mexico a small military force was moved by sea against the enemy's coast, but neither then nor during the war with the Southern Confederacy was there any hostile navy to be reckoned with. And so, when the problem came to be solved in 1898, it was discovered that if all essential technical knowledge was at hand, which is by no means certain, the tools were surely lacking. Not in thirty years had a brigade of the United States army been moved in a body, and as for mobilising and transporting a whole army corps, that was a thing about which our officers might know from their researches in books, but only old fellows who had had general command in the Civil War possessed any practical experience of it. The very earliest days of the war indicated what the later experience proved, that while the line of the army was efficient, while officers and men were good marchers and good fighters, in the staff departments, in the bureaus of commissary and of transportation, we were wofully deficient. Nor was this situation materially improved, as the young and inexperienced men, owing their appointments to political favour, began to appear at the various camps, and take up the tasks of feeding, housing, and transporting the soldiers.

It is related of the great Von Moltke, that during the years of peace which preceded the Franco-Prussian War, he laboured incessantly, preparing plans for the mobilisation of the Prussian army on any frontier that might be menaced. Plans of the most elaborate detail were drawn up and corrected day by day. The location of every

Prussian regiment was noted, the distance and route to the place of rendezvous, the amount of rations necessary on the way, the time it would take to reach the point of mobilisation, and all the myriad particulars of vast importance in the aggregate, but each in itself seemingly insignificant, were connoted, and all emergencies prepared for. The story goes, and it is true in substance if not in detail, that, war being declared at midnight, an aide was sent to Von Moltke's quarters to inform him of the fact. The general was in bed. He listened to the officer's tidings in silence. "Very well," said he tranquilly, when the situation was explained. "Look in the third pigeon-hole of the left-hand side of my desk," and therewith returned to his slumbers. This done, there were discovered in perfect form, and with the greatest amplitude of detail, the plans for mobilisation of the army on the French frontier, even to the orders to the various corps commanders, so that while Von Moltke slept the despatches went winging forth, and the troops began to move to the battle-ground.

Nothing so systematic as this was perhaps possible in the United States, since detailed plans for the mobilisation of an army can hardly be prepared without knowledge of the size and disposition of the army, and our army was, in the main, created after the declaration of war was promulgated. Yet it is impossible to doubt that prudent forethought might have obviated many of the difficulties which arose at Tampa, and much of the resulting suffering. The probability of war with Spain had been sufficiently great for a year before the actual event to justify the War Department, which is never overpressed with business, in preparing several alternative plans for the mobilisation of the army and the invasion of Cuba. In that event camps would not have been established in spots destitute of water and of shade, like Hempstead Plains, Long Island, nor in localities naturally unhealthful, like Chickamauga. And had the difficulty of embarking an expedition of 16,000 men been properly studied, it is not likely that the port chosen would have been one reached by only one line of single-track railroad, almost destitute of yard and shipping switching facilities,—a port where good drinking water was a marketable commodity, and where the burning sun sapped men's vitality and quickly ruined supplies. The Secretary of War, Hon. Russell A. Alger, himself said in June: "I do not believe that there ever was a nation on earth that attempted to embark in a war of such magnitude, while so utterly unprovided with everything necessary for a campaign." The Secretary of War went on to extol his department and the army for the manner in which the initial disadvantages had been met and overcome, and indeed notably good work was done in repairing the faults resulting from a notable failure to take precautions when time was plenty. We may note and condemn the obvious faults of the War Department without in any degree underestimating the worth of its many successes; we may show the weakness of our army without forgetting the fact that, despite all weakness, it accomplished speedily and thoroughly the task set it. Criticism of the military methods of the United States in 1898 does not imply a quarrel with success, but rather an indication of the lessons that may be learned from the conduct of this war for the good of the nation should it ever unfortunately be forced into another.

While the soldiers of the United States by the tens of thousands were sweltering under the burning sun of southern Florida, clad in uniforms designed for service on the wind-swept plains of Dakota, the military authorities concluded to send arms and munitions of war to the Cuban insurgents,—a body of patriots of whom much was hoped, but from whom little was realised during the progress of the war. It is true that at this moment our own army was so badly equipped as to be the scoff and jest of the foreign attachés at Tampa. There were regiments without uniforms and without arms, regiments in which seventy-five per cent had never fired a gun, and one hundred per cent had never shot at an enemy. There were volunteers and regulars going into service side by side, armed with entirely different types of rifles, so that there could be no interchange of ammunition. The great body of volunteers were equipped with rifles that were useless within easy range of the Spanish Mausers. All this was known of all men; but the Cubans were in still worse condition, so, turning from the plight of our own people, we undertook to supply the needs of our allies.

For this purpose a steamer was obtained — the "Gussie," perhaps the most antiquated vessel then on the Gulf of Mexico. She was a side-wheeler, hence an easy target with all her vital machinery exposed. Her speed was such as to make a monitor seem swift in comparison. This craft, being freighted with several thousand rifles, fifty mules, a number of horses, a quantity of ammunition, and other things useful to a people at war, took on 100 men of the First United States Infantry under command of Captain Dorst, and three members of the insurgent commission, who were to aid in opening communication with the Cubans. Then she set forth to seek a landing-place on the enemy's coast, but not before all the correspondents had learned of her mission, and telegraphed about it to their papers, whence it speedily reached General Blanco *via* Madrid. As the ship made first for Havana, before disembarking her cargo, and there steamed about in full view of the observers on shore, it was but natural that the Spaniards thereafter kept a sharp watch on her movements. Up and down the coast her progress was signalised by the quick flashes of the heliographs on the hills, and much of the way bodies of cavalry attended her down the beach. It was therefore not extraordinary that when, on the 12th of May, she cast anchor near

FORWARD TURRET OF MONITOR "TERROR."

Mariel and prepared to lower boats, a considerable force of Spaniards appeared on the beach ready to oppose any landing. The two auxiliaries which accompanied the "Gussie" cracked away with their one-pounders at the troops on shore until they took to flight, but the expedition moved on to another spot near the entrance of the harbour of Cabañas before landing. Here again failure attended its effort, for the utter lack of secrecy that had characterised the methods of the expedition from the very start had put the Spaniards all along the coast on their guard. Mr. Zogbaum, the well-known artist, had accompanied the expedition as a correspondent for "Harper's Weekly," and tells of the scene as witnessed from the deck of the ship thus picturesquely:

"It is well on in the afternoon as we near the entrance to Cabañas Bay, and it is decided to attempt a landing on Arbolitos, the point on the western side. Sounding constantly, the big red hulk of our ship creeps closer and closer in towards the reef. With a roar of chain and upward splash of spray the anchor takes the ground, and we swing slowly abreast the beach — in sea parlance, 'close enough to shy a biscuit on shore.' The gunboat, with gentle, easy dip and roll, lies just off our quarter; a little further out to sea the graceful lines of a diminutive cruiser, the United States gunboat 'Wasp,' show up in a gray mass on the unbroken surface of the sea. Of course the 'Gussie' is short-handed, — who ever knew of a hired transport that was n't? — and it takes some time to lower the boats. Amid some confusion, for there seems to be no one aboard experienced in such matters to direct their movements, two of the boats are filled and manned by the soldiers, the boat first 'shoved off' moving up the reef, as if seeking an opening, the second pulling direct for the shore. As it nears the reef the swell begins to lift it, sending it in quick-succeeding leaps rapidly forward, until in a burst and smother of foam it plunges right into the surf, almost disappearing from view. For a moment we on the ship hold our breath in anxious expectation; then, as we see one blue-clad form after the other boldly plunge overboard and rush through the water, stumbling, falling full length, picking themselves up again, in eager emulation to reach the land, while others grab the gunwales of the boat on either side, and shoving it along between them, carry it bodily up on the strand, an enthusiastic shout bursts out, as cheer on cheer goes up for the first American soldiers to set foot on Cuban soil.

"Meanwhile the first boat seems to be hard and fast on the reef, teetering up and down in the swell like the 'Gussie's' walking-beam; but the fine athletic fellows are out of her in a jiffy, and soon, strung out in long skirmish-line on the beach alongside their comrades, move forward into the bush. The Cubans are quickly landed, and the task of setting the horses ashore begins. . . . On the hurricane-deck of the ship, lined up under cover of the hay-bales, the men who form the covering party have been watching the proceedings with anxious interest. Suddenly some way up the beach, right on the edge of the brush, we see something moving. Two or three blue figures emerge partly, and are running forward, arms at a trail; one drops on knee; with quick, jerky movement up goes rifle to shoulder, and we see the flash of the discharge. 'By God, they're attacked!' speaks a voice at my side, and simultaneously the air about us is filled with a whirring, humming sound, followed by a distant pattering noise, like fire-crackers on Independence day. Zip! hum! buzz! the angry bullets come flying, and a thin blue haze floats over the brush just beyond where one of the boats has been hauled up on the shore. 'Tenshun!' The hardy figures behind the hay-bales become rigid. 'With magazines, load!' A momentary rattling and clicking of steel on steel. 'Aim just to the right of the boat on the shore! Steady! Fire!' and like the discharge of a single piece the volley hits back at the attacking enemy. Again and again, quietly and as on drill, the men respond to the orders. The fire on shore rolls here and there, now falling, now rising again, slacking finally to a few scattering shots, then dying away. The enemy's attack is repulsed, and he has retired, leaving behind him the bodies of an officer and two soldiers, victims of the first encounter between American and Spanish soldiers on Cuban shores. But, victorious as are our men for the time being, their position on shore is exceedingly precarious. Our morning's work has shown us that the country is swarming with Spanish soldiery. Cabañas is not far distant, the enemy knows our force, and it will not be long before he can confront us in overwhelming numbers. We must try to make the woods too hot to hold him, and so word is sent to our friends of the gunboats with request to shell and drive him away, while dispositions are made to re-embark.

"It is a pretty sight to witness as the two gunboats move slowly broadside to the beach. Their fire sweeps the entire length of the jungle, and the boom of the guns, the whir of the projectiles, and the sharp burst of the shells as they plunge in among the trees mingle in one continuous roar, and are added to by the rumble of the storm over the land yonder. Time presses, the afternoon is waning, the tide is falling, and the roar of the surf strikes heavier and heavier on the ear. Lieutenant-Colonel Dorst, the officer in command of the expedition — his boat upset on landing, casting him and all its occupants into the sea — stands with the Cubans by the trees where the horses are.

"Word had been brought off to the ship that our allies, alarmed by the presence of the enemy, hesitated to carry out the mission for which they had been put ashore; but now we see them saddling the horses, and soon they mount and ride off up the shore, picturesque figures in their wide-brimmed hats and loose cotton garments. Our men have gone forward into the bush again, ready to repel the enemy should he renew the attack; but now the bugle sounds the recall, and we see them emerging from the trees and gathering in squads on the beach. It is going to be more difficult to re-embark even than it was to land. The boats have to be shoved out to the reef, where the water deepens abruptly, and the surf is angry and growing more violent every moment as the swells run in from the open sea. The men wade into the water, pushing the boat before them, until the reef is reached, and scramble in; some, up to their necks in the water, throw their rifles into the boat, and clinging to the gunwales as the light craft is driven out over the swells, are dragged in by their comrades. A boat from the 'Manning,' as close in to the reef as it can get, lies on its oars waiting to take Dorst off, and I own to a grateful feeling of relief when, after struggling neck-deep through the surf, I see him safe in the stern-sheets of the 'Manning's' boat, the last to leave the shore."

At Tampa, in the long dull days of preparation for the start, the air was full of rumours. No one knew where the American attack would be delivered, but the general opinion was that Havana would first be taken. That was the natural expectation, though we know now that from the first the authorities at Washington had decided against besieging the Cuban capital. Captain Sigsbee and General Lee, both of whom had exceptional opportunities to judge of the strength of the defences, have left on record the opinion that it could have been taken easily at the beginning of the war. Every day's delay, however, was diligently improved by the Spaniards in extending the fortifications, and as they undoubtedly expected the American attack would be delivered against that city, it was no doubt the part of military wisdom to strike somewhere else. Where that would be was the subject of hourly conversation at Tampa; and Porto Rico, Cienfuegos, Santiago, and Matanzas had each its partisans. The secret was, however, well kept until the last minute. Being destitute of facts on which to base criticism of the plan of campaign, the disapproval of the idlers at Tampa was therefore directed against the wearying delay which continued day after day and week after week. For that criticism there was abundant justification. Swift action might have lodged an invading force in Cuba before Cervera's fleet could get across the Atlantic to menace it. That golden moment gone, it was still essential that action should be immediate in order that the campaign — which all knew would be short — might be ended before the Cuban rainy season with its attendant pestilence should set in. But the Spanish weakness for procrastination seemed to have infected the War Department, and the orders to move were delayed time and again, until the nation began to growl ominously. Early in May the plan was for a reconnaissance in force to the southern coast of Cuba to establish communication with General Gomez. That was abandoned when the news of Cervera's departure from the Cape Verde Islands was received. Then a month of drill and monotony followed, the commissary department meanwhile trying to catch up with the work before it. "Even as late as May 21st," writes General Shafter, "some of the regiments were without arms or uniforms." May 30th the moment for action seemed to have arrived. News came from Washington of the blockade of Cervera at Santiago, and the Fifth Corps was ordered to proceed to Santiago and assist in capturing the town and fleet. At the same time came word from General Nelson A. Miles, the major-general commanding the army, that he would take train for Tampa at once.

Then began the work of preparing the expedition for its departure. The United States had never seen such a spectacle, nor had the officers of its army ever had such a problem to grapple with. The point of embarkation was Port Tampa, nineteen miles from the camp. A single-track railroad connected the two points, and at the port ran out on a long pier which extended into navigable water, so that the great transports could lie easily by its side. The first plan was to sail on the 8th of June with 10,000 men, and all were embarked, after heart-rending confusion and delays, and some of the transports were well out to sea, when a telegram arrived from Washington ordering a halt. Somebody had seen some vessels out in the St. Nicholas channel which were suspected of being Spanish men-of-war, and the loaded transports were hurried back to the safe shelter of Port Tampa. We know now that no Spanish cruisers were at large at that moment, but the precaution was nevertheless a wise one. Even a single hostile torpedo boat might do dire damage in a fleet of crowded transports. Again on the 10th the fleet started only to turn around and steam ignominiously back to its moorings, with all the good-byes to be said over again, the cheering and the patriotic airs with which the troops were bidden Godspeed by those left behind all expended untimely. These repeated delays could not but have a tendency to demoralise the men, and they certainly put a heavy strain on the quartermaster's department. The troops were provided with rations for the voyage to the point of landing, which a few knew to be Santiago, but they were not fitted out for a week's stay in port and then a voyage on top of that. The single-track railroad which connected the long pier with civilisation and markets was overtaxed by this new and unexpected demand. In a sandy country hemmed in by salt water potable water was scarce and precious — two cents a gallon was the price the owner of the only considerable supply demanded for his fluid. Accordingly the water on the ships was stale, ill-smelling, and unhealthful. Colonel Astor offered to buy enough for all the ships at this price if it would be accepted; but General Shafter, feeling doubtless that there was a limit to the amount of financial assistance that soldiers of the nation should accept from even the most patriotic millionaire, declined the offer. So drinking doubtful water, most scantily fed, cooped up on ships, with little shade and less room for exercise, the men waited most impatiently for the order which should really mean "Forward."

It came June 14th. By this time the fleet and the army had grown in size. An army of 17,000 men was embarked on thirty-two troop ships, convoyed by fourteen men-of-war. The troop ships were great floating barracks with berths in tiers, built of pine, and men by day swarming over every part of the ship. At night — the hot calm nights of the tropics — all who could slept on deck, so that there was scarcely room for the seamen to pass amid the recumbent forms. Circling about the flotilla were swift torpedo boats and converted yachts, like cowboys riding about a herd keeping all in place, while the great battleship "Indiana" and the other heavier vessels of the convoy kept pace with the flotilla and watched cautiously for any sign of an enemy. The light-heartedness with which the American people had embarked on this war characterised their method of conducting some of the most vital movements in it. Though within fifty miles of a hostile coast, this great flotilla of ships went steaming along night after night, with all lights burning, men singing lustily, and often a band playing to while away the time. True, the convoy was vastly superior to any Spanish naval force that could by any possibility be in those waters, but the opportunity for a dash by a torpedo boat or even an auxiliary fitted with rapid-fire guns was such as has seldom been offered a belligerent. Ordinarily the fleet was so extended that the vessels in the rear were lost to sight for hours at a time, while at one point the contour of the channel was such that the forty-eight large ships were crowded into a strait only seven miles across. But perfect weather and an absolute quiescence on the part of the Spaniards contributed to make the voyage absolutely uneventful. It was another opportunity lost to the enemy, — another instance of such entire lack of audacity or even ordinary naval alertness on the part of the Spaniards as to make it clear that the United States, because of their easy victory over that power, must not feel themselves ready to grapple at a moment's notice with a really first-class military and naval nation.

June 20th the great fleet arrived off Santiago, and the blue jackets of the blockading squadron climbed on the rails of the great steel ships and cheered for the coming army. Admiral Sampson made haste in his launch to call on General Shafter, and arrangements were at once made for a joint visit to the Cuban General Garcia, whose camp was not far away. Boats put ashore the admiral, the general, and a small army of newspaper correspondents alert for this historic interview. A ride of two miles up the hills into the interior brought the party to the patriot camp. On either side ragged native soldiery lined the road, well armed, showing signs of discipline, and of course intensely interested in the arrival of the Americans who were to win for them the liberty for which they had so long and manfully striven against heavy odds. General Garcia himself was absent when the camp was reached, and his officers vied with each other in their efforts to contribute to the comfort of the visiting officers until he could be summoned. They had little in their scanty commissary stores to offer, but all they had was pressed upon the visitors with almost pathetic insistence. Cocoanuts, limes, pineapples, mangoes, and coffee were about the scope of the list of Cuban delicacies in Garcia's camp, and while the new arrivals were devouring these in a hut thatched with palm-trees and looking down to the sea, there was a stir without, and Garcia came. The Cuban general was straight and gaunt of frame, dark and grizzled of face, with white hair, a flashing eye, and, carved deep in his forehead, a bullet wound marking his effort to kill himself once when, a prisoner in Spanish hands, he sought rather certain death than the mercy of his captors. His dark face was set off by a heavy white moustache and imperial, giving him a pronounced resemblance, one of the spectators noted, to Caprivi, the German chancellor and successor to Bismarck. He wore a linen uniform and high military boots, with a slouch hat. However uncouth the exigencies of a starveling commissary might make his troops appear, Garcia was always in dress the officer and the gentleman. It may be said that this scrupulous neatness in dress was a characteristic as well of most of the Cuban officers of elevated rank. Contrasted with the spare form of the Cuban leader was the ponderous Shafter, a very leviathan of a man in the sober blue garb of a United States major-general. Admiral Sampson, in immaculate white duck, slight and turning gray, made the third in a trio of figures destined to become historic in the annals of the western hemisphere. Garcia had with him about 4000 Cuban soldiers, moderately well armed, but sadly destitute of rations and clothing. They had some cattle on the hoof, but in the main subsisted on fruits and roots. His presence at that point was the first useful result of the mission of Lieutenant Rowan, some account of which has been given in an earlier chapter. He instantly put himself and his men at the disposal of the American commanders, saying that he regarded this moment as the culmination of his long struggle for liberty, and that he believed victory now assured. General Shafter replied that he was without authority to conclude any arrangement with the Cubans other than to accept their aid if freely offered, but he wished particularly the benefit of Garcia's superior knowledge of the topography of the country and the numbers and disposition of the Spanish forces. On these subjects the three commanders talked for some hours, the Cuban generals Rabi and Castillo being summoned to the conference, with the result that at the end a plan of campaign was determined upon and formulated in the following memorandum:

"About 12,000 Spanish soldiers at Santiago and vicinity. Spaniards can concentrate at any moment about 4000 on the west. Proposal made of a feint of 3000 or 4000 men at some point west of Santiago de Cuba, and then land expedition at Daiquiri and march on Santiago. Plan proposed for General Castillo to have about 1000 men at Daiquiri, while navy bombards, and will capture escaping Spaniards. General Shafter then proposed a plan that on the morning of the 22d he would have the navy bombard Daiquiri, Aguadores, Siboney, and Cabañas, as a feint, and land whole expedition at Daiquiri. About 5000 Spaniards between city and Daiquiri. General Garcia says Daiquiri is the best base, and General Shafter accepts it. The following numbers of Spaniards were then given by General Castillo: force at Daiquiri, near wharf, 300 men; at Siboney, 600 men; Aguadores, 150 men; Jutici, 150 men; Sardinero, 100 men. It was then decided that General Castillo will take on board the transports 500 men from Aserraderos, to be landed at Tajababo and joined to his command now there and 500 strong; with this 1000 men he will be at Daiquiri, and assist at landing on the morning of the 22d. General Rabi will, on 22d, make a demonstration at Cabañas (to the west) with 500 men, while navy shells. It was then decided by General Garcia to bring his men, about 3000 or 4000 strong, from his camp near Palma to Aserraderos, and be ready to embark on the transports the morning of the 24th, and then be taken to Daiquiri, to join General Shafter. To-morrow (the 21st) navy will make transfer of 500 men to Tajababo, under General Castillo; 500 men under General Rabi will make demonstration on Cabañas on the morning of the 22d."

The interview terminated, the guests, followed by the retinue of correspondents and foreign attachés who had been industriously taking notes and making snapshot photographs the while, started for the coast. Garcia mounted his horse, and rode along, while the ragged army was drawn up in double lines along the road to do the new allies honour. Once back at the ships, immediate steps were taken to give the plan of campaign effect. Two thousand rations were sent to the Cuban camp, and the next day 500 Cubans were carried by the navy to join the 500 under command of General Castillo at Tajababo. Then some of the transports steamed down towards Cabañas, as if to threaten a landing there, while the navy made demonstrations at divers points along the shore in order to divert the attention of the Spaniards from the real landing-point, which was to be at Daiquiri. Then there was rest of a sort on the crowded transports, for every man knew that the next morning at six o'clock the work would begin of landing through the rolling surf or a beach probably lined with hostile sharpshooters.

CHAPTER X

The Landing at Daiquiri — Flight of the Enemy — Good Fortune attending the Invaders — Difficulty of landing Stores — The Advance into the Interior — Conference at Siboney — March of the Rough Riders — Fight at Guasimas — Bravery and Heavy Loss of the Americans — The Regulars in Action — The Losses and the Value of the Victory.

THE merits of the campaign of Santiago, judged from the view-point of the military critic, will probably be long the subject of controversy. To begin with, there is at least a reasonable doubt whether or not the army should have been called upon at all. The town was of importance to the United States only because in its harbour lay the Spanish fleet. That fleet once destroyed, Santiago was of the very least value to us. As the effect of the tactics employed by our forces, the Spanish fleet was compelled to leave the harbour, and instantly fell into the clutches of Sampson and Schley, who suffered not one ship to escape. But this triumph, though won at slight expense to the navy, cost the army dear; and the question arises why the army should have been called upon to perform a task which seems to have been naturally that of the navy. It is true that Cervera lay under protecting batteries, but so did Montojo at Manila. It is possible that the harbour was mined, but so was the harbour of Mobile on that hot afternoon of August when Farragut shouted, "Damn the torpedoes! Go ahead!" Looking back upon the operations about Santiago, and counting their cost, it seems that the part of common-sense would have been for the ships to go in after the enemy instead of waiting a month for the army to painfully force him out. However, the latter was the course determined upon at Washington, and the war was fought from Washington, — an innovation which a distinguished British admiral remarked is ominous for the future of naval tactics.

The task that the strategists at Washington set for General Shafter and his army was to land near Santiago, secure, and intrench a position commanding the city, and finally take it by assault or siege. Already an American force was intrenched at Guantanamo Bay, where the marines from the squadron landed and established Camp McCalla. But this was too far from the objective point, and a nearer landing-place was sought. Daiquiri, twelve miles east of the entrance of Santiago Bay, was selected, chiefly because there was there a small pier, and roads ran thence through the dense thickets into the interior.

June 22d, the morning of the landing, was clear and scorching hot. On every transport the men were up early, and eagerly scanning the mysterious shores that held for them all the possibilities of war. They saw a mountainous coast sloping abruptly to the beach, cut at two points down to the water-level by narrow slots, at the mouth of which little villages could be dimly made out, — villages for the most part of thatched huts scarcely distinguishable from the dense forest surrounding. A few red-tiled roofs peeped out from the trees, and clouds of smoke rising into the still hot air from each little settlement told that the Spaniards were burning their houses as they fled to the woods. Those woods were menacing. Thick and impenetrable, they afforded the best possible cover for sharpshooters, and the steep hills suggested many a point of vantage for a battery to contest the right to land, or to cut to pieces any marching column that should attempt one of the narrow roads leading off towards Santiago. One village was about five miles distant from the group of transports. That was Siboney. Immediately in front of the anchored ships a little pier extended some 500 feet into the water. This was Dai-

GENERAL WILLIAM R. SHAFTER

quiri, where a very considerable mining-industry had been conducted by Americans before the revolution ended peaceful industry in Cuba.

Through the quiet air, quivering with heat, came the sound of distant cannonades, for the navy had been asked to attack fiercely several small harbours in the neighbourhood, that the Spaniards might be kept busy and their attention diverted from the actual point of landing. But the men on the ships had little time to study the tropical landscape presented to their view, nor to speculate concerning the possibilities latent in the jungles alongshore, for the command soon came to pack and prepare to land. The smaller vessels of the navy ran close inshore and searched the bushes with insistent shells, while from the larger ships strings of boats, with a launch at the head of each to tow, could be seen making for the transports. The facilities for landing other than those supplied by the navy were exceedingly inadequate. General Shafter had ordered three tugs and two barges brought for this purpose, but only one tug and one barge arrived; but the friendly aid of the navy made good the lack. By and by the men on the crowded decks began to show themselves, girt about with rolls carrying their slender luggage — there was little enough of it, for they thought they understood the Cuban climate; but four hours after the roads about Daiquiri were strewn with the little they did take, and the army went stripped to its shirt, trousers, and shoes. The Eighth Infantry was the first to land, and the First, General Shafter's old regiment, followed. Those still on the ships looked eagerly after the vanguard. All expected a fierce fight at the water's edge. From the "Seguranca," the headquarters ship, the correspondents and foreign attachés who had not been permitted to land watched through their glasses for the volley which all felt sure awaited the first boat when it should reach the surf. "They are waiting to see the whites of their eyes," said some one, reminiscent of colonial tactics at Bunker Hill.

On the high ground commanding the beach was a Spanish block-house, so there could be no doubt that the ground was known to the enemy. But the boats drew up to the pier without a sound from the shore, and hung there bobbing up and down in the heavy surf, while the men clambered out and catching up their rifles made for the beach as fast as possible. Still no sign of an attack. Some blue-coated figures disappeared in the forest, and in a minute there resounded the crack of rifles. Was the expected battle open at last? Apparently not, for immediately the Americans were seen clustering about the block-house, and presently a small United States flag rose and fluttered above it, while all the whistles in the fleet shrieked shrilly, men cheered hoarsely, and the foreign attachés who had come across the Atlantic and the Pacific to see a real war settled disappointedly down to the conviction that the Spaniards would not fight at all. It is needless to say that this erroneous opinion was corrected at San Juan and El Caney a day later.

It being apparent that no resistance was to be apprehended at the moment, the work of landing proceeded apace. The spot was not the best imaginable. The pier at Daiquiri was so high above the water that the men had to throw their rifles on it first, and then clamber up the piles from a boat which was bobbing up and down in a high rolling surf. The terrible execution which Spanish sharpshooters in the woods could have done during this deliberate operation shocks the imagination. At Siboney was no pier at all, and at neither landing-place was there any anchorage, so that the transports were compelled to steam up and down to prevent being blown out to sea or on shore. Fortune favoured the invaders here again, for though it was the season of hurricanes and even a moderate storm would have cut the army in two, half being carried out to sea and the rest left to the mercy of a superior force of Spaniards on shore, the weather remained calm and the Spaniards were as quiet as the winds. It must be remembered, too, that the landing of the men and the horses was the easiest part of the undertaking. The former, with the quick adaptability of the American soldier, devised means for overcoming the difficulties of the situation, while the latter were landed by the simple process of being thrown overboard and compelled to swim for their lives. The mules, long trained to follow a mare hung with a bell, were guided in their swim by men who walked the beach ringing a dinner-bell with might and main, while the horses responded readily to the word of command. About twenty animals were lost in the process of landing, and two men who fell from the boats while trying to scale the pier were carried down by their heavy equipments and drowned. So light a loss in so large an expedition silences criticism of the plan. It was another of the many cases in our war with Spain in which good luck took the place of good management.

The lack of facilities for quick and safe landing proved more serious, however, when the stores came to be put on shore. An army of 16,000 men on land with one day's rations in their packs and everything else — artillery, ammunition, rations, ambulances, medical stores, and the like — on thirty ships afloat without anchorage on an unprotected and dangerous coast in a season of high winds, is in a serious position. Freight cannot under the best circumstances be landed from small boats with expedition, and many circumstances combined to make the landing of the stores unusually slow. To begin with, there was a great shortage of boats. One big scow towed from Tampa was the main reliance, and to it for awhile were added several old lighters which the chief quartermaster had found on the beach. But the management of these vessels was put in the hands of soldiers, landsmen all, with the result that the lighters were speedily stove against the pier or swamped in the surf. Then the small rowboats of the transports were employed to land tons of freight — naturally a slow and difficult task. It was not made easier by the captains of the transports, who, not being enlisted men but merely hired with their ships, conceived their first duty to be to the owners of their craft, and with an excess of caution lay from three to ten miles out at sea, often out of reach of any signal and never able to comprehend the wigwagging of the navy code. This could have been remedied had General Shafter exerted the authority he undoubtedly possessed, and put every captain under military authority; but he did not do it, and much of the time of the boats was spent in chasing steamers over miles of sea for another load of needed munitions. Another grave weakness, discovered of course when discovery cost most, was the fact that in loading the ships no effort had been made to put the things likely to be needed first where they could be most easily come at. Moreover, articles belonging to the same branch of the service, as for example medical stores, were scattered among twenty vessels, so that each would have to be ransacked to find a given thing. This led to the gravest results. When fever broke out in the trenches before Santiago, it was almost impossible to get medical stores. Cots for the sick, surgical instruments, medicines, and disinfectants were least obtainable when most wanted, and the frantic surgeons who rode through the woods to the shore to seek for themselves could not even get boats in which to go to the ships in search of what they needed. It is probable that, though there was never a sufficiency of medical stores on the field, large quantities were carried back to the United States in the returning transports, simply because they had not been found in season to be of use. Certainly an immense quantity of miscellaneous stores were thus sent back. As for the difficulty of keeping the army supplied with rations, General Shafter in his report admits that "it was not until nearly two weeks after the army landed that it was possible to place on shore three days' supplies in excess of those required for daily consumption."

The strategic plan of campaign is less open to criticism than the details of the arrangements for landing the army, nor, indeed, can an unprofessional student of military events presume so justly to comment upon it. The substance of General Shafter's plan was to attack Santiago from the landward side. It has been urged since that a wiser strategy would have been to proceed down the railway which runs along the coast to Aguadores, and thence proceed westward along the coast, under cover of the guns of the fleet, to Morro at the mouth of Santiago Bay. At that point, without attempting to storm or reduce the castle, he could go inland to the shore of Estrella Bay, and seize the shore station from which the submarine mines were operated. With this once in the hands of friends, the fleet could enter the harbour and aid the army in fighting its way up to the city. This plan viewed superficially seems to be admirable. The aid of the fleet, which could concentrate upon any point in the front of the advancing army a fire of 100 projectiles a second, would have made resistance almost impossible; the transports could have kept pace with the troops, and the supplies would therefore have been at all times near at hand, and the proximity of the open sea might have averted those malarial diseases which, as we shall see later, almost destroyed the army in its pestilential trenches. Two objections to the plan suggest themselves. Much of the railroad line to Aguadores passed over a long trestle which the Spaniards burned, and the other roads were even worse than the direct ones to Santiago which the troops followed. Furthermore — and this is General Shafter's own explanation of his plan — the orders to the army directed the capture of the Spanish forces. An advance by the coast would have left General Linares, who commanded in Santiago, ample opportunity to abandon the city and retreat into the interior with all his army, in case of serious reverses. Should he do so, the war would be prolonged for another year at least, for in the rainy season, then approaching, no American force could follow him. By attacking the city from its landward side, all opportunity for retreat was denied the enemy. It is true that the event showed the Spaniards not at all anxious to take to the forests and prolong the war. When opportunity came to surrender, not only the force caught in Santiago was delivered up, but all the troops in that military district, thus indicating an entire willingness to submit to the inevitable after Spanish honour had been satisfied. However, this disposition on the part of the enemy could not have been foreseen, and the wisdom of General Shafter's course depends upon the question whether the advantage derived from capturing the enemy was a fair set-off to the loss to his own campaign due to the selection of a difficult and miasmatic line of attack.

The plan actually adopted by the general took the men into the interior as fast as they were landed. Cubans were employed as scouts, while back of them were small detachments of our own men deployed on either side of the road and keeping closely in touch all along the line. By night of the first day of the disembarkation, 6000 men were ashore and trudging along the narrow road, walled in by almost impenetrable banks of foliage, in which poisonous, thorny, saw-edged, and matted greenery made the progress of the pickets slow and painful, and clattering land-crabs scuttled about, startling the soldiers with their hideous looks. The army was one of regular soldiers almost wholly; the Second Massachusetts, the Seventy-first New York, and the First Volunteer Cavalry or Rough Riders, being the only volunteer organisations in the corps. The cavalry regiments fought on foot, for no horses had been brought except for pack trains. On the first two days, as the commands made their way from the landing-places at Siboney and Daiquiri to the villages of the same names a few miles in the interior, there was little resistance offered. Both towns had been held by the enemy, but from both they had discreetly retreated as news of the American advance preceded the column, and such of the houses as were not burned by the navy's shells or the torches of the fugitives served as quarters for men who had been crowded on stifling transports for a week, — a utilisation of doubtful value, as the huts harboured the germs of more than one epidemic disease.

On the 23d the Cubans in advance of General Young's division, slipping through the jungle toward the threatened city, had come upon a body of Spaniards, clearly the rearguard of the retreating army. Rifles had flashed, and bullets flew; but neither party was eager for a fight, and the Spaniards continued their flight, while the scouts returned to Siboney to notify General Wheeler, who was in command there, as General Shafter was still aboard ship, that the enemy was in the front. There was a consultation that night between Wheeler, General Young, Colonel Wood, and General Castillo, whose Cubans brought the news. The latter described the country to his colleagues. From Siboney two roads perforated the forest toward Santiago. One, a mere trail, useful for packhorses, but impassable to anything on wheels, runs straight up over a high ridge to the north of the town and turns west to a point about four miles away, where it joins the other, a wagon-road which has reached the same spot by a more circuitous route around the base of the hills. The junction is called Guasimas. Colonel Wood was ordered to take his Rough Riders over the hill. In General Shafter's original plan the Rough Riders had no business to be there in the van at all; but that restless body, instead of loafing about the beach on landing and letting others take the road ahead of them, had made a forced march at night and reported at the rendezvous at Siboney ahead of many commands which landed before them. While these eager volunteers were to scale the hills, the regulars, consisting of four troops each of the First and Tenth Cavalry, with four Hotchkiss guns were to take the wagon trail. Both parties started about sunrise.

A Cuban guide led the way, and immediately behind him came Sergeant Hamilton Fish, of Captain Capron's troop, a young New Yorker of an historic and wealthy family, a mighty athlete in college, and a famous "man-about-town" since his graduation. Under him were four men, as scouts. Then followed Capron's troop, chosen for the difficult post of vanguard because of the experience and courage of their commander. Then a gap, after which came General Wood, Colonel Roosevelt, aides, and two newspaper correspondents. Then the body of the Rough Riders in single file, for the trail was narrow and steep. Usually in the advance of a column through a hostile country, men are thrown out on either side as flankers, to see that none of the enemy are passed and left in the rear, but in this march this was impossible. The thickets on either side were too dense for men to make their way through. At one point a log spanned a stream, and over it the men filed one by one. The column advanced steadily without anything in the demeanour of officers or men to suggest that the first serious battle of the war was at hand. The men talked of the novel country through which they were passing, and discussed its hunting possibilities until the word came from the head of the column to keep silence in the ranks. Then a halt and an order to fill magazines. That meant fight, but no excitement was manifested in the ranks. "The men," says Colonel Roosevelt, "were totally unconcerned. . . . I could hear the group nearest me discussing in low murmurs, not the Spaniards, but the conduct of a certain cow-puncher in quitting work on a ranch and starting a saloon in a New Mexican town." Edward Marshall, a correspondent who was shot down early in the fight, writes:

"These volunteers had been so long in preparation, so many weary days had elapsed since they first buttoned their uniforms over hearts beating with tremendous primary patriotic enthusiasm, that now they were taking things calmly, and talking about dogs and the imperfections of army shoes. One

GENERAL LEONARD WOOD.

man persistently blew paste balls at his neighbours. (Two hours later I saw him lying livid and dead in the high grass. He had been hit by a different kind of missile.) Spaniards and fighting seemed as far away to them as the cities of Asia Minor do to the school-boy studying geography, they had been carrying idle guns and ammunition so long. Indeed, it was hard for any of us to realise the actuality of the enemy.

"'——! Would n't a glass of cold beer taste good?' said one, whereupon others threw pebbles and sand at him for suggesting such an impossible ecstasy. There was much good-humour."

The halting-place was one of the few points on the trail at which the surrounding underbrush gave way so that a view of the neighbouring country could be had. On the right of the column the tropical foliage sprung up thick and impenetrable to a height of fifteen feet. On the left was a stout wire fence shutting off broad fields of high grass, into which here and there the jungle foliage cut in little islets and peninsulas of denser green. Wood and Capron dismounted here, and went cautiously down the trail ahead. The men in the ranks began to grow more serious, and those of Capron's troop brought their guns to a ready and knelt by the side of the fence, peering across the fields to the thickets beyond, as though suspecting danger. Presently the officers returned. Signs of the Spaniards were plentiful, a dead body being discovered in the road just ahead, presumably at the point of yesterday's skirmish with the Cubans. So the main force of the Rough Riders was deployed in line of battle to the left of the road where the open fields lay. Lieutenant-Colonel Roosevelt with three troops was ordered into the dense forest on the right. Capron continued down the trail. The men had hardly secured the positions to which they had been ordered when the storm burst with a rattle of Mauser rifles and a singing of bullets through the trees. "The noise of the Mauser bullet," writes Edward Marshall, who not only heard many but felt one, "is not impressive enough to be really terrifying until you have seen what it does when it strikes. It is a nasty, malicious little noise, like the soul of a very petty and mean person turned into sound." It was an irritating sound, however, and at it and the sight of leaves cut away about them by the flying bullets, some of the men began to swear. "Don't swear, men," growled out Wood; "SHOOT!" That raised a laugh, and restored self-possession to any who might have been about to lose it. The fire was a galling one, the more so because the absolute freedom of the Spanish powder from smoke made it impossible to tell whence came the stinging darts that struck men down. The high penetrating power of the Mauser bullets made them doubly deadly. They would cut through a palm-tree without losing anything of their murderous force, and many instances are recorded of two or more men struck down by the same vicious bolt. The attack fell first on Capron's men. Sergeant Fish fell at the first fire, shot through the heart. "It would be just my luck to get put out in the first fight and see nothing of the war," he had said at Tampa. Captain Capron, a gallant young soldier of a family of soldiers, found in that volley his death-warrant. Next day his father left for a brief time his battery before the Spanish lines, and came over to where the body of his son lay on the rank grass. He looked a moment on the still features, then stooped and kissed the icy face. "Well done, boy, well done!" was all he said as he went back to the battle.

The men in the road were being cut to pieces, and it was evident that the Spaniards knew the topography of the region perfectly, so accurate was their fire. Though not more than eighty yards away, they could not be seen by any of the Americans. The troops with Roosevelt in the bushes were suffering less, partly because the men were more widely deployed and offered a less conspicuous target, partly because the foliage that made progress difficult also impeded the enemy's aim. What was going on in the other parts of the field they could only guess by the sounds. Once the hum of machine guns was heard. All supposed that the Hotchkiss cannon, of which Lieutenant Tiffany had charge, had been brought up and were opening on the Spaniards. "Poor fellows! Now will they be good!" were the cries arising from the American lines; but it was not till night that they learned that it was the Spanish Gatlings opening on the men in the road the deadly fire that struck down Capron and Fish. For the men in the woods the advance was almost a matter of individual direction. If one could keep in touch with the man to the right and the one to the left of him, it was the utmost possible; farther down the line the palms, the softly waving vines, the gay flowers hid all in a vernal shield. The opportunity was tempting for skulking, but few yielded. In the main the line pressed on, men crawling under boughs where the limbs hung low, dropping to the ground when the fire was heavy, and running eagerly forward when some open space invited a dash. The difficulty of the ground and the impossibility of maintaining communications with all parts of the army caused some costly confusion. At one point in the battle an officer came running, crying to the men to stop firing, that they were shooting down their own comrades. Of course they stopped, horror-struck at the thought; but after the battle a Spanish captive taken on that part of the line commented on the curious custom of American soldiers of advancing without firing. At another moment a column of the enemy passed within easy range of the men with Roosevelt, but it was so absolutely impossible to determine that they were not Cuban allies that the fire of the troopers was withheld. At last the men on the right broke from the thickets and came in view of the Spanish position. A ravine separated the enemy from the Riders, and on a ridge beyond the Spanish lines were fixed in a sort of obtuse angle, the apex of which extended towards the gap which lay between Wood's lines and those of General

Young. Here was a large red-tiled building, which seemed to harbour an enemy; so with a cheer and a rush — the very sensation of being in the open where a rush was possible was invigorating — it was charged and taken. It was found deserted, but with great heaps of empty cartridge shells, showing that earlier in the fight it had sheltered a considerable and active body of the enemy. The battle was by this time approaching its end.

Meanwhile the column of regulars under General Young had swung along down the wagon-road until they too encountered the enemy. That day the doubt whether the Spaniards would fight or whether they could shoot was effectually dispelled. The route was more open than that which the Rough Riders had followed, and the enemy was discovered at a greater distance. A row of battered straw hats appearing over a stone wall a quarter of a mile away was the enemy's first appearance to General Young, and after examining the phenomenon a few moments he ordered up the Hotchkiss cannon, and sent word for the troops to follow in ten minutes. It was more like civilised fighting — if any fighting is truly civilised — on that front, and less like bushwhacking, than the tactics to which the Riders were reduced. There was a pause after the guns came up, for General Young did not wish to go into action until the men with Wood and Roosevelt on the other road should be engaged. But when the first cannon opened the response was so swift and accurate that one of the artillerymen fell where he stood beside his piece. The Spaniards evidently had the range of that position accurately. Then the First Cavalry rushed forward, and the fight began.

It is probable that no troops in the world are superior to the American regulars in action. Our army is so small that recruiting officers are enabled to be exclusive, and the men enlisted are picked men of their class. As the term of enlistment is short, those who are not fit for a soldier's life or who have a distaste for it quickly drop out, and the

American soldier who re-enlists is apt to do so for the love of a calling for which he has special aptitude. This campaign against Santiago was fought in the main by regulars, and this battle at La Guasimas was the first engagement of regular troops against a foreign foe since the war with Mexico. But these men, particularly those whose shoulder-straps or chevrons showed sign of long service, were veterans nevertheless. They had fought Indians on the arid plains of the Southwest and the bleak and wintry prairies of the North, and had seen service against bandits on the Mexican frontier. The business of war was no new thing to them, and they went about it in the unaccustomed surroundings of a tropical forest with professional calmness. They moved forward coolly, losing heavily, it is true, but driving the enemy from one position after another. After a few minutes the sound of guns on the left gave tidings that the volunteers were engaged as well, and now and then a shout and once a guidon waved from a tree told where the Rough Riders were pressing the foe. Finally a charge up a hill sent the Spaniards fleeing down the road to Santiago, the left of the Tenth Cavalry and the right of the First Volunteer Cavalry were joined, and thus the coloured regulars and the cow-punching, club-haunting volunteers in happy harmony dashed madly off in fruitless pursuit. The field of La Guasimas was won, and to the phrase which gained currency in the Civil War, "The coloured troops fought nobly," was added a new one, — "Cowboys, dudes, and football players make good soldiers."

Somebody has said of the campaign against Santiago that it was fought and won by the individual soldiers. The purport of the phrase is that the generals' plans had little to do with the victory. This may be, and doubtless is, an overstatement; but the battle at Guasimas was, beyond doubt, one in which the devotion and intelligence of the private soldier were all important. The difficulties of the ground and the impossibility of detecting the

Spanish positions because of the smokeless powder, threw upon the men who carried rifles the duty of winning the fight by sheer tenacity of purpose, advancing as seemed to them best, and trusting to break the Spanish lines when they were encountered. Because of the great part that individual valour played on this field, the many illustrations of it told by eye-witnesses are as important as interesting.

Captain Capron, being struck down early in the action with a wound he knew to be mortal, called to a man near by to give him the rifle that lay by the side of a dead soldier. Propped up against a tree, he continued firing with this weapon at the enemy until his strength gave out, and he fell forward to die. A very similar display of courage was made by Private Heffener, who fought leaning against a tree until he bled to death. Trooper Rowland, a cowboy from New Mexico, was shot through the lungs early in the action. Saying nothing about it, he kept his place on the firing-line until Roosevelt noticed the blood on his shirt and sent him to the hospital. Soon he reappeared. "I thought I sent you to the hospital," said the officer. "Yes, sir, you did, but I did n't see that they could do much for me there, so I came back," was the response; and back he stayed until the fight ended. Then he went again to the hospital, where the doctors, to his intense disgust, decided that he must be sent back to the States. That night Rowland secured his rifle and pack, slipped out of the hospital, and made his way back to his command, where he stayed. Nobody talked again of sending him to the States. Edward Marshall, the newspaper correspondent, struck down with a wound which the doctors pronounced mortal, employed the moments when he was not writhing in convulsions of agony in dictating the story of the battle to be sent to his paper. When he was being carried in a canvas hammock to the hospital, he noticed that one of the bearers of his litter, Trumpeter Cassa, had suffered the loss of two fingers near the middle joints, and was grasping the rough canvas with the bloody stumps. In Marshall's story of his experiences is a dramatic description of a scene in the field hospital where sorely wounded men lay crowded together awaiting their turns under the surgeon's knife:

"There is one incident of the day which shines out in my memory above all others now as I lie in a New York hospital writing. It occurred at the field hospital. About a dozen of us were lying there. A continual chorus of moans rose through the tree-branches overhead. The surgeons, with hands and bared arms dripping, and clothes literally saturated, with blood, were straining every nerve to prepare the wounded for the journey down to Siboney. Behind me lay Captain McClintock, with his lower leg-bones literally ground to powder. He bore his pain as gallantly as he had led his men, and that is saying much. I think Major Brodie was also there. It was a doleful group. Amputation and death stared its members in their gloomy faces.

"Suddenly a voice started softly:

> 'My country, 't is of thee,
> Sweet land of liberty,
> Of thee I sing.'

Other voices took it up:

> 'Land where my fathers died,
> Land of the Pilgrims' pride —'

"The quivering, quavering chorus, punctuated by groans and made spasmodic by pain, trembled up from that little group of wounded Americans in the midst of the Cuban solitude,— the pluckiest, most heartfelt song that human beings ever sang.

"There was one voice that did not quite keep up with the others. It was so weak that I did not hear it until all the rest had finished with the line,

> 'Let Freedom ring.'

Then, halting, struggling, faint, it repeated slowly:

> 'Land — of — the — Pilgrims' — pride,
> Let Freedom —'

"The last word was a woful cry. One more son had died as died the fathers."

The battle of Guasimas ended thus in complete victory for the Americans. They had met the Spaniards on their own ground, had triumphed over ambushes and intrenchments, had driven the enemy back, and had taken an advanced position on the road to the goal. They had proved that coloured regulars would fight with the dash and courage of Anglo-Saxons. They had shown that a volunteer regiment composed of such material as the Rough Riders would not only be brave, but would maintain discipline in battle. For all this they had paid dearly. Of the 964 men engaged, 16 were killed and 52 wounded, the Rough Riders alone losing 8 killed and 34 wounded. How great was the enemy's loss cannot be told exactly. The official report made by the American commander put it at 45 killed, while the Spanish report was 9 killed and 27 wounded. Colonel Roosevelt asserts that he saw eleven dead Spaniards on the field after the battle.

Out of this affair — as unfortunately out of almost every battle during the war — sprung some controversy as to the tactics employed. General Shafter being on board the "Seguranca" when the news of the affray between the Cubans and the Spanish rear guard was brought to Siboney, General Wheeler ordered the advance that brought on the battle. In Shafter's plan the Rough Riders were not assigned any such position in the van as fell to their lot that day, and there has been discussion as to the propriety of Wheeler's action in sending them forward. The military men will, no doubt, continue to debate the phases of this point of etiquette long after the mass of the people have settled down in the conviction that what the Rough Riders did afforded ample justification for their employment, and that whatever variations in the original plan of advance may have been caused by General Wheeler's action, they were excused by the result. General

Shafter himself, while saying that the battle was no part of his original plan, remarks: "The engagement, though unimportant, had an inspiring effect on the army, showing, as it did, that the Spanish troops could not stand against us. It proved to the men that they could whip the Spaniards if they could get at them."

CHAPTER XI

SAN JUAN, EL CANEY, AND AGUADORES — WAITING FOR SUPPLIES — THE POSITION AT EL CANEY — GENERAL LAWTON'S DISPOSITIONS — EFFECT OF MAUSER BULLETS — STORIES OF THE BATTLEFIELD — THE CAPTURE OF EL CANEY — THE ATTACK ON SAN JUAN — PLAN OF THE BATTLE — THE SLAUGHTER IN THE SUNKEN ROAD — THE CHARGE ON THE HILL — EXPOSED POSITION OF THE AMERICANS — THE QUESTION OF RETREAT — THE SCENES AT BLOODY BEND — THE DEMAND FOR THE SURRENDER OF SANTIAGO — NEWS OF CERVERA'S DEFEAT.

NOW ensued days of preparation for the really decisive action of the campaign. The Spaniards had fled not only from La Guasimas, but from Sevilla, a little village a few miles farther up the road toward Santiago, and the country in the immediate front of the invading army was open to its advance. General Wheeler with his cavalry division was ordered to a point a little beyond Sevilla, and directed to stop there, keeping his front well picketed and reconnoitring the country before him. Just beyond Sevilla on the crest of a ridge was the group of farmhouses known as San Juan, and here the enemy was evidently established in force. Farther to the right on the crest of another hill was the block-house of El Caney, a massive structure of stone defended by Spanish riflemen. The main road from Siboney to Santiago split at a ford called El Poso, one fork branching off to El Caney, the other continuing directly on to San Juan. The surrounding country to within a few hundred yards of these posts was a typical Cuban jungle, the spaces between the great palms thickly matted with clinging thorny vines, the saw-edged palmetto and the needle-pointed Spanish bayonet. Immediately before the two forts extended a broad expanse of open hillside, plentifully obstructed by fences of barbed wire, — a new defensive material which the Spaniards used freely in all their fortifications. Upon these open spaces, swept by the fire from the trenches at the crest, the roads debouched from the forests, a single opening to each as clearly defined as a door in a stonewall. Of course the Spaniards had well noted the range to each of these openings, and any body of troops coming out in a dense column would have a murderous fire to encounter. On the 1st of July battles were fought at both San Juan and El Caney, besides a skirmish at Aguadores. The three, though simultaneous, were in fact distinct actions.

The days from the 24th to the 30th of June were filled full by the work of landing supplies and getting what the soldiers called "the cracker line," by which rations were sent to the front, into good running order. This was vitally important, of course; but the delay it caused was endured with the utmost impatience by the men in the front, who could see that the Spaniards were utilising it by strengthening their lines in every imaginable way. Why no artillery was sent to the front to interrupt the enemy's industry in building rifle-pits has never been satisfactorily explained. The heavy siege-guns brought from Tampa the commanding-general never had landed, seeming to consider them useless; but he had four light batteries at the front which could have kept the Spaniards engaged during these days of waiting. However, the enemy peacefully dug his trenches and our men bloodily took them.

On the 29th, the landing of supplies having proceeded far enough to make an advance practicable, General Shafter, who had thus far remained at Siboney, rode forward as far as a high hill near El Poso to examine the country. Prior to this time the reports of reconnoitring officers had supplied him with knowledge of the topography of the country that was satisfactory, at least to him, though some vigorous criticism has been directed against his failure to examine more in detail himself. The general was physically handicapped by his great bulk, which in that torrid climate was a serious disability, and by an attack of gout which made every movement excruciating torture. His campaigning had to be done chiefly from a cot in the rear, or, in instances of unusual activity, from a buckboard. The climate by this time had begun to tell upon even the enlisted men, though they were young and picked for their robust physical health. The almost daily rains, the mists that rose from the water-logged soil, the bivouacs on sodden ground, the wretched and insufficient food which drove the soldiers to the unhealthful tropical fruits, all combined to bring on the army those first signs of a breaking down that were so fearfully watched for at home and in the field. The experience of the Spaniard for years past had not been lost upon our people. They knew what campaigning in Cuba in the rainy season meant to troops from the temperate zone, and every day of delay before San Juan was discussed anxiously in a hundred thousand homes in the United States, while every morning's paper was scanned eagerly and laid by with relief if no report of the coming of the dreaded yellow fever appeared in the news from the front.

On the afternoon of June 30th there came to the commanding officers of the 12,000 men encamped along the sides of the road to San Juan, orders to move at four and take up positions in the woods before the enemy's lines, ready to attack at dawn. General Lawton was sent with his division to attack the Spaniards at El Caney, and by marching all night was ready to attack at six o'clock in the morning. With him was Capron's battery and Bates's brigade. As the fighting at this point began before that at San Juan, we may conveniently first consider it.

A stone fort on the crest of a steep hill was in the centre of the Spanish position, and from it the "flag of gore and gold" floated defiantly. On either side yellow lines of fresh earth told of trenches filled with riflemen whose bullets were deadly at two miles' distance. Beyond and north of the fort, and separated from it by another valley, was the village, built of stout stone and adobe houses, huddled together almost as if intended to take the form of a fortification. An old stone church with a high tower pierced for musketry stood in the town. The two valleys, that before and the one behind the fort, were mainly open fields of grass waist high, broken here and there by groves of cocoanut and mango trees. The stronghold was defended by about a thousand Spaniards; estimates vary, and the stubbornness of the defence inclined the men who charged up and down those slopes that midsummer day in the tropics to set a much larger figure, but this seems to be approximately correct.

Early in the morning of July 1st the guns of Capron's battery began to thunder against the antiquated stone fort that crowned the hill. Masonry is of little use against modern artillery, and it might have been expected that the usefulness of that fort would have been terminated before the infantry was sent in to the attack. For some reason, however, the artillery proved ineffectual. There were but four guns, and these, says Captain Arthur Lee, the British military attaché, "were served with such deliberation, five and ten minutes elapsing between successive rounds, that it was of little material assistance to the infantry attack." When the fort was finally carried by assault, it was found to be shattered indeed, but still tenable. During the firing Lieutenant Hobson from his cell window in the prison of Santiago could see the fort clearly. "It was a fine sight," he writes, "to see the billows of smoke dart out of the hillock (where the battery was stationed), and then, after an expected pause of five or six seconds, see the puff-balls of gas at the blockhouse; then came another pause of ten or twelve seconds; then the peal, followed shortly by a sharp, strong echo from the mountains behind."

The plan of battle adopted by General Lawton, who commanded the American right which fronted El Caney, involved the almost complete surrounding of the enemy by the attacking lines. Chaffee's brigade enveloped the north and east sides, and Ludlow the south and west. At the first shot of Capron's battery the Spaniards, who prior to that signal had been coolly disporting themselves in front of their trenches as though ignorant of the presence of an enemy, plunged for the earthworks. In a few moments all that was to be seen of them was the row of big straw hats peering over the crest of the banked-up clay redoubts. But their alertness was made known by the stinging fire that came without sign of smoke from those sheltered lines. The Americans responded in kind, and for about three-quarters of an hour the battle took the form of a duel between infantry at about 600 yards. The assailants, however, were continually creeping forward, but every foot of advance was dearly paid for. The Spanish shooting was excellent. At one point on the American line eight sharpshooters crept forward to take position on a little knoll, and five were hit within five minutes. At another part of the field a hedge obstructed the advance of the Seventh Regiment. Seven men broke through it, and an immediate volley killed three and wounded all the rest. General Chaffee, who kept erect and on the firing-line, seemed to bear a charmed life. One bullet snipped a button from his coat, and another passed through the cloth under his shoulder-straps. The colonel of the Seventeenth Infantry was hit three times within a few seconds. Five men volunteered to take him to shelter, and before they had completed the task three were shot down. The troops advanced literally, as Napoleon said an army moved, on their bellies. Worming their way slowly through the high grass, running forward a few feet with trailing arms where the nature of the ground or a lull in the firing seemed to promise success, they fought for their ground, yard by yard, as stubbornly as ever a

GENERAL ADNA R. CHAFFER.

Yale football eleven struggled for an advance on the goal line of Princeton. The attitude of the men and the tremendous penetrating power of the Mauser bullets led to some curious and shocking wounds, for the conical steel-clad bullets entering at the top of the body, as the victim stooped over, would range the whole length of the man's trunk, often passing down the leg to some distance. Sometimes striking a bone, these vicious projectiles would double on their course, describing almost a circle within the body. It is worth noting, however, that the wounds inflicted by the Mausers, though seemingly more extensive than those caused by the larger-calibre and slower-speed bullets of earlier days, were less deadly. The channel was more cleanly cut, and the shock of the impact less. Men were sometimes seriously hit without knowing it until faint from loss of blood. Men shot in the stomach would complain that they had been kicked, perhaps by a comrade in the rank before them, and would be astonished to learn that a bullet had drilled them through and through. The officers, debarred in the main by military custom from shielding themselves as did the men, suffered severely in this fight. The story of one young lieutenant's death, told by the friendly captain whom England sent to see if America had any new message of military value for the old world, is worth retelling:

"Close in front of me a slight and boyish lieutenant compelled my attention by his persistent and reckless gallantry. Whenever a man was hit he would dart to his assistance, regardless of the fire that this exposure inevitably drew. Suddenly he sprang to his feet, gazing intently into the village; but what he saw we never knew, for he was instantly shot through the heart and fell over backward, clutching at the air. I followed the men who carried him to the road and asked them his name. 'Second Lieutenant Wansboro, sir, of the Seventh Infantry, and you will never see his better. He fought like a little tiger.' A few convulsive gasps and the poor boy was dead; and as we laid him in a shady spot by the side of the road, the sergeant reverently drew a handkerchief over his face and said, 'Good-bye, lieutenant; you were a brave little officer, and you died like a true soldier.' Who would wish a better end?"

Non-combatants on that hard-fought field have told graphic stories of the carnage and of the calm manner in which the men met wounds or death. It seemed that the same cry went up from each who felt the shock of a bullet. "I've got it," most would cry, dropping heavily to earth or rolling over clutching the wounded part, though some struck in the head or other mortal spot would raise a pitiful cry to God. As the wave of battle swept on, the field behind presented an appearance never seen until this Cuban war, for the bodies, dead or still living, were mostly half-stripped and lay gleaming white against the green grass. This came from the distribution to each soldier of "first aid" bandages, with instruction how to use them while waiting for the surgeons or hospital stewards to arrive. As a result, every wounded man who had sufficient vitality tore off that part of his slender raiment which covered his hurt and strove to stanch the blood. Captain Lee, whom I have already quoted, gives in his article in "Scribner's Magazine" a description of the field hospital at El Caney that is illuminating in the light it throws on the methods of hospital work and on the fierceness of the fire that day:

"About noon I crossed over to their position, and on nearing the sunken road noticed that it was full of men lying down. I asked an officer of the regiment who was coming down the road if those were his reserves I saw, and his reply was somewhat startling: 'No, sir, by God, they are casualties.' And indeed they were. On reaching the spot I found over a hundred killed and wounded laid out in as many yards of road, and so close were they that one could only pass by stepping over them. There was a strange silence among these men, not a whimper or a groan, but each lay quietly nursing his wound, with closed eyes and set teeth, only flinching when the erratic sleet of bullets clipped the leaves off the hedge close above their heads. Many looked up curiously at my strange uniform as I passed, and asked quickly and quietly, 'Are you a doctor, sir?' I could but shake my head, and they would instantly relapse into their strained intent attitudes, whilst I felt sick at heart at the thought of my incompetence. Some of the slightly wounded were tending those who were badly hit, and nothing could have surpassed the unskilled tenderness of these men. I was astonished, too, at their thoughtful consideration. 'Keep well down, sir,' several said, as I stopped to speak to them. 'Them Mausers is flying pretty low, and there's plenty of us here already.'

"But the worst feature of it all was the scarcity of doctors. Hour after hour these wounded men had lain in the scorching sun, unattended, and often bleeding to death. Their comrades had in many cases applied the first-aid dressings in rough and unskilled fashion, but so far as one could see there had been no medical assistance. The nearest dressing-station was three-quarters of a mile to the rear, and while the medical staff there was undoubtedly more than busy, it was chiefly with such cases as were slightly enough wounded to walk down for aid.

"One man I noticed lying very quiet in a great pool of blood. A comrade with a shattered leg was fanning him with a hat and keeping the flies off his face. I sat down beside them, and seeing the man was shot through the stomach, knew there was nothing I could do beyond giving him a little water. I asked him how he felt, and he replied with difficulty, 'Oh, I'm doing pretty well, sir.' His companion then said: 'Well, sir, if you can you might send a doctor along to see this man. He was one of the first hit, about eight this morning and no one has seen him yet.' The wounded man here broke in: 'That's all right, Mick; I guess the doctors have more than they can do looking after them as are badly hurt, and they will be along soon.' I looked at my watch, and it was nearly one o'clock."

But to return to the battle, — back again to the firing-line whence came those brave fellows whose patience in the hospital so moved the representative of England.

All the morning the battle had raged. The Spaniards in the trenches with the regularity of automatons were rising up to deliver a volley and then sinking back to safety, leaving more of our brave fellows writhing on the ground. The situation was becoming intolerable, for the advance of our men, though steady, had been so slow that there was no prospect of forcing the Spaniards from their position unless more dashing tactics were adopted. At one o'clock came a disquieting order from Shafter. The troops before San Juan were finding hotter work than they had expected, and Lawton was directed to leave El Caney and make a junction with the forces of General Wheeler. That meant retreat. It meant an admission that American troops could not carry a stronghold manned by Spaniards. It was a thing not to be thought of. Lawton instantly gave Chaffee discretion to charge the fort in his front, something that Chaffee had been waiting for. The tidings quickly passed along the line and cheered all the men in their work. The artillery briskened up, and its shells tore great rents in the stone fort as Captain Haskell's battalion of the Twelfth Infantry led the charge. It was not a spectacular charge. There were no long lines of cheering men in regular formation, with battle flags waving, as at Gettysburg for instance. Instead the spectator on the flank who from a position of comparative safety watched the advance saw a few men without formation advancing in groups slowly, while behind them some twenty paces followed a larger body of soldiers, who would run forward bent almost double for a few rods, then drop to the ground and crawl and wriggle on a bit, then rise and dash on again. A barbed-wire fence stopped the advance for a moment near the crest of the hill; but this was speedily cut, and the assailants dashed through the breaches. Then the Spaniards could be seen rising on the high ground behind their trenches and turning in flight. The fort had long been silent and its flag had been shot away, but soon through glasses the men back on the firing-line could see a man in civilian garb entering the fort while the storming-party danced and cheered from the top of the earthworks and from the outside of the stone citadel. The civilian who thus led the assailants was James Creelman, a correspondent for the " New York Journal." He found fort and trenches filled with dead and wounded Spaniards who made no effort at resistance. The scene spoke volumes for the courage of the defenders, for fort and trenches were literally paved with their bodies. None of the men who were engaged in the attack on the hill at El Caney ever afterwards expressed doubt whether the Spaniards would fight.

But the jollification on top of the hill was cut short when the Spaniards recommenced without ceremony their exposition of the fact that valour and pertinacity in battle are not the exclusive possession of any one people. The elated victors suddenly discovered that the battle was not ended, and that they had captured for themselves a most exposed position, against which the enemy from other block-houses on his line and from the houses and church tower in the village were now directing a galling fire. The bullets spattered against the stone fort, and one slipping in through an embrasure wounded Creelman, who was within. There was no cover for the large party which had by this time gathered at the dearly won position, and the best they could do was to drop to earth and pump away with their repeating-rifles at the enemy in the streets of the town. But the first success had stimulated the other troops on the American line, and they began to stream across the hollow and up against the Spanish lines. Such was the enthusiasm and dash of the assault, that the enemy fled from every block-house and streamed away through the city streets in full retreat, with the rifles of the Americans blazing down pitilessly from the captured heights. There was little attempt at pursuit, for no cavalry was at hand and the men were worn out with a long day of hard fighting. In all 158 prisoners were taken, each of whom made ready for instant slaughter, as had been the pleasing practice in the Cuban war before quixotic Americans introduced new customs. We had lost in this hot day's fight nearly 500 in killed and wounded out of 3500 engaged. The enemy lost half of the thousand men in his trenches. It was a heavy price in human life to pay for one step on the way to Santiago.

Meanwhile at San Juan had been raging a battle almost as sanguinary and quite as fierce. When Lawton's division had branched off to the north on its way to the hard-fought battle-field of El Caney, that part of the army which was designed for the capture of San Juan went straight ahead down the worn and sunken road which led direct to the enemy's stronghold at Santiago. It was not a good road at the best, for on either side of it rose banks three or four feet high, as if it were a ditch — which indeed it further resembled, from the fact that the rains which had now set in had left two or three inches of water at the bottom which the tramping feet of thousands of men soon churned into mud. At points the road was forty feet wide, but at others it was only ten; and as the columns proceeding down it were continuous, the narrowest width fixed its total capacity. The troops marched in columns of twos down either side of the river of mud, while up and down the middle galloped mounted aides carrying orders, and now and then a pack train with ammunition, spattering with mire the plodding men as they passed. In those patient, toiling columns were the dismounted cavalry regiments under Generals Sumner and Wood, including the Rough Riders, and six regiments of regular infantry under General Kent. Their task for the first day was to march to the edge of the woods fronting the Spanish position at San Juan. There they were to bivouac for the night, and in the morning attack, when they heard Lawton's guns at El Caney. It was expected, when the plan of battle was formulated, that the little stone fort on the hill would delay Lawton only briefly, and when he had run over El Caney the troops before San Juan were to swing in behind him, and completely invest the city on the north. But both at El Caney and at San Juan the enemy's stand was unexpectedly plucky, the headquarters plan was smashed, and, but that the soldiers and regimental commanders took authority into their own hands and adopted the tactics that the situation on the field of battle dictated, the day might have been lost. The men who saved the day were ill fed, half clothed, left by the inefficiency of their superiors without food to maintain their health or medicines to restore it when lost. The utterly insufficient methods of maintaining communication with the base of supplies at Daiquiri had resulted in the troops being kept on half rations during the days of the heaviest fighting, — a time when, if ever, a soldier should be supplied with everything needed to keep his physical strength at the highest point. The cheerfulness of the army under these circumstances was the marvel of the foreign attachés. The men accepted half rations or no rations at all, with only a little good-natured grumbling, and the loud cheers which greeted the arrival of a wagon train supposed to be rations changed but little in their note of enthusiasm when the load proved to be ammunition, or even, as in one case, an observation balloon, which in the end served only as a means of making the enemy's fire more accurate and murderous.

San Juan was a typical Spanish stronghold. Along a ridge ran lines of earthworks connecting block-houses which stood on little peaks rising above the general crest of the hill. Before the trenches were entanglements of barbed wire to catch and hold an assailant while the deadly Mausers from the heights beyond did their work. For some hundreds of yards the ground sloped away in front, largely denuded of trees and brush but covered with grass waist deep. The road from Siboney debouched on this clearing at a point in full command of the Spanish guns. To either side of the road extended heavy thickets, through which shells and Mauser bullets could indeed make their way easily, but the passage for men was painful and slow.

The attacking force had spent the night in the vicinity of El Poso. From there to Santiago it was about three miles, and from the place of bivouac the soldiers could see the lights glittering in the streets of the city which was to be their goal. How heavy a toll of human life was to be exacted for passage over that short stretch of quiet country road! Half-way to Santiago was San Juan. Dawn found the troops turning out, cooking a hasty and insufficient breakfast and preparing for the advance. Through the rising mist, ominous foreteller of malarial ills to come, they could look across to the enemy's works, see the Spanish flag floating proudly, and mark the morning smoke rising gently above the red roofs of San Juan. Wheeler's cavalry division — then in command of General Sumner, Wheeler being ill — lay on the hill of El Poso about the guns of Grimes's battery. Kent's division had bivouacked near the road farther back. The task of the morning for these commands was to proceed down the road to a specified point in the enemy's front, there deploy to right and left until Sumner's right should join Lawton's left — the latter officer being expected to have run over the little fort at El Caney by that time — and Kent's left touch the right of Duffield, who was expected to drive the Spaniards from a position they held at Aguadores. Thus completed, the line was to sweep over San Juan and on to Santiago. The first and chief obstacle to the complete fulfilment of the plan was the stubbornness of the Spanish defence at El Caney, where Lawton was held until late in the afternoon instead of being ready to co-operate with Sumner and Kent by nine o'clock, as was hoped. A second obstacle was the failure of Duffield to carry his objective point at all. This did not, however, materially affect the final result, though, had the Spaniards been as aggressive as they were plucky in defence, they might have taken advantage of Duffield's failure to outflank our lines on the left with possibly disastrous results.

Grimes opened fire at sunrise. A great cloud of smoke indicated his position with precision to the enemy, who responded at once with well-aimed shells. The effect showed the onlookers the unwisdom of stationing unsheltered troops near a battery in action, for the enemy's fire fell heavily upon the Rough Riders and other cavalry commands on the hill. They speedily deserted that position and swung into the road, where already the men of Kent's command were trudging manfully along toward the front. The road was choked with marching men, among whose ranks the spiteful bullets were searching insistently for victims. At the head of the column the troops were deploying out into the fields and forest on either side of the road and forming the line of battle. General Shafter, far in the rear, had defined the night before the exact limit of the advance, and had directed that, that spot attained, the army should wait for further orders. The difficulty with this arrangement was that the spot indicated was exposed to the fire of the enemy, who had the range exactly, and the further orders never came. General Shafter says, however, that his plan of the night before was disarranged by the delay at the fort of El Caney, and that when it was found that Lawton would not be able to lead the attack on San Juan, Kent and Sumner were ordered to go on without waiting for him. "They understood," continues the general, "that they were to assail the Spanish block-houses and trenches as soon as they could get into position, for there was no longer any intention of waiting until Lawton should come up on the right." There seems to be some doubt whether Kent and Sumner did understand that they were to make an assault. At any rate, the misunderstanding was such that for a long time the troops were halted under a heavy fire from the enemy, many of them being in the crowded road where a bullet or a shell did double execution. From the long line of Spanish breastworks, from the block-houses on the hill, and from sharpshooters in the bushes and trees came a deadly fire. The rattle of machine guns rose above the din of battle, and their streaming bullets sped down the road, leaving rows of wounded and dead men behind. No wreath of smoke gave a hint of the position of any Spanish gun. A sharpshooter might be perched in a tree within fifty yards of our lines, and if he kept his body hidden he could pick off our men in entire safety. It appeared that many of these sharpshooters had secured hiding-places in the rear of our troops,—a condition always galling and demoralising to the men who suffer. This General Shafter doubts, saying that the long range of the Mausers gave the dropping and almost spent bullets the appearance of coming from the rear; but this explanation seems hardly plausible. There had been so little reconnoitring or skirmishing in the neighbourhood that it is entirely probable an army advancing by night down a single narrow road might have left hundreds of concealed sharpshooters on its flanks and rear.

Under the most advantageous circumstances the advance of a large body of troops along a narrow road is but slow. On this scorching July day, when the sun seemed as pitiless as the bullets, the advance seemed to be at a snail's pace. Well disciplined as the men were, the dropping of a man checked for a brief moment the advance of those behind him, and men were dropping fast. There was no stopping to care for the wounded. The utmost that could be done was to lay them to one side of the road, where they remained until the hospital stewards came along and painfully carried them to the shore of the little brook where the field hospital was established,—"Bloody Bend," the soldiers dubbed it. As the opening of the road into the fields before San Juan was approached, the men defiled through gaps in the fences into the woods on either side, where they spread out to right and left. They were invisible to the Spaniards there, but their position was well enough known, and the fire was pitiless. Every shot from an American rifle furnished the enemy with a target, and many a man on the field cursed the lack of prevision in the department at Washington which had left to the soldiers of a nation boasting itself the most progressive, the old-fashioned and dangerous black powder, while antiquated Spain — "poor old Spain," this Spain which we described as old-fogy, "moss-backed," everything that expressed lack of progress and enterprise — had the best smokeless powder, the best rifles, and plenty of both. But we had some modern engines of war — or at least we flattered ourselves we had. With the Rough Riders was an engine of destruction called the dynamite gun. Its name suggested terrifying possibilities, and its appearance, being unlike any form of artillery known to soldiers, stimulated the imagination of men. But its accomplishments were disappointing. In the hands of a body of picked men of unusual intelligence, enthusiasm, and energy, it still failed to perform any feats of carnage. It was too heavy to get into effective position, its range was limited, and from some fault in construction it was continually getting choked and put out of action. There was also a balloon that was expected to be of inestimable service in reconnoitring. This was not a wholly new idea, as balloons were often employed during the Franco-Prussian war; but it may be said that our use of the balloon with Shafter's army was entirely novel. For on this day of hard shooting and heavy loss, when our lines were within almost point-blank range of the enemy and enjoying only a little immunity from loss because the thickets hid them, the balloon was sent up some fifty yards immediately above a road packed with soldiers. Some of the enemy's marksmen intelligently reasoned that at the point where the controlling cord of the balloon touched the earth there must be men, so they fired there with results profitable to them and disastrous to us. Others let fly at the great ball of silk itself, and their bullets dropping to earth behind fell among our men far back on the road. As an invitation to effective musketry that balloon has not been equalled in military history, and an eye-witness avers that when it had at last been happily disabled by a shot, the officer descending it reported, as the sole fruit of his observations, that he had seen " men over on those hills firing upon our lines," — a fact already sufficiently established by the testimony of our dead and wounded.

A fearful sight was that road after the tide of battle had swept on. Lined on either side with blankets, coats, ponchos, belts, food, and the various impedimenta which the men rushing into battle had thrown aside; the soft soil trampled into mud and soaked at many a spot with a redder and warmer liquid than ever fell from the skies or gushed from the lush stems of tropical plants; dotted all too often with dead men, — some, calm of face, lying on extended backs gazing up into the blue mystery of the heavens, others frightfully distorted as though death had come amidst excruciating pains; here and there a dead horse, or, more pitiful still, a sorely wounded one with a look of dumb suffering and patient wonder in his eyes; the bushes on the side scarred by flying bullets, and even the larger trees shot through and through, — all formed a picture which could never be forgotten by him who beheld it, a picture of war at its deadliest, a picture which showed how the fairest face of nature could be made frightful when man and his hatreds had their way with it.

For hours the devoted soldiers stood in the road of death or lay firing ineffective volleys from the cover of the woods. No order to advance came. The sound of battle coming across the country from El Caney gave no indication that Lawton had carried that point. The bullets cut savagely through the grass, and snipped the leaves from the trees and bushes as fast as though expert wielders of a sickle were there at work. Men whose duty compelled them to expose themselves erect to the enemy's fire were falling fast. Captain O'Neill — " Bucky," most picturesque of the Rough Riders — received a bullet fair in the forehead just as he had boasted, " There is no Spanish bullet made that can kill me." It became plain to the rawest soldier in the ranks that to remain still under that fire meant obliteration. To retreat was not to be thought. A trooper lying flat on his face in a row of his fellows put the feelings of all in a phrase when he grunted, " Boys, I have got to go one way or the other pretty damned quick." But there was only one way for American soldiers in the face of the enemy to go, and suddenly it appeared that all along the line this conclusion was reached at the same moment, and all sprung forward in a desperate charge.

By whom the advance was ordered is a matter not made clear by either the official reports or the accounts of observers on the field. It was seemingly much such a spontaneous act of all on the line as was the capture of Lookout Mountain by Grant's troops, not only without, but in defiance of, the general's orders. Inspector-General Breckinridge in his report says only : " About one o'clock, after a delay of nearly two hours waiting for the troops to reach their positions, the whole force advanced, charged and carried the enemy's first line of intrenchments." General Wheeler in his report says: " It was evident that we were as much under fire in forming the line as we could be by an advance, and I therefore pressed the command forward from the covering under which it was formed." General Kent, whose report gives the best official account of the action, describes the charge as simply part of the general forward movement ordered by him. Some correspondents were inclined to ascribe the assault as due to the sudden initiative of comparatively subordinate officers; thus in the story as told by one appears this description of Colonel Roosevelt's part:

"Colonel Roosevelt, on horseback, broke from the woods behind the line of the Tenth, and finding its men lying in his way, shouted: 'If you don't wish to go forward, let my men pass, please.' Captain Bigelow and the other junior officers of the Tenth, with their negroes, instantly sprang into line with the Rough Riders, and charged at the blue block-house on the right."

Another saw, or thought he saw, General Hawkins wave his hand toward the breastworks, and set that tide of men in blue to rising slowly but irresistibly up the hill. The matter is immaterial. However the order came, the men were ready and eager for it, and the hills were won by the men who carried guns. The charge was not spectacular. The troops advanced by rushes, one platoon running a few yards forward, then falling on its face while at its right another platoon would rise, dash beyond it, and in turn sink to earth. The dismounted cavalry, Roosevelt's men and the Tenth, or coloured cavalry, who supported them on their left, went up almost as individuals; the colonels in the front, Roosevelt mounted and "yelling like an Indian," as one admirer telegraphed home, the men following, stooping low, sending a shot ahead when occasion offered, falling to earth when the enemy's fire grew too hot, and running when there seemed a chance to make a few yards. They fell fast indeed, and the slope behind them was dotted thickly with writhing men or bodies strangely silent, but the advance was uninterrupted. On the left could be seen General Hawkins going up at the head of his brigade of infantry, his erect stalwart figure and determined mien giving his white hair the lie. To his support went speedily the Third Brigade under Colonel Wikoff, who fell ere the crest was reached. Lieutenant-Colonel Worth succeeded him in command, and quickly in death too. So also of Colonel Liscum, the third in command. The Spaniards were firing in volleys, and their machine guns were rolling with devilish zeal from every block-house. Now the point of interest is on the right, where the watchers can see that the Spanish fire from the San Juan fort, as one block-house was called, is slackening. Through glasses the defenders can be seen straggling out of the trenches there and running down the hill, and our men with a new burst of speed swarming around the ends and into trenches and house. It is the cavalry that has been victorious there, for first the yellow flag and then the bright-coloured guidons of the different troops can be seen fluttering on the hill. It can be seen, too, that the end is not yet reached. In the midst of the cheering the victors falter and seem to fall back, as though they had taken a position they were not strong enough to hold. But they quickly pulled themselves together and returned. Meanwhile on the rest of the line the men were rapidly nearing the crest. Here and there a bugle sung notes of encouragement and command. Officers moved along among the men, fairly pushing them forward. To the men left behind, that rising line seemed to be growing perilously thin as it neared the top. Sometimes it seemed about to disappear altogether, broken up into fragments as a great wave is shattered among rocks. It lagged, and the men who still struggled on could be seen to be sorely tired, while the little heaps of dead and wounded grew more numerous minute by minute. In the very front strode a young lieutenant of the Sixteenth Infantry, and by him, shoulder to shoulder, up the slope marched the standard-bearer of the regiment proudly bearing a great flag, while on the other side marched a private and a flute-player, the latter a boy of sixteen who looked years younger. Near the crest the private fell. Lieutenant Ord turned in answer to a faint cry from him. The wound was clearly mortal, and the officer was about to turn away, when the soldier said painfully: " I'm done for, Lieutenant. But you had better take my steel nippers. There may be another wire fence beyond the hill, and I won't be there to cut it for you." The little musician struggled on with his commander, marched by him until in the hour of victory a Spanish prisoner whom he was about to help shot the young officer dead. And still the boy sat by the body. "I was going back," said the little flute-player, when asked how he, so weak and so useless, had joined in that fierce charge. "I wanted to go back to the hospital and look after Colonel Egbert when he fell wounded, and I was doing no good at the front, for my flute is ruined with the mud and rain. But just as I started I heard Mr. Ord say, 'Now, all the boys who's brave will follow me; all the boys who's brave, follow me;' and then he rushed ahead, and kept that up about half an hour, resting a little while and then rushing ahead. And every time he started up he would shout back, 'Now, all the boys who's brave will follow me.' So all the boys followed him, and as I was lighter I got farther ahead than most." "Weren't you afraid, sonny?" asked an officer. Stephen Bonsal tells the story. "I was very fearful, sir, but I was n't afraid."

Soon the Americans were established along the crest which had formed the advanced line of the Spanish position. The enemy retired to a second line, and kept up a vicious fire while our men intrenched themselves as well as might be with their bayonets and hands while awaiting the arrival of intrenching tools from the rear. The glory of the day had been won by the regulars, the Rough Riders alone of the volunteer organisations having any share in it. An unfortunate feature of the day's work was the action of the Seventy-first New York Volunteers, out of which a bitter controversy afterwards arose. It can best be described here in the words of General Kent's official report. After detailing the situation on the road near the ford, he says:

"I hastened to the forks made by this road, and soon after the Seventy-first New York Regiment and Hawkins's brigade came up. I turned them into the bypath indicated by Lieutenant-Colonel Derby, leading to the lower ford, sending word to General Hawkins of this movement. This would have speedily delivered them in their proper place on the left of their brigade, but under the galling fire of the enemy the first battalion of this regiment was thrown into confusion and recoiled in disorder on the troops in the rear. At this critical moment the officers of my staff practically formed a cordon behind the panic-stricken men, and urged them to again go forward. I finally ordered them to lie down in the thicket, and clear the way for others of their own regiment who were coming up behind. This many of them did, and the Second and Third battalions came forward in better order, and moved along the road toward the ford. One of my staff officers ran back, waving his hat to hurry forward the Third Brigade, who upon approaching the forks found the way blocked by men of the Seventy-first. There were other men of this regiment crouching in the bushes, many of whom were encouraged by the advance of the approaching column to rise and go forward. . . . The head of Wikoff's brigade reached the forks at 12.20 P. M., and hurried to the left, stepping over the prostrate forms of men of the Seventy-first."

It was unfortunate for the good name of this regiment of volunteers — one of the "swell" regiments of New York City — that the first fire fell upon officers unused to war, and who seemed to be without the cool courage which would enable them to meet the situation. The men were demoralised by the failure of their leaders. Among them were many who keenly felt the disgrace which they saw coming upon their regiment, and who took their guns and fell in with other commands which were more fortunately led. But the defection of the Seventy-first as a body left the field of San Juan one which was won by regulars almost without aid. The Rough Riders alone carried the standard of the volunteer army high and proudly.

Mid-afternoon found our men in position all along the ridge. The enemy's retreat had been precipitate, but there was no effort at pursuit. General Wheeler reports of his men that after having carried the ridge " they were absolutely unable to proceed farther." Moreover, the question of holding the position won was one which took precedence over any possible pursuit. The enemy had only retired to another line nearer the city, and from thence continued the fire upon the unprotected captors of the hill. The victors had possession of long rows of rifle-pits, facing the wrong way, and several block-houses pierced for firing toward our own lines, but blank on the side of the enemy. The Spanish artillery quickly showed how little shelter the block-houses would offer, and suggested that the fight for possession might have been less bloody had the American troops been as well supplied with cannon. The men lay flat on the crest of the hill, panting with their exertion, and wondering what next. They could not rise to retreat; it would have been madness to go forward. A rush of Dillenback's battery to the crest of the hill gave promise of support, and the men cheered wildly, as the heavy guns came rumbling up the slope, the bright guidons flying, horses galloping, whips cracking, and all swung into position and let fly with a roar. But it was a brief diversion. In full view from the Spanish trenches the artillery men were easy targets for the Mausers, and they fell too fast for their fire to be effective. Limbering up again, the battery rushed back to the spot whence it had come. The Mauser rifle makes artillery useless at the old close range. It was mid-afternoon, and since dawn the men had had nothing to eat, nor was there anything now available, for no rations had come from the rear, the mule trains being busy hurrying ammunition to the front. Later in the day General Wheeler arrived among the rifle-pits which held the men of his cavalry division. He had risen from a bed of sickness to hasten to the sound of the firing, and now went up and down the lines speaking words of encouragement to the men. It was on this day that the wiry veteran of the Civil War delighted his men by climbing a tree despite his sixty-odd years, and shouting from its top: "They're running! They're running! See the Yanks — no, no, I mean the Spaniards, run." When the guns were roaring, the memories of the days when he fought with Lee against the forces of the Union sometimes confused the gallant defender of the Stars and Stripes in Cuba.

General Shafter, too, was drawn from his cot by the news of the battle, and from the hill at El Poso sent orders to the front to intrench, and to the rear to hurry forward the intrenching tools. He expected the Spaniards would attack furiously in the morning, and every nerve was strained to prepare for them. The men who had fought all day worked in relays all night digging trenches. About midnight Bates's brigade, which had fought at El Caney, came up, after a hard march, and was sent in on Kent's extreme left. Lawton, after settling the affair at Caney, had started at once for the scene of battle in the centre, but encountering unexpected resistance, had retraced his steps, and come up from the rear. The march took him until noon of the 2d. General Shafter tells a story illustrative of the tireless patience of the soldiers who fought and marched on those two bloody days. A correspondent, as the Tenth Cavalry was coming into position on the 2d, noticed one of the sergeants, a tall muscular black, carrying a little dog, the regimental mascot, in his arms. "Sergeant," he asked, "did n't you march all night before last?" "Yes, sah." "And did n't you fight all day yesterday at El Caney?" "'Deed, I did." "Did n't you march all night last night too?" "Yes, sah." "Then why are you carrying that dog?" "Why, boss, the dawg's tired."

But while the men to whom the battle left strength and high spirits were working with pick and shovel, or dragging guns into new position, or bringing up more ammunition, or foraging for food, there were sorry sights in the hospitals, and in the spots where the dead were brought for identification and burial. The day had been one of heavy losses. That ridge which now displayed the tattered flags of the victorious regiments had cost dear. Of the infantry, 12 officers and 77 men were killed, 82 officers and 463 men were wounded. Of the cavalry, 6 officers and 40 men were slain, and 223 men wounded.

That night there was grave discussion among the American officers whether the position so gallantly won should not be abandoned. The heavy losses of the day were depressing; the fact that between the heights and the town lay the very strongest point on the Spanish line of defence, the apparent activity of the enemy in preparing to attack in the morning, and the knowledge that not far away were 5000 Spaniards marching to reinforce Santiago, with only the Cubans to keep them out, all combined to make even the stoutest-hearted doubt whether the San Juan ridge could be held, or was worth the holding. It may be noted here that the Cubans failed to cut off the Spanish reinforcements, as indeed throughout the operations before Santiago they failed signally to be of service to our forces. During the night following the action, General Duffield's failure to carry the Spanish works at Aguadores became known, and the officers recognised that the American army occupied the perilous position known in military technology as "resting its left flank in the air." But while these doubts and these problems harassed the minds of the general officers, the company officers and men were working sturdily at the trenches, and the morning of the 2d found the troops on the ridge safely intrenched. The east was just turning gray when the Spaniards opened a heavy fire on our works. Our men withheld their fire except when some especially rash Spaniard offered a target that could not be ignored. Not a cannon sounded from our lines. It was seen that there might be long work and hot work before the city nestling snugly in its nest of hills could be taken, and the word was passed to be saving of ammunition. On the night before, indeed, there had for a time been grave apprehension lest ammunition might actually give out, and our soldiers in this new war for liberty be left as defenceless on the crest of San Juan hill as were the patriots on Bunker Hill a century and a quarter ago. Frederick Remington, the well-known war artist, tells of the enthusiasm with which a pack-train coming from the rear with ammunition was hailed by men who were half starved and who knew well enough that a road crowded with ammunition trains would not get through any rations that night:

"The wounded going to the rear, cheered the ammunition, and when it was unpacked at the front, the soldiers seized it like gold. They lifted a box in the air and dropped it on one corner, which smashed it open.

"'Now we can hold San Juan hill against them garlics — hey, son!' yelled a happy cavalryman to a doughboy.

"'You bet — until we starve to death.'

"'Starve nothin' — we 'll eat them gun-teams.'"

With cartridge belts filled anew, the defenders of the hill crouched all day in the trenches, watchful for an assault and keeping up just enough of a response to compel the enemy to be cautious. Far away on the southwest the deep thunder of the navy's guns could be heard. The fleet was engaging the Socapa battery. In the harbour the hapless Cervera was getting ready to make his dash the next day, and at the rear of our lines General Shafter was considering whether a retreat would be necessary. At half-past nine at night the Spaniards made a vigorous sortie, and drove our men for a few minutes from several points on the line. The positions were retaken, however, and the Spaniards driven back with heavy loss. Shortly afterwards at El Poso a council of war was held to discuss the wisdom of withdrawing to a more protected position. General Shafter had cabled to the United States that the enemy had been driven from his works, but that the American lines were so thin that he might be compelled to take a position farther to the rear. The situation was so abruptly changed the next day by the news of the destruction of Cervera that the general was bitterly condemned for his despatch, and even for considering a retreat at all. The facts seem to show this criticism to be unjust. Many of the officers at the front, including General Wheeler, whose course throughout the campaign came in for the most generous laudation, are said to have advised retreat on the afternoon and night of the 1st. General Shafter himself, so far from being the originator of the plan to withdraw, opposed it. That his cable message was unwise is doubtless true, for it needlessly alarmed the officials at Washington, and would have greatly alarmed the people, and correspondingly have encouraged the Spaniards, had it been published by itself. Happily, however, when the newspapers secured the despatch, the news of Cervera's annihilation was made public as well. It is enough to say of the controversy over the proposition for a withdrawal, that whatever may have been the individual opinions of the division commanders on the afternoon and night of July 1st and through the day of the 2d, when they came to express themselves officially on the night of the 2d, each with one accord voted to stick to the trenches on the ridge. Perhaps the greeting of a soldier whom Shafter passed on his way to the conference, and whose bleeding wounds suggested the price paid for that ridge, even as his words indicated the pride of the men who took it in their achievement, may have had something to do with General Shafter's determination to stick. "They gave us a hell of a fight, General," said the poor fellow, in a weak voice, "but we drove them out." The general saluted and rode on, visibly affected, says one who rode by him.

No battle-field of history, perhaps, has had its incidents, stirring, pathetic, or ridiculous, so fully commemorated in story as this of Santiago. In an age when all men write, and a multitude write well, it was the hunting-ground of an army of correspondents, magazinists, and novelists who dressed with more or less skill the incidents they saw and the anecdotes they heard. The horrors of the field hospital at Bloody Bend have been described by many skilled pens, until behind them the service of those who suffered there that human liberty might make a new and a giant stride seem almost hidden. There had been no expectation of such a great number of wounded as fell at Santiago, and the inevitable cruelties of a field hospital were multiplied threefold. For lack of ambulances, rough wagons, destitute of either springs or cushions, were employed in bringing the sufferers to the hospital. On the hard board floors of these jolting vehicles they slid helplessly about, often jolting down into one bleeding, suffering, screaming mass at the end. At the hospital where the Red Cross flag waved, often without proper respect from the enemy, the surgeons worked all night by fitful, spluttering lamps. The wounded came faster than the swiftest knives could work, and they lay in long rows waiting for attention. For those whom a glance showed to be beyond aid there was little care given, — brutal it seemed to pass them by with a hopeless gesture which too surely told the dying his hopeless state, — but mercy to those whom mercy might aid compelled it. There was dearth of anæsthetics, dearth even of surgical instruments. There was, as at Bingen-on-the-Rhine,

". . . lack of woman's nursing,
There was dearth of woman's tears."

But there was courage amid all the suffering, manliness in the midst of death in its most cruel form. The lives that were yielded up in that hospital were lives mankind could ill afford to spare, for they were the lives of men who had been ready to die for their country.

The next morning, July 3d, General Shafter sent by a flag of truce into the lines of the Spanish a demand for the surrender of Santiago. "I have the honour to inform, you," said the American commander in this communication, "unless you surrender, I shall be compelled to shell Santiago de Cuba. Please instruct the citizens of all foreign countries, and all women and children, that they should leave the city before ten A. M. to-morrow." An audacious demand this, considering that it followed within a few hours a serious consideration on the part of the Americans whether they could hold the line they had won. Audacious too for the fact that, despite the threat of a bombardment, Shafter had really but few heavy siege-guns, and the bombardment by the navy had proved wholly ineffective. It is noticeable that in reporting the despatch of his demand for a surrender General Shafter says he informed all the division and brigade commanders of the fact. It may be presumed justly that the demand was made quite as much to restore the morale of the American troops as in any hope that it would be fruitful. But the flag of truce had been gone but two or three hours when along the lines passed suddenly a rumour that the Spanish fleet had gone to destruction, and Santiago's chief defence was demolished. The news came to General Shafter from Lawton's lines. He sent out at once this bulletin, — a phrase of which adds to the evidence that he felt need of cheering the men in the trenches in every possible way:

"Lieutenant Allen, Second Cavalry, from our extreme right where he overlooked the bay, states that Admiral Cervera's fleet steamed out this morning and engaged our fleet. The French consul who came into our lines yesterday informed General Garcia that Admiral Cervera said yesterday that it was better to die fighting than to sink his ships. Rush this information all around our lines at the front."

The mere news that the Spaniards had gone out to fight was hailed by our men as though it were the tidings of a victory, and when later in the evening the actual intelligence of Schley's glorious triumph arrived, there was pandemonium on the lines. Men leaped to their feet and executed wild war-dances on the crest of the Spanish trenches in full view of the sulking Spaniards, for the truce was still on and no jealous sharpshooter could cut short the rejoicing of any. The bands played patriotic airs, and especially a music-hall ditty which had come to be almost the official air of the army in Cuba, — " There 'll be a hot time in the old town to-night." Bonfires blazed, salutes were fired, — most of them without the connivance of the commanding officers, for there was still a likelihood that graver use might be found for all the available ammunition. Though the response of General Toral, who had succeeded Linares in command of the Spanish forces, came in the midst of the rejoicing, and though it bore a refusal to surrender, it checked the celebration not a whit. The foreign consuls in the city asked that the armistice then in force should be continued longer than had been offered by General Shafter, in order that the women and children might be moved to places of safety. This was agreed upon, and a temporary peace settled down over the battle-scarred field. Both sides employed the lull in strengthening their works. General Shafter moved reinforcements to the front, put mortars and siege-guns in place, brought up reserve rations, and prepared for a long wait. From Washington came orders to consider no terms except unconditional surrender.

CHAPTER XII

Rigidity of the Blockade — The Bombardments — The Marines at Guantanamo — Cervera's Dash for Liberty — The Fleet Alert — Absence of the Flagship and the Admiral — The Controversy over the Honours — Destruction of the "Infanta Maria Teresa" — Capture of Admiral Cervera — Gallant Fight of the "Gloucester" — The Annihilation of the Torpedo Destroyers — The "Almirante Oquendo" Beached — The End of the "Vizcaya" — Magnificent Work of the "Oregon" and "Texas" — The "Cristobal Colon's" Fight for Life — The End of the Spanish Squadron — Effects of American Gunnery — The Disposal of the Prisoners.

OUTSIDE the entrance to the harbour of Santiago de Cuba the men on the great steel ships had been sweltering in enforced idleness, while their brethren of the army had been enjoying and enduring so much. Life on a battle-ship in the latitude of the south side of Cuba in the months of June and July is not like summer yachting. The great ships in their war-paint absorbed instead of radiating the heat, and the atmosphere in the crowded berth-deck and even in the compact little state-rooms of the officers was stifling. Happy were they who could get permission to sleep on the superstructure, where some air at least found passage. The daily routine for both officers and men was quite as arduous as if it were not wholly destitute of anything like glory. Night and day the mouth of the harbour had to be watched. From every ship a certain number of alert eyes were at all times riveted on that point. Columbus in those West Indian waters peered no more eagerly from the bow of his caravel for the first sight of land, than did fifty pairs of keen American eyes gaze toward that gap in the hilly coast of Cuba, looking for the first sight of the advancing vessel that should give signal for a battle by which all that Columbus did for Spain would be undone.

The blockade established by Admiral Sampson was iron in its inflexibility. A 350-foot channel was to be watched, and he closed the doors on it effectually. " I . . . maintained the blockade [at night] as follows," he says in his report: " to the battle-ships was assigned the duty, in turn, of lighting the channel. Moving up to the port at a distance of one or two miles from the Morro, dependent upon the condition of the atmosphere, they threw a searchlight beam directly up the channel and held it there. This lighted up the entire breadth of the channel for half a mile inside of the entrance so brilliantly that the movement of small boats could be detected. Why the batteries never opened fire upon the searchlight ship was always a matter of surprise to me, but they never did."

This, by the way, was also a matter of surprise to the foreign naval attachés upon our flagship. Captain Paget, the British attaché, standing once on the deck of the " New York " when this performance was going on, gazed on the broad shaft of light penetrating the enemy's harbour, and then on the battle-ship lying within easy range of the guns in Morro, and exclaimed fervently, " What d——d impertinence !"

" Stationed close to the entrance of the port were three picket launches, and at a little distance farther out three small picket vessels, usually converted yachts, and, when they were available, one or two of our torpedo boats. With this arrangement there was at least a certainty that nothing could get out of the harbour undetected. After the arrival of the army, when the situation forced upon the Spanish admiral a decision, our vigilance increased. The night blockading distance was reduced to two miles for all vessels, and a battle-ship was placed alongside the searchlight ship with her broadside trained upon the channel in readiness to fire the instant a Spanish ship should appear."

Early in the days of the blockade, before knowledge of Spanish marksmanship or experience with the unwillingness of the defenders of the fort to provoke a conflict had inspired contempt, Admiral Sampson ordered a bombardment in the expectation of so damaging the enemy's works that the ships might lie well in shore without danger. It was this bombardment that Hobson watched from his cell, and in which he came near meeting his end from a shell that struck within a few feet of his window. June 6th was set for the attack, which began shortly before seven in the morning. The fleet attacked in two parallel columns, the works on the east side of the harbour's mouth being bombarded by the column under Admiral Sampson, in which were the "New York," the "Iowa," the "Oregon," the "Yankee," and the "Dolphin,"—two battle-ships, one armoured cruiser, one auxiliary, and one despatch boat. This squadron delivered its fire against Morro, the most imposing but not the most formidable of the harbour defences, the batteries at Estrella Point, and those on Gorda Point. Commodore Schley, in the "Brooklyn," led the second squadron, which included the "Massachusetts," the "Texas," the "Suwanee," and the "Vixen,"—two battle-ships, one armoured cruiser, and two auxiliaries. Later in the engagement the "New Orleans," the British-built ship bought from Brazil, went into the action with her smokeless powder, to the envy of all the other ships, and the cruiser "Marblehead" was permitted a short taste of the pleasures of action. The morning was hot and wet, with frequent gusts of rain and wind, the showers sometimes falling so heavily that the ships were hid from the batteries and from each other. The ships steamed directly in toward the harbour, firing from their bow guns as they advanced, and turning to east and west as they came within a range of from 2000 to 2500 yards, letting fly their broadsides as they made the turn. The fire was deliberate, the greatest attention being given to accuracy of aim. Indeed, the affair had

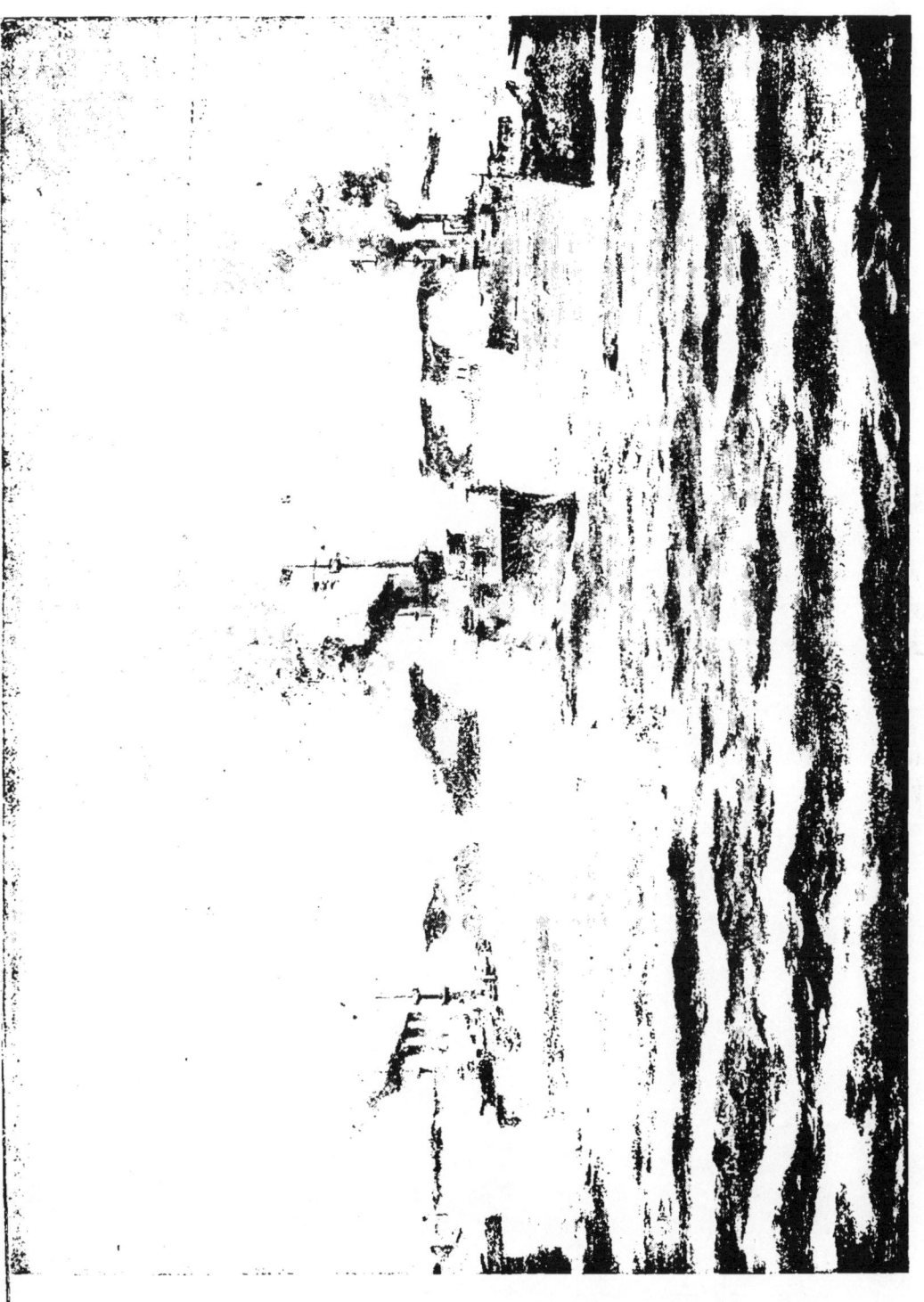

BOMBARDMENT OF MORRO CASTLE, SANTIAGO, BY ADMIRAL SAMPSON'S FLEET.

its chief value, as appeared later, in being a sort of target practice under fire. The attack was kept up for about two hours and a half, the batteries of the enemy being silenced early in the action. But here, as so often in the war, our seamen discovered how empty a triumph it is to "silence" a battery. Looking eagerly from his cell in Morro, Lieutenant Hobson had an excellent opportunity to watch the effect of the American fire, and his story is very convincing on this point. After describing the terrifying effect of the stroke of a 13-inch shell, — "it would raise a great yellow cloud of earth and débris, sending forked shafts of gas out and up for a hundred feet, while for many seconds afterward the fragments would continue to drop about Morro and in the water," — he writes:

"The fire seemed to slacken for a moment; then the enemy opened, and again the fire set in strong against the Socapa sea battery, and I came out, and climbed to the window once more, in time to see the crews of the enemy's guns leave them and run to a pit in the rear. Then I watched for the next lull. Sure enough, up they came again, and fired away. Then our guns reopened in full force, and again the crews retreated to the pit.

"This occurred over and over; and then I realised, even more than in the bombardment of San Juan, that ships cannot destroy shore batteries without coming into machine-gun range. It is necessary actually to strike the gun itself in order to put it out of action. I saw some of our shells literally bury guns with dirt and yet do virtually no injury. Our marksmanship was excellent, — splendid line shots, that tore up the shrubs and earth along the whole front of the battery, — but I did not see a single gun disabled, and every time we would slacken, the Spaniards would come up and fire away. I understood how they could thus make the vaunted 'last shot.'"

In the main the bombardment was fruitless so far as any injury to the batteries was concerned. One or two heavy guns are said to have been destroyed, but most were simply dismounted and quickly replaced after the fleet withdrew. Lieutenant Staunton, assistant chief of staff on the flagship, notes that "a 12-inch shell from the 'Texas' exploded under a 6-inch gun in the Socapa battery, blew it into the air and capsized it, and, it is said, killed all of its crew. Two days afterward that gun was again remounted and ready again for service."

The Spanish cruiser "Reina Mercedes," which came gallantly to the strait at the harbour's mouth to aid in the defence, suffered more severely. A shell burst under her forward turret, and killed one officer, Captain Acosta — who had been particularly courteous to Hobson when that officer was a prisoner on the ship — and sixteen men, and wounded another officer and eleven sailors. Some of our shells fell in the streets of the city, but seem to have done no damage. Mr. Frederick W. Ramsden, the British consul in the city, who by the way made a noble record for self-sacrificing and arduous labours in the cause of humanity during the siege and died shortly after of exhaustion, says in his diary of that date:

"Many shells fell in the bay about three-quarters of a mile distant from our office.... I can't say how many shots have been fired, but firing was continuous from eight to half-past ten, and a lot of powder has been wasted.... The first lieutenant of the 'Reina Mercedes,' Acosta, has been killed. A shell took off his right leg, but he continued to give orders for the care of the other wounded until he died. The ship ... caught fire three times.... Emma wanted to know what the sound like a railway moving in the air was, and was considerably surprised to find it proceeded from the shells flying about."

The ships drew off virtually unhurt by the Spanish response to their fire. On the 14th of June and for a day or two thereafter the attack was renewed in the same deliberate manner. To those on the vessels it was only a more exciting variety of target practice. The men in the forts have not recorded the emotions excited in their breasts by the storm of projectiles, grading from 13-inch shells downward, but Consul Ramsden in his diary describes the striking of one shell in the water which threw up a column of spray as high as the mast of a ship, and further notes the very disquieting fact that "any quantity of shells of all calibres are being picked up intact." He instances one 13-inch shell which he saw himself unexploded. But despite the noise and the prodigious expenditure of ammunition, the batteries that kept guard over Santiago were as strong after the several bombardments as they were before.

The bombardments, however destitute of results, were an excellent expedient for keeping up the spirits of the men, and steadying nerves sorely strained by the ceaseless watchfulness and apprehension of the blockade. Though the inexplicable inertness of the Spaniards resulted in a month of absolute immunity from attack, the ships were at all times exposed to danger, and the nervous strain was almost as great as if a more active enemy had been confronted. Most of the time the ships were within easy rifle-range of the batteries, and while the armoured hulls were impervious to small projectiles, the upper works, where because of the heat many men slept, were vulnerable to Mauser bullets. The men who operated the searchlights, too, were absolutely without protection from any form of firearm the Spaniards might see fit to employ against them. Night after night the most conspicuous thing on the coast was the great eye, gleaming white, and sending a long beam of fierce light straight into the harbour. No armour protected the delicate apparatus of this beacon, nor the men who served it; but not once did the Spaniards try with Mauser or with great guns to demolish it, though it was within easy range of either weapon. But the men in the tops of the searchlight ship did not know how long the gunners on shore would resist what must have been a temptation to any expert artillerist, and they expected a shot at any minute. Of course the small boats plying close in shore as pickets, particularly charged with watching out for torpedo attacks, kept their officers and crews under a continual strain. On them the Spaniards did indeed try their marksmanship, with negative results as a rule, but with a sufficient percentage of hits to keep the targets alert. The knowledge that in the harbour lurked the much dreaded torpedo boats was also a continual source of anxiety. Not only the danger to the picket boat should one slip out unperceived, but the certainty that any failure in watchfulness might result in the loss of a great battle-ship, kept the commanders of the scouts keyed up to the highest pitch. A torpedo boat at night is a phantom object, and many a phantom has been taken for a torpedo boat by even cool officers when charged with heavy responsibility. Men who are constantly looking for something are apt to find it, even if it is trouble; and so now and then some officer, after peering anxiously through a pitchy-black night for hours at a time in expectation of a Spanish torpedo boat, would see one coming perfectly distinctly, and then all the small guns on that ship would roar, and the signal to look out for a torpedo attack would flash high up in the air, and all the other vessels would move anxiously and begin to spit fire and bellow noisily like a herd of elephants when a mouse runs across the floor. One night a railroad train running along the road bordering the sea caused the alarm, and the shot-riddled cars were shown next morning in Santiago in evidence of Yankee barbarity. Another night the back hollow of a cave, with the white breakers tumbling on the rocks at its entrance, suggested to a picket boat well in shore that a dark torpedo boat was coming out at full speed with a tremendous bone in her teeth. These things were humorous in the telling afterwards, but at the time they were deadly earnest, and the men who went through them found the blockade anything but unexciting.

In the naval service of every nation is a body of amphibious soldiery who serve aboard ship — the marines described by Kipling as "soldier and sailor too," and the butts of many a Blue Jacket's scoff and story. In the earlier days of naval warfare the chief duty of the marine was to act as a sort of ship's policeman, keeping order aboard in time of peace and serving as a rifleman in battle. To some degree these functions are still filled by the marine corps; but it has become more of a martial organisation than of old, serving at rapid fire-guns during battle, and always the first to be landed when a shore party is needed. For weeks a detachment of marines had been stewing in the hot confines of the transport "Panther" at Key West, awaiting the discovery of some point at which they could be of service. When the news that Cervera was cooped up at Santiago reached Sampson, they were hurriedly sent for, and had no sooner reached the fleet than a task was assigned them which tested all their qualities of individual bravery and discipline.

Not quite forty miles east of Santiago lies the bay of Guantanamo, with a small town of the same name at its upper end. It is an excellent harbour, then not at all formidably fortified, and offering a safe shelter for warships and an easy landing-place for troops if such were needed. In the early days of June Admiral Sampson thought that such a landing-place would be needed. He knew that the army was painfully and slowly mobilising at Tampa, and that a great fleet of transports was gathering there to bring General Shafter's corps to the neighbourhood of Santiago. It occurred to the admiral to prepare the way at Guantanamo. If the army did not like that landing-place, possession of the harbour would still be useful to the navy, for coaling and repairing. So the "Panther" had hardly reached the blockade with her 600 marines aboard before they were ordered to Guantanamo, where the cruiser "Marblehead" and the auxiliary "Yankee" had been preparing for their reception by diligently shelling the earthworks the Spaniards had thrown up on the shore. It was impossible to tell how vigorous a resistance the enemy would offer to the landing-party; so the "Oregon," the "Yankee," the "Yosemite"—with a crew of naval militiamen clear from Michigan—the "Scorpion," the "Dolphin," and the supply-ship "Supply" were sent along. They were not needed. The Spaniards made no resistance —indeed, throughout the war they never fought our troops at exactly the moment when resistance would have been most effective, namely, when we were landing from boats. With hardly a rifle-shot, and while the band played cheerily "There'll be a hot time in the old town to-night," the marines landed, pitched their tents, and went into camp. It was as peaceful as a picnic. The Spaniards, when driven away by the fire from the "Marblehead" and the "Yankee," had left a flagstaff standing, and there the Stars and Stripes were run up, while the marines stood in line at a "present," and the ships in the bay fired a salute and cheered the colours. That was really the first landing of our troops on the south side of Cuba, for this was on the 10th of June,—twelve days before Shafter began landing his troops. The camp was named Camp McCalla, in honour of the commander of the "Marblehead," and the men set to work making it tenable for a long stay by burning infected Cuban huts in the vicinity, landing provisions, and fixing the camp kitchens. The spot seemed so peaceful that about evening many of the men, hot and wearied with a long day's work, stripped and went down to the beach to bathe. While they were disporting themselves, a Cuban came running into camp closely pursued by Mauser bullets. From the brush on the hills sounded the crack of rifles, and the vicious whistle of the bullets rung in the air. Naked men caught up rifles and cartridge-belts, and ran to where the officers were forming the companies and sending company after company out to the firing-line. They were absolutely green men, most of these marines, and the attack was a complete surprise; but they responded like veterans to the word of command, and poured their volleys into the bush with coolness and precision. The fighting was not long that afternoon, for the enemy soon drew off; but two of our men had fallen, — the first to lose their lives on Cuban soil, — James McColgan, and William Dunphy, privates both. At night the enemy returned to the attack, not charging or attempting to carry the American position in any way, but lurking in the bushes and potting away at the tents and the dark figures of our men outlined against the sky. All night this was kept up, effectually preventing the marines from getting any rest after their hard day's work. About midnight Surgeon John B. Gibbs was killed, the first United States officer killed in action in Cuba.

The next morning Colonel Huntington concluded to move his camp to lower ground, where the men would not form such conspicuous targets. The task was a wearing one. Never had the tropic sun been hotter than it was while the marines were painfully carrying tents, boxes, and bedding down the blazing hillside, while the Spaniards in the bushes popped away with their Mausers. Crouching in the bushes, with palm-leaves tied about them and using smokeless powder, the assailants were literally invisible to the Americans. Though the ships joined with the men on shore in shelling the bushes, the aim was at random, and if it did any execution did not check the Spanish fire. Neither did two raiding-parties sent out through the bush put an end to the persecution. It was like fighting a lot of gnats. All day of the 11th and the 12th this fighting went on. At night the Spanish fire slackened but little. Not even the American burial-parties were sacred to them, and their bullets poured quite as fiercely upon the men who drew up beside the chaplain at the grave of the dead as upon those on the firing-line. The marines dug trenches and landed their three field-guns, but to little effect. The "Marblehead" ransacked the bushes by night with searchlight and shell, but still the nagging stream of bullets flew from the thickets. Machine guns had as little effect. It began to look as if the marines would have to learn to ignore Mauser bullets altogether or take to the ships again.

However, a scouting-party learned that the Spaniards had a sort of base not far from the camp, where there was a reservoir of drinking-water, the only supply in the neighbourhood, and a heliograph for communication with the fort at Caimanera at the head of the bay. With a small company of Cubans, who fought bravely, a force of marines marched against this post, and destroyed it, burning the block-house, smashing the water-tank, and capturing the heliograph. Seventeen Spaniards and one officer were taken, and sent aboard the "Dolphin," which had followed the expedition along the coast. It was learned that the Spaniards had 2000 men in the vicinity, and people wondered why they had not swooped down on the 600 marines and gobbled them up. But, as General Garcia said in a conference on the "New York," "The Spaniards never attack. Remember that. The Spaniards *never* attack." How many they had lost in the four days of fighting was never known. The Cubans claim to have counted the bodies of fifty dead.

This much having been accomplished towards making the camp at the mouth of Guantanamo Bay tenable, the navy concluded to finish the job by running up to Caimanera at the head of the bay and smashing the Spanish forts there. The "Texas," "Marblehead," and "Suwanee" undertook this task, and after a three hours' bombardment silenced the fort in the traditional way. The garrison ran away promptly, some rushing down to a train for Santiago which was in full view of the ships, and at which the "Texas" sent a 6-inch shell as it pulled out. At the end the forts were still formidable had the garrison chosen to return to the defence, but apparently the

BATTLESHIP "MASSACHUSETTS."

commander of that district was content to abandon the neighbourhood, for thereafter the navy used Guantanamo Bay without molestation and the marines' camp was not disturbed. It is interesting to note that in their way up the bay both the "Texas" and the "Marblehead" fouled contact mines with their propellers. Neither mine exploded, though, when hauled on deck and dissected, each was seen to be powerful enough to sink any ship under which it should be discharged.

On all the ships about Santiago harbour were now heard the two questions, "When will the army come?" and "When will Cervera come out?" All lingering doubt about Cervera's presence — though, indeed, there was little left — was ended by the daring reconnaissance around Santiago of Lieutenant Victor Blue, undertaken on the 13th of June. This young navy officer had already distinguished himself by slipping through the Spanish lines on a mission to General Gomez. In his second expedition he crawled through dense thickets, infested with guerrillas, passed through the Spanish lines where if taken he would have been instantly hanged as a spy, found a spot on the crest of a hill whence he could look down on the harbour and count all the Spanish ships that were known to have sailed from Cape Verde, with the exception of the torpedo destroyer "Terror," and then returned to the sea west of the city, having made a complete circuit of Santiago. The exploit was one of the most daring of the war. Its success makes all the more inexplicable the apparent lack of just such expeditions in front of the army before it advanced on Santiago.

On the morning of the 20th fleet tugs came up to the blockade, bringing news of the presence of the army expedition in the offing, and a few minutes later the "Detroit," one of the convoying ships, came up with the same tidings. Admiral Sampson went down in a cruiser to meet the incoming armada, and the hills of Cuba resounded with the salutes of the warships to the general and the cheers exchanged by sailors and soldiers. It was a historic moment, this meeting of the two wings of the armed service of the United States on that distant foreign coast. It was the beginning of the end of Spanish misrule in Cuba; that was patent to all beholders of the monster armament there gathered. Sampson in a launch went off to call on General Shafter, and shortly afterwards the headquarters ship, "Seguranca," came up to the blockade, and the admiral and the general made that visit to Garcia's camp which has been described already. Thereafter for a day or two the navy was employed in shelling the coast defences preparatory to the landing of the troops and in assisting the actual disembarkation. The one incident of interest in this extended bombardment was the explosion on the "Texas" of a 6-inch shell, one of the few hits scored by the Spaniards in the war and the cause of the death of the first man killed afloat in the Santiago campaign. The "Texas" was bombarding the enemy's works at Cabañas, and ten transports lay in the offing as though awaiting an opportunity to land their cargoes. So vigorous and well directed was the Spanish fire that the affair which was intended as a mere feint developed into a fierce duel between the ship and the artillerists on shore. The range was about 5000 yards, and while the aim of the navy gunners was good, their lack of explosive shells enabled the enemy to stick to his guns. At last a 6-inch shell struck the battle-ship on the port bow about five feet below the main deck. It pierced the steel plate, at that point about an inch and three quarters thick, and exploded in the forward compartment, where fifteen men were standing at quarters. The steel-clad room was instantly filled with flying bits of iron. A great steel stanchion was cut in two, a 4-inch hawser and the oaken core on which it was wound were cut as with axes. The side of the ship opposite that by which the shell entered was bulged out three inches, and bolt-heads, gun-fittings, ribs, everything that came in the way of the storm of steel disappeared in general ruin. A man who was directly in the path of the missile was blown to atoms, and eight others were wounded; but the wonder is that any in that pent-up room with bits of steel and iron flying like grape-shot escaped alive. It was natural that when the officers came to gaze upon the scene, the first opportunity any of them had had to view the effect of a big modern shell in a warship, they should remember that projectiles twice as large were fired from every battle-ship on that station. "Well, if that is the work of a 6-inch shell," said Captain Philip of the "Texas," "I wonder what a 13-inch would do?"

The drama which was being enacted around Santiago was now rapidly approaching its denouement. The men on the great gray ships that clung so closely to the narrow entrance to the harbour knew that before many days the Spaniards must come out and fight, unless they intended to await the capture of the city by the American troops, and be compelled to blow up their vessels at their berths. But they did not know that during these very days the cable, which no American ship had been able to find and cut, was bringing from Madrid orders to Admiral Cervera to make the dash for freedom. Cervera had indeed protested. None knew better than he how inadequate were his ships to meet the storm of fire that lay in wait for them beyond the shelter of Morro. The days that he had lain quietly at anchor had been to him as the period in jail before the day of execution is to the convicted criminal. He is said to have wept, when he entered Santiago, knowing that his squadron would never escape; and he received now, as July was ushered in, the orders of General Blanco to make the dash, with resignation and without hope.

On paper the fleet which Admiral Cervera had under his command was a formidable one, but its actual strength was materially less than that with which it was credited in the naval manuals. Instead of the speed of from 18 to 20 knots with which his ships were credited, they proved, when put to the test, to be slower than our 16-knot cruisers. His flagship, "Cristobal Colon," was without the 11-inch guns for which she was fitted, but which the Spanish navy authorities, though war had been imminent for more than a year, had never had mounted. The discipline of the crews was of the most slovenly, and their marksmanship, as was proved later, was beneath contempt. It had never been the practice in the Spanish navy to buy powder and shot just to shoot away in target practice. Notwithstanding all weaknesses, however, the squadron was the strongest body of modern men-of-war that had up to that time been despatched from any European port on a mission of war. The flagship, the "Cristobal Colon," was an Italian-built armoured cruiser. The armour belt on her hull was six inches thick, on her barbettes five inches. Her complement was 500 men; her armament, in the main battery, two 9.84-inch and ten 5.9-inch rapid-fire rifles; secondary battery, six 4.7-inch rifles, ten 6-pounder and ten 8-pounder rapid-fire, and two Maxim guns. The displacement of the "Colon" was 6800 tons, or about that of the "Texas." The three cruisers that followed the flag of the "Colon"—the "Vizcaya," "Almirante Oquendo," and "Maria Teresa"—were sister ships, so alike in proportions and appearance that in Havana harbour Captain Eulate of the "Vizcaya" told Captain Sigsbee that his ship could only be distinguished from the others by some trifling differences in the gilding on the stern, and the carving of the woodwork. The description of these magnificent ships was: displacement, 7000 tons; length, 364 feet; speed, 18.5 knots; complement, 500 men. Guns: main battery, two 11-inch Hontoria, ten 5.5-inch Hontoria rapid-fire guns; secondary battery, eight 6-pounders, ten 1-pounder rapid-fire, and several machine guns. Added to this squadron o fighting craft were two torpedo destroyers, "Furor" and "Pluton," sister ships, of 380 tons, manned by 67 men each, carrying two 14-pounders, two 6-pounders, two 1.45-inch automatic guns, and two torpedo tubes each. All the Spanish ships had the usual complement of torpedo tubes. On paper — that phrase must constantly be returned to, for the estimated qualities of the Spanish ships differed so greatly from their actual accomplishments in battle — on paper there were in this squadron elements of actual superiority over their foes. It was equipped with smokeless powder, a great advantage. The Hontoria guns were regarded by naval experts, the world over, as better, weight for weight, than the American guns, being more rapid in action, and of greater muzzle velocity. In speed — again on paper — the Americans had only two ships equalling the Spanish vessels. On the day of battle one of these ships, the "New York," was absent from the blockade, and the other, the "Brooklyn," had one engine uncoupled and useless. What in more daring hands would have been a notable element of superiority in the Spanish fleet were the two torpedo-boat destroyers, splendid vessels of their class, and unmatched by anything in the United States navy.

The American fleet that engaged Cervera on his appearance at the harbour's mouth was notably superior in weight of metal, besides outnumbering the Spaniards. The "New York" may be left out of the calcalation, as she was absent from the blockade when Cervera made his dash, and came up only after the surrender. The fleet actually engaged was composed of three first-class battle-ships, one second-class battle-ship, one armoured cruiser, and a converted yacht. The descriptions of the ships engaged are as follows:

Iowa, battle-ship, 11,340 tons; complement, 505 men. Armour: belt, 14 inches; barbettes, 15 inches; turrets, 15 inches. Guns: main battery, four 12-inch, eight 8-inch, six 4-inch rapid-fire; secondary, twenty 6-pounders, four

1-pounders, four Colts. Two torpedo tubes. Speed, 17.1 knots. Commander, Captain Robley D. Evans.

INDIANA, battle-ship, 10,288 tons; speed, 15.5 knots; complement, 473 men. Armour: belt, 8 inches; deck, $2\frac{3}{4}$ inches; barbettes, 17 inches; turrets, 15 inches; casements, 6 inches. Guns: main battery, four 13-inch, eight 8-inch, four 6-inch slow-fire; secondary rapid-fire battery, twenty 6-pounders, six 1-pounders, four Gatlings. Torpedo tubes, two. Commander, Captain Henry C. Taylor.

OREGON, battle-ship, 10,288 tons; speed, 16.8 knots; complement, 473 men. Armour: belt, 18 inches; deck, $2\frac{3}{4}$ inches; barbettes, 17 inches; turrets, 16 inches; casements, 6 inches. Guns: main battery, four 13-inch, eight 8-inch, four slow-fire 6-inch; secondary rapid-fire battery, twenty 6-pounders, six 1-pounders, four Gatlings, and two field-guns. Torpedo tubes, three. Commander, Captain Charles E. Clark.

TEXAS, second-class battle-ship: displacement, 6,315 tons; speed, 17.8 knots; complement, 389 men. Armour: belt, 12 inches; deck, 2 inches; turrets, 12 inches. Guns: main battery, two 12-inch, six 6-inch slow-fire; secondary rapid-fire battery, six 1-pounders, four 37-millimeter Hotchkiss, two Gatlings. Torpedo tubes, two. Commander, Captain John Philip.

BROOKLYN, flagship of Commodore Schley: displacement, 9215 tons; speed, 21.9 knots; maximum coal-supply, 1461 tons; complement, 516 men. Armour: belt, 3 inches; deck, 3 to 6 inches; barbettes, 8 inches; turrets, $5\frac{1}{2}$ inches. Guns: main battery, eight 8-inch, twelve 5-inch; secondary battery, twelve 6-pounders, four 1-pounders, four Colts, and two field-guns. Torpedo tubes, four. Commander, Captain F. A. Cook.

The "Gloucester" and "Vixen," which completed the roster of the vessels available for meeting Cervera, were converted yachts. The former mounted four 6-pounders. Under the command of Captain Richard Wainwright, who had been with Sigsbee on that dreadful night when the "Maine" was assassinated in the harbour of Havana, she did gallant service in the day of battle.

To the layman the American squadron seems vastly superior, — an impression which is, of course, strengthened by the completeness of the victory it won. But just as the naval experts, even in our own service, at the beginning of the war thought the Spanish and United States navies very equally matched, so students who made their estimates of the comparative strength of the two squadrons at Santiago from the data set down in the books were not inclined to attribute any overwhelming superiority to the Americans. Mr. H. W. Wilson, a well-known English authority on naval affairs, writing after the battle, declares that the Spaniards were not so very deficient in anything except the skill to fight their ships. He makes an interesting comparison of the number of shots each squadron could deliver in five minutes, which shows that if the Americans had more guns, the Spaniards, by virtue of having more of the rapid-firing type, could discharge more projectiles in a given time. The exact figures for the space of five minutes, leaving out of the question the very small guns of the secondary batteries, are: Americans, 290.5 shots, with a total weight of 39,400 pounds; and Spaniards, 367.5 shots, with a weight of 31,200 pounds. Nor was the difference in the weight of metal hurled so great an advantage to the Americans as might appear, as it proceeded chiefly from their possession of more heavy guns, — the 12-inch and 13-inch calibres. As a matter of fact, only two shells from cannon of these great calibres hit their marks, so that the possession of these guns to the Americans was of but slender value.

It is worth while to consider these comparisons before taking up the story of the battle, because they are the sort of estimates our officers had been making for days and weeks before the crucial time of battle came. With access to all the latest naval statistics they were able to figure out exactly — so far as calculations in which the comparative gallantry of men must remain an unknown factor can be exact — the chances of the battle that was coming. When it was over, and won so completely and with so little loss, there was a tendency on the part of many to think it had been a most unequal affair, after all. It was unequal only because the Yankee seamen had planned to fight it as if they were meeting an enemy actually their superior. It was easily won, not because of the heavier guns of our ships, but by the better shooting of our gunners. We suffered little, not because our armour was thickest, but because every man from captain to powder-boy gave force and effect to Farragut's maxim, "The best defence against an enemy's fire is the fire of your own guns."

It was Sunday morning, July 3d, and on all the ships, as they floated heavily in their great half-circle, eight miles long, about the mouth of Santiago harbour, the men could be seen swarming out on the decks, clad in fresh, clean white clothes for general muster. The iron ring was not drawn as tightly as usual, for about nine o'clock the "New York" had hung out the signal "Disregard flagship's movements," and steamed off toward the east. She had gone to take Admiral Sampson to a conference with General Shafter, for which the general, whose troops that morning were just resting after the bloody assault on San Juan hill and El Caney, had long been asking. The absence of the "New York" made the blockading line west of the harbour ragged and weak. The little picket boat "Vixen" was there, and the "Brooklyn" lay to the southwest of the harbour. The "Texas" was directly south, and the three big battle-ships, "Iowa," "Oregon," and "Indiana," made a curve from the "Texas" inshore east of the Morro, with the "Gloucester" farthest east and nearest inshore. It was, perhaps, the most ragged appearance the blockading line had presented since the cordon was drawn nearly five weeks before. None of the ships had full steam up, the

"Iowa" and "Indiana" had both reported some trouble with their forward turrets, and the "Brooklyn's" forward engines were uncoupled. It is not probable that there was any conscious relaxation of watchfulness, but it is evident that conditions were about as favourable as they could be for an effort to break the blockade. Probably the general expectation was that when Cervera did make his dash he would make it at night, but he has himself said that the blockade seemed more impenetrable at night than by day. This morning saw the one ship which was supposed to be able to compete with the Spaniards in speed absent, and a broad gap in the blockading line. Cervera, under peremptory orders to sail, doubtless figured that he could leave the heavy battle-ships behind, and if the "Brooklyn," which alone was supposed to have a chance in a race, should pursue him, he could turn and overwhelm her with his superior force.

All the night before the lookouts on the fleet had reported fires burning on the hills, and this morning Commodore Schley, who had command in Admiral Sampson's absence, had signalled to the "Texas," "What is your theory about the burning of the block-houses on the hill last night?" The commodore sat on the deck of the "Brooklyn" awaiting an answer to his signal, and incidentally watching a cloud of smoke which was rising from the interior of the harbour behind the hills. It was a phenomenon to be watched, but it did not necessarily mean anything serious, for about that time in the morning a tug was apt to make a visit to the Estrella battery. There had been so many other hot and quiet Sundays that all hands concluded that another one was there, with attention to general muster the most serious business for the officers, and the danger of being caught at inspection in a badly washed jumper the gravest peril to the Jackies. But nevertheless the smoke was watched, and presently, when the quartermaster on the forward bridge said quietly to the navigating officer, "That smoke's moving, sir," that officer thought it worth while to take a peep himself. What he saw nearly made him drop the glass. The moment for which the fleet had waited five weeks, the hour of trial for which some of those blue and white clad men had been educating themselves for a quarter of a century, was at hand.

"After-bridge there," he bellowed through a megaphone, "tell the commodore the enemy is coming out."

No need to repeat the message. It was heard all over the ship, and not only the commodore but the powder-boys were rushing for their stations. The cry rung out, "Clear ship for action," and the gongs and bugles which call to general quarters clanged and pealed on the quiet air. From the other ships, so lately peaceful in the Sabbath calm, came echoes of the same martial sounds. The signal "The enemy is escaping" ran to the masthead of the "Brooklyn," the "Texas," and the "Iowa" at the same moment, for on all three ships keen eyes were fixed on that suspicious smoke. Apparently all the vessels on the blockade caught the alarm at the same time. Down came that signal from the flagship, and up went another, "Clear ship for action." Vain trouble! On every ship the men were rushing to quarters, without waiting for the commodore's commands. On every ship men were running to their places, dropping off the white clothes in which they had been prepared for general muster. Everything wooden was tumbling overboard all along the line, water-tight compartments were rumbling shut, battle-hatches were being lowered, hose was being coupled up and strung along the decks to fight fire, ammunition hoists were going, and — greatest of all miracles — while all this was accomplished in the midst of deafening turmoil in less time than it takes to tell of it, at the sudden blast of a bugle the men stood silent at their posts — 500 and more men to a ship, and each one where he would be most needed in battle and each as silent as a mute.

A huge black hull appeared thrust forth from beyond

Estrella Point. It came out far enough to show a turret, and from the turret came a flash and then the boom of a heavy shot. Almost at the same moment a 6-pounder rung out from the "Iowa." The battle was on, and "Fighting Bob" Evans had fired the first shot.

There has been some discussion as to the commander to whom credit for the victory won at Santiago should be awarded. Zealous partisans of Admiral Sampson have contended that though he was absent at the moment of battle it was his plan that was followed in the combat, and that to him therefore attaches the glory. On the other hand, adherents of Commodore Schley have insisted that as the flag officer present at the battle he should reap all the honours. But at the risk of ignoring naval etiquette and of descending beneath the dignity of history, which should perhaps painstakingly judge the merits of this controversy and award the guerdon, I will express the opinion that to no flag officer, present or absent, does there attach any especial and peculiar glory except in the purely formal and perfunctory way that a superior is given credit for the work of his subordinates, even though he has not actively directed it. For the plan of battle that Admiral Sampson had decreed in the event of a dash by the enemy was simply for each ship to make for the harbour's mouth and engage the enemy as they came out. Surely that was a plan not requiring any notable tactical skill to devise, — a plan which left to the individual ship commanders the real responsibility for the outcome of the action. As for Commodore Schley, his greatest glory proceeded, not from any commands which he gave the fleet, but rather from the gallant way in which he rushed the "Brooklyn" to the front, although she alone was weaker than any two of the vessels coming out. It was a day when the fleet commander was effaced and the captains were in their glory. Even the signal that the enemy was coming out was made from at least two of the battle-ships as soon or sooner than from the flagship, and the commodore's signals to clear ship for action and to close in and attack the enemy were in both instances anticipated by every ship in the squadron. For these reasons the acrimonious controversy between the friends of Schley and of Sampson which, as these pages are being written, is raging in the newspapers and in the halls of Congress with such fierceness that deserving navy officers are being deprived of well-earned advancement because of it, will be ignored here. It will be forgotten while the victory off Santiago is still fresh in the memory of man. The officers and men will not be soon forgotten. As Schley well said, " There was glory enough for all."

The first ship out was the " Maria Teresa." Behind her came the " Vizcaya," the " Cristobal Colon," and the " Almirante Oquendo." To meet them all the ships of the blockading fleet were standing in toward the harbour, firing rapidly from every gun that could be brought to bear. According to the plan of the blockade, the American vessels were lying still and had to get under way, — a slow process for a 10,000-ton battle-ship when the enemy is forging past under full headway. Which way the Spaniards would turn when they passed beyond the shoals that extend for half a mile beyond the harbour's mouth, was the vital question then. If they turned eastward, they would have to run into the midst of the most formidable ships of the squadron. If they went directly west, they might outrun the battle-ships and escape. The " Brooklyn," which was fastest of the ships on the blockade, was also in the best position to head off the enemy should they take this course. She was no match for the number of the enemy's ships that would be in a position to engage her when she came up to them, but Schley showed no sign of hesitation. It was possible that his ship would be lost — he says that the contingency entered very clearly into his calculations — but in sinking the " Brooklyn " the Spaniards would be delayed long enough for the battle-ships to come up with them, and once in the clutch of these monsters there was no reason to fear their escape. The difficulty with the "Brooklyn's" manœuvre was that, as it brought her up with the Spaniards on a parallel course and going in a directly opposite direction, she was compelled to make a complete circle in order to chase them. Had they possessed the speed with which they were credited in the naval manuals, this would have put the "Brooklyn" out of the fight, for one of her engines was uncoupled and her speed was greatly reduced. As a matter of fact, however, the Spaniards fell so far behind their estimated speed that not only was the "Brooklyn" able to circle about and still overhaul the fleetest of them, but the "Texas," our slowest battle-ship, was able to hold its own in the race.

The "Maria Teresa" rounded the shoals and turned west. That settled the first problem of the day so far as she was concerned. But was the whole Spanish fleet going to take the same course? Might not Cervera, knowing that in a fleet action we were too strong for him, scatter his ships, in the hopes that the fortunes of war might enable one to defeat her adversary, or at least to slip away through the American lines? That was the next anxiety, and professional students of the battle have since agreed that that was the best course the Spaniards could have pursued. The fortune that overcame Cervera that day, however, impelled him to take his whole line of ships to the west, and the situation for the Americans was cleared of all perplexities. "Close in and engage the enemy," was quite as explicit an order as any captain had need of that day.

The little "Vixen," which lay near the "Brooklyn," let fly with her 6-pounders when she saw the huge bulk of the "Maria Teresa" turn towards her, and then prudently slipped away. But the rest of the American ships, with funnels belching black smoke, and turrets, hulls, and tops spurting out red flame and yellow smoke, came rushing down towards the enemy. Noble work was done by the men whose most important but not spectacular duty it is to feed the roaring fires that drive the great floating forts. In the engine-rooms and stoke-holes of those men-of-war that scorching July day, men worked naked in fiery heat. They could hear the thunder of the guns above them, and feel the ship tremble with the shock of her broadsides. How the battle was going they could not see. Deep in their fiery prison, far below the lapping waves that rushed along the armoured hull, they only knew that if disaster came they would suffer first and most cruelly. A successful torpedo stroke would mean death to them, every one. The clean blow of an enemy's ram would in all probability drown them like rats in a cage, even if it did not cause them to be parboiled by the explosion of their own boilers. A shot in the magazine would be their death-warrant. All the perils which menaced the men who were fighting so bravely at the guns on deck threatened the sooty sweating fellows who shovelled coal and fixed fires down in the hold, with the added certainty that for them escape was impossible, and the inspiration which comes from the very sight of battle was denied them. They did their duty nobly. If we had not the testimony of their commanders to that effect, we still should know it, for they got out of every ship not only the fullest speed with which she was credited under the most favourable circumstances, but even more — notably in the cases of the "Texas" and "Oregon," which, despite bottoms fouled from long service in tropical waters, actually exceeded their highest recorded speed in the chase. On the "Oregon," when she was silently pursuing the "Colon" at the end of the battle, Lieutenant Milligan, who had gone down into the furnace-room to work by the side of the men on whom so much depended, came up to the captain to ask that a gun might be fired now and then. "My men were almost exhausted," said Milligan, "when the last 13-inch gun was fired, and the sound of it restored their energy; and they fell to work with new vigour. If you will fire a gun occasionally, it will keep their enthusiasm up." On most of the ships the great value of the work the men in engine and boiler rooms were doing was recognised by the captains' sending down every few minutes to them an account of how the fight progressed. Each report was received with cheers and redoubled activity. On the "Brooklyn," when the "Colon" was making her final race for life, Commodore Schley sent orderlies down to the stoke-holes and engine-rooms with this message: "Now, boys, it all depends on you. Everything is sunk except the 'Colon,' and she is trying to get away. We don't want her to, and everything depends on you." The "Colon" did *not* get away.

As the enemy came rushing out of the harbour, the American vessels to the eastward steamed down as fast as possible, maintaining a fierce fire the while from everything that could be brought to bear. The batteries on shore turned loose at the Americans, but no attention was paid to them. Nearest the shore was the "Indiana," and she, too, was nearest the leading ship of the enemy at the moment of beginning the battle. The water about this battle-ship fairly boiled with the flood of projectiles that poured down from Morro and sped from the broadside with which the "Maria Teresa" opened. The "Indiana" scored more than one hit on the "Teresa," as that ship was making her turn to the west, and then gave her attention to the "Vizcaya." All the American ships were engaged by this time, and it was almost impossible, in the dense smoke and the storm of projectiles, to make out the success that attended the efforts of any single vessel; but Commander Eaton, who was watching the fight from the tug "Resolute," says: "As the 'Vizcaya' came out, I distinctly saw one of the 'Indiana's' heavy shells strike her abaft the funnels, and the explosion of this shell was followed by a burst of flame, which for a time obscured the afterpart of the stricken ship." Straight toward the fleeing enemy steamed the "Iowa" and "Oregon," belching forth great clouds of smoke until they looked like huge yellow clouds on the water. Then came the time when a cool head and a clear eye were necessary for the captain of an American ship. As the battle-ships closed in on their prey, they overlapped each other, and careless use of the guns or a failure to make out accurately the target might have resulted in one of our ships firing into another. But so skilfully were our ships handled that at no time were they put in jeopardy from either the guns or the rams of each other, though at one time the "Oregon" was firing right across the decks of the "Texas."

The hapless "Maria Teresa" was the first ship to leave the harbour, and her end was swift and frightful. Upon her for a time the fire of all the American squadron was concentrated. The shells from the great turret-guns for the most part went wild, but the 5-inch and 6-inch shells and the storm of smaller projectiles searched out every part of the doomed ship, spread death and ruin on every hand, and soon had her woodwork ablaze. Her gunners for a time stood manfully to their guns, and the scarlet flames jetted viciously from her sides like snakes' tongues. Little smoke hung about her, and she stood out bold and black against the green background of the hills, a perfect target. A shot from the "Brooklyn" cut her main water-pipe; a shell, supposed to be from the "Oregon," entered her hull and exploded in the engine-room; a 6-inch shell from the "Iowa" exploded in her forward turret, killing or wounding every man at the guns; while the tempest of smaller projectiles made the decks untenable, and by the din of their bursting silenced the officers' commands. Admiral Cervera himself was on this devoted ship. "He expected to lose most of his ships," said one of his officers afterwards, "but thought the 'Cristobal Colon' might escape. That is why he transferred his flag to the 'Maria Teresa,' that he might perish with the less fortunate." Another officer who stood by the admiral's side that murderous morning, told an American journalist afterwards some stories of the effect of the American fire. Of a shell from the "Brooklyn" he said: "It struck us in the bow, ploughing down amidships; then it exploded. It tore down the bulkheads, destroyed stanchions, crippled two rapid-fire guns, and killed fifteen or twenty men." And of a shell from the "Iowa" he says: "It struck the 11-inch gun in the forward turret of the cruiser, cutting a furrow as clean as a knife out of the side of the gun. The shell exploded half-way in the turret, making the whole vessel stagger and shake in every plate. When the fumes and smoke had cleared away so that it was possible to enter the turret, other gunners were sent there. The survivors tumbled the bodies which filled the wrecked turret through the ammunition hoist to the lower deck. Even the machinery was clogged with corpses. . . . All our rapid-fire guns aloft soon became silent, because every gunner had been either killed or crippled at his post and lay on the deck where he fell. . . . There were so many wounded that the surgeons ceased trying to dress the wounds. Shells had exploded inside the ship, setting fire to the woodwork, and even the hospital was turned into a furnace. The first wounded who were sent there had to be abandoned by the surgeons, who fled for their lives from the intolerable heat."

The "Teresa" had come within the zone of the American fire at about 9.35 A. M. Within fifteen minutes smoke was rising from her ports and hatches, indicating that she had been set afire by the American shells. The shot from the "Brooklyn" that had cut her water-main made it impossible to extinguish the flames, and, the fire from the American ships growing more accurate and more deadly every minute, she was beached at 10.15 and her flag hauled down. On the "Texas" the men raised a shout of joy. "Don't cheer, men," said Captain Philip from the bridge; "those poor fellows are dying." Admiral Cervera's own race for life and liberty lasted less than forty minutes. Clad in underclothes only, he tried to escape to the shore on a raft, directed by his son, but was captured and taken to the "Gloucester," where he was received with honours due his rank. His voyage away from Santiago covered exactly six miles and a half, and his brief experience with American gunnery cost nearly half his officers and crew.

Behind the "Maria Teresa," at an interval of about 800 yards, came the "Vizcaya," — that crack cruiser which had been sent to New York as an offset to the "Maine's" visit to Havana, and from the decks of which in the harbour of the Cuban capital Spanish officers had looked down with idle curiosity and careless indifference upon the sunken wreck of that gallant battle-ship. We may well believe that when the prow of Captain Eulate's ship came ploughing out from the bay, Wainwright, late of the "Maine," on the little "Gloucester" aimed some shots at her with a special ill-will. But his particular game was of another sort, as we shall see, and the "Vizcaya" under gathered headway rushed on to the west, passing the heavier battle-ships "Iowa" and "Indiana," but receiving terrible punishment from their guns. In a newspaper interview on his arrival as a prisoner in the United States, a lieutenant of the "Vizcaya" spoke of the murderous effect of the shells from the "Indiana." He thought them the 13-inch shells, but it is more probable that they were the 8-inch missiles. "They appeared to slide along the surface of the water and hunt for a seam in our armour," he said. "Three of these monster projectiles penetrated the hull of the 'Vizcaya,' and exploded there before we started for the shore. The carnage inside the ship was something horrible and beyond description. Fires were started up constantly. It seemed to me that the iron bulkheads were ablaze. Our organisation was perfect. We acted promptly, and mastered all small outbreaks of flame until the small ammunition magazine was exploded by a shell. From that moment the vessel became a furnace of fire. While we were walking the deck headed shoreward, we could hear the roar of the flames under our feet above the voice of artillery. The 'Vizcaya's' hull bellowed like a blast furnace. Why, men sprang from the red-hot deck straight into the mouth of sharks."

But the "Vizcaya" lasted longer than the "Almirante Oquendo," which followed her out of the harbour. While the former ship made her turn at the harbour's mouth and headed west on the coast, with the "Brooklyn," "Oregon," and "Texas" in full pursuit, the latter fell an immediate prey to the fire of the "Indiana" and "Iowa." Though accredited with speed equal to that of her sister ships, she lagged that day of all times, and received a fiercer baptism of fire than fell to the lot of any of her ill-fated comrades. She bore the punishment five minutes longer than the "Teresa;" then, with flames pouring out of every opening in her hull, she made for the beach, hauling down her flag in token of submission, while men were dropping from her red-hot decks to the water. Two great Spanish war-vessels were thus destroyed in the first three-quarters of an hour, and the American fleet, as though hungry for more victims, was concentrating its fire now on the two that were left. From the conning-tower of the "Iowa," "Fighting Bob" Evans passed the word through the speaking-tubes to the men in the bowels of the ship, telling them of the victorious progress of the fight thus far; and the cheers that came from below were followed by the forward leap of the ship, as she responded to the increased pressure of steam the willing and enthusiastic stokers coaxed out of the boilers.

Leaving the "Teresa" and the "Oquendo" flaming and smoking on the beach, the chase swept on. The "Vizcaya" was still making a gallant running fight, and the greatest of all the Spanish ships, the magnificent "Cristobal Colon," named after the man who had given to Spain this western domain she was now in process of losing, the ship which alone Admiral Cervera had hoped to save from the wreck he foresaw, was racing along the coast near the shore, and protected from the American vessels in some degree by the "Vizcaya." While she fled, disaster fell upon the two torpedo-boat destroyers, "Pluton" and "Furor." And the story of the destruction of these vessels is also the story of the cool judgment and magnificent courage of Richard Wainwright, late executive officer of the "Maine," then commander of the converted yacht "Gloucester."

As the cruisers came out, Wainwright joined in the general cannonade with his little six- and four-pounders, but he did not join in the chase. With quick comprehension of the situation, he determined that the torpedo destroyers were his fair game, and he determined to await their appearance, meanwhile letting steam accumulate in his boilers in order to have plenty of speed when the crucial moment should arrive. The destroyers were slow to come out. For some reason, yet unexplained, Cervera, schooled tactician as he was, failed to handle them in the only way in which they might be made of service. Instead of bringing them out of the harbour on the lee, or protected, side of the heavier vessels, and letting them slip out when our ships were nearest, he left them to make their appearance alone and undefended. As if this were not enough to insure their impotence and their certain destruction, the destroyers themselves were manœuvred with an entire lack of that audacity and even desperation which alone can make one of these vulnerable craft formidable. Instead of dashing at the nearest American ship, and trusting to the rapidity of their progress and the small target they offered for their safety, both the "Pluton" and the "Furor" followed the example of the cruisers, and turned along the shore to the westward. A torpedo boat is often likened to a serpent, because of its sinister method of attack and of the deadly hurt which it can inflict. But, like the serpent, it is least dangerous in flight. Coiled and ready for a spring, a rattlesnake is a thing of deadly potentialities. Extended at full length, with its long, slender vertebræ exposed, and brittle to the lightest blow, it is easily slain. So with the torpedo boat. Coming head on, at a speed of twenty-five knots, with two deadly missiles ready to let fly, either one of which striking will end the stoutest warship, it is an enemy to unsettle the aim of opposing gunners. Running away, it is only an animate and interesting target. Cervera's torpedo destroyers ran away. The gunners on the larger American cruisers sent a storm of projectiles from the secondary batteries after them, but the real, serious attack was left to the little "Gloucester" and Wainwright. In a cloud of smoke from her own guns, the former yacht sped forward, receiving and ignoring shots from the batteries and the nearer Spanish cruisers. One 6-inch shell would effectually terminate her career, and many were fired at her; but her captain had eyes only for the two destroyers, and only one desire, to come to close quarters with them before they could either be sunk by our battle-ships or strike our vessels a blow. Either of the destroyers was more than a match for the "Gloucester." Their batteries alone were of twice the power, without considering at all the engines of destruction which they could let slip from their torpedo tubes. In a few minutes from the moment the enemy was sighted, Wainwright was engaged with the two destroyers at short range, and under the fire of the "Socapa" battery. The battle-ships which had been firing at them from their secondary batteries soon saw that the "Gloucester" was equal to the task, and desisted. In a very few minutes both destroyers began to smoke ominously, and the rapidity of their fire fell off. Then the "Furor" became erratic in her course, as though her steering-gear had been cut. Wainwright closed in savagely, and his men at their unprotected guns redoubled their efforts. Suddenly, amidships on the "Pluton," there shot up a prodigious cloud of smoke and flame, with a deafening roar and shock that could be felt across the water despite the thunders of the guns. A shell from one of the battle-ships — three afterwards disputed for the honour — had struck her fairly, and exploded either the magazines or the boilers, or both. Broken in two by the rending blast, she sank like a stone. Balked of half his chosen prey, Wainwright pursued the other craft the more relentlessly. She was already clearly crippled, and made pathetic efforts to escape. At last, fairly shot to pieces, she hauled down her flag, and ran for the line of breaking surf, where her men leaped overboard to escape the fierce flames that were sweeping resistlessly from bow to stern below. Changed in an instant from a relentless enemy to a succouring friend, Wainwright manned his boats, and went to the rescue of the survivors on the burning ship. Many were saved, and the Americans had barely left the smoking mass of scorching steel and iron, when it blew up with a resounding roar, and the Spanish torpedo destroyers had vanished. They lasted just forty minutes under the American fire, and at no time had been a serious menace to any American ship. An officer on the " Pluton " afterwards told of the plans and the fate of the destroyers in an interview, some part of which may be quoted here:

"The two torpedo-boat destroyers were to stay behind the armoured cruisers until the American ships closed in, and then they were to dart out, heading straight for the nearest enemy. That was the plan, but see how it failed! We were shot to pieces before we got within half the torpedo-striking distance of the American ships. We found ourselves riddled, and could not strike a blow in return. . . . Our vessel, without armour, offered no place of refuge. On one of the armour-clads a man feels somewhat safer on the lee side of a turret, or with the conning-tower between him and the enemy; but our men were just as safe on the open deck, safer indeed than below, for the shots soon shattered our steampipes, and escaping steam scalded to death the stokers and engineers. . . . We had prepared our torpedo tubes, but before the 'Texas,' now the nearest enemy, was within 1500 yards of us — much too far to use a torpedo against her — our steering-gear was crippled, half of our crew were killed, and our engines were mortally hurt. We steered for a time by the twin screw. We then tried to get behind the 'Oquendo,' not to save our lives, but to save our torpedoes until we could use them. But before we could take the position we intended, the 'Pluton' became unmanageable. The 'Oquendo' used smoke-producing powder at the beginning of the battle, solely to enable the 'Pluton' and 'Furor' to hide. But the smoke did not lie on the water. It rose in fleecy clouds that rendered our position all the plainer to the enemy in the clear strip of the blue, clean water below. . . . The biggest shells were fired so as to ricochet along the water. We could see them coming at us by the enormous splashes they made, and they came straight. Finally, a shell from the 'Brooklyn,' I think, literally stove the torpedo boat to splinters. It passed through the boiler-room, splitting the boiler itself, and letting out steam and scalding water upon the crew to stab them like sword-blades."

The action had now continued for about three-quarters of an hour. The "Infanta Maria Teresa" and the "Oquendo" were blazing on the beach with their colours struck. The two torpedo destroyers were annihilated. The battle-ship "Indiana," which had been distanced by the enemy in his rush to the eastward, had been signalled to turn in toward the shore, and give aid to the survivors on the burning ships. Two Spaniards only were still afloat, — the "Vizcaya," running and fighting bravely in a hopeless struggle for life, and the great "Cristobal Colon," which was rushing, with the momentum of a planet in its course through space, down the coast to the westward. In the chase of these two vessels, the "Brooklyn" held the place of honour. Her station on the blockade when the enemy came out was such as to give her a commanding position, and her speed kept her well to the front throughout. Next to her at the outset was the "Texas," a battle-ship which for years the newspapers had been describing as unlucky and "hoodooed," but which in this battle developed marvellous speed and fought with reckless gallantry. The "Oregon," third in the race at first, by a dash which no one thought possible for a ship of her weight and structure, passed the "Texas," and actually came up with the "Brooklyn," whose tars turned out on deck and turrets to cheer the wonderful fighter from a Pacific coast dockyard. The fire of these three vessels as they sped along, and that of the "Iowa," which was only a short distance in the rear, was concentrated on the unhappy "Vizcaya." She had passed inside the "Oquendo" and the "Teresa" when those two doomed ships were receiving the attention of the entire American fleet, and had, until they were sunk, escaped serious injury, but now with the fire of four of the biggest and best fighting-machines in the world concentrated upon her, the stanch and beautiful vessel began to go to pieces. Her great frame quivered under the repeated blows of the heavy shells that struck it and rung like a boiler-shop in full operation with the incessant clangor of the smaller projectiles. An hour had passed. Of the American ships that started in the chase, only the "Brooklyn," "Texas," and "Oregon" were hanging like hounds on the flank of the quarry. The "Indiana" had been left behind. The "Iowa," too, had stopped to give aid to the burning and drowning men on the two blazing warships. The "Colon" was steaming ahead with no sign of weakness, but the "Vizcaya" seemed like a ship in distress. On her the fire of the three pursuers was concentrated. Admiral Schley, peering around the lee of the conning-tower on the "Brooklyn," said to his captain, "Get in close, Cook, and we'll fix her." The range was then about 1400 yards. A moment before Commodore Schley had asked George H. Ellis, a ship's yeoman who was assisting the navigator, what was the range. The shells were flying fast, but Ellis stepped unhesitatingly from behind the lee of the forward turret, where he was sheltered, and adjusting his stadimeter, turned with the report, "Fourteen hundred yards to the 'Vizcaya,' sir." There was a low moaning sound in the air as a shell came on, a vicious spat, and the man's headless body fell heavily to the deck. "Too bad," said Schley, sorrowfully; but there was time for no regrets. It had been George Ellis's lot to be the one man to offer up his life in exchange for the victory of Santiago.

The word was passed to the turrets and tops of the "Brooklyn" to aim at the "Vizcaya" only. The ship was carried in until the range was less than 1000 yards, or little over half a mile, and the effect of the shots at that distance began to tell. "I don't see any of the shots dropping into the water," complained one of the gunners to the lieutenant in charge of that turret. "Well, that's all right," was the reply; "if they don't drop into the water, they are hitting." And hitting they were. Inside the "Vizcaya" the beautiful woodwork, which had awakened the admiration and at the same time the professional disapproval of Captain Sigsbee when he visited her at Havana, was all in a blaze. The turrets were full of dead and wounded men, the machinery shattered, and the hull pierced below the water-line. Reluctantly abandoning the fight, for he was a brave officer and a gentleman, Captain Eulate turned his ship's prow toward that rocky and inhospitable shore on which already lay piled the wrecks of the "Teresa," the "Oquendo," and the "Furor." As the ship swung about, a shell from the "Oregon" struck her fairly in the stern. The enormous mass of steel, charged with explosives of frightful power, rushed through the steel framework of the ship, shattering everything in its course, crashed into the boilers, and exploded. Words are inadequate to describe the ruin that resulted. Men, guns, projectiles, ragged bits of steel and iron splinters and indescribable débris were hurled in every direction, while flames shot up fiercely from every part of the ship. Between decks she was a raging hell of fire, and when she struck the beach the watchers from the American men-of-war could see what looked like a white line reaching from her bow to the water, which was in fact the naked men dropping one after another over the side to seek the cool relief of the ocean from the fiery torment they were enduring. So the "Vizcaya" dropped out of the fight. Anticipating a little the course of our narrative of the fight, we may tell of the final death-struggle of the ship as it was described in conversation by Captain Evans after the war:

"We had put in toward the 'Vizcaya' after she was beached," said "Fighting Bob," "thinking that since the 'Colon' was in the hands of our fellows we would see what we could do to save some of the poor devils of Spaniards who were grilling there in the burning ship. I had the boats lowered away, and the men went over to the 'Vizcaya' and took off all the Spaniards they could reach. Some of them had almost to be pried off the ship, they were so panic-stricken. In one of the first boats that came to the 'Iowa' was Captain Eulate. He was about half clothed, and had been wounded a little — nothing serious at all, a mere scratch. Why, the Spanish surgeon who tenderly assisted him up our ladder was twice as badly hurt, — had his whole arm shot away, — but was sticking to his commander with dog-like fidelity. Well, Eulate was depressed, of course; but I tried to cheer him up, told him he 'd made a good fight, and had our surgeon look after him. But he was persistently gloomy. Finally I asked him to come down to my cabin and take a drink. He acquiesced, and just as he turned to leave the deck, stopped, looked over to where his ship was smoking and flaming away, and raising his whole arm in the air, said, in a sort of theatrical fashion, 'Adios, "Vizcaya"! Adios, adios!' Well, sir, at that very instant the whole hull of that ship seemed to be lifted in the air by a most tremendous explosion, and she fairly vanished in a cloud of smoke and flying débris. I suppose her main magazine had been reached by the fire, but the event could not have occurred at a more dramatic moment if it had been timed and the explosion regulated by a stage-manager."

Thus the "Vizcaya" dropped out of the fight, at 11.06 according to the timekeeper on the "Brooklyn." One hour and a half had been the period of her endurance of the American shells. The "Colon" was now left alone. Thus far her career had not been glorious, for she had simply run away, not making any effort to stand and give battle to her pursuers, and not even keeping up a very fast fire from her guns. In her speed was her one hope of escape, and her captain trusted to it wholly. From the very first shot of the battle the Spaniards had done nothing but run. Their fire, such as it was, was only intended as an aid to their escape. Had Cervera come out of Santiago intent upon fighting a desperate battle, he might indeed have lost all his ships, but in all probability he would have taken at least one of the American vessels to the bottom with him. His running fight only resulted in the loss of all his ships without inflicting the slightest loss upon the Americans. The "Colon" adhered strictly to the plan which had thus far characterized the Spanish tactics. It was quickly evident to those on the foremost of the pursuing ships that there could be no escape for the fugitive. Even had not the Americans developed unexpected speed, the course of the ships was such that the "Colon" would inevitably be cut off. A cape jutted out into the ocean at some distance before her, which she would have to round. The "Brooklyn," being farther out to sea, was headed for that headland in a direct line, while the doomed "Colon" had a long curve to make to reach it. Commodore Schley saw that the prize was his, and began to lighten the strain on his men, who had fought so well. Firing was stopped, and the men were called out on the superstructure to see what had been done by the guns of the fleet and to watch the chase. Out of the turrets, up from the magazines and engine-rooms, poured the stalwart fellows, smoke-begrimed and sweaty. Far astern they could see the smoking wrecks of the "Oquendo" and "Teresa." Almost abeam was the "Vizcaya," with men dropping from every port. Ahead on the right was the "Colon" fleeing for dear life, while the "Brooklyn," responding to the work of men below for whom there was yet no rest, rushed after relentlessly. As the men crowded on turret top and along the decks to see the wonderful spectacle, they all of a sudden and spontaneously set up a cheer for Admiral Schley. The admiral's eyes moistened as he looked down upon them from the bridge. "They are the boys who did it," he said to one who stood beside him, and he spoke truly. Then the men cheered the "Oregon," which was coming up gallantly, and from that ship the cheers were returned. Signals of a social and even jocular character were exchanged between the three ships that were still in the chase, for now all felt that not even the last of Cervera's ships could escape. A signal from the "Brooklyn" suggested to the "Oregon" that she try one of her 13-inch guns on the chase. The great cannon flashed and roared from the forward turret, and the shell, which rushed past the "Brooklyn" with a noise like a railway-train, fell short. On they sped a little farther, the "Oregon" visibly gaining on the fastest ship of the Spanish navy, a battle-ship built for weight and solidity overhauling a cruiser built for speed. Presently another shell was tried. It fell nearer the fugitive, near enough for the captain of the fleeing foe to read in its splash in the water the death-warrant of his ship. At such a moment some men would turn fiercely and sell their lives as dearly as might be, but that instinct was lacking to the Spaniard. Instead he turned his almost uninjured ship toward the shore and beached her, hauling down his flag as she struck. Either before the surrender or after, her engineer's crew opened and broke the sea valves so as to destroy the ship. If this was done before the flag was hauled down, it was a legitimate and proper act; if after, it was dishonourable and treacherous. Captain Cook went in a boat to take possession of the prize, his crew being ordered not to cheer or exult over the vanquished. The ship had been struck but eight times, and not by shells of large calibre, and she would have been a useful prize but for this sly work below. There were plain indications that officers and men had been drinking heavily. An effort was made to save her by the "New York," which came up just after the surrender. Captain Chadwick, seeing the ship beached and fearing that she would slip off and sink in deep water, laid the nose of the "New York," up against her stern and pushed her gently but firmly up the shelving strand. The manœuvre was useless. Before another day the great cruiser had filled and rolled over on her side and lay a perfect wreck on the desolate and uninhabited shore of Cuba at the mouth of Rio Tarquino. It was the exact spot where the ill-fated "Virginius" expedition tried to land. More scores against Spain than that set down on account of the "Maine" were wiped out that day.

So ended, after less than four hours' fighting, — for the "Colon" surrendered at 1.15 P. M., — a naval battle that possesses many extraordinary and unique qualities. It completed the wreck of Spanish naval power which had been in slow and interrupted progress since our Anglo-Saxon progenitors strewed the Channel with the wrecks of the Invincible Armada. It dealt the decisive stroke in the war which deprived Spain of her last remnant of American colonies. It was of absorbing interest to naval experts in all parts of the world, because it was the only considerable battle in which heavy men-of-war of the modern type and with modern armament had ever been pitted against each other on anything like equal terms. And it was unique in that while the defeated fleet lost six ships, more than 600 men killed and drowned, and 1800 prisoners, many of them wounded, the victors had but one man killed and one wounded. Small wonder was it that when the flag of the "Cristobal Colon" went down and the decks of the American ships were covered with men cheering in a very delirium of joy, gallant Captain Philip of the " Texas " called his officers and crew about him, and, baring his head, said in reverential tone: " I want to make public acknowledgment here that I believe in God, the Father. I want you all to lift your hats and from your hearts offer silent thanks to the Almighty."

Much that was picturesque in the story of this most remarkable naval battle of modern times must be passed over hastily. The gallant effort of the " New York " to catch up with the fighters and retrieve her ill-luck in having been absent when the battle began, merits a passing word. Though technically in command, Admiral Sampson was by bad fortune absolutely out of the battle from beginning to end, near enough to see the fighting but too far away to join in it. He reached the leading ships just as they were closing in about the beached " Colon." Much might be said too of the gallantry shown by men of the " Iowa," " Indiana," " Gloucester," " Vixen," and " Ericsson " in rescuing the Spanish from their burning ships. Never perhaps in the history of war has such dreadful suffering fallen on defeated seamen. Scores were literally roasted alive, for the whole interior of the ships " Vizcaya," " Oquendo," and " Teresa," became like iron furnaces heated white hot. The wounded burned where they lay, for even the decks were red-hot. Men caught below, in engine or furnace room, by the jamming of the battle gratings were condemned to a slow and frightful death. The sight of the carnage and agony crazed men who were otherwise unhurt and in possession of their faculties, so that they were unable to intelligently respond to efforts for their rescue. Men clinging to a ladder on the side of a scorching hot ship had literally to be dragged away before they would loose their hold and drop into a boat below. The American Blue Jackets worked amid flames, on blistering decks, amid piles of ammunition continually being exploded by the heat, and under guns which might at any moment send out a withering blast. It is not too much to say that in their work of mercy the Blue Jackets encountered dangers quite as deadly as those they had met in the fury of the battle.

The poor gunnery of the Spaniards saved our ships from any serious test of their shell-resisting qualities. The "Brooklyn," according to Commodore Schley's report, was struck by shells about twenty-five times, and bore in all some forty scars of the combat. But she was ready to continue, or to begin all over again, when the "Colon" turned over on the shore. The "Iowa" received two wounds, that did not imperil her structure at all, but which it seems impossible could have been sustained without loss of life. One shell exploded on the berth-deck and ripped things up in wholesale fashion. Another entered the coffer-dam, but fortunately did not explode. The "Texas" was hit three times, one shell smashing her chart-house and another puncturing her smoke-stack. The injuries to the other ships were even more trivial. When the complete destruction of the Spaniards is contrasted with this comparative immunity of the American ships, the measure of our superiority in gunnery and our better fortune is suggested. An officer on the "Vizcaya" asserts that shots struck that doomed ship at the rate of one a second. But superior as our gunnery was, a table of hits compiled by an expert for the "Scientific American" from the official report of the Survey Board, shows how far we fell short of that ideal gunnery which figures so generally in newspaper accounts as "making every shot tell." After counting with the utmost care all the shot-holes on the wrecks that were above water or visible, the Board reported the following "palpable hits," classified according to the size of the calibre of the striking shells:

Size of Gun.	Number of Hits on each Vessel.				Total Hits by each Calibre of Gun.	Number of Guns of each Calibre in Action.	Number of Hits per Gun.
	Teresa.	Oquendo.	Vizcaya.	Colon.			
6-pounder	17	43	13	4	77	42	1.83
1-pounder	2	..	..	..	2	13	0 15
4-inch	1	7	4	2	12	3	4.00
5-inch	3	3	7	1	15	6	2.50
6-inch	1	1	..	1	3	7	0.43
8-inch	3	3	5	..	12	18	0.67
12-inch	2	..	..	..	2	6	0.33
13-inch	..	..	..	..	..	8	0.00
Totals	29	57	29	8	123	103	

The impressive facts shown by this table are, first, that our 13-inch guns did no execution at all, and our 12-inch guns scored only two hits; second, out of at least 6000 shots fired, only about 300 were effective. Allowance must be made for shots beneath the water-mark that could not be identified by the investigators and for those that did execution by bursting above the decks. But they change the results little, and the statistics of the wounds in the defeated ships demonstrate that, good as the Yankee gunnery was, it took many a shot to make a hit. It shows, too, that the maximum of execution was done by the rapid-fire and small-calibre guns. The slaughter on the Spanish ships and the flames which made them untenable came from the storm of small projectiles which relentlessly searched out every part of their structures. So completely were they riddled by these projectiles, and so destructive was the work of the flames they kindled, that, despite the eagerness of the Americans to save and repair one ship as a trophy, the only one which seemed to offer the slightest hope that the endeavour could be made successful was the "Teresa." She was raised by Lieutenant Hobson after costly and tireless efforts, but on her way North to be refitted she encountered a storm and was abandoned by her commander as sinking. Nevertheless she floated sixty miles and went ashore on Cat Island, where after another survey it was thought inexpedient to try to raise her. So of the more than $12,000,000 worth of Spanish ships and fittings destroyed that day, the Americans were unable to save anything. For them is only the remembrance of a victory so complete and so extraordinary that no trophy is needed to keep it fresh in the minds of the people. The almost 2000 prisoners were kept humanely and kindly cared for on the American ships until a great ocean-liner could be sent from the North to take them to their prison camp on an island in the harbour of Portsmouth, New Hampshire, the officers going to Annapolis. In their captivity they fared better, as we shall see, than the soldiers of General Shafter's army in their hour of victory.

CHAPTER XIII

CLOSING IN — THE SUFFERINGS OF BELEAGUERED SANTIAGO — THE LAGGING NEGOTIATIONS FOR SURRENDER — THE OUTPOURING OF REFUGEES — THE BOMBARDMENT — SURRENDER OF THE SPANIARDS — THE STARS AND STRIPES ABOVE SANTIAGO — THE WRECKING OF THE ARMY BY SICKNESS — THE FLIGHT TO THE NORTH — THE INFAMY OF THE TRANSPORTS — MONTAUK POINT AND CAMP WIKOFF — FEVER CAMPS IN THE UNITED STATES.

MEANWHILE about the beleaguered city the American lines were being drawn tighter and tighter. Reinforcements were landing at Siboney, and hurrying forward to the front. The news of the complete success of the navy so encouraged the men in the trenches that they stood ready to defend their positions at all hazards. The one moment when the Spaniards might have regained their lost ground — the afternoon of July 2d — passed without effort on their part, and thereafter the capture of the city became merely a matter of patience.

In the city was dire distress among non-combatants. Food was scarce and dear, and the poorer classes were reduced to devouring the most revolting scraps. The sanitary condition of the town was most alarming. To the effects of starvation was added the terror of a bombardment. Before Cervera went out to destruction, General Toral threatened that if the Americans should take the city by assault, he would turn upon it the guns of the ships, regardless of the thousands of women and children in its streets. This peril was averted by the result of the naval battle; but immediately thereafter came General Shafter's warning, that he intended to bombard the city from his trenches. Two days were given to the people to leave, — an act of humanity for which the general has been most unjustly condemned. It is true that the departure of the non-combatants left more food for the defenders and to that degree strengthened them; but the time has never been, when American soldiers wantonly bombarded a city full of women and children without giving them an opportunity to escape, and it is to be hoped it never will come. Consul Ramsden describes as heart-rending the scenes on the roads leading out of the city the morning set for the departure of the people. Toral had ordered that no carts or other vehicles should be taken, so the ways were packed with young and old, sick and feeble, plodding along on foot. "The scene was terrible," wrote Ramsden in his diary; "people flocking out, sick carried in chairs or as they could, children getting lost by the way, etc." Shelter was difficult to find, food still more so. El Caney, to which 18,000 to 20,000 fugitives flocked, was foul with the effluvium from unburied mules and horses, and even human victims of the battle. In the houses was not room enough for the people to lie down, and the nights were passed in sitting position on the floor. Food was scarcer than in the deserted town, and as the refugees had travelled on foot, none had more than three days' rations. The Red Cross Society, which had its agents on the ground, could not get its provisions up from the coast for lack of transportation, nor for that matter could the army. Small biscuits sold for $2 each, and $7 was refused for a chicken. On every hand children died for lack of food. General Shafter did all that could be done to alleviate the distress, though his first care was for the army. Like distress was reported from Guavitas, Dos Bocas, and other neighbouring villages. In all, about 35,000 people had left Santiago, mostly, of course, women, children, or helpless persons. In a war-racked, impoverished, and desolate country their sufferings were such that they soon began to appeal to the American commander for permission to return, preferring the perils of a bombardment to the slow agonies of starvation.

The bombardment, indeed, had gone on but slowly. A few shots, and then a flag of truce, with renewed negotiations for a surrender, was about the daily routine. Some of the soldiers grew impatient. "Now that we've got those dagoes corralled, why don't we brand them?" inquired one of the Rough Riders in the language of the cattle camp. The almost hourly interchange of notes under flags of truce was jeered at from the trenches, where the hot, hungry, and water-soaked men were naturally anxious for a conclusion to their efforts and relief from their discomforts. General Shafter, however, pursued a course which was at once cautious and humane. To assault would have cost heavily in human life, the more so since Garcia and his Cubans had failed to head off the expected reinforcements from Manzanillo, and 4000 fresh troops under General Escario had entered the city on the night of the 3d. To push the bombardment with the assistance of the navy, would perhaps have hastened the surrender, but the American general was assured by the foreign consuls that Toral was eager to surrender already, and was actively urging such a course upon Madrid by cable. Shafter accordingly determined to wait a reasonable time, in hope of taking the town without further sacrifice of life.

On the 6th of July the impatient men in the trenches saw that one of the flags of truce, at least, had borne fruit. Up a narrow trail from the city came a cavalcade of men, at the sight of the first of whom the crowd of soldiers who had been gathered there waiting in the heat for hours, went mad with joy. It was a throng of yelling, dancing, laughing, ay, and weeping, men that greeted Lieutenant Hobson and his seven comrades of the "Merrimac" exploit, when they came into the army's lines, after having been exchanged for seven prisoners taken at San Juan. As the band on the very foremost line struck up "The Star-

CITY AND HARBOR OF SANTIAGO.

Spangled Banner," all the new-comers, and those who had gathered to welcome them, stood silent at a salute, but when the music died away bedlam broke forth. To crowd about the heroes, to make the tropical forests ring with cheers, to shake each one by the hand, seemed to be the dearest wish of every man in blue uniform that day. From the ambulance in which they held their triumphal progress, the seven happy Blue Jackets yelled words of compliment and congratulation to the tattered and dirty soldiers, who shouted back applause. It was a glorious episode in the lives of these men, and its culmination came when, reaching the fleet after dark, they found the ships' companies turned out as though an admiral, at least, were coming to visit; and as their launch was seen advancing from the shore, the cheers of their messmates made the hills of Cuba ring almost as had the thundering fire that Morro and Estrella had levelled against them nearly six weeks before.

Day by day the American lines were growing stronger. The right had been extended until the city was bound in an iron ring, and men could get neither in nor out. The navy, freed from any apprehension of an enemy afloat, was able to give its undivided attention to the Spanish works, and on the 6th arrangements were made for the ships to bombard the town, while the troops did the same from their trenches. Every day, guns were placed in position along the American lines, which were now within three hundred yards of the Spanish position, and easily in range of the city. Three new batteries, twelve mortars, and the dynamite gun were thus trained on the beleaguered town, ready for the bombardment. On the 6th General Toral asked for terms of capitulation. The bombardment had been planned for this day, but at his urgent request for time to communicate with Madrid, it was deferred. The second day thereafter, he offered to surrender the city, but not his troops. They, according to the terms he suggested, were to be permitted to march away with their arms and unmolested, as far as Holguin. It seems strange, in view of the unconditional surrender of three days later, that this offer was favoured by General Shafter and all his division commanders. But by this time the continued rains and the pestilential climate were beginning to tell upon the soldiers, and the gravest apprehensions of an epidemic in the trenches were felt. If yellow fever, the ally so long of the Cubans against the Spaniards, should now turn against the American invaders, the army might be sacrificed and Santiago lost, after all. So reasoned the commanders in the field; but the authorities at Washington, convinced that Spain was about ready to sue for peace, refused to consider the proposition, and Toral was so notified, and warned to prepare for a resumption of hostilities at 4 P. M. on the 10th. Reinforcements continued to come from the United States. General Randolph, with the regular artillery, which would have been of the greatest service earlier, arrived, but was delayed at Siboney. The Ninth Massachusetts, Thirty-fourth Michigan, Eighth Ohio, First Illinois, and First District of Columbia volunteers came, all eager to see some active service. On the afternoon of the 10th the bombardment began from shore and sea, and continued until noon the next day. Singularly, little injury was done. Some few houses were destroyed, and others badly damaged; but the soldiers in the trenches suffered little. From the fleet the dynamite cruiser "Vesuvius" sent some of her monster explosive projectiles, but beyond making huge holes in the ground, and naturally shaking the nerves of the Spaniards, she accomplished little. The bombardment indeed was rather without spirit, since the idea had become firmly rooted in the minds of the commanding officers that the Spaniards intended to surrender.

Both belligerents were suffering heavily from causes other than bullets and shells. In the American ranks malarial fever had made its appearance, and spread like wild-fire. In the hospitals were more than 3000 men, down with wounds or fever. Men died for lack of medicines which were abundant eighteen miles away. Every day new cases were reported, and the surgeons began to look grave. The defenders of the town were in even more desperate condition. General Linares, who was still nominally the Spanish commander, though prevented by a wound from active service in the field, in a despatch to Madrid advising surrender, said: "Troops weak; sick in considerable proportions not sent to hospitals, owing to the necessity of keeping them in the intrenchments. Horses and mules without the usual allowance of forage; in the wet season with twenty hours' daily fall of rain, in the trenches which are simply ditches dug in the ground, without any permanent shelter for the men, who have nothing but rice to eat and no means of changing or drying their clothing." He closed his picture of the wretchedness of the troops with a recommendation for a surrender. The United States meanwhile had offered that if the Spaniards would surrender they should be returned to Spain at the expense of this government.

General Miles, the major-general commanding the whole army, had by this time reached Siboney. A story which indicates something of the conditions under which the men in the trenches were existing, is told of his visit to the front. At one point a battalion of naked men turned out solemnly and saluted. Somewhat startled, the general inquired the meaning of this remarkable spectacle. He learned that as it rained every day and the men had no change of clothing nor any place in which to dry it, they had become accustomed to strip at the first shower, putting their clothes under the shelter tents and going in nature's garb until the downfall was over. The fact too that the clothing supplied the troops was intended for winter use in North Dakota had something to do with their readiness to discard it. There was no change in the command of the army, owing to General Miles's visit. He had come simply on a visit of inspection, and left General Shafter's plans undisturbed. In company with the latter he rode out to a tree in the valley between the lines, where by appointment General Toral met them to discuss terms of surrender. The Spaniard quibbled so much on little points, and was so insistent upon time to consult Madrid, that General Miles impatiently told General Shafter he believed the whole discussion was for the purpose of gaining time, and recommended that an assault be ordered immediately. General Shafter, however, had been convinced, by conversations with the foreign consuls, that the Spaniards really wished to yield, and he accordingly agreed to a final armistice until the next day at noon. For once the Spaniards were not dilatory. At nine in the morning came a flag of truce to say that Toral was ready to surrender, and at two Generals Wheeler and Lawton and Captain Miley, as commissioners for the United States, met General Escario, Lieutenant-Colonel Fortan, and Albert Mason, the British vice-consul, who acted in a like capacity for Spain. The task of drawing up the articles of capitulation was a tedious one, consuming all that day and the better part of the next; but the reward was greater than had been expected, for it appeared the Spaniards were ready to surrender not only Santiago, but all the troops in Eastern Cuba, thus including in the surrender at least 12,000 men against whom not a gun had been fired. By evening of the next day, July 16th, the details of the surrender were all formulated, and approval of the terms fixed came from Madrid. The city was to be turned over to General Shafter and the American forces the day following. The Spanish officers were to be permitted to keep their side arms, and all soldiers were to retain their personal property. The United States government assumed the task of transporting the surrendered troops, in all about 24,000, back to Spain. As General Shafter justly said in his despatch to the President announcing the surrender, this ended the war. There was not another battle worthy of the name, nor any further serious opposition to the American arms in Cuba.

The surrender took place, July 18th, on a level spot between the opposing lines. With General Shafter to the meeting-place went the general officers with their staffs and a detachment of 100 men. General Toral brought out with him a similar escort. On the ridges crested by the American lines our army was drawn up under arms, — about 20,000 men. General Toral, who looked broken and worn, announced his surrender in the briefest formula that would express the idea. He did not deliver his sword, as the articles of capitulation had expressly protected the officers of the defeated army from this humiliation, but with his adherents he stood at "present arms" while making his brief address. There was no cheering on the ridges where stood the American troops watching this act in the tragedy in which they had played so great a part. This interview over, the official party rode into the city, past the ragged Spanish soldiers who lined the roads, and looking pityingly upon the groups of haggard half-starved Cubans who had barely managed to survive the privations of the siege. At noon, in the presence of a crowd that was rather stolid than hostile, the Stars and Stripes were raised over the governor's palace, while the band played "The Star-Spangled Banner." There was but little excitement, even in the American lines. Perhaps the men knew that with victory won the hardest and most costly part of their service was yet to come.

By this surrender a city of about 70,000 inhabitants in time of peace was won for the United States, — or rather for the Cubans, for whom the United States took up arms, — with a territory contiguous and surrendered with it of 5000 square miles. Nearly 24,000 troops with their arms and accoutrements, saving those of the officers, were also delivered to the conquerors. Had our army been able to retire at that moment, the loss in proportion to the extent of the triumph would have been light. Examination of the enemy's line of defence showed how wise had been the action of General Shafter in postponing from day to day an assault in hopes of the surrender which finally came. The Spaniards seemed to have a genius for devising defensive works. The whole territory before the American lines was cut with trenches and enmeshed with barbed wire extending in every imaginable direction. During the days of battle the defenders had given abundant evidence of their bravery in the trenches. They lacked that quality which impels soldiers to the assault, but in a defensive fight they won the admiration of their foes. Had the American army been compelled to take the city by assault, 5000 lives at least would have been the price paid. Nor would the navy have been able to round out its victory of the 3d of July by an entrance to the bay without heavy loss. A reconnaissance made by Admiral Schley and Captain Cook as soon as the flag was hauled down over Morro showed that the fortifications were practically uninjured by all the shot that had been hurled at them. After a careful examination of the ground which they had so long and so fiercely pounded, the navy officers reported that "over two million dollars' worth of ammunition thrown at the batteries defending Santiago harbour was absolutely harmless in its effect, so far as the reducing of the batteries was concerned, and simply bore out the well-known fact that it is a waste of time and money to bombard earthworks." The mines in the channel were found intact and well placed. It is just to set down the fact that the Spaniards were still equipped for a vigorous and costly defence, for in the newspapers and in some of the books of military history published at the time General Shafter was severely criticised for having waited so patiently for Toral to consult his home government. It was thought that for the American army to march into Santiago at any time after July 3d would have been a mere promenade. The fact is, it would have meant a battle bloodier than any fought in Cuba.

With the Spaniards disarmed and pacified, it might have been expected that the condition of the American troops about Santiago would at once become tolerable if not wholly comfortable. So, at any rate, the people at home thought, and they were not prepared for the stories of suffering, of dire sickness, and of death that began to come North from a camp supposed to be the scene of rejoicing over a complete victory. The pestilential climate which had enabled the hardened Cubans to stand out for so many years against the fresh troops sent by Spain to sicken and die, was beginning to tell upon our men. The rainy season had set in, and that meant that the trenches in which the men had been sleeping and living since the beginning of the siege were wet ditches, sodden and malarial. When the army embarked for Cuba, the most explicit scientific instructions were given to the soldiers for the preservation of their health against the ills of a tropical climate. They were to boil all water before drinking it, but they who offered the rule did not give the soldiers anything to boil the water in, nor suggest any way of building a fire where matches were scarcer than snowballs in Cuba, nor any method of keeping it going in constant rain without cover. So the men drank the water as they could find it, often from open brooks into which the offal of the camp drained; and as their rations were largely salted food, they drank a great deal. And the food! That was another subject upon which the prudent authorities on army hygiene had given explicit directions. The men were to eat only wholesome things; but the commissary department some days left them with nothing at all to eat, and then supplied them with beef preserved in such a revolting way that the commanding-general of the army referred to it as embalmed beef. Vegetables bought for the army spoiled before they were delivered. Especially were the soldiers warned against the fruits of the country, but there were days when they could get nothing else. So, too, the caution against sleeping directly on the ground affected men little who were given no opportunity to make floors for their tents, and who furthermore slept in wet trenches most of the time. As for the warning against wet clothes, it was met in many instances by wearing no clothes at all, — the only way it could be heeded.

Under ordinary circumstances Santiago is subject to the epidemic diseases of the tropics. At the time of the siege it was in a particularly unhealthful condition, its streets filthy beyond description and the air burdened with disease. For days during the negotiations leading up to the surrender, refugees from the city passed through our lines, leaving infection behind them. In Siboney and along the route of the army were the huts and houses of Cubans in which case after case of fatal yellow fever had occurred. These pest-houses, instead of being burned down, were used as headquarters, offices, and even hospitals, and frequently visited by our soldiers. Apropos of this fact, the superior caution of the navy may be noted. When the marines were landed at Guantanamo, every house on the beach was burned with all its contents, and barrels of Spanish wine which were found there were spilled. All water was distilled, and every tent was floored. The navy commanders took no risks, and the marines stayed in camp in a region naturally as unhealthy as that about Santiago without one case of yellow fever in the thirty-five days of their occupation.

But in the lines of the army the dread disease, and a virulent malarial fever akin to it, made their appearance even before Santiago fell. At that time the fever was making such headway in our ranks that had the Spaniards been well informed they might have held out with the certainty that a week's delay would put the army *hors du combat*. As a matter of record, in less than one week after the surrender there were 5000 men in the Fifth Corps ill with fever, and Colonel Roosevelt reported that of his hardy troops not more than one-fifth were fit for duty. Not all the sick men were in the hospitals, of course, but their illness was none the less grave because they tried to suppress it. The malady spread until at last the number of new cases reported reached 850 in one day. Early in August eight general officers in the Fifth Corps joined in a " Round Robin," in which they declared that illness had so enfeebled the army that it was without strength, that an epidemic of yellow fever was in sight which would surely destroy it, and that unless moved to the United States it must inevitably perish. In contemporary publications the unusual and unmilitary character of this document was construed as an attack on General Shafter, but he has said that it was drawn up with his knowledge and with his hearty acquiescence as a more emphatic protest against the proposition of the War Department that the army should spend the summer in Cuba. So unqualified was the opinion of the officers on this subject that one even urged that the general should ignore the Washington orders, seize all ships that were available, and start forthwith for the North. The " Round Robin," however, proved sufficient. With the accounts sent in by correspondents of men dying like sheep amid an utter lack of the necessary surgical attention, and deprived of the food and dainties which alone could build up their wasted constitutions, it roused the whole nation to irresistible indignation, and the management of the department under which such a condition could arise, and which in the face of it could seriously propose keeping the army in Cuba until the few well soldiers should become sick and the sick should die, was bitterly condemned. A situation in the camp which held the flower of the American army such as was disclosed by General Shafter's own admission that on August 8th, barely six weeks after landing, seventy-five per cent of his troops were unfit for service, was an intolerable, an inexcusable thing. So said every one with opportunity to give public expression to his views, and in the face of such general and just wrath the War Department could no longer hesitate. The regiments at the front were ordered relieved as fast as transports could be sent to bring them home and the shipment of the Spanish prisoners made a reduction of the force at Santiago safe. To hasten the latter condition, regiments of immunes were sent to serve as a garrison for the city. According to General Shafter's published statement, the losses of the army — of 20,000 men — up to this time were, "13 officers, 296 men, and 9 civilian employees died of disease; 24 officers and 226 men were killed, 83 officers and 1214 men were wounded, only 13 deaths resulting from wounds received in action."

But now the flames of public indignation lighted by the revelations of inefficiency in those who directed the commissary and surgical arrangements of the Santiago campaign were fanned higher by the stories of suffering on the transports and hospital ships. It had been bad enough for the field hospitals to be inadequately supplied with medicines and surgical appliances, but much of that failure was excused on the plea of faulty transportation. So, too, the lack of proper food at the camps, though regarded as an evidence that somewhere there had been incapacity, was condoned in view of the magnificent results of the campaign. But when the transport "Seneca" came into New York from Santiago, a story was told that seemed to show incredible indifference to the health of the men who had fought for the country. She carried 100 sick and wounded. The limited quantity of medical supplies she had was obtained from the Red Cross ship at Santiago, as the authorities had supplied none for the transport. Her condensers were inadequate to supply the fresh water needed, and wounds had to be washed in salt water. There were no bandages aboard; and when wounds were opened by the rolling of the ship, passengers tore up their clothing to supply bandages. An operation was necessary at one time during the voyage, and the surgeon, having no instruments, performed it with his pocket-knife. The cry of righteous wrath which this almost

incredible story of official neglect aroused, had not died away, when the ship "Concho," sailing from Siboney, July 29th, with 175 convalescents, arrived. She was literally a pest-ship. Her drinking-water was that shipped at Tampa when the Santiago expedition sailed early in June, and it had been stagnating in her tanks ever since. She had no ice. The conditions prevailing on the "Seneca" existed in equal barbarity on this ship. People began to ask whether Secretary of War Alger or the Spanish Mausers were the more deadly enemy of the American soldier.

Events such as this, and the ever-increasing volume of testimony from Siboney, that the situation there was growing worse daily, at last stung the War Department into belated activity. At the eastern end of Long Island, where the fresh ocean breezes blow unceasingly across the narrow strip of land between the Atlantic and the Sound, a great camp was laid out for the reception of the homecoming soldiers. The spot was well chosen, — its one weakness being a lack of a natural water supply, though that was easily met by stationing a condensing-ship in the harbour while wells were being driven. But the same incapacity that had decimated the army in Cuba by failure to plan transportation, commissary and medical service in proper proportion to the size of the problem involved, was manifested at Camp Wikoff. It was known, when the first load of lumber was placed on the ground, that this was to be a camp for sick and enfeebled soldiers. Nothing should have been permitted to stand in the way of having it ready in season and perfectly adapted to its purpose. But a contractor was allowed to quarrel with his workmen over a question of wages until a hospital was so much delayed that men sick with typhoid fever had no place to sleep. Departmental red tape so complicated the issue of supplies that within a hundred miles of the best market in the United States, sick soldiers were forced to eat bacon, hard tack, and worse than doubtful beef, because all the rations issued for use in Cuba had not been consumed, and fresh rations could not be issued until these were eaten. When the transports bearing the shattered remnants of General Shafter's army began to arrive, it was found that they were as overcrowded as the earlier ships that had come into New York. The most populous section of the United States thus had the horrors of war brought home to it, and the efforts of the people to remedy the stupid and positively criminal blunders of the War Department were at once noble and pathetic. Rich men and women sent great consignments of fresh vegetables to the camp where sick men were being fed on the coarse fare of stevedores. Whole neighbourhoods clubbed together to buy dainties for the soldiers. The people along the New England coast volunteered by hundreds to take the sick into their own homes,—a method of relief which, of course, army red tape prohibited. All that private initiative could do to correct official incompetence was done, but to the last the history of the War Department's management of Camp Wikoff was a record of stupidity and brutality. Pages could be filled with evidence of the justice of this characterisation. It is enough to close with a reference to the fact that the last act in the history of Camp Wikoff showed as little comprehension of the necessities of the case as the first. The troops were sent home by rail, the whole length of Long Island, over a notoriously uncomfortable railroad, in the burning hot days of September, although there is an excellent harbour at Montauk Point, and New York was full of comfortable vessels that might have been chartered for transports. Many of these troops were from seaboard States, and might have been taken to their own doors by water. For months after Camp Wikoff had become but a memory, men were dying at their homes from the result of the treatment there accorded them.

I have referred to the superior skill and intelligence

manifested by the navy in dealing with its problems of sanitation and hygiene. The contrast between its methods and those of the army could not better be drawn than by placing in close juxtaposition with this outline of conditions at Camp Wikoff the description, by Dr. Carroll Dunham, of the method by which the Navy Department prepared to take care of the prisoners taken from Cervera's fleet:

"At Portsmouth, on less than two days' notice, barracks were built and every preparation made to receive 1100 Spanish prisoners of war sent up from Santiago, where they had been captured at the time Cervera's fleet was destroyed. When the prisoners arrived, their barracks had been built, roofed in, and furnished — barracks, not tents — the kitchens were not quite done, but the cooking-ranges were in place and ready for use. These Spaniards have been kept there for some two months in a comfort which would have saved many lives if our own soldiers could have fared as well as these captives of the navy."

Not at Santiago or at Montauk Point alone did the men of the army pay a heavy price in health and life for the incompetence with which the bureaus of the War Department were honeycombed, — incompetence in some cases bred of long years of official idleness, in others the fruit of the appointment by the President of inexperienced and often notoriously inefficient persons to important offices as a reward for political services rendered by them or by their relatives. Many of the camps in which were kept the more than 200,000 volunteers who never saw active service nor ever left the borders of the nation, developed into pest-holes. Such notoriously was the case at the greatest camp of all, — that at Chickamauga. Lack of water, company camps improperly laid out so that contagion was spread by insects and even by the breeze, bad food, — the offscourings of Chicago packing-houses with which millionaires to increase their fortunes poisoned the soldiers of the nation, — unfit clothing furnished by contractors chosen through political favoritism and conscienceless in their zest to make money at the expense of the army,— all these conditions united to drag down to sickness and incapacity men who were picked out of thousands for their physical health. At Camp Alger, near Washington, like conditions obtained. Open sewers ran down the aisles between the tents in which the men slept, polluting the air and spreading the germs of typhoid fever everywhere. The story of the sanitary mismanagement of the war demands a volume to itself. It is summed up by the fact that ten times as many men were killed by disease as by the enemy.

CHAPTER XIV

THE PORTO RICO CAMPAIGN — TROOPS EMPLOYED — THE BOMBARDMENT OF NIPE — LANDING AT GUANICA — PLAN OF THE CAMPAIGN — CAPTURE OF PONCE — FRIENDLINESS OF THE INHABITANTS — CAPTURE OF GUAYAMO, COAMO, AND MAYAGUEZ — THE ENEMY'S STAND AT ABONCITO — THE NEWS OF PEACE — COMPLETE SUCCESS OF THE CAMPAIGN — THE PEACE NEGOTIATIONS — THE PROTOCOL — EVACUATION COMMISSIONERS.

SANTIAGO having fallen, the people of the United States looked for the attack on Havana which all had supposed would be one of the first strokes of the war. But again it was postponed — this time in order that General Miles might invade and subdue Porto Rico. This island is the most easterly of the Lesser Antilles, and had at the time of the Spanish war a population of about 900,000. The last official census prior to the war was taken in 1887, and showed a population of 437,933 whites, 246,647 mulattoes, and 76,905 negroes. As in Cuba, the aboriginal population had wholly disappeared before the civilising methods of the Spaniards. In area the island is of about 3600 square miles. Its population is about as dense as that of Connecticut and a little more dense than that of Delaware. The climate, though hot, is more salubrious than that of Cuba, and the higher parts of the island are healthful for persons of northern birth. The principal city is San Juan, which it will be remembered was bombarded by Admiral Sampson during the search for Cervera.

It will be remembered that the resolutions of Congress which preceded the war contained a paragraph expressly disavowing any purpose to make of the struggle an excuse for seizing the territory of Spain. The United States declared themselves animated by motives of the purest philanthropy, and denied any ulterior plans for territorial aggrandisement. But as the war progressed, there grew up among those in power in Washington a feeling that when victory was won and peace re-established the nation should have something to show for its sacrifices. Ethically and in entire honour a free and contented Cuba would have been a sufficient exhibit; but the Administration thought the people wanted a slice of the spoils after the fashion of the land-grabbing nations of Europe, and the Porto Rico expedition was expressly planned to gratify this desire. The word was given out semi-officially that this island when captured would not be handed over to its people for self-government, but would be kept by the United States as a nucleus for a colonial system.

General Miles had taken with him to Siboney the material and the greater part of the personnel of his expedition. July 21st he sailed. He had with him an army made up largely of volunteer troops — the Sixth Illinois, Sixth Massachusetts, four light batteries of the Third and Fourth artillery (regulars), 275 recruits who had been sent for the Fifth Corps and arrived after the need for them was past, Battery B of the Fifth Artillery, 60 men of the Signal Corps, and the Seventh Hospital Corps — in all, 3415 men. By way of transports and convoy he had the "Massachusetts," "Dixie," "Gloucester," "Cincinnati," "Annapolis," "Leyden," "Wasp," "Yale," and "Columbia." From Charleston about 3000 men had already sailed to join the expedition, and General Schwan's brigade set out from Tampa. These forces were to unite under command of General John R. Brooke, who sailed from Newport News about a week later with about five thousand men, including cavalry troops A and C of New York, the historic Philadelphia City Troop, and the Governor's Troop of Pennsylvania. General Schwan's brigade was made up wholly of regular troops. It comprised batteries, troops, and companies from the Seventh Artillery, the Second Cavalry, and the Eleventh and Nineteenth Infantry. It was the plan to send 35,000 men to Porto Rico, — almost twice as many as were given to Shafter, although there were fewer Spaniards to be encountered and the country was not so difficult. The arrangements for engineers, surgeons, and supplies were also vastly more perfect and comprehensive than they had been for the Santiago expedition. Whether this seeming improvement in the methods of the War Department was due to an intelligent profit from lessons hard learned, or whether it was that the major-general commanding the army was able to exact more of the authorities at Washington than a mere junior major-general could, is a question that was hotly debated at the time. Certainly General Miles went to Porto Rico equipped for any emergency. That the temper of the island people and the speedy negotiation of peace made his expedition a mere pleasure-jaunt, does not detract from the wisdom nor the skill manifested in planning it.

It had at first been planned to establish a base on the coast of Cuba. The port of Nipe, on the northern coast nearly opposite Santiago, had been selected for this purpose, and a naval expedition made up of the "Topeka," "Annapolis," "Wasp," and "Leyden," was despatched to take it. They engaged the batteries and one gunboat, the "Jorge Juan," which defended the bay, and very speedily silenced all opposition. The gunboat was sunk after a gallant resistance occupying but fifteen minutes, and the fort showed a white flag after the second shell fell among its defenders. In the end Nipe was not used for the purpose planned, and the engagement, which took place on the 21st of July, has interest and importance only because it was the last naval battle off the coast of Cuba.

On the 25th of July, after a voyage of four days, the portion of the Porto Rican expedition which had sailed from Siboney with General Miles entered the port of Guanica and prepared to land. This was a surprise to every one on board except the few in the General's confidence, and it was a surprise to the people at Washington too when they heard of it, for the expectation had been that the expedition would be landed on the north side of the island near San Juan, while the point selected was as far from that city as possible. It is probable that General Miles concluded that the practice of following to the letter an elaborately formulated programme which had been in the hands of the enemy for some weeks, might properly be abandoned. Certainly the people of Guanica were quite as much surprised as any one could be when the fleet steamed into their quiet little post and the "Gloucester" let fly a terrific three-pounder at the only Spanish flag in sight. There was no defence to speak of, for there was no artillery at the point, and a landing-party from the "Gloucester," after a lively brush with some Spanish soldiers in the streets, soon occupied the town, building a barricade in the main street. When the American flag appeared over the one block-house, the transports came into the harbour, and the work of landing began. The town was found to be a picturesque little village of one street, lined with red-roofed and party-coloured houses. The people were amiable; nothing was further from their minds than manifesting any hostilities to the invaders, and the volunteers for their part let their imagination run riot in inventing tales of the vast benefits which were to accrue to the people of Guanica when they became part of the United States.

Among the many advantages which the army in Porto Rico enjoyed that had been denied to the army in Cuba, was a very exact topographical knowledge of the country. In May, Lieutenant H. H. Whitney of the Fourth Artillery had travelled through the island in many disguises, studying the land and the harbours, mapping out roads and gathering data that would be useful to an invading

GENERAL NELSON A. MILES.

army should the time for invasion come. All the material he had gathered was in the hands of General Miles, and the campaign could be, and was, planned with the exactness of a game of chess. The first point to be struck after the landing at Guanica was complete, was Ponce, a small town fifteen miles due east. Ponce had importance because of its excellent harbour, and because from it a broad, level, and hard military road extended 85 miles to the metropolis of the island, and the chief seat of Spanish power, San Juan. Ponce fell a prey to the navy, Commander Davis with the "Dixie," "Gloucester," "Annapolis," and "Wasp," taking it on the 28th without resistance. Indeed, the habit of surrendering without resistance was found to be pleasingly prevalent in Porto Rico. There is a picturesque story that a beardless navy officer just out of the Academy compelled the surrender of Ponce by telephone from the port, making fierce threats of bombardment by the ponderous cannon of the "Gloucester;" but the official record denies this glory to Ensign Curtin, and gives to Commander Davis of the "Dixie" the honour of receiving the surrender of the town. It was a bloodless victory in either case; and when the troops came marching over from Guanica to occupy the town, they discovered that the inhabitants saluted them with volleys of flowers instead of bullets, and that there was not such a thing as a Spanish flag in the place.

After a few days spent in devising a military government for Ponce and in getting the affairs of the city in orderly progress once more, General Miles began the serious work of his campaign. This campaign was never finished, but so far as it did progress before the news of the armistice interrupted it it was successful, and conducted without varying a hair's breadth from the plan as originally formulated. The objective was the city of San Juan, at the other side of the island. But to take the city alone would not complete the purposes of the invasion, else it might have been done from the sea, or at any rate from a landing-place much nearer than Ponce or Guanica. The Spaniards all through the island had to be killed, captured, or pacified. Few were killed, many captured, more invited pacification. To have possession of a seacoast town while the enemy held the interior would be unprofitable; hence the plan of campaign. This involved, briefly, the division of the army into four columns which should swing out to right and left of Ponce and converge on San Juan, driving the Spaniards before them into that city. There was no danger that the army thus divided would be beaten in detail, for the Spaniards had not force sufficient for the purpose, and the interior lines of communication would enable our troops to concentrate at the word of danger in sufficient force to meet any probable attack. It was clear that the enemy could expect no aid or even sympathy from the inhabitants. On the 31st General Miles cabled to Washington, " Volunteers are surrendering themselves with arms and ammunition. Four-fifths of the people are overjoyed at the arrival of the army. Two thousand from one place have volunteered to serve with it. They are bringing in transportation, beef, cattle, and other needed supplies. The custom-house has already yielded $14,000. As soon as all troops are disembarked they will be in readiness to move."

Every effort was made to maintain the friendship so freely proffered by the people. The customs regulations of the port were revised so as to encourage trade, and burdensome restrictions and taxes levied by the Spaniards were repealed. The natives were hired at good wages, and their property purchased when needed for army use at fair prices. The people found that the American troops brought order and prosperity, and the news preceded the columns advancing through the island, with the result that everywhere the resistance met was only that made perfunctorily by the Spanish regulars.

The military road from Ponce to San Juan passed

through a point in the mountains called Aboncito, where the Spaniards, taking advantage of the nature of the ground, prepared to resist the American advance. General Miles's plan of advancing by separate but parallel roads furnished exactly the right method of meeting and overcoming this resistance, for as the columns to right and left of the centre advanced, the Spaniards would find themselves outflanked and would be compelled to retreat. The advance on the right was led by General Brooke, who went by sea to Arroyo, where he landed with 1200 men and pressed northward into the interior. At a little town called Guayama they encountered 500 Spaniards, who fled after a show of resistance by which one officer and four men were killed. At the other extreme of the American line the regulars of General Schwan's division fought a skirmish with the enemy in the outskirts of the considerable town of Mayaguez, losing two men and capturing fifty. In the centre General Roy Stone worked his way along to the northward, carrying Adjuntas in a midnight skirmish, and preparing for greater things by keeping 500 natives at work behind him changing the wretched trail over which his troops had advanced into an admirable road, — for in his own country this volunteer general and veteran of the Civil War was widely known as an expert road-builder. The town of Coamo on the road to San Juan was taken by the Sixteenth Pennsylvania Volunteers after a defence that was little more than perfunctory. Indeed the Spanish retreat was so precipitate that four unarmed correspondents entered the town and received the submission of its Alcalde before the American troops came up. A block-house in the suburbs engaged the attention of the artillery for a time, but soon burst into flames, whereupon the Spaniards fled. One detachment in an earthwork fought stubbornly enough to check the American advance until their commander — a brave man who rode about disdaining cover — was killed, when they promptly surrendered. There was little fight in the enemy at any stage of the Porto Rico campaign.

What the Americans might have suffered at Aboncito cannot be told. That was evidently the spot at which the Spaniards had planned to make their most determined resistance. From friendly natives came warnings of mines in the road, and torpedoes hidden in the bushes by the wayside. Toward this stronghold the converging columns took their way. General Wilson's men felt the enemy's sting first, coming into a zone of fire from artillery and rapid-fire guns posted on the mountain-sides about three miles in advance of the city. Wilson set his artillerists to drive the enemy out. The Spaniards were intrenched. Major Lancaster's battery went into position in an open field, and opened fire at a range of 2000 yards. The duel was lively, for the gunners on each side could see their enemy without glasses; but comparatively little damage was done, and the sun went down with the Spaniards still in position.

August 13th bade fair, when the sun rose, to see some hard fighting in Porto Rico. General Wilson had drawn his lines in preparation for a sharp attack on the enemy at Aboncito. General Brooke confronted a strong force at Pablo Vasquez, near Guayama, and intended to assault the hill held by the enemy, knowing that it was vital to the plans of General Miles that he break through and effect a junction with Wilson. At Cape San Juan forty American sailors, with the help of shells from the ships off shore, were holding their ground against the assaults of eight hundred Spaniards. Near Guayama, B Battery of the Pennsylvania artillery was about to open the day's fighting with a shot at the line of earthworks faintly discernible on a distant hill. The guns were shotted and aimed; the gunner of one stood with lanyard in hand awaiting the command to fire. There was a sound of a galloping horse on the road to the rear, and an officer came into view shouting something and waving his hand emphatically. "Cease firing! Cease firing!" the artillerists heard him shout as he came nearer. "What for?" inquired the captain of the battery with natural curiosity. "Peace has been declared," was the response, which the soldiers of that particular command, who were just getting into action and desired to see what their fine new cannon could do in the field, did not receive with proper enthusiasm. Carlyle says that if there is one thing more incredible than all others, it is that governments should be able to find men willing to give up their entire lives to studying the art of killing other men and getting ready themselves to be killed. In war the philosopher would have found a thing more incredible yet; namely, that a sudden interposition of peace in time to prevent a battle which promised to be desperate and bloody is often hailed with disappointment by men who stand an excellent chance of falling in the fight they courted. The peace of August 13, 1898, came suddenly upon men in the act of battle on the American lines at many points. At Manzanillo in Cuba the navy was vigorously bombarding the town. At Havana the batteries were engaging the blockading fleet, and one shell struck the "San Francisco." At far-off Manila, though of course the fact of the armistice was not known for days after its conclusion, the Spanish forces were engaged and defeated the day after the peace protocol was signed at Washington.

So the expedition to Porto Rico was ended abruptly by the interposition of diplomacy, yet not so abruptly as to deny to the American invaders ample opportunity to demonstrate their power to drive the Spaniards from the island. The plans of the commanding-general were being executed like clock-work when the end came. The commissary and medical departments showed no sign of that collapse which made the Santiago campaign disastrous even in the face of its success. General Miles summed up the whole in a paragraph of his report thus:

"During nineteen days of active campaign on the island of Porto Rico a large portion of the island was captured by United States forces and brought under our control. Our forces were in such a position as to make the Spanish positions untenable, outside of that of the garrison of San Juan. The Spaniards had been defeated or captured in six different engagements which took place, and in every direction and position they had occupied up to that time. The success of the enterprise was due largely to the skill and good generalship of the officers in command of the different divisions and brigades. Strategy and skilful tactics accomplished what might have occasioned serious loss in any other way. The loss of the enemy in killed, wounded, and captured was nearly ten times our own, which was only 3 killed and 40 wounded. Thus the island of Porto Rico became a part of the United States."

The campaign in Porto Rico was long enough, too, to demonstrate that the United States would have only a thoroughly friendly people to deal with in establishing its authority over the island. The towns in which there were no Spanish garrisons surrendered with such promptitude and were so eager to hoist the American colours that General Miles was compelled to telegraph to Washington for a fresh supply of flags. Everywhere there was haste to assume American airs. At Ponce one of the newspapers rubbed out its record of the past, and appeared with a new name, "volume one, number one," the day after the surrender. Every endeavour was made to encourage this feeling among the people, and the work done in establishing orderly conditions, in framing a military government, in building roads and enforcing hygienic conditions, and in reforming the custom-house methods so as to encourage trade was even more important and quite as arduous as the work done with rifle and cannon. But the story of the reformation and development of Porto Rico is something distinct from this short chronicle of its conquest.

The peace which came thus suddenly to the men at the guns in Porto Rico and Cuba had been a matter of current discussion at Washington and Madrid for nearly a month. Rumours that it might be sought by Spain filled the columns of the newspapers of the world, but were of course strenuously denied by the Spanish authorities. To the people of Spain, and particularly to the commercial and financial classes having interests beyond the borders of the country, the hopelessness of the conflict became apparent immediately after the destruction of Cervera and the fall of Santiago. The government still clung to the forlorn hope of dragging some other European country into the quarrel with the United States, but with notable prudence and justice all held aloof,—a result that was by many ascribed to the avowed friendship of Great Britain for the United States at that time. It was evident that whatever nation came to the aid of Spain would have England also to deal with. As for the wishes and hopes of the United States, they were frankly enough for a speedy end to the conflict. President McKinley said immediately upon the news of the fall of Santiago, "I hope for a speedy peace now."

It was not as speedy as it might have been, for that very delicate sentiment "Spanish honour" had to be handled most tenderly, and moreover there were political conditions in Spain which made the ministry desirous of proceeding somewhat cautiously. Negotiations were opened through the French Ambassador at Washington, M. Cambon, who from the beginning of hostilities had acted for the Spaniards in this country. Just an afternoon call on the President by this gentleman with the remark that Spain had requested him to suggest that it was ready to open the question of a treaty, was enough to send Spanish securities up on all the bourses of Europe, and when a day or two later M. Cambon announced that he had been formally authorised by the government of Spain to represent it in the discussion of the conditions upon which peace should be resumed, everybody saw that the end of the war was at hand. The Spaniards were anxious that during the discussion of the preliminaries an armistice should be declared, and their papers bitterly berated the United States government for not agreeing to this; but it was evident to the authorities at Washington that at the moment M. Cambon made his first overtures on the part of Spain — on the 26th of July — there was every reason to prosecute the war with energy. To stop pending diplomatic negotiations meant that the expedition of General Miles to Porto Rico would be paralysed, and if the negotiations failed it would be doubly hard to resume it. Accordingly they insisted that before the declaration of an armistice a protocol preliminary to an actual treaty should be agreed upon by the representatives of the two governments. This protocol should enumerate the conditions of peace which the United States would be willing to accept and which Spain would be willing to consider, — for it was made clear, by implication at least, that Spain, as the party suing for peace, would be the one compelled to make concessions and sacrifices. This protocol, after repeated conferences between members of the President's cabinet and the French Ambassador, was finally formulated and sent to Spain for the consideration of the Ministry. There was brief discussion there. By the 7th an answer suggesting some slight changes in the document was received at Washington, and five days later in the President's room at the White House the commissioners for the two nations, Judge William R. Day, Secretary of State, and M. Jules Cambon, Ambassador of France, affixed their signatures to the document which ended the war in fact, though not formally. The substance of this document, shorn of its official redundancies, will be sufficient here. It was drawn in six clauses:

First. Spain renounced all claim to sovereignty or other rights in Cuba.

Second. Spain to cede to the United States Porto Rico

TORPEDO BOAT "ERICSSON."

and all other Spanish islands in the West Indies and one island in the Ladrone Archipelago, to be selected by the United States.

Third. The United States to occupy Manila, its bay and harbour, until a treaty of peace should determine the disposition of the Philippines.

Fourth. Spain to immediately evacuate Cuba and other West Indian islands.

Fifth. Both nations to appoint peace commissioners to meet at Paris not later than October 1st to negotiate a treaty of peace.

Sixth. Hostilities to be suspended on the signing of the protocol.

The alterations in this protocol which Spain had unavailingly pleaded for included an article which would have relieved her of all debt incurred on account of Cuba and Porto Rico, a provision which would have saddled the people of the former island with a debt of $550,000,000 incurred in the effort to make them submit to misgovernment; an article permitting her to retain possession of Luzon, the largest of the Philippine islands, and an article granting to her troops the right to leave Cuba and Porto Rico with the honours of war, and to remove all war material from those islands. To all of these proposed amendments the United States returned an emphatic negative, and the protocol as finally signed was, in effect, that first suggested by the American government.

Immediately upon the completion of the protocol, indeed before the commissioners left the White House, the President affixed his signature to the proclamation announcing an armistice, and telegrams were sent to the commanders in the field. How sudden a check they put on the operations of the army under Miles has already been related. The despatch to Admiral Dewey was cabled to Hong Kong, and thence carried to Manila by a fleet steamer, but it reached the seat of war only after a decisive battle had been fought. In that case, as in others,

Dewey profited by the slow communication with Washington. If the President's order had reached him on the 13th instead of on the 16th, he would have been checked in the very act of taking Manila, and the political difficulties of his situation, which in any case became most perplexing, would have been multiplied fivefold.

Very significant was the order sent at this time to Admiral Sampson. He was directed to abandon the blockade, and to take to New York the ships "New York," "Brooklyn," "Indiana," "Oregon," "Iowa," and "Massachusetts." The heaviest fighting-ships of the navy were thus ordered withdrawn from Cuban waters. The monitors were to be left in a safe harbour in Porto Rico, and the marines were relieved from the post at Guantanamo they had stuck to so persistently, and sent North. By a later order the "Texas" was added to the list of vessels ordered to New York, and when the fleet reached the entrance to the noble harbour of that port, they found a magnificent ovation awaiting them. At the first news that the ships and men by whom the great victory over Cervera had been won were to visit the harbour of the metropolis, the people of New York and all the neighbourhood cried out that there should be such a triumph as ancient Rome decreed to her home-coming conquerors. The Navy Department was persuaded to order the vessels to proceed in column up the broad expanse of the North River to a point opposite the stately tomb erected on the hill for the body of General Ulysses S. Grant. There they were to fire a salute, and turning, return to the navy anchorage at Tompkinsville. This insured to the millions of people who live within a few minutes' ride of the great city an opportunity to see the fleet of veterans, and right eagerly they availed themselves of it. New York was crowded the night before, until there seemed not roofs enough to cover the guests. The streets were gay with bunting, the docks and piers early in the morning were black with people, while on distant city roofs other crowds hung to precarious perches, and watched eagerly for the ships. Never, perhaps, in history, since the days of the gorgeous Roman pageants, did conquerors have a more brilliant reception. The air throbbed with the crash of cannon, the roar of cheering multitudes, and the shriek of steam whistles. Every imaginable craft was pressed into service by sight-seers, and about the ships, as they made their stately way up the river, crowded a fleet of yachts, tugs, great excursion steamers, trim launches, steam canal-boats, every imaginable thing that would float and move, all packed by a cheering throng. At night officers were banqueted, and the success of the navy drunk in brimming bumpers. For days thereafter, the Blue Jacket was the guest by common consent of the people of New York, and in doors and out the best of everything was freely forthcoming to any who wore the uniform of the United States navy.

The first duty under the protocol was to provide for the immediate evacuation of Cuba and Porto Rico. To accomplish this, commissions were named by each nation. The commissioners appointed on the part of the United States to effect the evacuation of Cuba were Major-General James F. Wade, an officer who had been in command of the great camp at Tampa, during the war; Rear Admiral William T. Sampson; and Major-General Matthew C. Butler, a civil appointee to the army, but a veteran of the Confederate service, and a former United States Senator. The Porto Rico board was composed of Major-General John R. Brooke, who was already in service on that island; Rear Admiral Schley, and Brigadier-General William W. Gordon, another Confederate veteran. The task was no easy one in either case, and the work of the Cuban commission was made additionally difficult by the action of the Spanish government, which threw repeated obstacles in the way of a prompt and peaceable evacuation of the island. It was well into January, 1899, before the last of the Spanish troops left Cuba, though before their final departure the island was under the domination of the United States, and General Ludlow in Havana and General Wood in Santiago were struggling with the problems presented by a people reduced to the point of starvation, communities in which the first essentials of sanitation were unknown, and a business situation which combined almost complete lack of money with almost equal lack of opportunities for employment.

CHAPTER XV

The Philippines again — Dewey's Position in Manila Harbour — His Work in Diplomacy and War — The Part played by Aguinaldo — The Coming of the American Troops — The Quarrel with the Germans — The Capture and Occupation of Manila — Growing Discontent of the Filipinos and their Final Revolt — The Problems presented to the United States by the Situation in the Philippines.

AT anchor in the harbour of Manila, with the Spanish fleet destroyed, the Spanish fortifications at Corregidor and Cavite demolished or in the possession of his marines, Admiral George Dewey found himself at once master and victim of the situation. Without troops there was nothing more of a warlike sort for him to do. He could reduce the city, but he could not hold it, and a bombardment under such conditions would have been but wanton slaughter of the innocent. The Spanish military authorities gave prudent heed to the admiral's warning, that if his ships were fired upon, he would destroy the town, and no provocation was given. But the Spanish flag still floated defiantly from the corner of the bastion of the walled town, and Manila was still a Spanish city, though it lay at the mercy of the American commander. As for the country behind, that was the spoil alternately of the Spaniards and the insurgents. As the admiral himself described it, his authority extended just as far as one of his ships could throw a shell, and no farther.

This situation was necessarily irksome, and the prolonged delay in sending troops, which irritated even the people at home, must have been almost unbearable to the admiral. With notable patience and self-restraint, however, he held his peace, making neither appeals nor complaints, and doing the best with the material at hand. The insurgents for a time seemed to offer a means for opening the way to Manila to our troops when they should arrive, and Aguinaldo was permitted to arm his men as fast as they were enrolled from the store of captured arms in the Cavite arsenal. This fact formed one of the counts in the insurgent indictment of the United States for bad faith when the relations between Aguinaldo and the American commanders reached the point of open war.

Not for more than three weeks after the victory of May 1st did the first detachment of United States troops sail from San Francisco to Dewey's relief. The voyage consumed more than a month, so that for exactly two months the admiral was left with a hostile city under his guns, a force of undisciplined insurgents operating in the surrounding country, with at least a colour of countenance from him, and the warships of several European nations, some of which had openly expressed sympathy for Spain, anchored by his side, their commanders watching eagerly for the first sign of weakness, or the first disaster of which they could take advantage to intervene. Months after, when Manila was occupied by American troops and the United States flag was everywhere displayed and respected, Admiral Dewey said to a friend, looking contemplatively upon the wrecks of the Spanish ships, " That was the least of my troubles down here."

The story of Dewey's diplomacy in Manila harbour during the long period of suspended war will, when it is fully told, be one of the most creditable chapters in the history of the American navy. In these later days of cables and telegraphs the commander seldom has an opportunity to display much individual initiative. To Dewey a great opportunity was given, and by him it was greatly improved. Against the persistent nagging of the

PASIG RIVER AT MANILA.

German commander he set up a frankly expressed readiness to defend the rights and the dignity of his country's flag in distant waters at the mouth of the cannon, even though by his act the two nations should be plunged into war. His treatment of the insurgents, though sympathetic, stopped short of formal recognition, while in his relations with the Spanish authorities of Manila he bore himself with the firmness of one who knows that the victory is his, though he may have to wait patiently for its fruits. Nor was there any relaxation of the admiral's attention to strictly naval details amid all these puzzling diplomatic duties. Though his men could not get ashore, their daily regimen was so carefully watched that the health of the squadron remained perfect. Though the Spaniards were pledged to respect the ships on penalty of the destruction of the city, there was never a moment, night or day, when a single ship in the squadron could have been caught unaware by a torpedo attack. The two months' vigil of the American Blue Jackets in Manila harbour must ever stand as one of the finest achievements of naval history.

The grand strategy of war has so often been compared to a game of chess on a monster scale that the expression has become stale, but one situation during the war with Spain so strikingly illustrates the analogy that it is impossible not to call attention to it. That in a war waged over the comparatively narrow territory of a single nation, or indeed over a single continent, the movement of every considerable force on either side would at once have its effect in determining the action of an opposing force, even at a considerable distance, is only a commonplace, but the swift thrust and parry that went on throughout this war between the very antipodes has never before been paralleled in the history of strategy. That the movements of a fleet in the Mediterranean Sea should be properly chronicled as a part of the operations in the

Philippines seems at first sight incredible, but how just it is to award such a place to the story of the manœuvres of Camara perhaps nobody is better able to testify than Admiral George Dewey.

When Cervera sailed on his ill-fated voyage to the West Indies, there was left to guard the coasts of Spain what came to be known as the Cadiz fleet. Its most formidable ships were the "Pelayo," a battle-ship of the first class, and the "Carlos V," an armoured cruiser. A large number of cruisers, gunboats, torpedo boats and destroyers made up the squadron, which was under command of Admiral Camara. On paper — that qualifying term must always be used in speaking of the Spanish navy — this fleet was formidable, and its presence at Cadiz compelled the retention along our northern coast of several cruisers even during the days when the blockade of Cuba made the demand for ships in West Indian waters continually pressing. It was, as the naval phrase goes, "a fleet in being," and as such had ever to be reckoned with. Its influence upon the tactics of the American fleets extended not only to those in the Atlantic, but to the fleet in the far-away waters of the Philippines as well; for by passing through the Suez Canal Admiral Camara could have brought his fleet into action against Dewey's squadron long before any reinforcements from our Atlantic coast could have reached Manila, and even before any ships from our Pacific seaboard could have made the long passage. Camara had, in short, the advantage of what is known in military terminology as an interior line of communication, and accordingly his fleet menaced both Dewey and Sampson at once.

His first move, however, freed the latter from apprehension, though for the time it added materially to the burden of worry upon Dewey's mind. Just as our forces under General Shafter were landing at Daiquiri, news came that Camara had left Cadiz, and swiftly upon the heels of the first intelligence came the tidings that an

English merchantman had seen the squadron steaming east in the Mediterranean. That meant, of course, that the Suez Canal was to be passed and the blow delivered against Dewey. The first effect of this discovery was to relieve the ships which had been guarding our northern coast, and to strengthen by so much the blockade of Cuba. But this advantage was more than offset by the apprehension of disaster to Dewey, whose fleet, wholly destitute of armoured ships, was not — on paper — equal to that of the Spaniards. The coast-defence monitor "Monterey" was at the time on the way from San Francisco to reinforce the American squadron at Manila; but her speed being slow, like that of all ships of her class, the probabilities were that the Spaniards would arrive before she did. As a matter of fact, while the Board of Strategy was anxiously discussing this danger in Washington, word came that the "Monterey" had been compelled to put back into Honolulu to repair.

The utmost that could be done then by the navy authorities at Washington was to hastily prepare another fleet to go in hot pursuit of the Spaniards. The organisation and despatch of such a fleet had two advantages. As its course to the Suez Canal would take it past the coast of Spain, which had been stripped of all naval defence by the departure of Camara, apprehension of bombardment of their seaport towns might impel the Spaniards to recall their squadron. Even if this did not result, the American vessels, being faster than those of the enemy, could reach Asiatic waters so soon after Camara that Dewey, being duly warned, might avoid battle until a juncture could be made. Accordingly Commodore Watson, with the flagship "Newark," was directed to form the squadron of relief, and the widest publicity was given to the purpose of the government to send a powerful fleet through the Mediterranean in pursuit of Camara.

How far the mere announcement of the American plan

of campaign affected the Spanish purpose cannot be told. Camara's expedition, threatening at first, soon became ridiculous, and ended in an almost inexplicable display of folly and vacillation. Arriving at Port Said, the squadron lay at anchor for several days, — difficulty in getting coal was the Spanish explanation of the delay, but later occurrences suggest that there was never any serious purpose to make the voyage. Finally the ships were coaled, the heavy canal tolls paid, and the armada — a really formidable squadron of fifteen ships including torpedo boats and transports — majestically entered the great water-way. That was the day before Cervera's fatal dash at Santiago. The result of that action in West India waters was to free all our battle-ships for operations on the coast of Spain or for pursuit of Camara, and the work of supplying them with ammunition was rushed forward in order that they might be ready for this service; but before it could be completed the amazing news came from Port Said that Camara had turned about and was coming back again, having paid the tolls both ways, $200,000, for no imaginable purpose. To this day it is not known what strategic end this singular and costly excursion through the canal was expected to serve.

Meanwhile Dewey in Manila Bay had been studying the problem presented by the reported approach of Camara. Without cable facilities he was not as well informed as the Washington authorities of the vacillations of that remarkable commander. For several days all he knew was that a Spanish fleet outnumbering his, with two armoured vessels where he had none, with a formidable force of torpedo destroyers was steaming toward him. He knew the "Monterey" was on her way to reinforce him, and that the "Monadnock" would follow; but he was aware of the extreme sluggishness of these vessels, and figure it as he would he was convinced that the Spaniards would arrive first. The commander, who had all the strategy of his attack on Montojo planned long before war was declared, was not the man to leave a problem of the importance of this unstudied. General Francis V. Greene, who accompanied the second army expedition to Manila, tells how the admiral purposed coping with the situation, which was complicated by the fact that at this time there were 2500 American soldiers landed on the shores of Manila Bay. Dewey was convinced that to meet the "Pelayo" without any battle-ships of his own would be suicidal. Accordingly he planned to abandon the harbour and take his fleet and the transports which had then arrived around to the north of the island of Luzon, and thence cruise eastward to meet the "Monterey." That ship once added to his squadron, he would come back to Manila and give battle to the Spaniards. In the meantime the American troops thus left without naval support in a hostile country were to be taken up into the hills, and there intrenched to maintain themselves until the ships should return. The news of Camara's retreat reached Dewey only July 22d, or just as he was about to put this plan into effect.

The Filipinos very early became a source of some apprehension to Admiral Dewey, who it must be remembered was absolutely without any information as to the policy of the United States government in dealing with the territory which he had brought to the point of conquest, or the insurgents who were making so gallant a fight for freedom. When Congress declared war for the purpose of re-establishing humane and civilised conditions in Cuba, no revolution was in progress in the Philippines. The leaders of the former insurrection were, as has been already noted, living in Hong Kong, watching, no doubt, for a favourable opportunity to reopen the struggle, but meantime making no sign. For this reason Congress did not put into the resolutions instructing the President to employ the armed forces of the United States any such disavowal of any purpose to acquire territory in the

Philippines or any such promise of aid in the establishment there of an independent government as was employed in treating of the situation in Cuba. In its relations to the Filipinos the United States was bound by no promise, expressed or implied. Only the principles of national ethics and the dictates of expediency could affect its action. As there was, and is, some radical difference of opinion concerning alike the ethics and the advantages of the situation, it was impossible for the admiral to conjecture what attitude the President and the country would assume towards the insurgents. Accordingly, as they became stronger, he became more cautious. It is impossible to free him wholly from responsibility for their presence in the field, for he brought them their most capable leader and he furnished them with most of their arms; but he speedily came to doubt the wisdom of his own course and treated his whilom allies with studied coolness.

Before the arrival of the first expedition from the United States, Aguinaldo had made such progress in arming and organising the natives that in a series of engagements around Manila the Spaniards were worsted, losing heavily and being driven into the lines immediately surrounding the city. Aguinaldo captured 1800 prisoners and an immense store of arms, including two batteries of artillery. By the last of May the exultant insurgents were within seven miles of the city, which their lines completely encircled, and their prisoners numbered almost 3000. Then the first damper was put upon their enthusiasm by Admiral Dewey himself. Fearing that if the city should be taken by the insurgents, there would result a sack and massacre which would compel the intervention of the other armed forces in the harbour, he sent word to Aguinaldo that the advance must be stopped. Between the Filipino front and the town lay the Malolele River. This stream they were forbidden to cross. "If you do," said Dewey, "I will send the 'Petrel' into the stream to bombard your lines and to shoot down your men." The order was for the time obeyed, but naturally it created great bitterness. But even thus checked, Aguinaldo kept up an active warfare, most harassing to the Spaniards, and resulting in greatly increasing his store of captives, whom he treated well and held for ransom. The Spanish governor, General Augustin, was at his wits' end. In the harbour was a fleet of American warships holding the city at their mercy. On the hills and in the forests completely surrounding the town were nearly 30,000 natives, desperate with the memory of centuries of wrong and drunken with the sense of victory within their grasp. There was no communication with the interior, — no hope of help from either sea or shore, nor any chance, however desperate, of escape. The water supply was stopped by the insurgents. Food shipments were stopped. The despatches sent to Madrid by General Augustin tell how fatal he felt his position to be, and show incidentally how considerable an ally the Americans had in the young insurrectionary leader, Aguinaldo.

The first military expedition to Dewey's aid set sail from San Francisco May 25th, — an unconscionable delay which might have led to the most serious complications had a less capable commander than Dewey been holding the position in Manila. The cruiser "Charleston" convoyed the expedition, which was composed chiefly of volunteer troops from Oregon and California, and a portion of the Fourteenth United States Infantry, all under command of Brigadier-General Thomas M. Anderson. Prior to this time Major-General Wesley Merritt, a West Pointer and a veteran of the Civil War, had been given command of the department of the Pacific, including all military forces which were to take part in the Philippine expeditions; but he did not accompany the first expedition. The plans of the administration for pressing the campaign in the Philippines involved the ultimate despatch thither of 20,000 men, — a colossal task for an army establishment which but a few months before had scarcely exceeded that number in its total enrolment. The difficulty of getting troops to Manila was further increased by the lack of suitable ships on the Pacific seaboard, and by the fact that war in Asiatic waters was so far from the minds of the Washington authorities, at the beginning of the conflict, that they had stripped the Pacific coast States of their volunteers.

Once begun, however, the despatch of military forces to Dewey's aid proceeded apace. General Greene with the second expedition — four transports carrying 3500 men, all volunteers except eight companies from the Eighteenth and Twenty-third United States Infantry — sailed June 15th and reached Manila July 17th. The third expedition, under command of Brigadier-General Arthur McArthur, sailed June 27th and arrived July 31st. It comprised about 4000 men, mostly volunteers. Indeed, it may be noted here that if the campaign in Cuba was fought mainly by the regulars, the conquest of the Philippines — both in the war with the Spaniards and the later sanguinary fighting with the insurgents — was effected by that volunteer army which has ever been the great military reliance of the people of the United States. The three expeditions thus far enumerated, comprised in all about 10,000 officers and men. Other detachments of troops followed, — indeed the persistence of the insurrection resulted in compelling the United States government to exceed materially its first estimate of 20,000 for the Philippines, but the capture of Manila was effected before any more troops reached the scene.

Only the first of these expeditions from San Francisco was convoyed by a ship of war, — a fact which, had the Spaniards been as enterprising as they were brave, might have resulted in disaster. All, however, reached Manila without even an incident to relieve the monotony of the long voyage, except General Anderson's expedition, which, by virtue of its naval force — the unarmoured cruiser

GENERAL WESLEY MERRITT.

"Charleston" — stopped on the way to capture a Spanish colony. The story is a curious one, and strikingly illustrative of the slovenliness of the Spanish colonial system.

In the western Pacific, ten days' moderate steaming from Manila and rather more than twenty days' from San Francisco, lie the Ladrone Islands, a dependency of Spain. The principal island is called Guam, and its chief town is known as St. Ignacio de Agano. Here were ancient and decrepit fortifications, and here, too, the Spanish colonial governor had his residence in a picturesque if somewhat dilapidated official palace. Into this harbour steamed the "Charleston," and let fly a six-pound shot at the Spanish flag that floated over the opera-bouffe fort. There was no response, nor was there any excitement. Presently a boat was seen coming from the shore and made for the "Charleston's" gangway. Out of it climbed the Spanish governor, and with great dignity asked to be presented to the commander of the "Charleston." He had come at once with a welcome and an apology, he said. The salute which the Americans had been so polite as to fire he knew should be returned, but unhappily his home government had neglected him and he had no powder with which to return it. He was highly sensible of the honour done his little colony by this call of a fine warship from the great American nation, and quite desolated by the sense of his inability to discharge the formal courtesies of the occasion, but would the captain not accept his apologies and do him the honour to dine at the palace? All this and much more to the same ingenuous effect the Spanish governor said to his amazed auditors, who could hardly believe that he was ignorant of the existence of the war, and that he had mistaken their shotted guns for a formal salute. The luckless governor was soon undeceived, and with his officials was carried off to Manila, while a force was left to hold the island. By the terms of the treaty which closed the war, Guam became an American possession, and will be turned into a naval station where, it may be presumed, enough powder will be kept on hand for saluting or other uses.

A correspondent who was on the American flagship when the white flag was hoisted over the defences of Manila on August 13th reports that Admiral Dewey said at the moment, "I feel that I have won a greater victory to-day than that of May 1st." Perhaps to the men of the army who for weeks had been living in water-soaked trenches, alternately baked by the sun and drenched by heavy tropical showers, the while maintaining a sputtering warfare with the Spaniards, the assumption that the victory was won by the navy may be irritating, but to a great degree it was just. Much of the immunity from serious loss enjoyed by the troops was due to the moral influence of the ship's guns looking down on a helpless city, and the surrender, finally made after an almost bloodless contest, was the direct result of negotiations carried on between the defenders and the admiral.

When General Merritt reached Manila, July 25th, and assumed command of the troops, he found this situation existing: In Manila were supposed to be about 12,000 men. The city was beginning to suffer for both food and water, as supplies of each had been interrupted by the insurgents, who had completely hemmed in the town. The American forces — other than the navy — then on the ground numbered about 6000, and occupied the ground along the bay shore from Cavite toward Manila. The insurgents, as first on the ground, were in possession of the most advantageous positions for an attack on the Spanish lines, and completely shut off the American troops from the city. There had been no fighting except between the insurgents and the Spaniards, for the enemy had carefully refrained from giving the admiral any cause to fulfil his threat of bombarding the town if the American ships or lines were fired upon.

After reconnoitring the field, General Merritt agreed with Admiral Dewey that the attack on the city should be postponed until the arrival of the "Monterey" and the third expedition from San Francisco, which was then almost due. But it was held desirable to get the insurgents out of the way, and to accomplish it if possible by diplomacy, for by this time Aguinaldo had become sensible of his strength and resentful of his grievances, real or fancied. To General Greene, whose line was "blanketed" by the Filipinos, this task was assigned, and by him it was accomplished without much difficulty, by explaining to Aguinaldo that the heavier artillery of the Americans in the trenches occupied by his men would be vastly more effective against the common enemy than the antiquated guns which he had mounted there. The insurgent chief acceded to the suggestion, and on the 31st of July the Filipinos withdrew that portion of their lines which had rested on the bay shore, and their places were taken by Greene's brigade, which, not content with the advanced position thus gained, pushed still farther forward and brought on an engagement in which ten men were killed and thirty-three wounded. The engagement was at night, and was fought with a furious fire of musketry. The Americans, becoming convinced that the enemy was advancing, fired 60,000 rounds of ammunition. The next day General McArthur's command arrived and was landed, and the work of pushing forward the trenches continued. The country was a most difficult one either for intrenching or for marching, being given over mostly to the cultivation of rice, which necessitates submerged fields. The roads are few and narrow, and the best line of approach to the enemy's position was along the beach, even though it was much of the time under water. From the 1st to the 7th of August the troops worked persistently at rectifying and advancing their lines, a sputtering fire being kept up meanwhile by the enemy. General Greene declares that at no time after the first of the month would the issue of the conflict have been in doubt had the Americans charged the Spanish lines, but Admiral Dewey insisted that the attack should be deferred until the arrival of the "Monterey," and accordingly the time was occupied with preparations far more elaborate than the task really demanded. On the 7th all of General McArthur's troops were landed, the "Monterey" had arrived and completed the slight repairs necessary to fit her for active service, and the moment for bringing the long wait to a close seemed to have come. Of the issue of the conflict there could be no possible doubt. The batteries of the ships enfiladed the Spanish trenches on the right, so that the advance of the Americans along the beach and the few narrow roads would be in a great measure covered. Seeing this clearly and hoping that the Spaniards possessed an equally correct appreciation of the situation, Admiral Dewey and General Merritt strove to avert bloodshed by sending to the Governor-General a summons to surrender, with a warning that in forty-eight hours the attack would be made if he refused. He was cautioned, furthermore, that if the night assaults on the American troops continued the attack might be precipitated even before the expiration of the time set, and he was urged to send the women and children in the city away to places of safety. The response of the Governor-General showed that he appreciated the hopelessness of his position, but dared not surrender without at least a show of resistance. He pointed out that with the city surrounded by half-savage insurgents there was no place of safety to which he might send the women and children, and he asked that the time before the assault be extended to give him time to communicate with the government at Madrid. This was promptly refused, and the preparations for the attack began, the Spaniards meanwhile abandoning their practice of night attacks on the American lines lest the day of reckoning be hastened.

It was during the preparations for the attack that the

British squadron in the bay gave another of those frank expressions of good-fellowship for the Americans that have done so much to break down the ancient hostility between the two nations. The harbour was busy with shipping moving to anchorages out of reach of the expected bombardment. The foreign consuls were actively engaged in embarking people of their nationalities on transports and taking them to places of safety out in the bay — and by the way an eye-witness notes that the number of German citizens thus cared for was ridiculously disproportionate to the powerful fleet which the Kaiser had thought it necessary to maintain there for their protection. A few hours before the time set for the attack, the British squadron of four ships, which had been anchored far across the bay from the Americans, weighed anchor and steamed over toward Cavite, where Dewey was moored. As the British flagship "Immortalite" steamed under the stern of the "Olympia," her band crashed out the strains of the "Star-Spangled Banner" and her men cheered the Yankees lustily. The American band responded with "God Save the Queen" and equally hearty cheers, and then, perhaps by accident only, the British took up an anchorage directly between the American ships and the Germans. The incident was one move — a trivial one — in the diplomatic game which went on concurrently with the game of war in Manila harbour.

The attack was not begun on that day, however. Some difficulty in securing an advantageous position for the troops under General McArthur compelled another delay. The time was not wholly lost, for before another forty-eight hours had passed Admiral Dewey had learned, through the Belgian consul, who was his intermediary in communicating with the Spaniards, that the city would be surrendered as soon as there had been enough of an attack and a defence to satisfy "Spanish honour," and incidentally to save the commander from a court-martial when he reached home. It was arranged, accordingly, that the ships should not fire upon the town, but should confine their attack to Fort San Antonio and the trenches immediately in the American front. The United States troops meanwhile were to be gathered under cover in their trenches, ready for an assault if one should be necessary. After a short bombardment the admiral with the "Olympia" was to move up close to the city walls and display the international code signal "Surrender." The response to this was to be a white flag on the corner of the Malate, the most advanced of the walls of the city. Should the Spaniards fail to display this signal, then the Americans were to advance to the attack; but if it was shown they would merely have to enter the city and take possession. While this programme was thoroughly understood by General Merritt, he nevertheless prudently made his dispositions for a real battle, apprehending that the Spanish officers might not be able to control their men, or that in some other way the arrangement might miscarry.

The point in the Spanish line of defence menaced by the American attack was directly south of the city, where the Spaniards had a line of earthworks and barbed wire extending from Fort San Antonio on the beach to a block-house on the bank of a small stream which ran parallel with the sea-shore and about a mile away from it. From that point the Spanish lines turned sharply northward, enveloping the city and confronted at every point by the insurgents. The United States forces concerned themselves only with that part of the enemy's line between the fort and the block-house. That was the most vulnerable point of attack, because the fort itself could have been demolished in half an hour by the fire of any of the men-of-war, and the whole line to the stream was within easy range of the cannon of the fleet. With this position carried, Manila would be at the mercy of the invaders, since nothing would remain to bar their advance except the antiquated walls of Malate.

The day of battle came gusty and showery. The soil, already waterlogged, was made even more difficult for the passage of troops, and the frequent showers of rain hid from the gunners of the ships the targets offered them. About nine o'clock in the morning the ships blossomed out with battle-flags at every point. With the "Olympia" in the lead, they steamed slowly down toward Fort San Antonio, the blare of the band from the British flagship, which accompanied them at a safe distance, lending an air of festivity to the scene. Soon the "Olympia," "Raleigh," and "Petrel" opened on the fort, quickly enshrouding themselves in a cloud of yellow smoke, which hung heavily about them in the damp and sultry air. The "Monterey" had steamed nearer to the city, and confronted in silence the central battery, where were mounted four formidable Krupp rifles. If the Spaniards held to their agreement, that battery would not open fire; but the "Monterey," with her heavy armour and 12-inch guns was stationed there to attend to it if the Spaniards proved forgetful. The "Concord" was north of the walled town, her guns commanding the fort at the mouth of the Pasig River, which intersects the city. Her part in the conflict, like that of the "Monterey," was destined to be a merely silent and precautionary one. The little gunboat "Callao," captured from the Spanish, lay close inshore, raking the enemy's trenches with her machine guns and preparing the way for the American troops who were to make the assault. For more than half an hour the bombardment continued without any answer from the shore. The American ships were putting in their heaviest shells, and great clouds of dirt could be seen thrown high in the air as the "Olympia's" 8-inch shells exploded fairly within the fort. The battle was as harmless and almost as unexciting to the sailors as target practice, for the defenders of the fort clung sullenly to their earthwork bombproofs and made not the slightest reply. At last there was a rattle of musketry from the shore, and after allowing the smoke to clear away, the men on the ships could see a column of men advancing up the beach toward the fort, in water up to their waists part of the time, but pressing forward with cheers, with colours waving, and with a band stoutly plodding along in their rear, from which there came faintly over the water the strains of that novel battle-song, "There'll be a hot time in the old town to-night."

This was the First Colorado Infantry, sent forward under orders from General Merritt of the night before to make a feint, or, if the Spaniards showed resistance, a real attack. Either because the understanding between the governor-general and the American commanders had not been communicated to the men in the fort, or because the Spanish officers were unable to control their men, a vigorous fire was opened on this column, but without checking its advance in the least. The Coloradans pressed on, throwing themselves flat to rest when they came to a piece of dry beach, and wading stubbornly through the surf that at points covered their sandy pathway. Now and then a man fell, but not many, for the Spanish aim was bad, and apparently only a part of the Spanish forces were firing. A small stream in front of the fort was promptly forded, and soon the watchers in the ships could see the Spaniards streaming out of the back of the fort, while the Colorado men with loud cheers rushed up and over the front. Almost instantly the Spanish flag came fluttering down, and a great American flag was run up to the top of the staff and saluted with cheers from the ships and the trenches.

On the right of the American line, out of sight of the ships and with little aid from their guns, the assailants were meeting a more serious resistance. There General McArthur's brigade was engaged. Massed in trenches, behind stone houses, and taking advantage of everything that offered protection, these troops waited until they saw the flag come down from Fort San Antonio. Then the guns of the Astor battery and a Utah volunteer battery were turned on the most formidable work in their front — a stone block-house — and quickly riddled it, after which the troops charged the Spanish lines and soon carried them. The Spaniards retreated before the advancing Americans, who did not stop in the captured trenches, but pressed on toward the city, sustaining meanwhile a heavy fire from the woods that bordered the road and from every farm-house or other covert they encountered. By the time the Spaniards had been driven from every halting-place the brigade had lost 7 men killed and 37 wounded.

Meanwhile the Colorado men with the First California and part of the Twenty-third Regulars had left Fort Antonio behind, and were pushing into the suburb of Malate, where they met a heavy fire from house windows and roofs. The situation was then a most anomalous one. In pursuance of the agreement with Admiral Dewey, the Spaniards had displayed a white flag on the corner of the wall of the old town, but directly under this flag the Spanish soldiers were continuing the fight, and the American troops were responding with heavy volleys. The navy had ceased firing, and at this very moment officers representing Admiral Dewey and General Merritt were on their way to the city hall to meet, by prearrangement, the Spanish officials and formulate the terms of capitulation; yet there was fighting in the streets of Malate, and large bodies of Spanish troops were standing irresolute, with arms in their hands, uncertain whether to reopen the conflict or not. The insurgents, who had not been much in evidence during the day, as the fighting was not on their lines, now began to crowd toward the breach in the Spanish position, and announced their intention of entering the city with the victors, — a purpose which General Merritt promptly interdicted, instructing his brigade commanders to keep them out at any cost. By night, however, these complications were all untangled. The Spaniards everywhere were informed of the surrender, the last Spanish flag in the city was hauled down, American troops garrisoned every fort, and patrolled all the principal streets of the city, and the insurgents, nursing a not unjustifiable resentment, were left in their trenches, confronting not only their enemies the Spaniards, but their friends the Americans. The sufficient justification for the restraint put upon the insurgents is the fact, that had they been admitted to the city before the American authority was complete, and arrangements for the protection of life and property perfected, they would beyond a shadow of a doubt have sacked and looted the town.

The terms of capitulation were arranged the following day. In effect they granted to the Spaniards the honours of war. Manila and its suburbs were surrendered to the United States forces, together with all public property, arms, and munitions of war. The Spanish officers were to be permitted to retain their side arms, horses, and personal property of every sort. The Americans charged themselves for the present with the subsistence of the prisoners pending the decision of the Washington authorities as to shipping them back to Spain. The duty of policing the city, protecting private property, and reopening the port to commerce was also assumed by the conquerors. The details of the surrender thus completed, Governor-General Augustin made a hasty flight from Manila on the German flagship "Kaiserin Augusta"—an incident that for a time added to the bitterness felt against Germany in the army, but it afterwards appeared that the flight was with Dewey's knowledge and connivance. When the German ship reached Hong Kong, however, her officers assured the American consul there that the situation at Manila was unchanged, although they had seen the American flag raised over the city some hours before their departure. Seemingly the German policy of unfriendliness could not stop short of petty falsehoods.

The capture of Manila is almost unprecedented in the history of warfare, for the great value of the prize and the small expenditure of human life in the winning of it. A city of 300,000 inhabitants, heavily fortified, was taken with a loss of twenty killed and 105 wounded, after a leisurely campaign covering 24 days. On the American side, exclusive of the navy, scarce 9000 men had been engaged, and they had taken 13,000 prisoners. Of arms and munitions of war there were captured 22,000 small arms, ten million rounds of ammunition, about 70 pieces of modern artillery, and several hundred antiquated bronze pieces. In the vaults of the city was about $900,000, — fair spoil of war. Nor was the extent of the triumph the greatest of the American achievements at Manila. Almost instantly conditions of peace were restored in the city. The strong hand of authority restrained alike the eager insurgents and the sullen Spanish soldiery. The custom-house was reopened, and shops took down their shutters. After the first moment of terror the inhabitants discovered that while the American occupation meant martial law it meant also protection to every man in the pursuit of his business. General Greene, who was most active in this work, writes:

"Within one week from the time the articles of capitulation were signed every branch of the government except civil courts was in operation. The police stations were open, and American soldiers were on duty as patrolmen. Police court was held every morning, and petty offenders were tried, and either acquitted, or convicted, sentenced, and sent to jail. The streets were being cleaned; the prisoners of war were quartered and fed; public property was inventoried and counted; public funds were secured and placed in the custody of officers under bonds; the custom-house was doing a large business; the streets were lighted; water was delivered through the pipes; the markets were open, and food in ample quantity was coming in from the country on one side and by sea on the other. . . . The day we entered the city all shops and buildings were closed, and they remained so the following day, which was Sunday. But on Monday a few venturesome shopkeepers threw open their doors, and finding that they were fully protected, the others followed their example on Tuesday. That afternoon the newspapers made their appearance, and the tramways resumed operations. On Wednesday morning the banks opened their doors, under a guard of soldiers to preserve order, which, however, was withdrawn two days later as being no longer necessary."

A curious fact about the capture and occupation of the city by the American troops is that it took place after the peace protocol had been formally concluded at Washington, resembling therein the famous victory of New Orleans which was won by General Jackson several days after the signing of the treaty of Ghent which concluded the War of 1812. Had the cable to Hong Kong been intact, it is doubtful whether Manila would ever have been taken, for it would have been the duty of the authorities at Washington to notify the forces in the Philippines immediately of the end of the war. There would have been a sorry time for the soldiers and sailors who had been working and waiting so patiently to put the finishing touch upon Dewey's victory of May 1st, and the map of the world might have escaped a radical change. Certainly the United States would in that event have been freed from grave problems and heavy responsibilities which have come to them as the result of their new possessions in the Philippines.

It is possible to give here only the most cursory account of the deplorable revolt of the Filipinos under Aguinaldo against the authority of the United States in the captured territory contiguous to Manila. As I have already pointed out, the insurgents became restive very early in the Manila campaign. As they gained in numbers and in confidence, they assumed authority which they could not maintain. During the long days when Dewey was waiting for troops from home it became only too clear that Aguinaldo thought the admiral greatly dependent upon him for support on shore. In more than one instance the insurgent chief attempted to assert his power in a way annoying to the admiral, but in every instance he was summarily rebuked. It was perhaps this tendency to independence shown by the Filipino leader that led the admiral to revise materially his first declaration, " These people [the Filipinos] are ten times better fitted for self-government than the Cubans."

However that may be, the extreme care taken by Admiral Dewey and later by General Merritt to avoid anything which would seem like recognition of the Filipino leader in his official capacity — he had proclaimed himself Dictator — undoubtedly suggested to Aguinaldo that the bright hopes he had formed of a native republic under the protection of the United States were doomed to disappointment. Through his envoy Agoncillo he was kept informed of the progress of the peace negotiations at Paris, and saw the American commissioners there calmly bargaining for the sovereignty of the Philippines, with apparently no thought of the rights or the wishes of their people. Against the terms of the treaty Agoncillo the diplomat filed a protest. Aguinaldo the soldier continued to co-operate with the Americans against Manila, but manifested suspicion and resentment by studiously avoiding any communication with the United States commanders.

Men who have known this remarkable leader have given the most conflicting reports of his character, and perhaps it is no more than natural that the estimates proceeding from American sources should have been almost uniformly eulogistic until the moment of his revolt, and thereafter almost invariably to his discredit. It is undeniable, however, that he is a man of marked native ability, which he has improved by arduous study of all that pertains to the tasks of the soldier or the statesman. He has power over men, and has ruled his followers with an iron hand. He has courage, and that lofty temperament which enables its possessor to go down cheerfully for an idea. He is imbued with the spirit of national freedom, else he would not have staked all on a hopeless revolt against the power of the United States.

It would be idle to deny that Aguinaldo and his followers had some excuse for feeling themselves betrayed when they learned that the opportunity to form a government of their own was to be denied them. They were at the outset treated with the utmost friendliness by the official representatives of the United States. The consul at Hong Kong was in constant communication with the Filipino leader, and furthered his plans for again taking the field against Spain. One of Dewey's ships brought him to Manila. His men were armed with rifles captured by the Americans. When a German ship checked a body of the insurgents in the act of capturing a Spanish post in Subig Bay, an American man-of-war took the post and delivered it over to the Filipinos. Perhaps in all this the representatives of the United States did not overstep the line between inofficial friendliness and official recognition, but the Filipinos can hardly be blamed for believing themselves an important factor in the Manila problem, — one that could not be ignored in the solution. The treaty of peace by which the United States paid Spain $20,000,000 to relinquish sovereignty in the Philippines gave to the revolutionists their first rude shock. A proclamation in the form of a letter from the President to General Elwell S. Otis, who succeeded General Merritt after the capture of Manila, only converted into certainty the suspicion of the insurgents that they were to be denied self-government. The President declared that the United States had succeeded to the sovereignty of Spain in the islands, announced that the Americans came, "not as invaders or conquerors, but as friends to protect the natives in their homes, in their employments, and in their personal and religious rights," and further announced that the " mission of the United States is one of benevolent assimilation,

GENERAL ELWELL S. OTIS.

substituting the mild sway of justice and right for arbitrary rule." In this was no word of comfort for the Filipino republic, which had been duly formed with Aguinaldo as President. The natives were prepared to admit that in exchanging the sway of Spain for the rule of the United States they had made a notable bargain, but they still cherished a hope that they, like the Cubans, might secure at least the opportunity to try a government of their own. Out of this sentiment grew inevitably an antagonism to the United States as bitter as any that had been felt for Spain. Feeling themselves deceived and outraged, unable with their limited horizon to discern the many reasons which had compelled the Americans to assume the position they had, the natives prepared to give battle to their new masters.

The first serious defiance of the authority of the United States occurred at Iloilo, the second commercial port of the Philippines. It had been held by the Spaniards during the armistice, but on the 24th of December was evacuated. Immediately a force of Filipinos entered the town and occupied its fortifications, refusing to evacuate them at the demand of a detachment of American troops which had been sent as soon as notice of the evacuation was received. A week later Aguinaldo issued a proclamation protesting against the American occupation of Manila, and calling upon all native Filipinos to continue the battle for liberty. Meanwhile Manila was honeycombed with plots. In one instance a Filipino in the service of the United States was noticed diligently organising clubs in all parts of the town. "To help maintain American supremacy," he explained when questioned; but a little investigation showed that they were revolutionary and designed to aid Aguinaldo. Outside the city the insurgents occupied the same trenches they had when they hemmed in the Spaniards and cut off their food and water. Now it was the Americans who were hemmed in, though a semblance of peace was preserved and the most imperative orders given to avoid a conflict. But the conflict was as inevitable as fire when inflammable materials are exposed to heat. On the night of the 5th of February there was a shot on the lines. From which side it was fired cannot be told with certainty, but as if it was a signal, it was followed by volleys and the United States, not yet fairly out of war with Spain, was at war with the Filipino insurgents. The outbreak was not unexpected, and the American commanders, by sea and shore, inflicted upon the new enemy such punishment as showed the insurgents that they no longer had Spaniards to deal with. As soon as day dawned the ships opened on the insurgents in the trenches. The "Monadnock," the "Charleston," the "Concord" and two captured gunboats were engaged, and their fire, with that of General Otis's troops, did cruel execution among the half-armed Filipinos. The enemy's loss was heavy. Though not definitely reported, it is known to have extended into the thousands, and Aguinaldo was driven from his lines about Manila. But he was far from being crushed.

At this time there were in the island of Luzon — the only one thus far affected by the revolt — about 30,000 Filipinos under arms. In discipline and in equipment the different commands varied widely, some being mere bands of savages armed with bows and arrows, others having a semblance of European organisation and carrying the Mausers captured by the Americans from the Spaniards. The force was a formidable one, nevertheless, vastly superior to that with which Garcia and Gomez had kept the Spanish in Cuba in check for three years. With perfect knowledge of the country, with acclimated troops and holding possession of everything outside a narrow belt around Manila, Aguinaldo threatened to make grave trouble for the United States in establishing its authority over the new domain.

Very quickly, however, the American commanders demonstrated to the insurgent general that he had men of a type very different from the Spanish to deal with. There was no building trochas, no clinging to the cities, no effort to subdue men under arms by starving women and children. The troops took up the new contest as if they had expected it. Blow followed blow, and the insurgents were forced back away from the city and into the interior. Five days after the outbreak at Manila, the insurgent stronghold at Caloocan was taken, and the day following Iloilo was captured. There was fighting every day, the enemy's forces being diligently sought and attacked fiercely wherever found. Either because of a lack of self-control or through pure bravado, Aguinaldo failed to adopt the Fabian tactics which the Cuban insurgents had employed so effectively. Confident of the strength of his forces, he seldom attempted to avoid battle, and accordingly his troops were pushed back day after day, losing heavily in every encounter. Early in February much of the sympathy which had been felt for him as a sincere and able if mistaken leader was alienated by the discovery of a plot among the Filipinos in Manila, to assassinate all foreign residents, regardless of sex, age, or nationality. The plot had progressed so far that the date for its execution was fixed, and its details were worked out with the utmost circumstance. Nations are not builded upon wholesale massacres, and a new St. Bartholomew would form but a sorry inauguration of an enlightened republic in the East.

The discovery of this plot had immediate effect in strengthening the determination of the Americans to put down the revolt without mercy; and the completion of the treaty of peace which soon followed, removed certain embarrassments in the way of the conquerors. Before the treaty the Tagals were rebellious Spanish subjects; thereafter they were in rebellion against the United States. Prior to the treaty General Otis could not negotiate with the insurgents, nor did he feel justified in waging a really aggressive campaign against them. The treaty once completed, however, the American forces took the field in earnest. By the middle of March all plans were ready for an advance into the interior of the island. On the 13th the town of Pasig, which is on the river of the same name, was captured, and during the two weeks following the fighting was continuous and deadly.

By the 1st of April it became apparent that the United States had encountered in the Philippines a situation more grave than had ever confronted the nation, except at the outbreak of the Civil War. Expedition had followed expedition to the far-off islands, until, instead of the 20,000 soldiers which had been thought enough to cope with the problem, we had nearly 45,000 there, including many regiments of regulars and a heavy fleet. To our people, unused to colonial wars and distrustful of a large army, this seemed a heavy price to pay for territory of doubtful value. It was, indeed, an expenditure of men in foreign warfare which might appall nations of a wider military experience than ours. The expedition of Lord Kitchener through the desert, which attracted the attention of all military Europe, numbered only about 8000 white troops, and some 12,000 natives. In their prolonged war on the frontiers of Afghanistan, the British employed only 32,000 troops, of whom only about 10,000 were white. The French put only 15,000 men into Madagascar, and the British subjugated the Zulus with a scant 7000. Even the Spaniards held the Philippines with fewer soldiers than we found necessary, for when Dewey entered Manila Bay there were not more than 20,000 Spanish troops in all the islands.

This condition naturally bred the greatest anxiety in the United States. The relatives of volunteers who had enlisted for the war with Spain bitterly denounced the policy which compelled these soldiers to remain in service months after that war was over, fighting a fight for which they had not volunteered and for which many had no sympathy. The so-called "anti-expansionists" or people who held that the United States should confine themselves within the natural continental boundaries, hailed each new embarrassment in the Philippines as additional proof of the justice of their contention that only disaster could follow the adoption of a colonising policy by the United States. About Manila the war was fought with bullets, at home it was waged scarcely less bitterly with pamphlets, speeches, and editorials. The administration withheld any definite declaration of its policy beyond a declaration of purpose to first put down the revolt and then consider what should be done with the Philippines. While the army and navy were intrusted with the primary duty, a commission was appointed to proceed to the scene and consider the political methods which would best serve to give the islands an orderly and civilised government. The members of this commission were men of notable attainments and high character. President Jacob Gould Schurman, of Cornell University; Professor Dean C. Worcester, of the University of Michigan, who had travelled extensively in the islands before the war; Colonel Charles Denby, long the Minister of the United States to China, made up the commission, together with Admiral Dewey. The commissioners arrived at Manila on the 4th of March, and great hopes were expressed that they would speedily affect an arrangement with the insurgents; but the pertinacity of the enemy again disappointed American expectations. Though beaten whenever brought to battle, they shifted their positions and fought on week after week, deaf to any suggestions of peace which involved their first laying down their arms. Though driven from their capital, Malolos, their villages burned, their ranks decimated in the most merciless fighting in which American soldiers have ever engaged, they stubbornly maintained their hopeless resistance; and as these lines are being written, the subjugation of Aguinaldo and his followers, though promised for an early date, is still a thing to be accomplished. More men by far were lost in the war against the insurgents than in that against the Spaniards, if the losses from disease be excepted; more troops have been employed, the fighting has been fiercer, and to-day the results are almost barren. Of the outcome there can be no doubt. In the end the limitless resources of the great Republic and the discipline of its army and navy will prove too much for Aguinaldo's half-clad soldiery; but the contest has been costly and not wholly glorious, the civil problems which will follow it will be harassing and difficult, and the profit, either material or moral, attending all is more than problematical.

CHAPTER XVI

The Peace Commission at Paris — The Completion of the Treaty — The Struggle in the American Senate — Some Lessons of the War — The Work of the Torpedo Boats — The Need for a Permanent Staff Organisation — The Part played by the Militia — The Future of the Army.

IN outlining the course of events in the Philippines after the declaration of the armistice on the 13th of August, 1898, I have to some extent anticipated the course of the historical narrative. While Merritt and Dewey were advancing upon Manila, the civil authorities in Washington were busily engaged in negotiating the protocol which resulted in preliminary peace; and while the earlier fighting between the insurgents and the Americans in Luzon was in progress, the peace commissions of the two nations at war were meeting in Paris to formulate a treaty, which in its effect upon the distribution of national power is second in importance to scarcely any instrument of the sort ever negotiated.

To all intents and purposes, the agreement upon the protocol ended the war except in the Philippines, where the news was slow to arrive. The armistice passed without incident into a permanent peace. Much in the way of formality had to be gone through with before the war could be declared at an end; but the fighting stopped that 13th day of August, and what remained to be done was the work of the diplomats. In an era of short wars this was one of the briefest. The Franco-Prussian war lasted five days over six months The Turco-Russian war of 1877 had a duration of nine months. The war between Japan and China ended with the ignominious defeat of the latter in eight months. Our own struggle with Spain reached its conclusion in less than four months, though already — May, 1899 — the sharp conflict with the Filipino insurgents has occupied a like period and seems likely to continue months longer. It is to be borne in mind that this period of four months is that of active hostilities only. Formally and of record the war is presumed to have continued until the interchange of ratifications of the treaty, which took place at Washington, April 11, 1899.

The treaty as finally agreed to by the United States Senate and the Queen Regent of Spain, who ratified it in the recess of the Cortes, followed closely the lines of the protocol. To formulate it, both governments appointed commissioners, who met in Paris in October. The United States commission included Mr. W. R. Day, who resigned the post of Secretary of State to undertake this task; Mr. Whitelaw Reid, editor of the "New York Tribune;" United States Senators Gray, Frye, and Davis, and Mr. John B. Moore, secretary. For Spain appeared Señor Eugene Montero Rios, president, General R. Cerero, and Señors de Garnoca, Arbazuza, and de Villaurrutia. Into the details of the prolonged discussion it is unnecessary to go. The determination of the United States government to insist upon Spain's renunciation of all sovereignty over the Philippine Islands led to the most violent disagreement, and would doubtless have broken off the negotiations had not Spain's case been so obviously helpless. The Spaniards urged, with some measure of justice, that the protocol, which was supposed to cover all the demands of the United States, did not demand the actual abandonment of the islands by Spain; but by this time public opinion in the United States had so clearly signified the desire of the people that the Philippine Archipelago should at least be freed from Spanish dominion, that the American commissioners were unyielding. A prolonged and brilliant effort was also made by the Spaniards to saddle upon Cuba that part of the Spanish debt which was supposed to have been incurred for the good of the island, including the money spent and the money stolen in the various efforts to put down Cuban rebellions. Against this, too, the American commissioners made a determined and successful resistance. It may be remarked here that the peace commissioners — like any diplomats accredited to foreign countries in this era of swift cable communication — were, in fact, supernumerary functionaries. Their instructions were cabled from day to day, and they had but the shadow of personal authority So wholly were they a representative body, expressing only the will of the central authority at Washington, that their instructions were radically changed after a Western journey had convinced the President that the sentiment of the country favoured a plan for the Philippines different from the one he had originally contemplated. Diplomacy is a very different art in the end of the nineteenth century from what it was at the beginning. An ambassador now, even a special one with so important a mission as the negotiation of a treaty of peace, is but a mouthpiece.

After weeks of haggling, the peace commission formulated a treaty, signed it December 10th, and adjourned. The essentials of the treaty followed closely the lines laid down in the protocol, its chief differences being in the clauses dealing with the Philippines. All claim to sovereignty in those islands was relinquished by Spain, and, in consideration of that action, the United States was bound to pay Spain $20,000,000. The future of the islands was left to the determination of the United States. Porto Rico was ceded to the United States, as were also all other West Indian islands then in Spain's possession, excepting Cuba, which was given freedom, and in addition the island of Guam in the Ladrones. The customary clauses securing civil rights to the residents of the territories ceded, and providing for special privileges to the vessels of the ceding nation in the ports of the countries relinquished, completed the treaty.

After a bitter fight in the United States Senate, growing out of the opposition of many Senators and public men to what seemed to portend the actual annexation of the Philippine Islands to the United States, the treaty was ratified and signed by the President, February 10, 1899. In Spain the Cortes was not in session, and indeed there was some doubt whether a ratification would have passed that body. Accordingly, the Queen Regent affixed her signature to the document March 17th, and it became effective.

An historic document, indeed, is this Treaty of Paris,— one that marks an epoch in the development of the United States, one that signalises a day of disaster in the history of Spain. To Spain it is the final decree of expulsion from the western hemisphere. The enormous territory which the Spanish had held as the fruit of the endeavours of their hardy explorers was at last dissipated. First the great Louisiana Territory ceded to France had passed into the ownership of the United States. Then by purchase, though almost at the cannon's mouth, the United States freed themselves from a troublesome neighbour, and Spain lost Florida. Next, by successful revolution, Mexico broke away from the control of Madrid, and by war the United States acquired much of the territory which Spain thus lost. Followed then, in swift succession, the revolutions by which the flag of blood and gold was dragged from its places of authority in the States of South America. At last Cuba and Porto Rico alone were left to hapless Spain, and these, as we have seen, were held by her largely by grace of the United States, until her sins grew so intolerable that the very power which had long protected her in occupation of American territory was compelled by considerations of humanity to sweep her out of it.

If to Spain the end of the war of 1898 seemed to mean

submission to spoliation and the sacrifice of her historic possessions in two distant seas, to the United States it means new problems, new responsibilities, new duties, and perhaps new evils. The event marked our first acceptance of territory beyond seas — for Hawaii had been taken during the war, and Porto Rico by the very terms of the treaty became a part of the United States. The relinquishment of Spanish sovereignty over Cuba and the Philippines meant for the United States a grave and perplexing problem. For both countries we became thereby responsible. Though pledged to give the Cubans a chance to govern themselves, duty commanded that we should maintain such a supervision over their first attempts at self-government as to assure the continuance of order and the permanence of the government. Should the Cubans prove unfit for self-government, — a most improbable supposition, — or should they prefer annexation to the United States, the graver question of our acceptance of the island as a State or a Territory would come up. But all the problems presented by the situation in the West Indies are dwarfed by those which the Philippines present. Those huge and undeveloped islands, 6000 miles from our nearest port, peopled by 11,000,000 natives, mostly savages skilled in warfare and loving it, pestilential in climate, and of little profit in trade, were by a stroke of a pen, following an unexpected development of the war, made wards of the United States. For years their people had been in revolution against Spain, and with alacrity they revolted against their new rulers. For the first time in its history the nation found itself confronted with the necessity of sending its sons to a far distant and alien land to fight naked savages in a jungle. People began to ask, " Is it worth while ? " and the territory which Dewey won from the Spaniards was described as another shirt of Nessus, very gay and beautiful in appearance, but which gave to him who put it on a fatal disease. The doubt was generally expressed whether

Spain had not received $20,000,000 for ridding herself of a province which she could not govern and which brought her no profit, and whether the United States had not paid that sum for the doubtful privilege of suppressing a revolution. But in response, the question was asked, "Would you have us return the Filipinos to Spain, to extortion, to torture, and to death?" Only one answer to that question could be returned; but as yet the final response has not been made to the more important query, which grows more insistent daily, "What shall we do with the Philippines?"

A nation which enters upon a war braves the unknowable. The issue of the conflict may perhaps be predicated with some certainty from an exact knowledge of the rival armaments, but the collateral results of the struggle develop most unexpectedly, and often in shapes which the most far-sighted statesman could not have foreseen, nor the most vivid fancy imagine. The United States embarked on the war with Spain formally disavowing any purpose of territorial aggrandisement. It emerged the possessor of Porto Rico, Guam, and the populous Philippines. It went to war to save the starving reconcentrados, and the exigencies of the struggle compelled a blockade which only made their condition more pitiful. It entered upon the conflict denouncing Spain for attempting to enforce an alien and hateful rule upon the Cubans, and it ended by enforcing upon the unwilling Filipinos a rule equally alien, and supported by cannon and rifles. Among the unexpected results of the war was the annexation to the United States of the Hawaiian Islands. This fertile and beautiful archipelago in the Pacific had been for years knocking at the door of the Union, to which, indeed, it belonged by interest, by the character of its population, and by its geographical position. Constitutional scruples in the minds of certain Senators had resulted in the defeat or indefinite postponement of every

HARBOR OF HONOLULU.

effort to ratify an annexation treaty. But Dewey's victory gave the Hawaiian Islands a new importance. They afforded the only sheltered spot between San Francisco and the Asiatic islands where a ship could put in for coal or repairs, the only rendezvous in the Pacific for the expeditions which it was foreseen would soon be following one another to the new dominion. Accordingly, constitutional procedure was stretched until, in the minds of some, it broke. By means of a resolution of both houses of Congress, the annexation of the islands was ordered, and on the 16th of July the President signed the resolutions giving them legal effect. The cruiser " Philadelphia" was despatched to the islands with the news, and on the 12th of August — the day the peace protocol was signed — the Hawaiian flag came down, and the Stars and Stripes went up over the government building in Honolulu for ever. There, as in the Philippines, the natives grieved over the downfall of their own government, but no resistance was made. For years the islands had been in form a republic, in fact a little oligarchy, all power being held by a few Americans who had seized the government by force from the hands of the native queen, Liliuokalani. Beyond the shadow of a doubt the administration of affairs by the United States will be to the advantage, both material and moral, of the islands and their people.

The war taught its lessons, military, naval, and political, not only to the nations concerned in it, but to all considerable powers. Perhaps the naval operations and combats were watched with the greatest interest, since this was the first opportunity ever presented for studying the value in combat of the complicated and delicate fighting-machines which compose modern navies. It is probable that one result of the war will be to destroy the favour — manifested it must be said only in the United States — in which ships of the monitor type are held.

Admiral Sampson curtly says that in his operations in the West Indies he was only hampered by the "Amphitrite" and "Terror." Captain Mahan, in his review of the naval lessons of the war, aptly points out that, however useful the monitors might be for harbour defence, they cannot be held for that purpose only; and as soon as they have to move, their slowness and small coal capacity make them a source of anxiety to the fleet commander who is burdened with them. It is true that the "Monadnock" and the "Monterey" crossed the Pacific safely; but they did so at so sluggish a pace that, as we have seen, Admiral Dewey was all but compelled to abandon his hard-won position lest the armoured vessels of Camara might arrive first. The thorough efficiency of the battle-ship for every use to which a monitor could be put was as fully demonstrated as was the inefficiency of the monitors when assigned tasks normally belonging to battle-ships.

The work of the torpedo boats and destroyers during the war left the efficiency of that arm of the naval service in grave doubt. The Spanish torpedo boats accomplished nothing. Perhaps it was because they were handled without either intelligence or dash, but the fact of their impotence remains. The one instance in which a Spanish vessel of this type made a really determined effort to torpedo an American ship was at San Juan, June 22d, when the "Terror" attempted to destroy the auxiliary "St. Paul" commanded by Captain Sigsbee. Although the threatened vessel afforded a huge target and was armed only with comparatively light guns, the torpedo boat was unable to get into effective distance of it, and was driven back to port in a sinking condition without an opportunity to let fly one of its deadly missiles. In this case there were dash and bravery in the Spanish attack, but not intelligence. Had the attempt been made at night, a different story might be told. At any rate, this was the nearest approach to the use of a torpedo boat for the purpose for which it was designed during the war. At Santiago repeated efforts were made to take the "Furor" out of the harbour at night, to break Sampson's rigid blockade; but the glare of the American searchlight defeated the purpose, and when the two destroyers came out with the other ships on the 3d of July, they fled like their companions, and like them died impotently.

On the part of the Americans constant use of torpedo boats was made for every purpose except that for which they were designed. They served as messengers and as blockaders; they bombarded fortifications, as in the case of the "Winslow" at Cardeñas, and the "Porter" at San Juan; they helped in cable cutting, and they examined rivers and harbours under the enemy's fire. The United States was not rich enough in vessels to employ each class on the service for which it was especially designed, and accordingly work was put on the torpedo boats for which they were not fitted, and the performance of which exposed their officers and crews to the greatest discomfort and danger.

But if on neither side did the torpedo boat prove in action the reason for its existence, a sort of moral proof was afforded by certain incidents of the war. The officers of the ships about Santiago harbour will bear testimony to the nervous strain which the mere knowledge of the existence of the torpedo destroyers with Cervera caused. One night a train gliding along the line close to the water's edge called out a furious fire from the fleet, because an officer thought it was a torpedo boat lurking in the shadows. Another night the white foam breaking on a ledge of rocks was similarly honoured for the same reason. If these errors show how constant is the menace in the possession of torpedo boats by the enemy, a graver blunder, narrowly averted, came near giving a sorrowful demonstration of the murderous power of the weapons of these midgets when rightly used.

It was during the first week of the blockade of

Havana, and the torpedo boat "Porter," commanded by Captain John C. Fremont, was acting as a picket. Out of the darkness there loomed up the form of a big ship, obviously from her outline a man-of-war. It was early in the war, and neither Fremont nor any of his officers had any definite knowledge where the Spanish squadron might be. The little low-lying leaden-hued "Porter" was invisible from the big ship. The cruiser lay at her mercy. But the vital question with which the minds of the men on the torpedo boat was charged was whether it was an enemy or a friend they saw before them. They pushed forward to within one hundred and twenty yards, and at eight hundred yards their torpedo would have been effective. Then they flashed the signal that all American men-of-war understand, and to which all usually speedily reply. There came no answer. Seemingly the men on the greater ship neither saw the little boat almost submerged in the water, nor did they catch sight of the glowing lamp which offered friendship or threatened danger according to the response returned. The torpedo boat drew nearer and nearer. Captain Fremont repeated his signal and still received no return. Had he let slip a missile, the ship before him would have gone to the bottom as went the "Maine." But being prudent and well informed as to the course of the war, he felt convinced that the enemy could have no ship of such great bulk in those waters. Therefore he held his fire, and swinging his craft around so that the stranger would come between him and the faint glow of the stars in the sky, he saw that she had three smoke-stacks. No Spanish ship had more than two, so that the question whether it was an enemy they confronted was thereby immediately settled. As it turned out in the end, the ship was the "New York," and with all her 500 men she had been for an hour almost absolutely at the mercy of a little craft that carried only thirty-two.

This incident shows what might have been accomplished

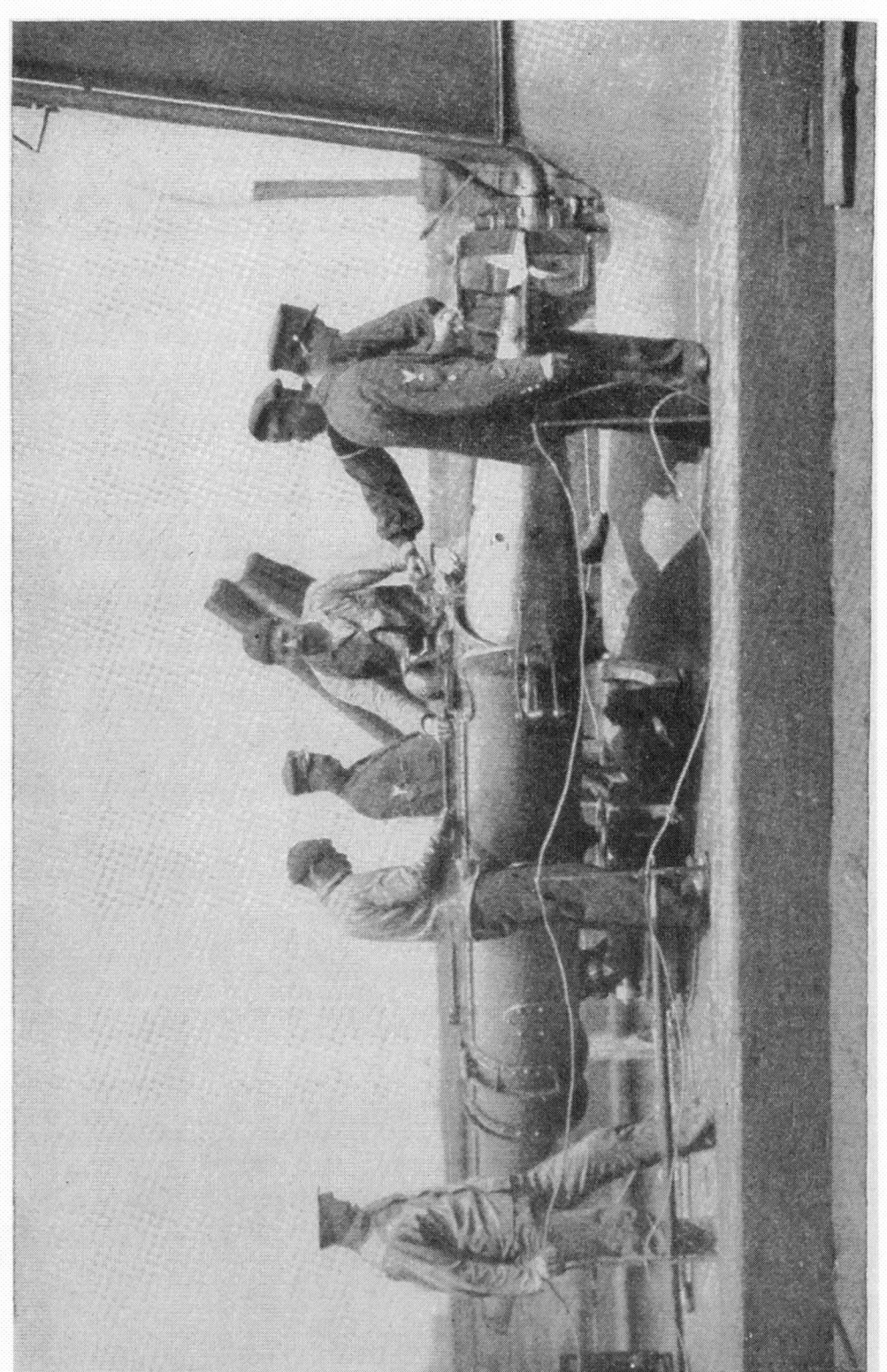

DECK TUBE AND PROJECTILE OF A TORPEDO BOAT.

by boats of this class had occasion arisen. The occasion did not arise, and so they did whatever service came first to hand, their officers with true American adaptability forcing the little vessels into the performance of duties for which they were but little fitted. It is not likely, however, that the fever for torpedo boats will again reach the point at which it stood before the Spanish war. It was clearly demonstrated that by day none of these craft could approach near enough to a ship of war to deliver an effective blow, and the modern devices for illuminating the neighbourhood of a warship at night seem to have made the chances for successful torpedo attack very small.

If the war had ended with the signing of the peace protocol, it is probable that the people would have felt it had demonstrated the grave weakness of the militia in time of actual hostilities. In the Santiago campaign the victories were won almost wholly by the regular troops. Of the three volunteer regiments engaged, the "Rough Riders" alone acquitted themselves with credit. There was noticeable, immediately after the close of this campaign, a very general inclination to underestimate the worth of volunteer forces, and to urge that the regular army establishment be largely increased. The hard fighting against the Filipino insurgents changed that national attitude. There the volunteers were in the vast majority, and they fought with a steadiness and gallantry that no regular troops could outdo. It is still too early to write the history of the war against the Tagals, but when it is written it will crown the American volunteer with such glory as he has had no opportunity to win since the dark days of the Civil War.

But if the volunteers failed at Santiago, the regular army in two of its most important branches proved itself far from impeccable. The transportation and commissary departments of the army approached as near absolute failure as could be possible without disaster. It is needless to recount here the story of the delays in getting troops and supplies to the points of rendezvous, or to rehearse the pitiful narrative of the wrecking of the army by bad food and faulty sanitation. It is enough to note that the one great military lesson of the war was the need for a permanent and highly trained staff, able to cope swiftly with all the details of the mobilisation, equipment, and subsistence of great bodies of troops. This should be distinctively the function of the regular army; the militia being trained rather in the less technical branches of military science. In some such device for dividing between the national guard and the regular army establishment the duties and responsibilities of military organisation in war-time probably lies the solution of the army problem in the United States. The antagonism of the people to a large standing army is ineradicable. Even in the glow of triumph over Spain Congress refused to accede to the President's request for a regular establishment of 100,000 men. It is unquestionable, therefore, that the course for those who are interested in the development of our military resources to pursue is to plan systematically for a closer co-operation between the militia and the regular army. By the terms of the army bill passed in the last days of the congressional session, the President is authorised to maintain a regular army of about 65,000 men for two years to come, and to enlist new volunteers to the number of 35,000. At the end of the time fixed, in default of new legislation, the regular army will be reduced to its normal peace footing, and all volunteers will be discharged.

When the people of the United States, unwillingly and after long and earnest consideration, turned aside from the paths of peace to take up the sword, to which for almost half a century their hands had been strangers, they declared they were going to war in the cause of humanity. They knew they were about to make heavy sacrifices, and in some ways the sacrifice has been greater than the most apprehensive among them imagined. But in the end the great purpose of the war will be amply fulfilled. If territory has come to us unexpectedly, its tenants — whether in Porto Rico or the Philippines — will be far better off than under the almost barbarous rule of Spain. If the inevitable savageries of war have inflicted upon Cubans and Filipinos sufferings more poignant even than they endured before our intervention, it has been such suffering as the surgeon inflicts to perform a radical cure. There need be no fear of a recurrence or continuance of the evil, as was inevitable under Spanish rule. The people whom we have rescued from Spain, and even the half-civilised people whom we are now striving to rescue from themselves, will find nothing but profit in their new situation. Whether to the citizens of the United States the results of the war will prove so unmixed a blessing, cannot be said with equal certainty. We have entered upon a new national policy, and its fruits will be slow to ripen. Distant colonies, in lands already densely populated with alien races, and in a zone which has never been the scene of successful nation-building, offer problems which may well daunt even the indomitable American spirit. The story of the war with Spain is only the least important part of the narrative of the results of our intervention in Cuba. The history of what we have done and shall do in our new possessions to justify our entrance upon them, and the record of the effect, if any, upon our home institutions, will be the more important chapter of the historical narrative. Loyal Americans will not fear that the chapter, when written, will be other than a glorious part of our national annals.

THE END

X 178

Printed in Great Britain
by Amazon.co.uk, Ltd.,
Marston Gate.